320.473
Sh2p

121143

DATE DUE			

POLICY AND POLITICS IN AMERICAN GOVERN ** MENTS

IRA SHARKANSKY
The University of Wisconsin, Madison

DONALD VAN METER
The Ohio State University

McGraw-Hill Book Company

New York St. Louis San Francisco Auckland Düsseldorf Johannesburg
Kuala Lumpur London Mexico Montreal New Delhi Panama
Paris São Paulo Singapore Sydney Tokyo Toronto

Library of Congress Cataloging in Publication Data

Sharkansky, Ira.
    Policy and politics in American governments.

    1. United States—Politics and government—Handbooks, manuals, etc. 2. Policy
sciences. I. Van Meter, Donald, joint author. II. Title.
JK274.S46   320.4'73   74-20696
ISBN 0-07-056428-0

POLICY AND POLITICS IN AMERICAN GOVERNMENTS

1234567890DODO798765

This book was set in Times Roman by Black Dot, Inc.
The editors were Robert P. Rainier, Helen Greenberg, and Phyllis T. Dulan;
the cover was designed by Anne Canevari Green;
the production supervisor was Dennis J. Conroy.
R. R. Donnelley & Sons Company was printer and binder.

To our children
Erica and Stefan Sharkansky
Joshua Stuart Van Meter

Contents

Preface

American governments have experienced a number of crises and conflicts during the past decade. These crises reflect the growing and changing character of American society: racial tension, economic instability, urban decay, poverty, pollution, energy shortages, countercultures, Vietnam and the domestic controversies it spawned, Watergate, and others. Most serious, however, is the crisis of confidence in American governments. We have long believed that any problem could be solved if enough American know-how was applied. The crises of the past decade have caused many people to question this traditional idea; they have begun to sense that things are getting worse, and that our governments are incapable of solving the many problems that cry for attention.

Not everyone is willing to admit to the flaws in the American political system. Some view criticism as a tearing down of all that is right and good in America. They regard critics as irresponsible radicals and defend their country with such slogans as "America—Love It or Leave It." Other critics, in contrast, find nothing worth defending. Arguing that American governments are "rotten to the core," they maintain that a better America can be built only after existing political structures have been totally dismantled. Yet, neither of these positions reflects the thinking of most Americans. Most people recognize the need for change; they sense that both government structures and policies must be altered if the United States is to realize its economic, social, and political objectives.

This book does not try to explain what is wrong with American governments or to defend the status quo. Different people will evaluate the political system in various ways, given their own observations, experiences, and political philosophies. Unlike many other American government texts, this one does not try to indoctrinate or support any one ideological point of view. Rather, it gives students a framework for organizing the data and understanding the complex, often conflicting, processes by which policies are made and delivered. These processes, in turn, determine how goods and services are distributed and cause the system to benefit some people more than others. With this background, students will be able to think critically about the policy-making process and to assess how well American governments perform.

To this end, we use the model of "policy delivery systems." This model is a simple framework that focuses on policy and helps clarify how private citizens, political parties, interest groups, and government institutions affect the system.

This text also provides an integrated examination of national, state, and local governments. All levels of government take part in making and deliverying policies, and there is both conflict and cooperation among them. Finally, this book encourages students to think critically about controversial issues: busing to desegregate the schools; involvement in Vietnam and the Middle East; revenue sharing; the ability of private citizens to influence governments; congressional reform; presidential power and presidential impoundment; and the impact of Supreme Court decisions.

We deeply appreciate the contributions of many people to this book. More than a thousand students in our American Government courses over the past decade contributed to its evolution through course syllabuses and lectures. For critical reviews of the manuscript, we are indebted to Edward S. Greenberg, Stanford University; Robert R. Holland, University of California at Riverside; Joe Klassen, Penn Valley Community College; Michael Lipsky, Massachusetts Institute of Technology; James P. Levine, University of Oregon; Carl E. Lutrin, California Polytechnic State University; Mark Nadel, Cornell University; William Prentiss, Valencia Community College; and Edwin Strong, University of Tulsa. We also wish to thank the following individuals, who read and commented upon particular chapters: Herbert B. Asher, Steven Ballard, Lawrence Baum, and Henry Marsh, all of The Ohio State University; and B. James Kweder, Cleveland State University. Doris Wells provided outstanding and timely typing assistance. We also owe a special debt of gratitude to Helen Greenberg, our untiring and adept editor. Finally, our indebtedness to our families cannot be measured. Our wives, Ina Sharkansky and Sally Van Meter, have endured our complaints and frustrations, explained to others our peculiar moods, and accepted a disproportionate amount of responsibility for domestic tasks while we completed the book. Our children, Stefan and Erica Sharkansky and

Joshua Van Meter, have also seen too little of their fathers. We recognize the many sacrifices made by the families of those whose teaching and research activities occupy so much of their time.

Ira Sharkansky
Donald Van Meter

Chapter 1

Introduction

The framers of the U.S. Constitution were guided by the belief that individuals have a right to control their own lives and that government activity must occur within strict limits in order to protect the individuals' rights. As the United States marks the two hundredth anniversary of its independence, these basic values are being challenged. While paying lip service to individualism, free enterprise, and limited government, we have evolved a massive array of public institutions that make themselves felt in every home in the country. Many Americans still sneer at the "cradle-to-grave" welfare programs of other countries; yet our own national, state, and local governments offer programs in the fields of health, income protection, employment, and education that cover some residents from first breath to entombment.

OUR EXPANDING GOVERNMENTS

The economic and social policies of the national government have changed our notion of a free enterprise system. The government sub-

1

sidizes preferred industries, limits increases in wages and prices, and competes with private industry in the production and distribution of selected goods and services. Beyond our borders, the "umbrella" of U.S. military forces means defense, aggression, massive expenditures, or simply political controversy to many nations in Europe, Asia, and Latin America. United States economic policies affect the well-being of countries that depend upon our markets for the sale of their products or use our currency to regulate the value of their own money and to trade with other nations.

The government of the United States, in terms of the basic outline of its institutions, is actually the oldest of all the major countries. When the Constitution went into effect in 1789,

> the French monarchy still stood; there was a Holy Roman Emperor, a Venetian Republic and a Dutch Republic, an Autocrat in St. Petersburg, a Sultan-Caliph in Constantinople, an Emperor vested with the "mandate of Heaven" in Pekin and a Shogun ruling the hermit empire of Japan in the name of a secluded, impotent and almost unknown Mikado.[1]

While there is still a monarchy in Great Britain that traces its lineage to the distant past, the powers of Gerald R. Ford are more like those of George Washington than are the powers of Elizabeth II like those of the absolutist George III. Yet, no one can claim that Ford's powers are very much like Washington's; nor does the present relationship between our national and state governments resemble that of 1789. Our governmental stability and age are apparent only when they are compared with greater changes elsewhere in the world.

Our changes compete with our stability for attention. We now have extended universal free suffrage to all citizens at least eighteen years old and no longer deny the vote for reasons of race, religion, or wealth. Throughout the nineteenth century, Congress generally dominated the policy-making process. However, since the Great Depression of 1929, we have seen the decline of Congress and the growth of the presidency. During the same period, the relationship between the national and state governments has changed tremendously. Washington has expanded the scope of its activities into areas previously reserved for state and local governments, and states have become increasingly dependent upon the financial resources of the national government.

THE SOURCES OF PUBLIC POLICY

It is difficult to explain the origin of these changes. Do they come from popular demands or from the preferences of government officials? The answer is, both. The United States has had no successful political revolution since the constitutional convention of 1789, and except in a revolutionary setting, public officials define public policies. However, many officials gain office by popular election and are subject to public pressures. Many other officials are appointed, not elected, to office. Since they do not face reelection, they may be less responsive to demands for change.

There are hundreds of power sources in government all the way down the line. They are constantly interacting among themselves and with the public, forming alliances that shift from week to week, month to month, year to year. Let us take a look at this diversity.

Local officials who develop zoning ordinances must frequently respond to indignant citizens. School board officials often deal with parents concerned about the curriculum or about the racial composition of the schools. However, public officials are sometimes guided by their own views as well. During the Vietnam war, the private views of many local draft board officials led them to grant or deny deferments to students, farmers, or conscientious objectors. The foreign policies of Presidents and bureaucrats have become matters of great concern in recent years. Budget decisions that affect all areas of life are made privately within the administrative, executive, and legislative branches. Many tax policies, in contrast, are hammered out in public, with officials clearly pressured by various interest groups.

Public officials, in turn, often join interest groups to influence decisions they do not make directly. The Governors' Conference, the U.S. Conference of Mayors, and the National Association of State, County, and Municipal Employees compete with other lobbies to influence legislators or administrators. Sometimes the government responds to the public; at other times it runs contrary to public sentiments; and at still other times it governs in the midst of public apathy. Often it is simply not clear which is more important: the public will or the private will of public officials.

THE RELEVANCE OF AMERICAN GOVERNMENTS

This book concentrates on activities at all levels of American government, using the study of *government* to begin the study of *politics.* This is logical, since governments provide the major targets and arenas of political activity; it is within government that some of the most intriguing and significant political developments take place. A sound knowledge of government structures and procedures is necessary to understand how politics shapes public policy.

One only has to think of the tensions surrounding a presidential election to appreciate the importance of government for the American people. The 1964 campaign saw the reincarnation of a basic conflict that many felt had been laid to rest in 1936: Barry Goldwater, a strident advocate of free enterprise and limited government, ran against Lyndon B. Johnson, an architect of extensive new social programs. In 1968, the bitterness and violence of the Democratic Convention reflected the agony of a nation divided by a continuing war in Southeast Asia. And the fundamental conflicts in the 1972 presidential election combined these thrusts, dealing with government regulation of the economy; the provision of education, health, and welfare services; the proper kinds of taxes; and again, American involvement in Southeast Asia.

The conflicts between supporters of different policies do not end on election day. Issues continue as a group losing in one area tries again in another election campaign or in a different area. Most elections merely decide who will occupy which seat in government. Policies become defined *between* campaigns in executive and administrative offices, judicial chambers, and legislative committee rooms. Interested citizens and government officials join in these continuing disputes, with the alleged sentiments of the people being only one of the criteria considered.

The war in Southeast Asia divided voters into bitterly dissenting groups. Many election campaigns focused on this issue, and voters may have felt that they had defined American foreign policies by means of their ballots. Such a belief was only partially correct; no single election settled the issue. Candidates with general positions on withdrawal, victory, or negotiation still had to bargain privately over sticky details involving American, North Vietnamese, South Vietnamese, and Vietcong interests.

In the field of income maintenance, problems abound. Is it right to provide anything like a "guaranteed annual income"? Will certain features of the program encourage or discourage clients from earning some money? What percentage of annual income should the federal government provide? How much can the individual earn and still qualify? How can the formulas regulating these percentages be made flexible enough to meet thousands of differing personal circumstances? Like Vietnam, this many-sided problem must be hammered out by a limited number of official and unofficial experts, and not by a public torn in different directions by the issues, personalities, and ballyhoo of an election campaign.

THE PERSPECTIVE OF THIS TEXT

For those who wish to understand why and how our governments have evolved in 200 years, and who are concerned about the things that governments do, or fail to do, the formulation and delivery of public policy is what it's all about. This book deals with the mechanisms that define and provide services, impose taxes, and constrain behavior. Government is not a neutral, antiseptic set of instruments. The people and procedures that formulate and deliver policies have a major impact on all our lives. Furthermore, these services, taxes, and regulations affect us unequally. Some get more service than others, some pay more taxes than others, and some are freer than others to act.

To Explain How the System Works

It is not our purpose to argue for a "proper" arrangement of government or for more "fair" policies toward various segments of society. We are not interested in advancing a set of prescriptions for change in American politics. We are more interested in explaining why and how the system benefits some people more than others. This book describes how various parts of the government formulate and deliver public policies, which determine how goods and services are distributed. Further, it shows how certain parts of this complex system depend upon and influence other parts.

What about the reader who now feels that he or she wants to change the system? This book can help in two ways. First, by understanding *how* government works, he or she can pinpoint where and how to agitate most effectively for change. Second, this knowledge can help the activist choose targets more intelligently and recognize when innovations may have unintended harmful consequences for areas where change might at first seem desirable. The person who understands the policy process is better equipped to identify those changes that will help achieve truly worthwhile goals.

> Without a sense of where power is now located, how it is used, what values and interests are dominant—and how change may come about in those respects—there is neither a rational basis for judgment between competing prescriptions nor any idea of how to bring them about in the real world.[2]

To Explore Our Stability and Flexibility

One additional perspective of the authors should be stated before proceeding further. Though we anticipate that some readers will resist this notion, we feel that the existence of both stability and change reflects the staying power and the worth of the American political system. This perspective carries with it an endorsement of the government's structure: the powers of national, state, and local officials and the rules that define the ways private citizens try to influence them. After all, since we have lived nearly 200 years without a successful domestic rebellion and more than 100 years without a serious attempt at revolution, we must be doing something right.

This is not to say that everyone is content, or should be. Studies indicate that the American people have become more distrustful and cynical about their government in recent years, a trend which is most striking in particular social groups—such as the young and minorities. Some see a system unable to meet the changing needs of a complex society, a government serving the interests of the haves and being unresponsive to the needs of the have-nots. Others see changes that destroy the familiarity of the past and cloud our view of the future.

The theme of change includes matters of great controversy. Some change appears in the form of public policies, and some in the economy and culture that are—at least partially—independent of government policies. The pace is slow. Southern blacks now have economic and political opportunities that were inconceivable to many observers as late as 1963, as the existence of a black mayor in Atlanta shows. Yet, blacks still have fewer economic and political opportunities than whites in the South and elsewhere. Other changes appear in the procedures used to formulate policies: up to 1971, eighteen to twenty year olds were denied the vote, and as recently as the early 1960s, federal courts tolerated unequal representation in Congress and state legislatures with some rural and small-town voters having many times the proportionate weight of urban voters.

Much of the strength in the American political system lies in its flexibility. While there is stability in its form and procedures, there is no rigor mortis. At no time will everyone be satisfied with the government and its distribution of benefits and costs. Individuals will vary in their evaluations and judgments of government and its policies. On numerous questions, the authors themselves hold very different views. But we share at least one perspective: an individual who is well informed about the workings of government is more able to bring about desired changes with the fewest unintended consequences. To accomplish this, an important goal for the beginning student is to identify those features of government and policy that are likely to remain stable, and those that are likely to change.

POLICY DELIVERY SYSTEMS

Before we can examine policy making in American governments, we must decide how to organize the vast amount of material to be considered. We need a framework to help select the information that is most important for our interests, and to clarify what each part means for the others. We want a format that is relatively simple and that will serve our needs without a surplus of sophisticated theory that becomes excess baggage.

We have chosen the model of *policy delivery systems* to guide our discussion of American governments.[3] The name itself has important implications. First, it emphasizes those features of American governments that shape the character of public policies. Second, it implies that there is no simple equation between the announced intentions of policy makers and services actually delivered. Policies must be *delivered* as well as formulated, and there are several factors that can interfere with their effective delivery. Third, the name indicates that policy-relevant elements fit together in *systems*. Citizens, legislators, administrators, and judges do not operate in isolation from one another; and officials at the national, state, and local levels cannot operate for any length of time without encountering other levels of government. Fourth, we consider *several* delivery systems. Conditions change with the situation. The system that produces national defense policies differs from that which delivers higher education or tax policies in the states. Indeed, the fragmented and diverse nature of policy making is a major component of political life in the United States. Not only are there numerous centers of governmental decision making that effect the character of public services, but there are countless private interests that seek influence in these councils. One consequence of this diversity is frequent conflict among policies. Since many people have an opportunity to make themselves heard in different areas of government, we seldom hear the "final word" on a topic. However, this does not ensure that *all* groups receive consideration. Depending on one's point of view about the issue at hand, this diversity can be a source of hope or frustration.

A policy delivery system is not a tangible body of persons and procedures clearly defined in the government. It is an abstract model that leads us to look for certain kinds of information, a framework that assists us in the organization of the materials selected for study. Figure 1-1 portrays a policy delivery system. Its components are: (1) an *environment* that both stimulates government officials and receives the products of their work; (2) *demands and resources* that carry stimuli from the environment to public officials; (3) a *conversions process*, including the formal structures and procedures of government, that transforms (converts) demands and resources into public policies; (4) the *policies* that represent the formal goals, intentions, or statements of government officials; (5) the *performance* of the policy as it is actually delivered to clients; and (6) the *impact* of policies and performances on the environment, which is then transmitted back to the conversions process as the demands and resources of a later point in time.

A beginning student may find that the meaning of these terms is

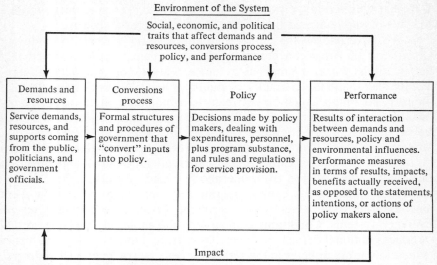

Figure 1-1 The policy delivery system.

unclear. So, in the remaining pages of this chapter, and in the two chapters that follow, we will describe and illustrate the components of the system, with particular emphasis on the relationships among them.

Environment, Demands, and Resources

The environment includes all the social, economic, and political factors that present problems to policy makers and help or hinder their efforts to seek solutions. The environment influences citizen demands and resources, the character of the conversions process, and policies and service performance. For example, certain cultures encourage political activism as a means of achieving personal and/or social goals; in other cultures, individuals are discouraged from or consider themselves incapable of influencing the government. Areas of high involvement are communities of upper-income, well-educated people, especially in those states with intense competition among political parties and respect for public officials. Less involvement occurs in poorer, less-educated areas, especially where there is single-party domination, a history of discouraging the participation of the poor and blacks, and a low regard for politicians.[4]

The nation's past also has a continuing effect on its politics. The notions of federalism and separation of powers were incorporated into our Constitution as a result of the founding fathers' experiences with despotism prior to 1787. They feared that a concentration of political power would lead to renewed tyranny, and they divided power in order to ensure democracy. Though the past two centuries have been marked by major changes in our government, we still see the fragmentation of power intended by the founding fathers.

Within the environment are individuals who pay costs (taxes) and receive benefits; the markets, which set costs for the goods and services to be delivered; the interest groups that seek to influence policy makers; and other political actors who show support for, or opposition to, a policy. At times, the environment appears benign; it generates proposals that aid policy making and help to solve problems. At other times, however, the environment produces conflicting demands and stubborn conditions that "harden" problems and frustrate policy makers' efforts to cope with them.

Demands and resources come from the environment to the conversions process. They include demands for goods and services; money, material goods, and manpower to sustain public policies; and support, opposition, or apathy toward governmental actions. Policy makers are pressured by political parties, interest groups, and periodic elections. They also feel the weight of civil disobedience, mass demonstrations, and political violence, as in the sit-ins, civil rights marches, civil disorders, and antiwar protests of the 1960s.

Conversions Process

The conversions process includes the institutions of government that respond to political demands and resources and convert them into public policies. Conversion takes place in the legislative, executive, administrative, and judicial branches of national, state, and local governments. Each of these branches receives separate, and often contradictory, stimuli from its environment, and each helps determine public policy. Yet none of these branches operate in isolation from the others. Congress depends upon the executive branch for the initiation of proposals, and the President is constrained occasionally by a Congress that may limit or refuse the funds necessary for his programs. Likewise, the President can direct his administration to ease up on the enforcement of school desegregation orders, or Congress can pass legislation granting the police greater flexibility in the use of wiretaps and search warrants. But in both cases, the courts can review these policies and rule them unconstitutional. And administrators can enforce the law either strictly or with a casual effort that suggests evasion.

Policy and Performance

It is necessary to consider *policy* and *performance* as two separate categories of the policy delivery system. Policies do not always produce the services intended, and conflicting policies may produce a net result of zero. Anti-inflationary policies of the Federal Reserve System may have little effect if federal spending levels are increased, or if tax cuts are introduced to deal with rising unemployment. The social or economic problems that are the targets of policies are often more substantial—and therefore harder to deal with—than first believed. Problems of poor or destitute families have proved intractable in the face of numerous policies that were thought capable of dealing with them. Health policies have not been sufficient to stop the spread of certain diseases. Conflicting demands from the environment lead officials to water down their objectives and pursue policies that are so weakened by compromise that they cannot perform as intended. This occurs for programs designed to control pollution, regulate business practices, or eliminate racial discrimination.

Policy represents actions taken by the government. It appears as governmental statements or actions, and is undertaken (at least partly) to change the quantity or quality of public services. Public officials cannot directly control the learning of schoolchildren or the well-being of welfare clients. They can only aim at these targets by policies that define expenses, salary levels, employees' workloads, and the rules and regulations that govern the treatment of clients. Not all these policies reflect the authorities' wishes. Spending depends partly on the money available, the constitutional and statutory controls on taxation, and the political climate.

Performance is the work that is actually produced. It usually reflects a mixture of policy intentions, plus other influences that complicate the delivery of such intentions. Like other elements of the policy delivery system, *performance* is multifaceted. The many goals of each policy make it difficult to measure performance. Every service has many components, each of which must be measured separately. Elementary and secondary education try to teach the basic skills of reading, writing, and arithmetic; substantive knowledge across a wide range of academic fields; technical skills under the headings of vocational training and automobile driving; an understanding of personal health and living; and a dose of patriotic love for nation, state, and community. Performance, then, is evaluated partly in terms of short-term academic achievements and partly by reference to long-term economic, social, and moral standards that cannot be measured precisely. The welfare field is only a bit simpler in its goals: various programs include providing food, clothing, and shelter; ambition and skills for employment; and the acceptance of certain moral standards. There are numerous ways to measure performance: by changes in the traits of clients as a result of a program; by how often services are made available; by how often these services are used; by the kinds of people who are served by a program; or by the continued existence of conditions (such as poverty) that a program is designed to abolish.

Impact

This final component in the policy delivery system reflects a policy's success or failure, and its effects on the environment that result in new demands later on. The crucial feature of *impact* is the influence of earlier policy and performance on the demands and resources at a later time. Existing tax legislation affects the flow of money to the government. Public services make citizens satisfied or dissatisfied and thus shape their future demands. For example, the failure to achieve high-quality education for blacks has led many of them to abandon the goal of integration, and demand instead black schools governed by the black community.

THE POLICY DELIVERY SYSTEM AS A FRAMEWORK FOR THIS BOOK

The policy delivery system, as we have said, is not simply the government officials included in the conversions process; it is the interaction among these officials and the other elements described in Figure 1-1. By thinking about government in a systems framework, we should discipline ourselves to ask about the relevance of the individual parts. What implications for *policy* and *performance* can we find in the various features of the *conversions process*? What factors determine how the *conversions process* responds to *demands and resources* originating in the *environment*? This kind of questioning leads us to appreciate the interdependence of environmental and political factors at all levels of government. A policy delivery system is a framework to aid us in our study of governments. With this system as a guide, we can collect information about items that seem to function as demands and resources, conversion components, policy, performance, and impact mechanisms. We can then see how these factors actually do interact with one another at various levels of government and under various conditions.

A PREVIEW

The remaining chapters of this book are organized around the policy delivery system. Chapters 2 and 3 use the system to examine two issues of great significance: the struggle to achieve school desegregation and American involvements in Southeast Asia and the Middle East. Chapter 4 emphasizes the roles of citizens, political parties, and pressure groups in policy delivery systems. There we focus on the ways that some of the most important demands make their way to the conversions process. Chapters 5 through 7 examine relationships among the three levels of American government and the similarities and contrasts in national, state, and local politics. Chapters 8 through 11 deal with the branches of government: the legislative, executive, and judicial branches that are described formally in the national and state constitutions, and the administrative branch that has increased in importance during recent decades. These chapters describe major features of the environments that surround each institution, plus the structures and procedures that convert environmental stimuli into public policies. Finally, Chapter 12 focuses on the performance of American governments. This concluding chapter also summarizes the nature of policy making in American governments, and evaluates the performance of our policy systems.

REFERENCES

1   D. W. Brogan, *Politics in America* (New York: Harper & Brothers, 1954), p. 1.
2   Kenneth M. Dolbeare, *Power and Change in the United States* (New York: John Wiley & Sons, Inc., 1969), p. 1.
3   The theoretical work that is most frequently cited in connection with the systems approach to political science is David Easton, *A Systems Analysis of Political Life* (New York: John Wiley & Sons, Inc., 1965). See also David Easton, *A Framework for Political Analysis* (Englewood Cliffs, N.J.: Prentice-Hall, Inc., 1965); Gabriel Almond and G. Bingham Powell, Jr., *Comparative Politics: A Developmental Approach* (Boston: Little, Brown and Company, 1966); Thomas R. Dye, *Politics, Economics, and the Public: Policy Outcomes in the American States* (Chicago: Rand McNally & Company, 1966); Richard F. Fenno, *The Power of the Purse: Appropriations Politics in Congress* (Boston: Little, Brown and Company, 1966); John C. Wahlke et al., *The Legislative System* (New York: John Wiley & Sons, Inc., 1962); and Karl W. Deutsch, *The Nerves of Government* (New York: The Free Press, 1963). The reader should realize that there are various ways of portraying a system for describing and analyzing politics. Figure 1-1, the model followed throughout this book, stresses how government units contribute to the formulation and implementation of public policies in the United States.
4   Daniel J. Elazar, *American Federalism: A View from the States* (New York: Thomas Y. Crowell Company, 1972).

Desegregating the Schools: The Agony of Busing

Few issues in recent years have created as much debate or controversy as school desegregation. During the past two decades, this issue has inspired both peaceful protest and violence, has led private citizens and public officials to act in open defiance of the law, and more recently, has resulted in a sharp increase in the number of black children attending racially integrated schools, particularly in the South. Critics of school desegregation assert the right to determine their children's educational environments; they see governmental desegregation efforts as both unwise and a violation of states' rights. Proponents of school desegregation argue that it is demanded by the U.S. Constitution. Only through racial integration, they insist, can a child's constitutional right to the equal protection of the laws be achieved.

A BRIEF HISTORY

Although a perennial issue on the American political scene, desegregation has taken on added significance in the 1970s. When the U.S. Supreme

Court ruled in *Brown v. Board of Education of Topeka* (1954) that enforced racial segregation in public education violated the Fourteenth Amendment, which guaranteed equal protection under the law to all races, the most direct and immediate effects were felt in the South. Southern states were the primary targets of most school desegregation policies coming from Congress and the White House during the 1950s and 1960s. In most instances, these policies were aimed at eliminating de jure segregation and discrimination—that is, racial isolation and discrimination that resulted from state laws.

It was not until 1970 that school districts throughout the nation began to experience the intense pressures for desegregation that Southerners had known for nearly two decades. Most school segregation outside of the South reflects segregated housing and neighborhood schools. Until the 1970s, this de facto segregation largely escaped the challenge of the law and the courts. While the Civil Rights Act of 1964 authorizes the withholding of federal funds from racially discriminatory programs, this authority does not extend to cases of de facto segregation. The Act defined *desegregation* as ". . . the assignment of students to public schools and within such schools without regard to race, color, religion or natural origin, but . . . shall not be construed to mean the assignment of students to public schools in order to overcome racial imbalance." This Act also stipulated that

> nothing herein shall empower any official or court of the United States to issue any order seeking to achieve a racial balance in any school by requiring the transportation of pupils or students from one school to another or one school district to another in order to achieve such racial balance.

While it is still too early to define precisely United States policy on school desegregation, de facto segregation is no longer safely beyond the reach of the law. In its highly controversial *Swann v. Charlotte-Mecklenburg Board of Education* decision (1971), the U.S. Supreme Court ruled that "desegregation plans cannot be limited to the walk-in school." The Court also ruled that so long as it did not endanger the health of students or interfere with the educational process, busing could be used to break down the discriminatory effects of de facto segregation.

With this decision, busing became the most emotional issue of the early 1970s. In Lamar, South Carolina, a school bus loaded with children was overturned; in Pontiac, Michigan, another school bus was fire-bombed. Throughout the nation, the school bus has become a symbol of federal interference in local affairs; it is seen as a tool to disrupt local communities and threaten the well-being of innocent children. This, of course, is misleading, since busing, far from being a new practice, goes back to 1869. In that year, Massachusetts became the first state to transport students at public expense. In 1969–70, more than 18 million public school children (43 percent) were being bused. It has been estimated that of these only some 2 or 3 percent were being bused for purposes of racial desegregation.[1] In many respects, however, busing is a straw man; few (if any) of its advocates support it for its own sake. Instead, they view it as the unsatisfactory but sole means by which school desegregation can be achieved. The issue, then, is not busing but racial integration.

Even though busing may be a false issue, for many it has come to be the central one, and it has spread conflict over racial integration to the whole country. Legislators who long favored desegregation in Meridian, Mississippi, or Birmingham, Alabama, now find themselves resisting similar programs that would antagonize their own constituents in Minneapolis, Detroit, or New Haven. Northern "liberals" who once saw the desegregation of Southern schools as a moral and legal imperative now hedge on integrating the public schools that their own children attend.

In this chapter, we examine the issues of desegregation and busing, using policy delivery systems as an organizing framework. Our primary focus will be school desegregation as a national issue—that is, as a product of the national government. This does not mean that we can ignore policy making at the state and local levels. However, when assessing state and local contributions to the policy delivery system, we shall be concerned with the *implementation*, or performance, of policy decisions; this, after all, is largely the responsibility of state and local officials.

THE ENVIRONMENT: RACIAL INEQUALITY AND AMERICAN EDUCATION

The environment that has produced school desegregation policy is extremely complex. For our purposes, three factors are most important: (1) the long history of racial inequality and discrimination in the United States; (2) the residential (de facto) segregation of minority groups— which is partly voluntary and partly imposed by discrimination in the sale and rental of housing—and the use of the neighborhood school; and (3) the fragmented character of American governments. The fragmented nature of government is a part of the environment in which racial policy is made, and also affects the conversion of demands and resources into public policy. We mention fragmentation briefly in this discussion of the environment and then treat it more thoroughly as part of the conversions process.

Inequality and Discrimination

Racial inequality is deeply rooted in American society. In 1776, Thomas Jefferson wrote that "all men are created equal." This concept was immediately repudiated by delegates to the Continental Congress, many of whom were from the South, where the economy depended on slave labor and the slave trade. In drafting the U.S. Constitution a decade later, the founding fathers gave constitutional protection to the practice of slavery. In Article 4, Section 2, they wrote: "No person held to service or labor in one State, under the laws thereof, escaping into another, shall, in consequence of any law or regulation therein, be discharged from such service or labor, but shall be delivered up on claim of the party to whom such services or labor may be due." They also decided that three-fifths of all slaves should be counted when determining a state's population for the purpose of apportioning seats in the House of Representatives.

The issue of racial discrimination continued to plague the United States throughout the nineteenth century. As the Western territories were opened, the conflict between free-states and slave-states worsened as each tried to tip the balance in its favor. It was this conflict over the developing frontier that helped to precipitate the Civil War.

While some whites urged the total elimination of slavery and full citizenship for black Americans, many were content simply to confine slavery to the area where it already existed—the South. Even Abraham Lincoln stopped short of calling for the abolition of slavery or the equality of races:

> I will say, then, that I am not, nor ever have been, in favor of bringing about in any way the social and political equality of the white and black races: that I am not, nor ever have been, in favor of making voters and jurors of negroes, nor qualifying them to hold office, nor to intermarry with white people. . . . there must be the position of superior and inferior, and I as much as any other man am in favor of having the superior position assigned to the white race.[2]

Eventually, Lincoln did call for the emancipation of slaves, but even then he saw it not as a moral imperative but only as a means of preserving the Union.

Reconstruction and After

The abolition of slavery, however, did not make the black American equal to the white. As he threw off the chains of an old social system, the former slave entered another system of political subjection. During Reconstruction throughout the South state and local governments enacted a series of

Black Codes which restricted the social, economic, and political rights of the freed slaves. Black people, most of whom had no land, money, or education, became tenant farmers or sharecroppers, living on the bounty of "white folks." As dependents, they had little choice but to go along.

Reacting to the unwillingness of Southern whites to protect and respect the rights of black citizens, the U.S. Congress enacted several civil rights laws and added three amendments to the Constitution. The laws, enacted between 1866 and 1875, guaranteed blacks "full and equal benefits of all laws and proceedings for the security of person and property, as is enjoyed by white citizens"; made it a federal crime to abduct a black with the intention of making him a slave; placed the U.S. Army in control of the South and ordered new elections under federal supervision; prohibited racial discrimination in registering voters; and declared that "all persons within the jurisdiction of the United States shall be entitled to the full and equal enjoyment of the accommodations, advantages, facilities, and privileges of inns, public conveyances on land or water, theatres, and other places of public amusement. . . ." The three constitutional amendments abolished slavery and involuntary servitude (Thirteenth Amendment); provided that no state "shall make or enforce any law which shall abridge the privileges or immunities of citizens of the United States, nor shall any State deprive any person of life, liberty, or property without due process of law, nor deny to any person within its jurisdiction the equal protection of the laws" (Fourteenth Amendment); and stated that the "right of the citizens of the United States to vote shall not be denied or abridged by the United States or by any State on account of race, color, or previous condition of servitude" (Fifteenth Amendment).

Plessy v. Ferguson

These laws and amendments had only a limited effect on black Americans. The failure of Reconstruction can be attributed to several factors, including the underlying racist attitudes of most white Americans, the success of Southern officials in circumventing federal laws, the economy of the South, and the very scope and complexity of the problem involved. Reconstruction's failure is nowhere better illustrated than in the decision of the Supreme Court in *Plessy v. Ferguson* (1896). At issue in this case was a Louisiana law that required railroads to provide separate but equal accommodations for whites and blacks. Homer Plessy, who was one-eighth black and whose appearance was that of a white man, was arrested when he refused to leave a coach reserved for whites. Hearing this case, the Supreme Court rejected Plessy's plea and ruled that the Louisiana law did not "re-establish a state of involuntary servitude" but that it implied "merely a legal distinction between the white and colored races." In defense of its "separate-but-equal" doctrine, the Court argued:

> We consider the underlying fallacy of the plaintiff's argument to consist in the assumption that the enforced separation of the two races stamps the colored race with a badge of inferiority. If this be so, it is not by reason of anything found in the act, but solely because the colored race chooses to put that construction upon it. . . . Legislation is powerless to eradicate racial instincts or to abolish distinctions based upon physical differences, and the attempt to do so can only result in accentuating the difficulties of the present situation. . . . If one race be inferior to the other socially, the Constitution of the United States cannot put them upon the same plane.[3]

As the one dissenter in this case, Justice John Harlan wrote: "In view of the Constitution, in the eye of the law, there is in this country no superior, dominant, ruling class of citizens. There is no caste here. Our Constitution is color-blind, and neither knows nor tolerates classes among citizens."[4]

For more than fifty years, *Plessy v. Ferguson* was the law of the land. As such, it serves as part of the environment for recent struggles for racial equality in American education. In the years immediately following World War II, civil rights advocates won a series of court decisions which held that black schools actually were inferior to those of whites. These inequalities were found in course offerings, buildings and other physical facilities, transportation, extracurricular activities, teacher quality and salary levels, and geographical convenience. In *Sweatt v. Painter* (1950), the Supreme Court ruled in favor of a black student who sought admission to the all-white University of Texas Law School, even though the state had established a separate law school for black students. The Court argued: "the University of Texas Law School possesses to a far greater degree those qualities which are incapable of objective measurement but which make for greatness in a law school. Such qualities, to name but a few, include reputation of the faculty, experience of the administration, position and influence of the alumni, standing in the community, traditions and prestige."[5]

Civil Rights: 1954 to the Present

The landmark *Brown v. Board of Education* (1954) was the watershed, repudiating *Plessy v. Ferguson.* The Court reversed its position on the separation-but-equal doctrine and declared that separate educational facilities are *inherently* unequal. Relying heavily upon sociological and psychological evidence concerning the effects of racial isolation upon black children, the Court held:

Segregation of white and colored children in public schools has a detrimental effect upon the colored children. The impact is greater when it has the sanction of the law; for the policy of separating the races is usually interpreted as denoting the inferiority of the Negro group. A sense of inferiority affects the motivation of a child to learn. Segregation with the sanction of law, therefore, has a tendency to retard the educational and mental development of Negro children and to deprive them of some of the benefits they would receive in a racially integrated school system.[6]

The effects of this decision varied considerably from one part of the nation to another. Urban school districts in the North and border states made serious efforts to integrate, often with considerable success. In the South, however, local school districts made little effort to comply with the Court's ruling. Noncompliance resulted partly from the fragmentation of political power—that is, the struggle between states' rights and federal demands—which characterizes the American policy delivery system. Another reason for the slow pace of integration was the fact that most white Americans were less than enthusiastic about it. Nationally, 41 percent of the people surveyed by the Gallup poll in July 1954 opposed the *Brown* decision. In the South, where the impact of this decision was to be felt most directly, 71 percent voiced opposition.[7] The underlying racial hostility that permeated American society, and that had been upheld by law for almost 100 years, frustrated efforts to achieve school desegregation.

The U.S. Civil Rights Commission's 1967 study of seventy-five cities found widespread segregation; three-fourths of the black pupils still attended schools that were 90 to 100 percent black, while four-fifths of the white pupils were in schools that were 90 to 100 percent white.[8] In some cases, this segregation resulted from state or local laws (de jure); in many more instances, however, it resulted from a variety of social and economic factors (de facto) that determined where black families lived. The Supreme Court's 1954 *Brown* ruling, and most of the civil rights laws of the 1960s, dealt primarily with de jure segregation. It was not until the 1970s that de facto segregation became the focus of federal policies.

RESIDENTIAL SEGREGATION AND THE NEIGHBORHOOD SCHOOL

De facto school segregation is caused mainly by the residential segregation of minority groups and the widespread use of neighborhood schools. Karl and Alma Taeuber have developed a residential "segregation index," which varies from 100 (complete segregation with no whites in black areas and no blacks in white areas) to 0 (random distribution by race).[9] Table 2-1 reports the average segregation scores for 109 American cities in 1940, 1950, and 1960, and shows that residents in most American cities are highly segregated by race. Three factors seem responsible for this: (1) most people prefer to live among members of their own race; (2) many blacks are unable to afford homes anywhere but in the poorest neighborhoods; and (3) racial discrimination, which ranges from polite discouragement to the hysteria of blockbusting. Stressing the importance of this final factor, Karl Taeuber has written:

> Negroes are excluded from many residential areas in which their economic status could allow them to live. . . . Discrimination is the principal cause of Negro residential segregation, and there is no basis for anticipating major changes in the segregated character of American cities until patterns of housing discrimination can be altered.[10]

Table 2-2 illustrates how residential segregation contributes to public school segregation in both the North and the South. Children living in black neighborhoods go to black schools, and children living in white neighborhoods go to white schools. Sometimes local school boards intensify existing segregation patterns. In Houston, for example, the school board constructs, refurbishes, and enlarges schools in the heart of the ghetto instead of building them on the periphery, where they would draw both white and black students. Milwaukee bused students from overcrowded schools in black areas to white schools, but segregated them in the receiving schools.

To date, there is no clear policy on de facto segregation. Some argue that it should remain beyond the reach of the law. Others advance alternative strategies for dealing with it, including compensatory education (i.e., more facilities and better teachers for ghetto schools) and busing. The obvious fact, however, is that the American social and

Table 2-1 Average Values of Indexes of Residential Segregation for Regions, 1940, 1950, 1960

Region	1940	1950	1960
Northeast	83.2	83.6	78.9
North Central	88.4	89.9	88.4
West	82.7	82.9	76.4
South	84.9	88.5	90.7
Total	85.2	87.3	86.1

Source: Reprinted from Karl E. and Alma F. Taeuber, *Negroes in Cities* (Chicago: Aldine Publishing Company, 1965); copyright © 1965 by Karl E. and Alma F. Taeuber.

Table 2-2   School Desegregation, 1971

Region	All-black schools	80–100 percent black schools	Majority white schools
		Percentage of black students attending	
North	11.2%	57.1%	27.8%
Border	24.2	60.9	30.5
South	9.2	32.2	43.9

Source: United States Bureau of the Census, *Statistical Abstract, 1972* (Washington, D.C.: Government Printing Office, 1972), p. 119.

economic environment, from its inception, has had a striking effect on the evolution of the school desegregation controversy.

FRAGMENTATION OF GOVERNMENT

Making and enforcing school desegregation policies have been influenced greatly by fragmentation in policy delivery systems. In the nineteenth century, this fragmentation was one cause of the failure of Reconstruction. While the policies were made in Washington, responsibility for implementing them rested with state and local officials. During the 1920s and early 1930s, the Supreme Court urged a more equal balance in the powers of national and state governments, and struck down many federal programs as unconstitutional.

The effects of governmental fragmentation appeared even more clearly after the Supreme Court's 1954 *Brown* ruling. Again, state and local officials were charged with implementing federal policies. In many instances, the law was simply ignored and replaced by a policy of massive resistance. In 1955, the Court aided this resistance by refusing to set precise deadlines for desegregation. Instead, it announced that because of local considerations, local school districts would be permitted "flexibility" in setting time schedules:

> The burden rests upon the . . . [local school officials] to establish that such time is necessary in the public interest and is consistent with good faith compliance at the earliest practicable date. To that end, the courts may consider problems related to administration, arising from the physical condition of the school plant, the school transportation system, personnel, revision of the school districts and attendance areas into compact units to achieve a system of determining admission to the public schools on a nonracial basis, and revision of local laws and regulations which may be necessary in solving the foregoing problems. . . .[11]

This decision was a great disappointment to those seeking an immediate and complete implementation of the Court's ruling. While it required local officials to make a "prompt and reasonable start toward full compliance," it stipulated that once a "start" had been made, delays could be authorized if "necessary in the public interest and . . . consistent with good faith compliance at the earliest practicable date." This ruling gave Southern officials a golden opportunity to resist and circumvent the Court's 1954 decision. Harrell R. Rodgers, Jr., and Charles Bullock describe what happened:

> In resisting *Brown* Southern solons displayed far more ingenuity, energy, and boldness than they ever expended in resolving the problems of poverty, illiteracy, malnutrition, and illness which have plagued the region. . . . In Texas the progress that had been made immediately after *Brown* was reversed by a state law that withheld state funds from school districts that integrated without prior approval having been registered by the district's citizens in a referendum. The Georgia, Alabama, and Virginia legislatures forbade desegregation even when ordered by Federal courts. Several states offered tuition grants to parents of white children wishing to send their children to private schools to avoid desegregation. In Arkansas and Virginia, where integration had been orders by the courts, public schools were closed, denying an education to both blacks and whites.[12]

Government fragmentation on desegregation policies appears not only in the division of power among federal, state, and local governments, and the powers given to state and local officials by the Supreme Court, but also in fragmentation at the federal level. It was not until 1957 that Congress enacted the first civil rights bill since Reconstruction. The Civil Rights Acts of 1957 and 1960 were relatively weak and essentially confined to voting rights. Not until 1964 did Congress pass a civil rights law that guaranteed blacks access to public accommodations, opened jobs and facilities to blacks, prohibited discrimination in federal aid programs, and strengthened voting rights laws. Throughout the 1950s, President Eisenhower voiced little support for the *Brown* decision that occurred near the beginning of his presidency, and he pushed the cause of integration only when forced into action by sheer state or local intransigence, as in Little Rock, Arkansas, in 1957. John F. Kennedy, in his 1960 presidential campaign, maintained that it was the President's responsibility to provide "a moral tone and moral leadership" in the field of civil rights. But once in office, he was slow to propose new civil rights legislation, largely because he recognized that Congress would not approve it.

By 1964, however, both the executive and legislative branches of government had joined the struggle for school desegregation. Under provisions of the Civil Rights Act of 1964, the Department of Health,

Education, and Welfare set guidelines for the allocation of federal funds to local school districts. Using its authority to withhold funds from those districts that failed to desegregate, HEW initiated action against a number of districts. These actions had a noticeable, though not overwhelming, impact on school desegregation in the South. In 1969, the Nixon administration asked the Supreme Court to permit Southern school officials to delay desegregation in their states. This request evoked intense criticism from most civil rights organizations, many of the administration's political opponents, some activists within the administration, and the Supreme Court itself. In *Alexander v. Holmes* (1969), the Court flatly rejected the administration's request, stating:

> Continued operation of racially segregated schools under the standard of all deliberate speed is no longer constitutionally permissible. School districts must immediately terminate dual school systems based on race and operate only unitary school systems. . . . [defined as one]: "Within which no person is to be effectively excluded from any school because of race or color."[13]

With this decision, the Supreme Court indicated its impatience with the deliberate pace of school desegregation. The Court demanded immediate and decisive action—not merely in the South, but throughout the nation. More than any other event or decision, this ruling altered the character of the desegregation struggle. It resulted in massive school integration in the South; and throughout the country, it led to the rise of a new controversy of unequaled proportions—the use of busing to achieve school desegregation.

DEMANDS AND RESOURCES

Race, particularly when it concerns school desegregation, is one of the issues that generates great conflict in American politics. Gallup polls find that inflation, Vietnam, environmental pollution, and the energy crisis have maintained visibility for months and sometimes years, but only race has been consistently seen as an important problem since the 1950s.

Attitudes toward the Principle of Integration

The racial attitudes of black and white Americans are the primary constraints facing policy makers. Admittedly, efforts to integrate the schools will prove costly. Yet, compared to outlays for public welfare, health, highways, and educational programs, the sum is small. The real costs of school desegregation are measured in social and political terms—people's willingness to accept racial integration in the public schools and to spend even modest amounts to achieve it. The American people are deeply divided on the issues of racial equality and integration; their attitudes in these areas are held more intensely than in most others.

These are also areas in which public officials feel strong public pressure. One study has shown that, compared to other issues (e.g., social welfare and foreign involvement), civil rights is an area where public officials understand the attitudes of their constituents and vote accordingly.[14]

Most white Americans now appear to support racial integration *in principle.* In 1942, fewer than one-third of those interviewed felt that white and black students should go to the same schools. By 1956, two years after the Supreme Court's *Brown* decision, this number had risen to 49 percent; and in 1963, to 63 percent. Throughout this period, Southern whites have been less enthusiastic than their Northern counterparts, although even among this group acceptance has grown—from 2 percent in 1942 to 34 percent in 1963.[15]

Attitudes toward Implementing Integration

It is one thing to support the principle of racial integration but quite another to endorse proposals to achieve it. As Table 2-3 shows, Americans are sharply divided—and in some instances intensely negative—on making integration a reality. The data indicate that a near majority of Americans feel that the federal government is moving too quickly, and that is morally wrong to force people to accept desegregation. Less than a majority of those questioned by the Harris survey approve of the Supreme Court's ruling in *Alexander v. Holmes* (1969), which stated that no further delays could be granted: "continued operation of segregated schools under a standard of allowing 'all deliberate speed for desegregation is no longer constitutionally permissable." In other words, fifteen years after the *Brown* decision, almost half the white American population defended the rights of states and localities to determine the speed of integration—and, in effect, to slow it down.

Many people strongly support de facto segregation. Sixty percent saw nothing wrong with this policy in 1970, while only 19 percent opposed it. This attitude is most important for school desegregation in the North, where racial isolation is largely a result of segregated housing patterns. Also, many people who support the integration of schools and transportation facilities continue to resist residential integration. A retired mason in eastern Pennsylvania, for example, approved of integrated schools but objected to a black person of equal education and income moving into his block. "I believe in equality, but not that much."[16]

The busing policy has few supporters. Approximately three-fourths of all Americans oppose it, many of them intensely. When asked to rate themselves on a 7-point scale ranging from intense support to intense opposition, 73 percent of the respondents in a 1972 survey chose the most negative (conservative) position; and only 11 percent placed themselves in any of the three more positive (liberal) categories.[17]

Table 2-3 Opinions on Race Relations and School Desegregation

From the Harris survey:

	Agree	Disagree	Not sure
The Supreme Court was pushing things too fast (in its *Alexander* decision), before people were ready for it. (February 1970)	49%	42%	9%
States and local communities rather than the U.S. Supreme Court shall decide when it is right to desegregate schools. (February 1970)	49	38	13
It is morally wrong to force desegregation on people who don't want it. (February 1970)	50	37	13

It has been pointed out that one way to integrate the schools is to bus children from one area to another. Suppose it could be worked out so that there was no more busing of school children than there is now in each community and in each state—would you favor or oppose using busing to achieve integrated schools? (March 1970)	Favor busing Oppose busing Not sure	19% 73 8

In the North, segregated schools result from whites and blacks living in neighborhoods which are all-white or all-black. Children go to schools in their home neighborhood. The result is called *in fact* segregation, even though there are no laws requiring segregated schools. Do you think this system in the North of separate black and white schools, due to neighborhoods being that way, is right or wrong? (March 1970)	Right Wrong Depends Not sure	60% 19 12 9

As you know, the U.S. Supreme Court has ruled that public schools which are segregated must become integrated now without further delay. In general, do you tend to approve or disapprove of this ruling for integration now by the U.S. Supreme Court? (March 1970)	Approve Disapprove Not sure	48% 38 14

From the Gallup poll:

Do you think the racial integration of schools in the United States is going too fast or not fast enough? (March 1970)	Too fast Not fast enough About right No opinion	48% 17 21 14
In general, do you favor or oppose the busing of Negro and white school children from one school district to another? (November 1971)	Favor Oppose No opinion	18% 76 6

Black Americans show more support than whites for the principle of integration and the programs to achieve it. In 1967, a Detroit study found blacks favoring integration by a ratio of 87 to 1; in a Buffalo study conducted among blacks at about the same time, the ratio was nearly 15 to 1. A fifteen-city survey in 1968 found that only 8 percent of black respondents preferred a neighborhood with no whites, and only 6 percent preferred a school where more than half of the students were black.[18]

While most blacks appear to believe in integration, many are pessimistic about the possibility of white acceptance. This pessimism about whites, and the pride in themselves, appears in the Black Power emphasis on racial identity and integrity, and the demand for community control of political and social institutions (see pp. 189, 197–199).

The degree to which both whites and blacks are questioning the desirability of integration is reflected in a 1972 study of racial attitudes in Detroit.[19] A sample of respondents was asked to describe their concept of the "best kind of race relations." All responses were grouped into three basic categories: (1) those favoring integration and close personal relationships across racial lines; (2) those calling for mutual respect and understanding, but stopping short of integration; and (3) those preferring "isolation, cultural domination, or separatism." Table 2-4 shows that a sizable portion of both white and black respondents favored the third arrangement; in the case of whites, nearly 50 percent voiced opposition to the ideas of racial integration, equality, and mutual respect. While fewer blacks called for separatism, only a third appeared to prefer the active pursuit of integrationist goals (group 1). It should also be noted that the proportion of blacks who saw integration as a desirable goal declined between 1967 and 1971.

In summary, most white Americans do not actively support integrationist goals. While a majority of them favor the *idea* of integration, support falls sharply when the discussion turns to *implementation*, particularly when the solutions are residential integration or busing.

THE CONVERSIONS PROCESS: GOVERNMENTAL FRAGMENTATION AND CONFLICT

National Demands versus States' Rights

The demands and preferences of white and black Americans do not simply become public policies. The process by which they are translated into policies includes the structures and procedures of governments; and as we have seen, fragmentation is found at all levels. School desegregation policies involve all levels of government. State and local officials are

Table 2-4 Respondents' Views on the "Best Kind of Race Relations" in 1967 and 1971 Surveys, by Race

	Whites		Blacks	
	1967 (No. = 282)	1971 (No. = 326)	1967 (No. = 183)	1971 (No. = 166)
Integration or close personal relationships				
Integration and integration programs	13%	15%	24%	14%
Personal relationships—*do things together, work out problems together, cooperative community projects*	7	6	12	20
Integration with a time qualifier or within socioeconomic classes	5	5	1	2
	25	26	37	36
Mutual respect and understanding				
Respect and dignity for blacks (by whites), color consciousness disappear	11	13	21	16
Mutual courtesy and respect; learn to understand each other	13	13	24	23
	24	26	45	39
Isolation, cultural domination, or separation				
Each race mind its own business; stop fighting; all obey the law	15	19	12	19
Blacks change to be like whites —have similar values	11	7	2	3
Separation or segregation	21	20	3	2
	47	46	17	24
Other	3	3	2	2
	99%*	101%*	101%*	101%*

*Totals do not sum to 100 percent because of rounding.
Source: Joel D. Aberbach and Jack L. Walker, *Race in the City* (Boston: Little, Brown and Company, 1973), p. 154.

responsible for drawing school district boundaries, assigning students and teachers to particular schools, and developing busing programs where necessary for integration. Federal officials are responsible for more general policy decisions, including those relating to the constitutionality and permissibility of de facto segregation, busing, and other programs designed to achieve racial balance. Many decisions of state and local officials serve to implement federal desegregation policies. However, such policies are usually vague enough to permit considerable discretion. For example, until the Supreme Court's *Alexander* decision (1969), states and local communities could determine the pace of integration pretty much as they pleased. Even today, state and local officials are generally free to select from among several methods of bringing about racial balance, not to mention their numerous opportunities for evasion and noncompliance with federal guidelines.

Fragmentation in National Government

The effects of fragmentation also appear at the national level. School desegregation policy is a joint responsibility of legislative, executive, bureaucratic, and judicial officials. Throughout the 1950s, the courts alone tried to achieve desegregation. Only with the passage of the 1964 Civil Rights Act did Congress actively support this effort. Also in the 1960s, administrators in the Department of Health, Education, and Welfare began to withhold education funds from districts that did not uphold its desegregation guidelines.

Busing: The Courts   Busing, the key issue of the 1970s, provides a focus for examining the fragmentation of the conversions process. The United States Supreme Court took a major step in its 1971 *Swann* ruling, which indicated that busing *might* be necessary to achieve racial balance in the public schools. The Court recognized the problem in such a program but argued that "all awkwardness and inconvenience cannot be avoided in the interim period when the remedial adjustments are being made to eliminate the dual segregated school system."[20] In succeeding months, numerous federal district courts used this decision as a basis for ordering school districts to initiate busing programs. In the most controversial of these cases, one federal court ordered the merger of two Richmond, Virginia, school districts—a suburban district that was predominantly white, and a central city district that was mainly black—with extensive busing employed to gain racial integration.

Busing: The President   President Nixon responded to the busing decisions by arguing that lower federal courts had exceeded the Supreme

Court's requirements by ordering massive busing. The President indicated his support for the Supreme Court's 1954 ruling, but he reiterated his opposition to busing as a means of achieving racial balance. In a rather curious comment, he noted that the Court had not yet made a definitive decision "on whether or not, or the extent to which, 'desegregation' may mean 'integration.'"[21] Beginning in 1970, the Justice Department challenged the courts on numerous occasions, asserting the anti-busing position of President Nixon and charging that lower courts were going beyond the still vague rulings of the Supreme Court.

Early in 1972, President Nixon sent two bills to Congress that would place severe limits on the courts' ability to order busing. These proposals called for a moratorium on all new busing orders by federal courts, and provided instead for a new program of "compensatory education" directed at the children of poor families. One proposal would impose permanent restraints on court-ordered busing: busing would be permitted only if initiated by local officials, and federal funds could be used to support only voluntarily adopted busing programs.

Busing: Congress   In busing, as in many other issues, legislative debates reveal a wide range of attitudes. Fragmentation is built into the bicameral structure of Congress, and appears further in the division of each house into committees. During the early 1970s, each house examined the problem on its own. In the House of Representatives, lawmakers approved strong anti-busing provisions for inclusion in the Higher Education Act. These measures had been bottled up in the pro-busing Judiciary Committee and the liberal Education and Labor Committee for more than a year. Under the rules of the House, the (anti-busing) Rules Committee could discharge a bill from a legislative committee by majority vote. Representative William M. Colmer (D., Miss.), chairman of the Rules Committee and a vigorous opponent of busing, felt that the Judiciary and Education and Labor Committees were stalling action on anti-busing measures. "This Congress should not adjourn without taking favorable action on this matter. It should be settled and not left as a political football to be kicked around in this election year."[22]

When the Judiciary Committee refused to act, the Rules Committee voted 9 to 6 to discharge the anti-busing measure and send it to the floor. Recognizing that the Rules Committee had the votes required to discharge its anti-busing legislation, the Education and Labor Committee subsequently voted to send an amended version of the President's equal opportunities bill—with its strong anti-busing provisions—to the floor of the House. The Rules Committee's action is particularly noteworthy since it represents only the fourth time in more than twenty years that this rule had been used to force a piece of legislation out of a House committee.

In November 1971 the House approved the higher education bill with its three anti-busing provisions: (1) federal education funds could not be used for busing; (2) the national government could not force states or localities to use their own funds for busing; and (3) all court-ordered busing should be postponed until all appeals had been exhausted. While the Senate accepted the anti-busing position of the House, it preferred a less-rigid law. Senators endorsed an amendment stipulating that busing was not required by law and declared that desegregation was to be implemented uniformly throughout the country, regardless of whether segregation was de jure or de facto.

Congress completed its action with the passage of a compromise bill in June 1972. Even though the House had threatened to reject any provisions not consistent with its earlier position, the report of the conference committee (composed of members of both houses) was accepted by a 218 to 180 vote. As approved, the anti-busing provisions were: (1) court-ordered busing would not be implemented until all appeals had been exhausted; (2) federal funds could be used for busing only if local officials requested them, and then only if busing involved no risk to the student's health and did not require him to attend a school educationally inferior to the school he had attended formerly; and (3) federal officials could not pressure local school boards to undertake busing "unless constitutionally required."

Who Has the Final Word? A fundamental question raised by this controversy is: What constitutional power allows the President or Congress to limit the authority of the federal judiciary? As we will see in Chapters 8 through 11, the Constitution established three separate, independent, coequal branches of government. This fact has led critics of anti-busing measures to argue that since the Supreme Court endorsed busing in 1971, jurisdiction rests with the federal courts; neither Congress nor the President can take it away from them. To do so, they assert, would make the courts subservient to executive and legislative authority.

Supporters of anti-busing proposals argue that since Congress has the constitutional authority to limit the appellate jurisdiction of the Supreme Court, it has the right to keep the courts from ordering busing to achieve racial balance. Before his appointment to the Supreme Court, Associate Justice William H. Rehnquist, then an Assistant Attorney General in the Nixon administration, proposed that anti-busing efforts take the form of a constitutional amendment. This would avoid many of the constitutional problems raised by legislation designed to limit judicial authority.

POLICY AND PERFORMANCE

With the Supreme Court's "integration now" decision in *Alexander v. Holmes* (1969), some observers felt that the next few years would produce great progress toward achieving integration. But looking back, this optimism seems unwarranted. The "go slow" policies of the Nixon administration, the resistance of Congress, the growing ambivalence of the Supreme Court, and the unwillingness of state and local officials to comply have all contributed to the retreat from active desegregation that has marked the 1970s.

The Word from the White House

President Nixon opposed busing and argued in favor of the neighborhood school; he condemned de jure segregation but called de facto segregation both natural and legal. In 1969 he instructed HEW officials not to withhold federal funds from school districts that failed to comply with desegregation guidelines. Instead, the administration announced its intention to sue these recalcitrant districts, a procedure that is both costly and time-consuming. In 1969 and 1970, the administration asked for a delay in desegregating several Southern school districts. As we have already noted, the Supreme Court rejected this request on both occasions.

Second Thoughts in Congress

The actions of Congress also show a retreat from the earlier, active pursuit of desegregation. After passing several school desegregation laws during the 1960s, Congress became more negative as integration became linked to the issue of busing. So long as civil rights programs affected only de jure segregation in the South, Northern Congressmen found it easy to pursue the cause of racial justice. But as the courts turned their attention to the de facto segregation in the North, many longtime integrationists retreated—at least temporarily. Illustrative of this shift are the cases of five Michigan Democrats, all with pro-civil rights voting records.

Four of the five—James G. O'Hara, Lucien N. Nedzi, William D. Ford, and John D. Dingell—voted for the amendment to the higher education bill, approved by the House in 1971, that delayed the implementation of court busing orders until all appeals had been exhausted.

The amendment was authored by William S. Broomfield (R., Mich.) specifically to delay any cross-district busing in the Detroit area. O'Hara and Ford previously had been opponents of anti-busing amendments.

The four Michigan Democrats, joined by Martha W. Griffiths (D., Mich.), later signed the petition aimed at discharging the Judiciary

Committee from consideration of the constitutional amendment barring busing.[23]

The Supreme Court in Retreat

The Supreme Court is also in retreat. Since the *Swann* decision (1971) that permitted, but did not require, busing, the Court has made two important rulings on school desegregation. In a pattern that is common during the evolution of law on controversial matters, each case decided certain points in particular controversies and signaled—sometimes clearly and sometimes ambiguously—what the general policy was to be in similar cases. In one ruling, the Court returned a Denver case to a federal district court for further consideration. In so doing, the Court served notice that Northern school districts *may* be subject to desegregation orders even though de jure segregation has never existed there. In its second decision, however, the Court placed limits on the authority of judges to order busing across county lines. In *School Board of Richmond v. Virginia State Board* (1973), the Court upheld the ruling of an appeals court that had overturned a district court order to consolidate the predominantly black Richmond school district with two predominantly white systems.

Following the *Swann* decision, President Nixon appointed two more Justices to the Court. With four Nixon-appointed members, the Court has tended toward a more conservative position on numerous issues. Although in most instances it has not radically rejected the major constitutional developments of the past two decades, the "Nixon Court" has changed judicial policy through the techniques of subtle erosion (see pp. 311–312). It would not be surprising, therefore, if Court rulings in pending desegregation cases signal a further slowdown in the active pursuit of school integration.

Evaluation

But even if the Supreme Court pushed the cause of school desegregation, public education throughout the nation would probably not be truly integrated. Court decisions are one thing, implementation another; progress depends upon other branches of governments, and upon state and local officials. President Nixon asserted repeatedly that his administration would hold forced desegregation to the *minimum* "required by law." Congress also appears to be prepared to resist vigorously Court efforts to achieve racial balance through busing. Without the cooperation of executive and legislative officials, there is little chance that white and black children will be educated in the same schools or that they will have equal educational opportunities in the schools they now attend.

If the branches of the national government do not unite on school desegregation policies, the states and localities probably will do little. In the years after the *Brown* decision, Southern officials showed great ingenuity in trying to avoid desegregation.

> Frequently opposition took the form of a flat refusal to obey the law, and sometimes it was cloaked in sophisticated arguments designed to make federal officials believe that the district could not obey the law. Misleading Federal officials became something of an art, and the Nixon administration was particularly vulnerable. Federal bureaucrats played into the hands of lagging officials by assuming that the latter could be expected to act in good faith. After a decade of dishonesty, the assumption of good faith was worse than naïve.[24]

In terms of percentage points, integration *appears* to be forging ahead. Between 1968 and 1970, the proportion of black students attending schools with predominantly white enrollments went from 23.4 to 33.1; in the South, it increased from 18.4 to 39.1 percent. However, these numbers may be misleading. One observer in 1971 pointed to "the new discrimination" that has replaced the old racial desegregation—at least in the state of Mississippi.

> Visible control of the schools is still white; during the past two years, more than half of all black administrators were fired, demoted, or placed in tangential positions.
> Non-tenured teachers were released for a variety of reasons. The State Department of Education reports a 5% decrease in black teachers, while independent surveys show the number to be 10–12% . . . [and] predicts a 5$1/2$% loss of regular teachers (over 1,000 teachers) in the coming year with a disproportionate number in majority black districts. . . .
> Over forty percent of black school children attend segregated classes and, cordoned off by the whites, felt the impact of separate tracking.
> Teacher recruitment from Mississippi colleges also changed. Black colleges placed 38% fewer certified graduates last year according to State Department figures, while white colleges increased placement 52%. These changing patterns make the future less hopeful for young would-be black teachers and the institutions to which they have gone for their higher education.[25]

IMPACT

During the 1960s, several Northern cities initiated school integration programs which involved the use of busing. In 1966, for example, Boston began its METCO program, which bused 1,500 black students from the central city to predominantly white schools in middle-class suburbs. Other communities which began integration programs voluntarily include White Plains, New York; Ann Arbor, Michigan; Riverside, California; and New Haven, Connecticut. These programs rested on the assumption that racial integration would increase the educational opportunities of black students; they took their rationale from the 1967 *Report of the United States Commission on Civil Rights*:

> Negro children suffer serious harm when their education takes place in public schools which are racially segregated, whatever the source of such segregation may be. Negro children who attend predominantly Negro schools do not achieve as well as other children, Negro and white. Their aspirations are more restricted than those of other children and they do not have as much confidence that they can influence their own futures. When they become adults, they are less likely to participate in the mainstream of American society, and more likely to fear, dislike, and avoid white Americans.[26]

However, the evidence on the impact of school desegregation and busing programs is not encouraging. One report suggests that integration and busing have had only limited effects, not all of which are positive. Drawing on the evidence of six Northern cities, the report discusses the effects of integration and busing on the academic achievement, aspirations, self-concept, racial attitudes, and educational opportunities of black children. None of the cities show that integration has had any effect on academic achievement as measured by standardized tests. However, this finding should not be terribly surprising since "there is no published report of *any* strictly educational reform which has been proven substantially to affect academic achievement; school integration programs are no exception."[27]

The evidence suggests further that bused students do not significantly raise their educational or occupational aspirations. While the findings vary slightly from one city to the next, the general pattern is that minority students do tend to have lower self-esteem and motivation, but also that these are not affected by integration. It has long been assumed that integration would increase racial tolerance, reduce racial stereotypes, and generally improve race relations. However, just the opposite seems to be true: "integration heightens racial identity and consciousness, enhances ideologies that promote racial segregation, and reduces opportunities for actual contact between the races."[28]

One area where integration and busing show some positive effects is in long-term educational achievements. In Boston, bused students were much more likely to start college than were nonbused students who attended predominantly black, central city schools. However, of those students who entered college, a much larger proportion of the bused students dropped out after the first year. "[T]he METCO program seems to have had a dramatic effect upon the impetus for college, and many more of the bused students actually started some form of higher education. But the bused drop-out rate was substantially higher, so that towards the end of the sophomore year the bused students were not much more likely to be enrolled full-time in college than the control group."[29] In spite of the dropout rate, however, bused students are more likely to be enrolled in higher-quality colleges, leading to the conclusion that educational experiences of black students in middle-class suburban schools may have a "channeling" effect not found in central city schools.

While these findings are not entirely clear or supportive of integration, they should not, by themselves, serve as a basis for rejecting integrationist goals. For one thing, we must realize that integration generally operates under contrived circumstances.

> In all of the programs reviewed, the integration has been induced by the actions of state or local agencies; it has not occurred in a more natural way through individual voluntary actions. The use of busing, the relatively instantaneous transition from an all-black to an all-white environment, the fact of being part of a readily identifiable group in a new and strange setting, may all combine to enhance racial solidarity and increase separatist tendencies from black students.[30]

Also, these data have been collected during a period in which the black community has come to question the value of integration. While a majority of blacks continue to support integration, a growing number (particularly among the young) favor black pride, black community control, and separatism. The attitude shifts identified in the above report may reflect these new ideas and not the results of busing per se.

The limited effects of integration and busing also reflect the several difficult problems of black students: incessant poverty, substandard housing conditions, and family instability, plus racial discrimination and inferior educational opportunities. It is unrealistic to expect one tool—school integration—to alter educational achievement, since these other social and economic conditions persist unabated.

SUMMARY

In this chapter, we have explored the politics of school desegregation, using policy delivery systems as an organizing framework. The problems of racial inequality and discrimination are deeply rooted in American society. While white Americans give lip-service to the notion that "all men are created equal," they have compromised—if not repudiated—this principle on many occasions. The struggle for racial equality has been a most difficult one, with the failures of Reconstruction, the barriers sanctioned by *Plessy v. Ferguson*, the initial excitement and eventual disillusionment with *Brown v. Board of Education*, the active pursuit of desegregation during the late 1960s, and the apparent retreat of the 1970s.

Racial desegregation in the public schools can result from laws (de jure) or from social and economic factors—particularly residential segregation of minority groups and the widespread use of the neighborhood school (de facto). For many years, governmental efforts have focused on de jure segregation; only since the late 1960s has de facto segregation been attacked. As such, the struggle for racial equality has become a national problem. With it has come busing as a tool for integrating the public schools.

Most white Americans, though supporting the principle of racial integration, do not seem to favor specific proposals to achieve it. Public opinion surveys have shown consistently that an overwhelming majority of white Americans are opposed intensely to busing. Numerous studies have also shown that more blacks than whites support integrationist goals and programs designed to achieve them. However, support for integration has dropped noticeably within the black community in recent years.

School desegregation policies are made and carried out in the midst of government fragmentation and conflict. At the national level, legislative, executive, bureaucratic, and judicial actors constantly debate alternative courses of action. The latest example is the struggle over the courts' authority to order busing. Since the Supreme Court sanctioned busing in 1971, opponents of this policy have endorsed congressional efforts to limit the scope of judicial authority.

Fragmentation is also seen in the relationship among federal, state, and local governments. While federal officials make general desegregation policy decisions, state and local authorities are responsible for implementing them. Since federal policies are usually quite vague, state and local officials enjoy considerable latitude; and their inability or unwillingness to comply with national guidelines serves as an important barrier to the achievement of school desegregation.

Finally, the impact of school desegregation and busing is not yet clear. At least one study has found that integration and busing have had little effect on the academic achievement, aspirations, self-concept, racial attitudes, and educational opportunities of black children. The one area where some positive effects have been identified is long-term educational achievement. Black students who are bused to predominantly white schools in middle-class suburbs are more likely to enroll in higher-quality colleges or universities.

REFERENCES

1 "Education for a Nation" (Washington, D.C.: *Congressional Quarterly*, 1972), p. 32.
2 Quoted in Richard Hofstadter, *The American Political Tradition* (New York: Alfred A. Knopf, Inc., 1936), p. 116.
3 *Plessy v. Ferguson*, 163 U.S. 537 (1896).
4 Ibid.
5 *Sweatt v. Painter*, 339 U.S. 629 (1950).
6 *Brown v. Board of Education of Topeka, Kansas*, 347 U.S. 483 (1954).
7 George Gallup, *The Gallup Poll: Public Opinion 1935–1971* (New York: Random House, Inc., 1972), vol. 2, pp. 1249–1250.
8 U.S. Commission on Civil Rights, *Racial Isolation in the Public Schools*, 1967, pp. 3, 5.
9 Karl E. Taeuber and Alma F. Taeuber, *Negroes in Cities* (Chicago: Aldine Publishing Company, 1965).
10 Karl Taeuber, "Residential Segregation," *Scientific American*, vol. 213 (August 1965), pp. 12–19. Copyright © 1965 by Scientific American, Inc. All rights reserved.
11 *Brown v. Board of Education of Topeka*, 349 U.S. 294 (1955).
12 Harrell R. Rodgers, Jr., and Charles S. Bullock, III, *Law and Social Change* (New York: McGraw-Hill Book Company, 1972), p. 72.
13 *Alexander v. Holmes*, 396 U.S. 19 (1969).
14 Warren E. Miller and Donald E. Stokes, "Constituency Influence in Congress," *American Political Science Review*, vol. 57 (March 1963), pp. 45–56.
15 Herbert H. Hyman and Paul B. Sheatsley, "Attitudes toward Desegregation," *Scientific American*, vol. 211 (July 1964), pp. 16–23.
16 Ibid., pp. 409–410.
17 These data have been taken from the 1972 election survey conducted by the University of Michigan's Institute for Social Research.
18 Joel D. Aberbach and Jack L. Walker, "The Meanings of Black Power," *American Political Science Review*, vol. 64 (June 1970), pp. 367–388; Everett F. Cataldo et al., "Social Strain and Urban Violence," in Louis H. Masotti and Don R. Bowen (ed.), *Riots and Rebellion: Civil Violence in the Urban Community* (Beverly Hills: Sage Publications, Inc., 1968), p. 293; and *Newsweek*, June 30, 1969, p. 20.
19 Joel D. Aberbach and Jack L. Walker, *Race in the City* (Boston: Little, Brown and Company, 1973).
20 *Swann v. Charlotte-Mecklenburg Board of Education*, 402 U.S. 1 (1971).
21 Quoted in *Civil Rights: Progress Report 1970* (Washington, D.C.: *Congressional Quarterly*, 1971), p. 16.
22 "Education for a Nation," p. 35.

23 Ibid., p. 36.
24 Rodgers and Bullock, op. cit., pp. 97–98.
25 Quoted in *Congressional Record*, Jan. 31, 1974, S931.
26 U.S. Commission on Civil Rights, p. 193.
27 David J. Armor, "The Evidence on Busing," *The Public Interest* (Summer 1972), p. 99. Copyright © by National Affairs, Inc., 1972.
28 Ibid., p. 102.
29 Ibid., p. 105.
30 Ibid., p. 112.

Chapter 3

Vietnam and the Middle East: Two Cases in American Foreign Policy

FROM 1787 TO 1945

By tradition, the United States is an isolationist nation. Between 1787 and the early years of the twentieth century, its foreign policy had two objectives: (1) to remain aloof from the political affairs of the major powers, particularly those in Europe; and (2) to carve out a special sphere of influence in the Western Hemisphere. In his *Farewell Address*, George Washington indicated that temporary alliances might be necessary in times of crisis, but he advised future leaders to "steer clear of permanent alliances with any portion of the foreign world." These isolationist sentiments dominated American thinking throughout the nineteenth century; the United States played only a limited role in world affairs.

As a corollary to isolationism, the Monroe Doctrine asserted the United States' intention to protect all North, Central, and South American countries from the interference and intervention of the European powers.

Declaring the Western Hemisphere "off limits" to the expansionist policies of European nations, President Monroe asserted that

> we should consider any attempt on their part to extend their system to any portion of this hemisphere as dangerous to our peace and safety. With the existing colonies and dependencies of any European power we have not interfered and shall not interfere. But with the Governments who have declared their independence and maintained it, and whose independence we have, on great consideration and just principles, acknowledged, we could not view any interposition for the purpose of oppressing them, or controlling in any other manner their destiny, by any European power in any other light than as the manifestation of an unfriendly disposition toward the United States.[1]

Thereafter, isolationism and dominance of the Western Hemisphere defined American foreign policy for more than a century. As European powers fought to gain more territory and expand their spheres of influence, the United States remained officially neutral. At the same time, it pursued policies within the Western Hemisphere that resembled the imperialism of the Western European powers. In 1901, Theodore Roosevelt argued that the United States should take a more active role in world affairs: "We stand supreme in a continent, in a hemisphere. East and West we look across two great oceans toward the larger life in which, whether we will or not, we must take an ever-increasing share."[2] Yet isolationist sentiments were not easily overcome. President Woodrow Wilson delayed American entry into World War I for more than two years and finally agreed to enter it as a moral crusade to make the world "safe for democracy." After the war, America refused to join the League of Nations and again turned inward. The 1920s and 1930s were marked by an emphasis on domestic problems. Americans isolated themselves from Europe and its problems, and many seemed oblivious to the developing threat of Hitler's Germany.

World War II did much to erode America's isolationist mood. In 1937, Franklin D. Roosevelt had warned that the United States would not escape involvement in the war, but it was not until Pearl Harbor that most Americans realized that the costs of isolationism were too great. Participation in World War II elevated the United States to world leadership. At the war's end, some Americans called for a return to a "go it alone" policy, but such a policy was unrealistic. The United States' role in the postwar world had already been determined, and retreat was no longer practical. The United States possessed great power in the world of international politics. It had a monopoly on nuclear power. Physically, it was untouched by the war; its economy was stronger than that of the

Soviet Union, not to mention those of the ravaged European nations. The rise of the Soviet Union as a world power, and the growing tension between it and the United States, further assured that there would be no turning back.

WHAT SUPERPOWERDOM MEANS

The United States has dominated international politics for the past three decades, with important consequences for Americans and others alike. The American people have provided the money and manpower required to finance foreign aid and to maintain large military forces. Many of our domestic crises have grown out of our international role. While some feel that our activities abroad are necessary for our national security, others believe that their number limits our ability to deal with domestic problems. They also argue that these activities deprive people of their "real" incomes by contributing to rapid inflation. Our involvement in Vietnam, for example, caused sharp domestic conflicts beginning in the mid-1960s and continuing after the withdrawal of American ground troops in 1973. Finally, our foreign policies can affect our economy through the actions of other nations, as demonstrated by the 1973–1974 Arab oil embargo against the United States because of our support for Israel.

THE VIETNAM AND MIDDLE EAST CRISES: DIFFERENCES AND SIMILARITIES

The Vietnam war and the Middle East crisis are two of our most significant foreign policy controversies since World War II. In some respects, these crises were very different. In Vietnam, the United States became involved directly in a massive land war that dragged on for more than a decade, but no American troops have fought in the Middle East. Also, while the Middle East crisis was largely a conventional war, Vietnam was a guerilla war, with no clear demarcation between the territory of friends and enemies, and with many political factors that resisted our overwhelming manpower and sophisticated technology. Finally, Israel is politically united; South Vietnam is not.

In spite of these differences, the similarities between the Vietnam war and the Middle East crisis are striking. Both crises represent recent flare-ups in long-standing controversies. Historically, the Vietnamese have long been locked in conflict with the Mongols, Chinese, Siamese, French, and—during World War II—the Japanese. Following Japan's collapse in 1945, Ho Chi Minh proclaimed from Hanoi the independence of all Vietnam, while at the same time, French troops reestablished control in large portions of the south. The refusal of the United States to intervene directly in support of the French colonial forces led to their catastrophic defeat at Dien Bien Phu in 1954. When the United States opted for military intervention less than a decade later, it merely marked the beginning of a new phase in the continuing struggle for control of Vietnam.

Similarly, the origins of the Middle East conflict go back several decades. The issue of Palestine was a troublesome one, beginning with Britain's pledge in the Balfour Declaration of 1917 to establish it as a "national home" for the Jewish people. At that point, many Jews had already established homes in Palestine. Some groups had lived there continuously since biblical times; others had fled the antisemitic pogroms of Czarist Russia; and still others to pursue the ideals of Zionism articulated late in the nineteenth century. Hitler's slaughter of 6 million Jews in his concentration camps caused many Jews to emigrate after World War II to Palestine, which they regarded as their traditional homeland. "The Jews were determined to establish a Jewish state, while the Arabs feared that the Jewish immigration would crowd them out of what they also regarded as their rightful homeland."[3] In November 1947, the United Nations partitioned Palestine into two independent states, one Jewish and the other Arab. Six months later, the British ended their mandate of Palestine and the Jews proclaimed the State of Israel. Refusing to accept this state of affairs, Arab armies invaded Israel. By the time of the subsequent armistice, the Israelis had lost access to part of Jerusalem but otherwise had added to the territory assigned to them in the earlier United Nations resolution. Since then, Arab-Israeli border clashes have been common, with major confrontations occurring in 1956, 1967, and, most recently, 1973.

Of even greater significance to the United States, the conflicts in Vietnam and the Middle East have occurred at two levels. First, each was a local conflict. The Vietnam war was, in part, a civil war between the Vietcong and the governments of North and South Vietnam. Similarly, the Middle East contest occurred between two hostile groups over a common territory. Second, each was also a confrontation of superpowers. In both Vietnam and the Middle East, the interests of the United States and the Soviet Union (and, in the case of Vietnam, China) were at stake. The American commitment in Vietnam was based less on a concern for the independence of South Vietnam than on the belief that the Soviet Union and Communist China would benefit directly from the collapse of the Saigon government, and that our own interests would be threatened. Likewise, the superpowers pursued their own interests in the Middle East by providing their allies with weapons, supplies, advice, or encouragement. From the American perspective, Eugene V. Rostow has written that the Middle East quarrel "has become not only a difficult regional problem, but . . . an important tool in the Soviet Union's effort to outflank NATO, divide Europe from America, and neutralize Western Europe."[4]

This confrontation of superpowers is a dominant feature of the American foreign policy environment. In this chapter, the Vietnam war and the 1973 Middle East crisis will be explored, again using policy delivery systems as an organizing framework. In contrast to our examination of desegregation and busing, here we can ignore state and local contributions to the system. Foreign policy is the province of the federal government; rarely do state and local policy makers have a voice.

THE ENVIRONMENT: COLD WAR POLITICS IN A NUCLEAR AGE

The Development of the Cold War

American foreign policy has two touchstones: the political conflict of the cold war and the ever-present threat of nuclear destruction. At the end of World War II, the United States envisioned a world of peace and cooperation among the "Big Three"—the United States, Britain, and the Soviet Union. However, this vision was never realized. Between 1945 and 1948, the Soviet Union imposed control over Albania, Bulgaria, Hungary, Poland, Roumania, and Yugoslavia. The Russians also asserted themselves with a pro-Communist coup in Czechoslovakia in 1948; the Berlin blockade which sought to limit American, French, and British access to that beleaguered city; and the pressure put on Greece, Turkey, and Iran.

The situation was similarly unsettled in the Far East. After years of intermittent fighting, the Communists gained control of China, sending Chiang Kai-shek and his American-supported Nationalists to Taiwan (Formosa) in 1949. The Communist takeover resulted partly from the corruption and inefficiency of Chiang's regime. As John Spanier has written:

> The government had alienated important segments of the politically articulate minority, especially the businessmen and intellectuals. The more inarticulate and passive peasants were tired of the constant fighting, the high rents and taxes. All three groups had either lost confidence in the ability of the government to take care of the problems of postwar China, or felt that the government was not interested in their welfare.[5]

The United States tried to save Chiang's government, but to no avail. In 1950, the struggle in Asia shifted to South Korea with an invasion by the Russian-equipped North Korean Communists. The United States alone went to the aid of the South Koreans, although several months later—after action by the United Nations Security Council—other nations provided troops and material. When American and United Nations troops carried the fighting into North Korea, hundreds of thousands of Communist Chinese troops joined the battle in a war that lasted nearly three years.

By the early 1950s, the shape of the postwar world had been clearly established: a global conflict between the "Communist Bloc" and the "Free World." This is not to say that all countries were members of or identified with one or the other. But these rival coalitions, each led by a "superpower"—the United States and the Soviet Union—dominated international politics; the so-called nonaligned nations provided a frequent battleground for quarrels between them.

It was not immediately clear how the United States would respond to growing Soviet hostility and to the expansion of communism in both Europe and the Far East. While some United States officials maintained that national security demanded an aggressive response, others felt that this would only intensify Soviet hostilities. The first clear indication of how the United States would react came from George Kennan, the State Department's foremost expert on the Soviet Union. Kennan argued that the Soviet Union and the Western world had few interests in common. Communist ideology had taught the Russians that "the outside world was hostile and that it was their duty eventually to overthrow the political forces beyond their borders. The powerful hands of Russian history and tradition reached up to sustain them in this feeling."[6] Therefore, Kennan argued, the struggle would be a long one. The Russians would not seek an immediate conquest; they would always be exerting pressure, seeking weak spots, trying to expand their control over people and land. "The main thing is that there should always be pressure, increasing constant pressure, toward the desired goal. There is no trace of any feeling in Soviet psychology that the goal must be reached at any given time."[7]

Kennan proposed a policy of "long-term, patient, but firm and vigilant containment." He argued that the United States should recognize the realities of the cold war and seek to prevent the expansion of communism beyond its postwar boundaries.

> The Soviet pressure against the free institutions of the Western world is something that can be contained by the adroit and vigilant application of counterforce at a series of constantly shifting geographical and political points, corresponding to the shifts and maneuvers of Soviet policy.[8]

Containment became the basis for America's postwar foreign policy. For more than a quarter of a century, the United States has been committed to resisting Communist expansion throughout the world. In economic, political, and military affairs, the competition between the United States and the Communists has provided the setting within which policy decisions are made. This contest is the basic reason for American economic and military assistance to Greece and Turkey; the initiation of the Marshall Plan; the creation of the North Atlantic Treaty Organization (NATO); and intervention in Lebanon, Cuba, Vietnam, and the Middle East.

The cold war's impact on American foreign policy can be seen in Townsend Hoopes' account of the United States' involvement in Vietnam. Hoopes argues that President Johnson was both uncomfortable and insecure when dealing with questions of foreign policy. He tended to "think about the external world in the simplistic terms of appeasement versus military resolve." Such a view was consistent with the thinking of his closest foreign policy advisers, above all, with the notion that

> the "Communist Bloc" remained an essentially cohesive international conspiracy manifesting itself primarily in military and paramilitary assaults against that other comprehensible entity, the "Free World." An important corollary was the belief that an accretion of "communist" influence *anywhere* must redound to the direct benefit of the main power centers in Moscow and Peking, for from this flowed the logic that counterthrusts in kind were everywhere and almost automatically necessary; otherwise a progressive, irreversible, unacceptable erosion of the world power balance could not be averted.[9]

As we have already observed, the situation in the Middle East is not very different. American policy toward that region is made with an eye on the Soviet Union. Our concern for the integrity of Israel is matched by our effort to contain Soviet influence. Through the years the United States has sold arms to Arab countries to limit their dependence on the Soviet Union. At the same time, arms sales to Israel were stepped up in response to the heavy Soviet investment in the rearming of the Arab states after the 1967 war. For some observers, the Middle East is presently the most unstable region of the world, and it is there that the dangers of a direct Soviet-American confrontation seem most acute.[10]

Many of the elements of the cold war have been transformed, if not eradicated, in recent years. The classic view of two cohesive blocs, each dominated by a single superpower, is out of date. The United States and the Soviet Union are no longer able to control the activities of their allies. The conflict between Russia and China, and the loosening of Russian control over several Eastern European nations, has undermined the Soviet position. Similarly, the United States no longer controls the activities of the Western world. The loosening of the Western alliance is seen in Western Europe's economic recovery and the creation of the European Economic Community; the erosion of NATO's position as a cornerstone of the Western world's defense system; the intensification of Franco-American disagreements; and the realization, after October 1973, that Arab oil might be more important than American friendship.

Despite these changes, our policy in Vietnam was affected greatly by the background of the cold war and the view of continuing threats from the Soviet Union and China. In the Middle East, many American officials saw the Soviet Union as the real force behind the Arab attack.[11] Similarly, they see pro-Communist activities in Africa, Asia, and Latin America as being directly caused by, and benefiting, the Soviet Union and Communist China. Thus, while many elements of the cold war may no longer exist in their original form, the competition between East and West remains a crucial factor in the making of American foreign policy.

The Bomb and American Foreign Policy

The threat of nuclear war is a second determinant of American foreign policy. The development of nuclear weapons did much to persuade people that large-scale war was too costly and dangerous a way of resolving disagreements among industrially advanced nations. The same, of course, could be said of wars before the nuclear age. But the ultimate threat of total annihilation, with no winners and all losers in a nuclear war, made it more urgent than ever to find other ways of resolving conflicts.

Some policy makers see nuclear weapons as "the 'absolute weapon' and . . . believe that a clear preeminence in its development would permit a power to dictate terms to any power which did not have it or was inferior in the development of it. . . ."[12] Thus, for more than two decades the United States and the Soviet Union have been engaged in a massive arms race. Each believes that its national security can be preserved only when there is equality or, even better, when one enjoys a position of nuclear superiority. However, it is a race that neither side can win. Perhaps realizing this, these two superpowers have begun a series of Strategic Arms Limitation Talks (SALT). It is hoped that these talks can help each nation better understand the other's intentions regarding the future development and use of nuclear weapons, control the development of new weapons that would upset the present balance of forces, and deescalate the arms race.

The threat of nuclear war has also affected the cold war. Neither the Soviet Union nor the United States desires a direct confrontation involving the use of nuclear weapons; the risks are too great to tolerate. Each is prepared, however, for military conflicts short of this, involving conventional weapons. A strategy which involves even less risk—and one which has been common in recent years—is that of "limited war," in which the superpowers confront each other only indirectly. In such situations, much of the fighting is done by the superpowers' allies, as in the Middle East. Where one of the superpowers becomes involved in the actual fighting, as in Vietnam, its adversary has been its rival's agent or proxy, not the other superpower itself.

DEMANDS AND RESOURCES

Public officials have more freedom in making foreign policy than in making domestic policy. Yet, they are still limited by: (1) economic and military capabilities; (2) public opinion; (3) the actions and reactions of allies; and (4) information about the probable consequences of different courses of action.

Economic Capabilities

A nation's ability to produce goods and services can have a vital effect on its foreign policy. It determines how deeply the nation can get involved in foreign commitments and what kinds of demands that nation can make on others. If the economy cannot sustain a war effort without a drastic cutback in domestic production or massive aid from other countries, the nation's foreign policy potential is seriously limited. In contrast, if the economy is strong and capable of producing goods and services for both the war effort and the home front, the nation's foreign policy can be much more ambitious.

The United States clearly falls in the second category. With a Gross National Product of $1.2 trillion in 1972, its capacity to turn out both "guns and butter" is unquestioned. Yet, like all other nations, its capabilities fall short of its needs; it is constantly faced with the problem of scarce resources. Both the Johnson and Nixon administrations tried to prevent the Vietnam war from becoming a drain on domestic programs, and for the most part, they succeeded. As military spending continued to rise, domestic spending remained fairly stable throughout the war years.

Midway through the war, however, the national economy, which had expanded rapidly during the 1960s, began to show some strain. In 1966, Richard Steadman, special assistant to Secretary of Defense Robert McNamara, warned that we had overextended ourselves and that if the war continued, shortages of certain skills and materials could be felt. If this happened, the federal government would have to impose wage and price controls and other anti-inflationary measures. Interestingly, though, the decision to deescalate the war in the late 1960s was largely political; our economic bind was largely ignored.

Why is it that in formulating foreign policy, economics takes a back seat? Is it because we are so rich? We can determine the answer most easily by considering the *character* of defense and foreign affairs. As budgetary figures make clear, our national defense and related foreign involvements have the highest priority, and money is often no object; policies are often based on considerations other than cost. But with domestic programs, policy makers often ask: Can we afford an expanded health care system, innovative education programs, and new income-maintenance programs? In defense and foreign affairs, they generally ask: Can we afford *not* to resist communist expansion throughout the world? Can we afford *not* to honor our international agreements by providing aid to our allies in Europe, the Middle East, and elsewhere? Professor Joseph Frankel depicts this dilemma as follows:

> It may well be true . . . that if some of the money devoted to foreign policy were spent domestically, it would benefit the states involved much more by strengthening them economically and socially. Nobody, however, can be quite certain that more limited defense may not spell moral danger, and more limited foreign aid, significant political advances by rivals and opponents.[13]

This being the case, enormous spending for defense and related matters will probably continue.

This is not to suggest that economics has little or no effect on defense and foreign affairs. In fact, its impact can be seen in a number of recent policy decisions. The SALT conferences reflect, in part, the limitations on our economy. Aside from contributing to national security and international stability, SALT is also seen as a means of deescalating an incredibly expensive arms race. The importance of economic factors can also be seen in the decisions to shut down certain military facilities both in the United States and abroad, to reduce military manpower levels, to reexamine American troop commitments in Western Europe, and to cut drastically the funds allocated for space exploration and many foreign aid programs.

Military Capabilities

Capacity and willingness to use military force also affect policy-making in defense and foreign affairs. A nation with a powerful military machine is obviously in a strong international position. The United States is in this enviable position. Its military strength gives its policy makers opportunities enjoyed by the leaders of only a few nations. Both the size of the American economy and its advanced technology make available the military hardware needed for virtually any situation. Every year the United States spends billions of dollars for military research and development. At stake are both the continued strategic arms race with the Soviet Union and the desire to be ready for any conceivable battlefield condition.

However, since even the American economy has its limits, policy makers are still subject to some constraints. During the Vietnam war, the demand for military goods, consumer goods, and domestic social services rose quickly. Realizing that the economy could not accommodate all these demands, and also that certain pressure groups were agitating for more money for domestic programs, both the Johnson and Nixon administrations recommended limiting the budget for the war effort.

Policy making can also be faced with manpower constraints. As the United States entered the Vietnam conflict, it anticipated a conventional war requiring no more than a few thousand men. But the buildup continued month after month, year after year. Ultimately, the draft was greatly expanded—a policy that aroused opposition to the Selective Service System and ultimately to the war itself.

> By 1967 a ceiling was reached in the number of men available through the draft and through enlistments. At this time General Westmoreland requested 200,000 more troops, a figure that could not be reached without mobilizing the reserves. Literally the United States ran out of men, and it was Johnson's refusal to put the country on a semiwar footing that was one decisive influence on his March 31 [1967] decision to reverse the escalation.[14]

Finally, the training of the Armed Forces can be a severe problem. The war in Vietnam was the first large-scale guerrilla war the United States had ever entered. It was not prepared for the kind of war that evolved. Until 1965, American officials did not question the United States' ability to win a clear-cut victory in Vietnam. Most of them remained confident even though quick victories are seldom achieved in a guerrilla war, in which the aim of the insurgents is "to capture the power of the government from within, and to do so by eroding the morale of the army and by undermining popular confidence in the government."[15] A French defeat at Dien Bien Phu in 1954 "demonstrated that guerrilla warfare could defeat the larger, stronger, conventionally equipped army of even a major power."[16] As the war progressed, an increasing number of American soldiers was trained for guerrilla warfare, and yet the debate waged on: "Walter Rostow concluded that a clear-cut victory could be won in a guerrilla war while George Ball argued that white, foreign troops could not win. By [July 1965], however, the debate was largely academic, for the first group troops had already been sent to Vietnam."[17]

Public Opinion

As we shall see in Chapter 4, most public opinion polls show that numerous Americans are uninformed about and uninterested in political affairs. On many questions, particularly foreign policy issues which tend to be remote and complex, many people do not even *have* opinions. For example, when a random sample was asked in July 1969 what the United States should do next in Vietnam, 29 percent said they had given no thought to the matter. A year later, another sample was asked if it favored or opposed a congressional resolution to withdraw all United States troops from Vietnam by the end of 1971; 21 percent had no opinion.[18] Further, it is likely that many who did voice an opinion lacked basic factual information about the issues involved.

Analyzing public impact on foreign policy, Professor Bernard Cohen argues that "public opinion as a political force" is marginal: it gives policy makers "some encouragements or limitations that facilitate or modify preferred behavior."[19] Because most people know little about foreign affairs, and are content to leave it that way, policy makers have wide discretion in this area. Many other factors contribute to this discretion. For one thing, when international events do attract widespread attention—namely, in crises—people tend to support government actions. The Japanese attack on Pearl Harbor, the flare-up of fighting in Korea, the entry of American troops into Lebanon, the Bay of Pigs invasion and the Cuban missile crisis, and the alleged attack in the Gulf of Tonkin generated a "rally-round-the-flag" effect which gave policy makers overwhelming public support. Unlike domestic crises, which often aggravate internal divisions and disagreements, international crises which threaten national security tend to make the public close ranks behind the actions of public officials.

This support can be seen in the results of numerous public opinion surveys. Following the Gulf of Tonkin incident in 1964, those favoring a complete withdrawal from Vietnam were outnumbered 6 to 1 by those calling for some form of continued war effort. By early 1965, support for the war effort had declined but was still favored by a ratio of nearly 4 to 1. After President Johnson declared in 1966 that the United States would not tolerate a Communist takeover of South Vietnam, 73 percent of the American people endorsed a continuation of existing policy or a major escalation of the fighting, while only 19 percent argued for the withdrawal of troops.[20]

The public's response to our pro-Israeli policies has been similarly positive. In July 1967, a month after the Six-Day War, a Gallup poll found "only one American in seven of the opinion that Israel should be required to give back the lands seized in the six-day war against the Arab nations."[21] When Gallup inquired in 1973 whether people's sympathies were with Israel or the Arab states, 50 percent sided with Israel, 7 percent supported the Arabs, and the remaining 43 percent had no opinion or responded that neither side had their sympathies.[22]

This support reflects, in part, the ambivalence that marks most people's thinking about American foreign policy. "Where individuals are uncertain about what is right and what is wrong, or where they do not have much information and have not given the problem much thought, they are likely to lean upon authority figures as a way of arriving at an opinion on the matter."[23] In the United States, the President is the highest authority figure. In crisis situations, the public tends to rally to his support, turning away from both his domestic critics and foreign detractors.

This tendency is illustrated by President Nixon's decision to send troops into Cambodia in spring 1970. The President's action created violent criticism and protests in many cities and campuses. Throughout the country, there was little enthusiasm for the Cambodian invasion, which many writers called one of the least popular actions of the entire war. But notice the gradual development of support. On the eve of the invasion, the Harris poll reported that only 7 percent of the American people favored it, while 59 percent were opposed. Another 23 percent felt that our commitment should be limited to sending advisers to aid Cambodia. After the President's decision was announced, the Harris poll found widespread skepticism about what the invasion would accomplish. Only 12 percent felt that the President would be able to remove all troops from Cambodia by the end of June (as he had promised to do), and an equal number thought that the invasion would end the war more quickly. But when the Harris organization asked whether the President had been right in sending troops to Cambodia, 50 percent said yes while 43 percent said no. "These data vividly illustrate the prestige of the President when he acts and the malleability of American opinion. The wide gap between the 7 percent who favored sending troops before they were sent and the 50 percent who approved the President's decision after he had decided to send the troops is a measure of the support he can arouse."[24]

This does not mean that foreign policy makers are never influenced by public opinion. Domestic support is vital for an effective foreign policy. As Henry Kissinger has written, public support is "the acid test of a foreign policy."[25] Vietnam provides a remarkably clear illustration of this point. In the face of the Buddhist crisis of 1966, the persistent political instability in South Vietnam, the Tet offensive of 1968, and the apparent inability of American officials to control—or even anticipate—

events in Vietnam, public opposition to the war intensified. As the war dragged on, President Johnson's credibility slipped more and more. Antiwar sentiment spread as a result of several factors, including rising economic problems at home and the deterioration of the "quality of life"—as shown in student demonstrations, racial and political violence, and the growth of a counterculture which challenged prevailing beliefs and values—and a growing sense that the war could not be won.

After the bitter taste left by Vietnam, the federal government may be slow to involve the United States directly in another war. Numerous Gallup surveys indicate that the American people are weary of such involvements, as shown in recent inquiries about the Middle East crisis. As we have already seen, the American people continue to sympathize with the Israelis, but there is also increasing support for the view that we should stay out of the conflict. In 1967, 41 percent of those questioned supported this position; in 1970, this percentage had grown to 58. The findings of a 1973 Gallup survey are even more revealing: "A late October survey, for example, showed the public voting by the ratio of about 7 to 5 against sending arms and material to Israel, and to be overwhelmingly against supplying arms and material to the Arab states."[26]

The Actions and Reactions of Allied Nations

American policy makers are also sensitive to the positions taken by our allies, particularly if it is *they* we claim to be defending. It is more difficult for the United States to pursue a war effort if it does not have the moral support—not to mention men and material—of allied states. Until the fall of Prince Sihanouk in 1970, we had no support in Cambodia; and Laos has been cool to the American effort throughout the Vietnam war. The United States did receive the support of other governments—including South Vietnam, South Korea, Australia, the Philippines, Thailand, and numerous European allies—but some of them were less than enthusiastic.

However, this factor has only marginal influence. President Nixon ordered the mining of the harbor of Haiphong in the face of criticism from our European allies, and the objections of South Vietnam and Cambodia did nothing to halt our deescalation in Vietnam. The 1973 Middle East conflict is still another example. In response to the 1967 Six-Day War, the United States and its European allies (with the exception of France) developed a coordinated diplomatic effort that was based on extensive and almost constant consultations. In 1973, the American response was noticeably different:

> Nothing mattered except the course of the war itself, and Soviet-American diplomacy. The United States did not undertake from the beginning an orchestrated and worldwide campaign, as it did in 1967 and 1968, to explain

its policy to the Atlantic allies and to other governments, friendly and not-so-friendly alike, and to develop common positions with them where possible. We had full public support only from the Netherlands and from Portugal. Europe as such was on the sidelines, neutral, or at odds with the United States.[27]

Information about Probable Consequences

Finally, policy makers are influenced by what they know, or think, the probable results will be. The problems are generally complex, and many alternate choices and outcomes must be weighed. At times, however, policy decisions are made with information that is either inaccurate or incomplete. This can have a limiting influence, as when policy makers tend to play it safe by taking low-risk actions. This tactic was particularly clear when the United States confronted the Soviet Union in the Cuban missile crisis of 1962. Possible courses of action included a "surgical" air strike against Soviet missiles already in place and a naval blockade to end Soviet weapons shipments to Cuba. President Kennedy and his aides spent many hours analyzing possible Soviet responses. Initially, the air strike received greater attention. In the end, however, the President chose to go with the blockade, largely because it presented fewer risks. As Theodore Sorenson has written:

> The air strike, unlike the blockade, would directly and definitely attack Soviet military might, kill Russians as well as Cubans and thus more likely provoke a Soviet military response. Not to respond at all would be too great a humiliation for Khrushchev to bear, affecting his relations not only at home and with the Chinese but with all the Communist parties in the developing world. . . .
> [The blockade] was a more limited, low-key military action than the air strike. It offered Khrushchev the choice of avoiding a direct military clash by keeping his ships away. It could at least be initiated without a shot being fired or a single Soviet or Cuban citizen being killed. Thus it seemed slightly less likely to precipitate an immediate military riposte.[28]

Despite all the money involved in its collection and analysis, information does not always lead to simple solutions. The *Pentagon Papers* show that American officials had some information on Hanoi's willingness to continue the war, regardless of cost. President Kennedy's intelligence reports indicated that an American escalation of the fighting would be matched by Hanoi. Some reports indicated that North Vietnam's agricultural economy, with its primitive but flexible transportation system, would not be destroyed by bombing. Yet other reports offered contrary projections.

The one area where information was lacking dealt with the intentions of the Soviet Union and China. The *Pentagon Papers* show that American officials were sensitive to potential Soviet and Chinese reactions and limited their actions accordingly. For example, President Johnson restricted bombing in North Vietnam so that American planes would not fly close to the Chinese border. We never seriously considered an invasion of the North, since it would draw in the Chinese. As time went on, however:

> Perhaps because of improved relations and increased contact between the Nixon administration and the Soviet Union and China, fear of their reactions was less important in the policy making of 1972. Possibly, secret contacts with leaders of these two countries convinced Nixon that they would not intervene. Possible reactions did not influence the president to modify his plans to mount a destructive bombing campaign against the North, with attacks very close to China, and to mine the harbors of Hanoi and Haiphong—a warlike act limiting the movement of Chinese and Soviet ships.[29]

CONVERSIONS PROCESS: PRESIDENTIAL PREEMINENCE IN FOREIGN POLICY

The fragmentation and conflict which surround school desegregation policies are much less evident in the field of defense and foreign affairs. While school desegregation and other domestic policies involve many actors at all levels of government, foreign policy decisions usually involve a few officials in Washington. The courts are rarely involved; and political parties and interest groups have only limited influence here. As we have already observed, public opinion also tends to have little effect on foreign policy—as the traditional weakness of Congress shows. Since each of these factors will be examined more thoroughly later, we shall restrict ourselves in this chapter to a brief discussion of policy making on Vietnam and the Middle East.

Vietnam

The Vietnam war illustrates how foreign policy making varies from one situation to another. During the Kennedy administration and the first two years of Lyndon Johnson's presidency, policy making on Vietnam was largely the responsibility of the President and his closest advisers. There was little involvement by Congress, much less by interest groups and the public. When President Kennedy opted for military intervention in Vietnam at the end of 1961, there was little congressional or public attention. The shift from a few hundred American advisers to more than 12,000 troops in 1962 aroused little controversy. It was not until 1964 that

Congress turned its attention to the war, and then it merely ratified decisions made by the President. In response to an alleged attack by North Vietnamese gunboats on two American destroyers in the Tonkin Gulf, President Johnson requested in August 1965 that Congress adopt a joint resolution which supported his position and authorized him "to take all necessary measures to repel any armed attack against the armed forces of the United States and to prevent further aggression." This Tonkin Gulf resolution was approved by both houses of Congress almost unanimously, in the Senate by 82 to 2 and in the House by 416 to 0.

During this first phase of the war, then, Congress functioned as a rubber stamp. Although the Constitution reserves for Congress the power to declare war, the President acted without any formal declaration. This fact appeared to concern only a few members of Congress, even in the face of ever-increasing demands for money. In spring 1965, for example, Congress approved a special $700 million military appropriations bill which was necessitated largely by the Vietnam war. The House passed the bill 408 to 7, the Senate 88 to 3.

If Congress was all too willing to defer to executive leadership during this period, the White House was equally happy to have it this way. Neither President Kennedy nor Johnson sought a formal declaration of war. Toward the end of the Johnson presidency, Under-Secretary of State Nicholas Katzenbach argued, in fact, that Congress's power to declare war had been made obsolete by the nuclear age; limited war, such as that in Vietnam, could be fought without such formalities. Furthermore, he argued that the Tonkin Gulf resolution had fulfilled the President's responsibility "to give the Congress full and effective voice."[30] Congress had already declared war, whether it knew it or not.

Nor did Presidents Kennedy and Johnson seek to involve Congress in policy making on Vietnam through serious consultation. When President Johnson asked Congress to approve the Tonkin Gulf resolution, he was less than straightforward about the "attack" on the American ships. As years passed, it became more and more difficult to prove that an attack had actually taken place. Perhaps most damning was the fact that the resolution had been prepared some time *before* the alleged incident; Johnson had merely waited for an opportune time to present it to Congress. Senator J. William Fulbright (D., Ark.) described the President's consultation with Congress during this initial period in the following manner:

> The President called the congressional leadership to the White House and had the Director of the CIA, the Secretary of Defense, etc., all demonstrate to us the reasons why the only course of action open to use was to bomb.

This was the consultation of the President with Congress on that important decision. Mike Mansfield and I were the only ones at that meeting to demur on the bombing . . . the President just did not give a damn.[31]

By mid-1965, the Vietnam war had begun to enter its second phase. No longer was it an issue that concerned only the President and his closest advisers. American troop commitments in Vietnam were growing steadily, both in numbers and in expense. The economy was beginning to feel the pressure of this war that we had almost drifted into. Television coverage of Vietnam was intensifying, and protest "teach-ins" on campus were being introduced. The war now assumed a prominent place in the consciousness of the American people. When they were asked in 1964 to name the most important problem facing the nation, only 8 percent mentioned Vietnam. In June 1965, this figure had risen to 23 percent. From that time until 1972, it remained as the most serious problem perceived by the American people.

In Congress protests against the President's handling of the war became particularly intense, and during the late 1960s and early 1970s, certain members of Congress tried repeatedly to restrain him. The Cooper-Church amendment sought to cut off all funds for the support of American troops in Cambodia. The McGovern-Hatfield amendment would forbid the use of funds to keep troops in Vietnam after the end of 1971. Although both of these amendments were approved by the Senate, they were ultimately rejected by the House.

It was not until 1973, after the Paris peace agreement, that Congress was able to challenge the President's preeminence in foreign affairs. Using the power of the purse, both houses of Congress accepted the Church-Case amendment, which forbade the use of funds for bombing in Cambodia, where no cease-fire had been achieved. Yet, this legislative victory was less than complete, since President Nixon vetoed the appropriations bill to which the amendment had been attached.

Most of the major decisions concerning the war were still being made by the President and his close advisers in the State Department, the Department of Defense, the National Security Council, and on the White House staff. The situation had not been altered that radically. But as Vietnam became a public controversy, these officials were subject to pressures and constraints not known previously. Public criticism seemed to influence President Johnson's decision not to seek reelection in 1968. It supported Nixon's continuing a policy of deescalation initiated by Johnson. Yet it did not prevent Nixon from committing American troops to Cambodia and Laos, and it did not preclude widened air attacks against population centers in North Vietnam and the mining of Haiphong Harbor. The Vietnam war remained in the hands of the White House; the

President remained the ultimate policy maker. But his decisions and actions were under closer scrutiny and constant attack from private citizens and public officials alike.

The Middle East

The Middle East crisis of 1973 illustrates the way in which foreign policy decisions are usually made. While the Arab attack on Israel of October 6, 1973, received widespread attention, it was President Nixon and members of a relatively small foreign policy elite who assumed responsibility for shaping the American response. The President had access to information not available to most members of Congress or the public. He could call upon the State and Defense Departments, the Central Intelligence Agency, the U.S. Information Agency, and personnel in the Agency for International Development and such departments as Treasury, Commerce, and Agriculture. Each of these units had representatives in American embassies throughout the Middle East and were in a position to transmit vital information to the President.

Furthermore, as Commander in Chief of the Armed Forces, President Nixon was able to act quickly and decisively. He immediately placed American troops throughout Europe on "alert" status and ordered American naval forces to standby positions in the Mediterranean Sea. Like his predecessors, Nixon also supported Israel, virtually committing the United States to its defense even though no treaties had ever been submitted to or approved by the Senate.

To be sure, the President did not have a completely free hand. As we have already noted, the American people's support for Israel in the Middle East crisis is tempered by their desire not to become directly involved. Furthermore, President Nixon was constrained by previous American actions. When he entered the White House in 1969, Nixon inherited commitments made during prior administrations to support the government of Israel; a reversal of policy would have been difficult. The President was also subject indirectly to pressures from Jewish organizations in the United States. Bernard C. Cohen has found that these organizations are most active in the State Department; government officials are sensitive to them and respect their political clout. Although he suggests that we should not exaggerate this impact on American foreign policy, he does note:

> One official talked about his contacts with Zionist organizations, but he summed up their impact not in terms of pressure-group politics but as a more generalized political fear of the electoral reactions of Jews in big cities, likening the situation to that of the Irish and United States policy toward Great Britain in the nineteenth century.[32]

Finally, the President recognized the importance of Israel as America's principal ally in an area that had attracted extensive Soviet commitments. Yet he also recognized that an open-ended commitment to Israel could drive the Arabs even further into the Soviet orbit. It could even endanger the Soviet-American detente or even precipitate a direct confrontation between them. Thus, there was much in the situation to assure considerable—but restrained—United States support for Israel.

POLICY

It is not our purpose to explore in detail American policy in Vietnam and the Middle East; such analyses can be found elsewhere.[33] Here we provide a brief outline of American policy in these two conflicts, emphasizing its consequences and assessing its effectiveness.

Vietnam

Looking back, it appears that American policy makers were not guided by a precise set of goals and objectives in setting our involvement in Vietnam. Rather, their decisions were a series of short-term responses—steps, or increments—to immediate problems. Policies were not shaped by the answers to such basic questions as: How large a commitment is the United States prepared to make, and what costs is it willing to endure?

Instead of asking these questions, American policy makers assumed that the interests of the United States and South Vietnam were inseparable and responded to a deteriorating situation with a series of short-range, progressively elaborate solutions: "first covert operations, then increasingly frequent 'retaliatory' air strikes against North Vietnam, followed by extensive bombing and, finally, the increasing use of U.S. ground forces in South Vietnam."[34] The Department of Defense estimates that between 1965 and 1974 total expenditures on the war in Vietnam came to approximately $112 billion. The figures in Table 3-1 show that outlays for Vietnam were $100 million in fiscal 1965 (July 1, 1964 to June 30, 1965); the next year they approached $5.8 billion. The peak in Vietnam spending was reached in fiscal 1969, the same year that American troop commitments surpassed 630,000. It was estimated that Vietnam expenditures would fall to about $4 billion in fiscal 1974 with the signing of the cease-fire agreement and with the withdrawal of most American troops.

President Eisenhower had initiated the American commitment with massive programs of economic and military assistance to support the government of South Vietnam. President Kennedy expanded that commitment by sending several thousand military "advisers" to South

Table 3-1   Cost of the War in Vietnam, Fiscal Years 1965–74
(Outlays in Billions of Dollars)

Fiscal year	Expenditures
1965	$ 0.1
1966	5.8
1967	18.4
1968	20.0
1969	21.5
1970	17.4
1971	11.5
1972	7.2
1973 (estimate)	5.9
1974 (estimate)	4.1
Total	$111.9

Source: Edward R. Fried, Alice M. Rivlin, Charles L. Schultze, and Nancy H. Teeters, *Setting National Priorities: The 1974 Budget* (Washington, D.C.: Brookings, 1973), p. 330. These data were taken originally from an unpublished computer tabulation provided by the Department of Defense (1973).

Vietnam and allegedly consenting to the overthrow of the Diem regime in the hope that a new military government would be better able to wage war against the Vietcong.

The most dramatic escalation of the war occurred during the Johnson presidency. In 1964, Johnson initiated retaliatory air strikes after the Tonkin incident; the next year American air strikes were intensified and troop commitments rose to over half a million men. The American objective throughout this period was a traditional clear-cut military victory. Not until the 1968 Tet offensive did President Johnson and his advisers concede that such a goal was unattainable. Rejecting the recommendation of an Ad Hoc Task Force on Vietnam that 200,000 additional troops be deployed immediately and that reserve call-ups, larger draft calls, and lengthened duty tours in Vietnam be initiated, the President announced to the nation: "I am taking the first step to de-escalate the conflict. We are reducing—substantially reducing—the present level of hostilities . . . unilaterally and at once."[35]

When Richard Nixon became President in 1969, it seemed that the American people would not accept a protracted war much longer. Yet, Nixon rejected pulling out all American troops immediately on the grounds that such action would lead to the collapse of the South Vietnamese government and the deterioration of the United States' reputation throughout the world. The deescalation strategy devised by the President and his chief foreign policy adviser, Henry Kissinger, had two parts. First, American ground troops would be withdrawn gradually from

Vietnam, thus reducing the war's costs in terms of both men and material. The President hoped that these troop withdrawals, coupled with continuing air action, would encourage Hanoi to negotiate an end to the conflict.

Second, the President initiated a policy of "Vietnamization," which was intended to upgrade South Vietnam's capacity to defend itself. It consisted of providing better training and more sophisticated armaments for South Vietnam's military. It was hoped that this would permit the South Vietnamese Army to assume primary responsibility for the ground war, although Washington realized that American economic and military aid—including air and naval support—would be required for some time.

On January 27, 1973, North Vietnam and the United States signed a cease-fire agreement that brought the war to a formal end. This agreement recognized the independence, sovereignty, and territorial integrity of Vietnam; called for an end to all hostilities and the withdrawal of all foreign troops within sixty days; mandated the return of all captured military and civilian personnel during the same period of time; asserted the right of the South Vietnamese people to choose their own form of government; supported the reunification of North and South Vietnam through peaceful means and without foreign intervention; and called for the creation of a Four-Party Joint Military Commission which would ensure that other provisions of the agreement were carried out. Although this agreement marked the formal conclusion of the Vietnam war, it did not end the political struggle for control of South Vietnam. As we shall see below, that struggle goes on, and some of the goals set out in the cease-fire agreement remain unrealized.

The Middle East

In contrast to Vietnam, American policy in the Middle East has shown great stability. Since 1948, the United States has been committed to aiding Israel. In part, this policy reflects empathy for Israel's precarious situation and the influence of the American Jewish community. It also reflects America's concern with the Soviet Union's growing influence in the Middle East. As we noted earlier, the American response to the ongoing Middle East crisis has been shaped greatly by the realization that serious Arab attacks on Israel would not have occurred without the explicit support of the Soviet Union.

Three concerns dominate the Nixon administration's policies in the Middle East. First, the United States is guided by its traditional support for Israel. In the wake of the October 1973 war, the President declared that an American effort to resupply Israel was essential "to prevent the emergence of a substantial imbalance resulting from a large-scale resupply of Syria and Egypt by the Soviet Union." With this in mind, he requested $2.2 billion in emergency aid for Israel, an appropriation that was approved by Congress in two months.

Second, President Nixon has sought to improve relations between the United States and the Arab nations. Following the Six-Day War in 1967, some Arab nations severed diplomatic relations with the United States and turned to the Soviet Union for increased economic, political, and military support. The 1973 Middle East crisis gave the United States an opportunity to reinforce its containment policy toward the Soviet Union. This was done both by aiding Israel militarily and—in taking an even-handed position in the Arab-Israeli negotiations—by trying to offer the Arab countries an alternative to a strictly Soviet alignment.

Talk of a more "even-handed" policy made Nixon highly suspect within the American Jewish community:

> He had, after all, been elected with only marginal help from American Jews, who traditionally backed Democratic Presidential candidates with both votes and lavish contributions. What the American-Jewish community suspected was that Nixon, unencumbered by political obligations, would impose a settlement on the Israelis that would force them off the vast lands they had captured in the 1967 six-day war without guaranteed security, just as Eisenhower had done.[36]

The President initiated economic aid to some Arab nations. Asserting that "we have an opportunity to achieve a significant breakthrough for world peace," Nixon recommended in April 1974 that $907.5 million in aid be divided among Egypt, Jordan, and Israel, with some aid possibly going to Syria after a military disengagement between it and Israel had been achieved. Specifically, the President's proposal called for:

Egypt—$250 million in security supporting assistance, including funds for clearing operations in the Suez Canal, farm and industrial goods purchases, and reconstruction of war-damaged cities.

Jordan—$207.5 million in military assistance and credit sales.

Israel—$350 million in military credit sales and security supporting assistance.

"Special Requirement Fund"—$100 million which could be used for peacekeeping forces, refugee aid, and other development projects. Some of this aid could go to Syria.

Third, President Nixon has tried to encourage closer cooperation between the United States and the Soviet Union in dealing with the Middle East crisis. The success of Washington's efforts at diplomacy depends, in part, on the Soviet Union's willingness to persuade the Arabs to negotiate seriously and to reach a settlement on such questions as the occupation of captured territories, the reopening of the Suez Canal, and the guaranteeing of Israel's future.

This concern with Soviet-American relations has been particularly evident in Secretary of State Henry Kissinger's many meetings with Secretary Leonid Brezhnev and other Soviet leaders. We have come to realize, first, that the Arabs will have little incentive to lessen hostilities and begin to negotiate seriously if the Soviet Union continues to supply them with sophisticated military and economic aid. Second, the Nixon administration sought to establish improved relations with the Soviet Union, a development in the cold war which has been discussed above. A broadening of the Middle East conflict could only harm the existing detente. Thus, the United States had encouraged the Soviet Union to join its diplomatic efforts in the Middle East. As already noted, however, while working toward detente, policy makers have not overlooked containment. Even though we have come to see the Soviet Union as something less than our blood enemy, we have not stopped viewing it as an aggressive antagonist that must be limited in its aspirations.

PERFORMANCE

As we discovered in Chapter 2, policy actions do not always have the intended results; this is particularly true in the case of foreign policy. Much of the controversy over Vietnam grew out of policy makers' inability to deliver as promised. Each new escalation in the war effort—the expansion of American troop commitments, the massive bombing of the North, and the invasion of Cambodia and Laos—was justified on the grounds that it would both shorten the war and facilitate American victory. While some officials were skeptical about these claims, others were true believers.

It is not our purpose here to examine competing assessments of American policy in Vietnam or the Middle East. By focusing on two specific aspects of policy, however, we can show not only how important it is to distinguish between policy and performance, but how difficult it is to assess performance. These two aspects of policy are: (1) our bombing in Vietnam; and (2) our effort to cultivate better relations with the Arab nations, thus stopping the dangerous rise of Soviet influence in the Middle East.

Vietnam

During the Vietnam war, bombing was used (1) to reduce the Vietcong infiltration of men and materials into South Vietnam, (2) to make the

North pay a high price for its support of the war in the South, (3) to break North Vietnam's will, (4) to encourage negotiations for an end to the war, and (5) to boost the morale of the United States and South Vietnam. With remarkable consistency, the American air war failed to produce anything like a uniform assessment of its success.

It is true that American bombing failed to disrupt the flow of men and supplies to the South. This failure can be attributed to at least three factors. First, North Vietnam is an underdeveloped, agricultural country and is, therefore, far less susceptible to massive bombing than a heavily industrialized country would be. It offered a few targets that could, with their destruction, halt a sophisticated interlocking system of production and transportation.[37]

Second, a large majority of the supplies entering South Vietnam from the North originated in Russia and China. Therefore, in attacking North Vietnam, the United States was striking at the pipeline, and not at the source itself. Finally, the North Vietnamese adapted to the American bombing in a resourceful and determined manner. As the *Pentagon Papers* report:

> Several hundred thousand workers were mobilized to keep the transportation system operating. Miles of by-pass roads were built around choke-points to make the system redundant. Knocked-out bridges were replaced by fords, ferries, or alternate structures, and methods were adopted to protect them from attack. Traffic shifted to night time, poor weather, and camouflage. Shuttling and transshipment practices were instituted. Construction material, equipment, and workers were prepositioned along key routes in order to effect quick repairs. Imports of railroad cars and trucks were increased to offset equipment losses.[38]

To be sure, the air strike imposed severe hardships on millions of North Vietnamese; it has been estimated that more than 52,000 of them were killed. Also, the bombing increased the cost of the war to North Vietnam. It may have limited the manpower and material flowing south, even if it did not stop the flow. The bombing also may have boosted the morale of the South Vietnamese government and the American military. But the bombing did not destroy Hanoi's determination to continue the war. On the contrary, it increased support for the North Vietnamese government and created a social cohesion that helped to compensate for the hardships brought on by the war. One study done by the Defense Department revealed that bombing had not made the leaders of North Vietnam more willing to negotiate and that any boost in morale experienced in the United States or South Vietnam was transient at best.

The Middle East

The American effort to establish friendlier relations with the Arabs may provide an interesting contrast to the bombing policy in Vietnam. Eight months after the 1973 Yom Kippur War, the United States seems to have made significant inroads into the Arab world. Diplomatic relations with Egypt, which had been severed after the 1967 war, have been reestablished. In accepting the credentials of the United States' first ambassador to Egypt in seven years, President Anwar Sadat observed that "this is an opportunity to open a new page in relations between our countries." The improvement of Egyptian-American relations is reflected, in part, in President Nixon's request to Congress for $250 million in aid for Cairo, the largest American grant in nearly twenty years. President Sadat's announced intention to end his nation's twenty-year dependence on the Soviet Union for arms could also result in closer ties with the United States. However, it is not clear that the United States is willing to become a large-scale supplier of arms to both Israel and Egypt. The volatile character of politics and the recent histories of several Arab countries make any predictions risky.

Egypt is not the only Arab country that has shown an interest in building better relations with the United States. During his successful efforts to achieve a troop-disengagement agreement on the Golan Heights, Secretary of State Kissinger found Syria's President Hagez Assad far less hostile toward the United States than has been the case in recent years. Yet Syria may be less ready to follow Egypt's lead in terminating its dependence on the Soviet Union for economic and military support. But even Syria is beginning to look to the West. It is interested not only in securing aid from the United States government but also—like other Arab nations—in profiting from the investment of private American capital and from American tourism. As *Newsweek* has reported:

> Syria still retains its tight links to the Soviet Union and an almost pathological hostility toward Israel. But even so, the Damascus government has begun to nudge open a door to the United States. . . . Sheraton has begun construction of a 350-room hotel in Damascus, and four other American hotel firms are in the midst of negotiations with the Syrian Government. American automobiles are being imported in growing numbers. And in the capital's rapidly proliferating nightclubs and discotheques, the vibes are pure American rock. "There is a tremendous anticipation of an economic miracle in Syria," one Damascus journalist told me, "and we expect the Americans to help us achieve this miracle."
>
> Syria's sudden move to woo the West is part of an ambitious development program designed to attract foreign capital, advanced technology and, in the near future, 1 million tourists a year from Europe and the U.S. Duty-free industrial zones have been plotted on the outskirts of Damascus

and Syria's other major cities. The government has promised potential foreign investors that their property and capital will not be nationalized and has even begun to rewrite specifications for projects in order to lure American firms. "Syria is looking for quality," said one American economist in Damascus, "and they aren't bound to go for the lowest bid. They will pay a bit more to a firm name they know."[39]

IMPACT

The Vietnam war and the Middle East crisis have had serious consequences for both the American people and the policy delivery system. The 1960s were marked by growing voter dissatisfaction, feelings of political powerlessness, and mistrust of government and political leaders. Vietnam has contributed greatly to this growing distrust and cynicism. The inability of public officials to deliver on their promises in Vietnam created a tremendous "credibility gap," leading to the intense frustration of voters, who felt powerless to change United States policy. American policy in the Middle East has not produced such alienation. But, by interrupting the flow of Arab oil, it led to serious economic problems in late 1973 and early 1974.

The impact of the Vietnam war can also be assessed in terms of its effect on the American economy and government expenditures for other activities. As we indicated earlier, spending for Vietnam in the mid-1960s was a source of some concern. It rose to the point where the economy became overextended, thus resulting in serious inflation and shortages in certain skills and materials. Professor Bruce Russett's analysis of the costs of American defense policy provides further insight into the impact of the Vietnam war. Examining data for 1939 through 1968, Russett found that increased defense spending—such as during World War II, the Korean war, and the Vietnam war—led to a significant decrease in private consumption and investment. In government, escalating defense expenditures typically resulted in reduced spending for such domestic activities as education, health, and public welfare. Russett writes: "It seems fair to conclude . . . that America's most expensive wars have severely hampered the nation in its attempt to build a healthier and better-educated citizenry. . . . A long-term effort has been made, and with notable results, but typically it has been badly cut back whenever military needs pressed abnormally hard.[40] More than a decade ago, just as President Johnson's policy of escalation in Vietnam was beginning to be felt, former Senator J. William Fulbright (D., Ark.) decried this fact when he admonished

the readiness with which the American people have consented to defer programs for their welfare and happiness in favor of costly military and space programs. Indeed, if the Congress accurately reflects the temper of the country, then the American people are not only willing, they are eager to sacrifice education and urban renewal and public health programs—to say nothing of foreign aid—to the requirements of the armed forces and the space agency.[41]

SUMMARY

Between 1787 and the early years of the twentieth century, American foreign policy reflected an isolationist spirit and a desire to prevent European powers from interfering in the political affairs of the Western Hemisphere. It was in the midst of World War I that the United States became actively involved in international affairs, although after the war it became isolationist again. This policy was abandoned forever with the attack at Pearl Harbor in 1941, when the United States began to assume a position of leadership in world politics.

While the United States has been faced by numerous international controversies in recent years, the Vietnam war and the continuing crisis in the Middle East have been two of the most trying and potentially explosive. In some respects, these controversies are quite distinctive: the United States became involved in a massive land war only in Vietnam, and the conventional warfare in the Middle East is quite different from the guerrilla tactics that predominated in Vietnam. And yet, Vietnam and the Middle East show some striking similarities. Most significantly, both crises reflect longstanding controversies which have been played out at both a regional and a global level. From a regional perspective, the United States has aided its allies—the governments of South Vietnam and Israel—which have been involved in limited conflicts within a geographically defined area. From a global perspective, the United States has tried to contain communist influence. Although the classic view of two cohesive blocs, each dominated by a single superpower, engaged in a cold war struggle for survival is now somewhat out of date, the United States has continued to see the Soviet Union (and, in Vietnam, Communist China) as the source of North Vietnamese and Arab hostilities. Thus, while some original elements of the cold war may no longer actually exist, the competition between East and West continues to be a critical factor in the making of United States foreign policy.

In formulating decisions, policy makers have many opportunities and constraints, some of which vary in importance from one situation to the next. They must be sensitive to their country's ability to produce the goods and services to sustain a war effort, and to do this without jeopardizing domestic production levels. Policy makers are also limited by their willingness to use military force. Still other factors are public opinion, the actions and reactions of allied nations, and the availability of information about the probable consequences of different courses of action. As we have seen, however, these limitations are less important than they might seem.

In most instances, foreign policy decisions are made by the President and his closest advisers, with little if any involvement of the courts, interest groups, and the public. Even Congress plays a minor role in crucial foreign policy situations. The early years of the Vietnam war and the 1973 Middle East crisis reflect this pattern of policy making. However, in some situations, as in Vietnam after 1965, foreign policy making involves many more actors and becomes a matter of widespread controversy.

The conflicts in Vietnam and the Middle East demonstrate that policy actions do not necessarily deliver what they have promised. In Vietnam the mixed success of the air war challenged the optimistic predictions of certain officials. American efforts to establish more cordial relations with the Arab world have been quite successful to date, although future developments in this area are most uncertain.

Finally, the two controversies explored in this chapter have affected the American people and the political system of which they are a part. Our greater distance in time from Vietnam allows us to write with more confidence about its domestic impact. Voter alienation and growing political cynicism can be attributed, in part, to this war, which also contributed to rapid inflation and general economic instability. As Professor Russett's analysis reveals, it has also had a depressing effect on government spending in many domestic policy areas, including education, health, and public welfare.

REFERENCES

1 Quoted in John H. Ferguson and Dean E. McHenry, *The American System of Government*, 12th ed. (New York: McGraw-Hill Book Company, 1973), p. 499.
2 Quoted in Donald Brandon, *American Foreign Policy* (New York: Appleton-Century-Crofts, 1966), p. 33.
3 John Spanier, *American Foreign Policy since World War II*, 6th ed. (New York: Frederick A. Praeger, Inc., 1973), p. 116.
4 Eugene V. Rostow, "America, Europe, and the Middle East," *Commentary*, vol. 57 (February 1974), p. 40.
5 Spanier, op. cit., p. 77.
6 Quoted in ibid., pp. 35–36.
7 Quoted in ibid., p. 37.
8 Mr. X [George Kennan], "The Sources of Soviet Conduct," *Foreign Affairs*, vol. 25 (July 1947), p. 576.

9 Townsend Hoopes, *The Limits of Intervention* (New York: David McCay Company, Inc., 1969), pp. 7–9.

10 See Robert W. Gregg and Charles W. Kegley, Jr. (eds.), *After Vietnam: The Future of American Foreign Policy* (Garden City, N.Y.: Doubleday & Company, Inc., 1971), p. 12; and Walter Laqueur, "Kissinger and the Politics of Detente," *Commentary*, vol. 56 (December 1973), p. 50.

11 Rostow, op. cit., p. 40.

12 George F. Kennan, "After the Cold War: American Foreign Policy in the 1970s," *Foreign Affairs*, vol. 51 (October 1972), p. 211.

13 Joseph Frankel, *International Politics: Conflict and Harmony* (Baltimore: Penguin Books, Inc., 1973), p. 83.

14 John R. Handelman, Howard B. Shapiro, and John A. Vasquez, *Introductory Case Studies for International Relations: Vietnam/The Middle East/The Environmental Crisis* (Chicago: Rand McNally & Company, 1974), p. 24.

15 Spanier, op. cit., p. 244.

16 Ibid., p. 240.

17 Handelman, Shapiro, and Vasquez, op. cit., p. 25.

18 John E. Mueller, *War, Presidents, and Public Opinion* (New York: John Wiley & Sons, Inc., 1973), pp. 93, 96.

19 Bernard C. Cohen, *The Public's Impact on Foreign Policy* (Boston: Little, Brown and Company, 1973), p. 26.

20 These and other surveys are cited in Mueller, op. cit., pp. 75–98.

21 *The Gallup Opinion Index*, January 1974, report no. 103, p. 12.

22 Ibid., p. 13.

23 Milton J. Rosenberg, Sidney Verba, and Philip E. Converse, *Vietnam and the Silent Majority* (New York: Harper and Row, Publishers, Incorporated, 1970), p. 25.

24 Ibid., pp. 27–28.

25 Quoted in Leslie H. Gelb, "The Essential Domino: American Politics and Vietnam," *Foreign Affairs*, vol. 50 (April 1972), p. 459.

26 *Gallup Opinion Index*, op. cit., p. 11.

27 Rostow, op. cit., p. 49.

28 Theodore Sorenson, *Kennedy* (New York: Bantam Books, Inc., 1965), pp. 772–773, 776.

29 Shapiro, p. 29.

30 Quoted in John Spanier and Eric M. Uslaner, *How American Foreign Policy Is Made* (New York: Frederick A. Praeger, Inc., 1974), p. 72. For a further discussion of this issue, see "The Legislative-Executive Foreign Policy Relationship in the 90th Congress," *Congressional Digest* (October 1968). Also see Louis Fisher, *President and Congress* (New York: The Free Press, 1972).

31 Handelman, Shapiro, and Vasquez, op. cit., p. 29.

32 Cohen, op cit., p. 104.

33 See Spanier, *American Foreign Policy since World War II*, pp. 234–280; Hoopes, op. cit.; Eidenberg, op. cit.; Theodore Draper, *The Abuse of Power*

(New York: The Viking Press, Inc., 1967); *The Pentagon Papers* (New York: Bantam Books, Inc., 1971); Marcus Raskin and Bernard Fall (eds.), *The Viet-Nam Reader* (New York: Vintage Books, Random House, Inc., 1965); Edwin O. Reischauer, *Beyond Vietnam* (New York: Vintage Books, Random House, Inc., 1967); Theodore Draper, "Israel and World Politics," *Commentary* (August 1967), pp. 19–48; Theodore Draper, "From 1967 to 1973: The Arab-Israeli Wars," *Commentary* (December 1973), pp. 31–45; and Walter Laqueur, "Russia Enters the Middle East," *Foreign Affairs*, vol. 47 (January 1969), pp. 296–308.

34　Spanier and Uslaner, op. cit., pp. 39–40.

35　Quoted in Hoopes, op. cit., p. 221.

36　Rowland Evans, Jr., and Robert D. Novak, *Nixon in the White House: The Frustration of Power* (New York: Random House, Inc., 1971), p. 87.

37　U.S. Department of Defense, Office of the Secretary of Defense Task Force, Vietnam, *United States–Vietnam Relations, 1945–1967*, 1971, IV.C.7(a), pp. 54–55.

38　Ibid., pp. 56–57.

39　*Newsweek*, vol. 83, no. 17, Apr. 29, 1974, p. 40. Copyright Newsweek, Inc. 1974.

40　Bruce M. Russett, *What Price Vigilance? The Burdens of National Defense* (New Haven, Conn.: Yale University Press, 1970), p. 153.

41　Quoted in Julius Duscha, *Arms, Money, and Politics* (New York: Ives Washburn, Inc., 1965), p. 18.

Chapter 4

Citizens, Political Parties, and Interest Groups as Policy Makers

One feature of the policy struggles explored in the two preceding chapters was the role of private citizens. For American involvement in Southeast Asia and the Middle East, as in most foreign policy situations, mass preferences had little effect on officials. The school desegregation struggle, especially as it involves the use of busing, is a contrasting situation where public pressures seemed most effective. Chapters 2 and 3 illustrate a point that we will see again: the importance of any part of the policy delivery system varies from one policy area to another.

Social scientists have long been concerned with grass-roots efforts to affect policy. Except in a revolutionary setting, it is a class of elites (public officials) who actually make and implement public policy. Thus, any examination of the public's ability to shape policies must focus on *linkages between* masses and elites. These linkages are complex and reciprocal: sometimes the public influences the thinking of elites, and sometimes the reverse. Often it is impossible to determine who influences and who is influenced. Stated simply, the questions are: Who governs? To what extent are policies shaped by political elites functioning independently of mass demands and preferences, and to what extent do elites respond to private citizens?[1]

Additional questions concern the mechanisms that unite private citizens so that they may deal effectively with government officials. The United States is not a popular democracy whose citizens deal with government on an individual basis. Few if any of us have the prestige, the information, or the resources to bring about major policy changes by ourselves. To be sure, we may receive a fair hearing on our individual claims and see administrators make special provisions for our particular needs. If no provisions of current statutes fit our cases, we may succeed in having Congress or a state legislature enact a "private bill" in our behalf. Individuals have also become famous when their cases produced landmark decisions of the U.S. Supreme Court. Clarence Gideon received considerable publicity when the Court invalidated his conviction on charges of petty larceny and ruled that indigents must be provided with legal counsel in cases when a serious penalty is involved; Danny Escobido gained fame when one of his numerous arrests led to a ruling that a suspect's right to counsel could not be abridged by denying him an opportunity to have his lawyer present while he was being questioned by the police.[2] However, it is unusual for individual citizens to shape policy. Most often it is through collective action that we tackle the policy delivery system. Industrial lobbies and public interest groups unite numerous individuals with common goals; pool their financial resources to buy the services of social and economic researchers, lawyers, and communications experts; and support the campaign necessary to elect a candidate or win a change in program. Ours is a complex government that is not vulnerable to amateur citizens. Unless we understand the organizations that citizens use to deal with government, our inquiry about grass-roots politics will not tell us a great deal about the policy delivery system. In this chapter we deal with two of the most important mechanisms that connect citizens with their government: political parties and interest groups.

CITIZENS

Private citizens are the lifeblood of democratic government. They make demands for public goods and services; supply the money to pay for them; and support or reject the leaders, institutions, and policies of the political system.

A democratic political system cannot survive for long without the support of a majority of its citizens. When such support wanes and underlying discontent is the necessary result, and the potential for revolutionary alteration of the political and social system is enhanced.[3]

Throughout the 1950s and much of the 1960s, most political scientists agreed that Americans exhibited an extraordinarily high degree of support for their political system. Compared to citizens in other nations, Americans were more likely to express great trust in their elected officials, confidence in policy-making procedures, and support for the policies enacted. They felt a clear obligation to participate in politics and believed that their participation would influence the government.[4] On campus, this was the period of the "silent generation," which seemed to be apathetic or acquiescent toward public affairs.

During the past decade, this trust in government has weakened. There have been massive urban disorders, violent demonstrations on college campuses, outbreaks of racial unrest, widespread discontent with American involvement in Southeast Asia, and since 1972, growing distrust of the Nixon administration. Spokesmen for the New Left challenge the legitimacy of a system that subsidizes wealthy farmers, huge corporations, and absentee landlords, while permitting millions to live in rat-infested slums, unable to make a decent living. They also charge that the United States persists in practicing racism at home while pursuing imperialistic policies abroad. Critics from the Right tell us that America has lost sight of individual virtues, that we are saddled with massive welfare and regulatory programs that enforce social conformity at the expense of individual freedom.

These two extreme groups hold very different views of American society. The Left decries a system obsessed with serving the interests of the haves while remaining insensitive to the desires and needs of the have-nots. The Right protests against a system too responsive to the desires of intellectuals and "do-gooders" seeking the creation of a socialist state. Yet, these two groups agree on one thing: the ordinary citizen has little control over the actions of his government; he is far removed from the arenas of power where policy decisions are made.

It would be wholly inaccurate to suggest that discontent and political alienation occur only at the extremes of American society. These feelings are readily found at all levels—the daily reports of the mass media, the rhetoric of many political campaigns in recent years, and most strikingly in the substantial support given to George Wallace in the 1968 presidential election and the early primaries of 1972.[5]

A decline of public trust in government is reflected in the responses to five questions asked during each of the last three presidential election years. Table 4-1 shows that an increasing number of Americans has come to question the competence, honesty, and fairness of government

Table 4-1   Trust in Government: A Comparison over Time

1 Do you think that people in the government waste *a lot* of the money we pay in taxes, waste *some* of it, *or don't waste very much of it?*

	1964	1968	1972
Not much	7.0%	4.0%	3.0%
Some	45.0	33.0	27.0
A lot*	46.0	57.0	68.0
Don't know	2.0	6.0	2.0

2 How much of the time do you think you can trust the government in Washington to do what is right—*just about always, most of the time,* or *only some of the time?*

	1964	1968	1972
Always	14.0%	7.0%	7.0%
Most of the time	62.0	52.0	45.0
Only some of the time*	22.0	37.0	45.0
Don't know	2.0	4.0	3.0

3 Would you say the government is pretty much run by a *few big interests* looking out for themselves or that it is run *for the benefit of all* of the people?

	1964	1968	1972
For benefit of all	64.0%	49.0%	43.0%
Few big interests*	28.0	39.0	48.0
Other; Depends; Don't know	8.0	12.0	9.0

4 Do you feel that almost all the people running the government are smart people who usually *know what they are doing,* or do you think that quite a few of them *don't seem to know what they are doing?*

	1964	1968	1972
Know what they are doing	68.0%	56.0%	53.0%
Don't know what they are doing*	28.0	36.0	42.0
Don't know	4.0	8.0	5.0

5 Do you think that *quite a few* of the people running the government are a little crooked, *not very many are,* or do you think *hardly any* of them are crooked at all?

	1964	1968	1972
Quite a few*	28.0%	25.0%	34.0%
Not very many are	48.0	55.0	46.0
Hardly any	18.0	20.0	16.0
Don't know	6.0	0.0	4.0

*Indicates response interpreted as cynical or distrustful.
Source: Center for Political Studies, Institute for Social Research, University of Michigan.

officials. For example, in 1964, 76 percent of those questioned believed that the government in Washington could be trusted to do what is right just about always or most of the time; in 1972 this figure dropped to 52 percent. Correspondingly, there has been a jump from 22 to 45 percent of those saying that such trust is warranted only some of the time. There has been an increase of 20 percent in those who feel that government is pretty much run by a few big interests looking out for themselves.

Some of this shift from confidence to uncertainty and cynicism can be seen as a temporary response to Watergate. Other observers perceive it as a deep-seated public concern with the government's seeming inability to deal effectively with a whole series of problems: Southeast Asia, urban and rural poverty, rampant inflation and ever-shortening boom and bust economic cycles, energy shortages, an increasing crime rate, and ever-present racial antagonisms. With a whole series of scandals emerging from Washington since the 1972 election, one can only speculate about the future of public confidence. The public mood in the late 1970s can hardly show much improvement if the American people continue to encounter public officials being charged with illegal actions, public funds being wasted on ill-conceived and badly administered programs, and party leaders who break the rules of democratic procedure.

Citizen Politics

The feelings of distrust and alienation do not affect all of us equally. Some of us know more than others about public affairs, and some of us participate more often and/or more intimately. It is useful to consider a "hierarchy of political involvement." As shown in Figure 4-1, this consists of fifteen different types of involvement, from the most common and least intimate (exposing oneself to political stimuli) to the most rare and intimate involvements (holding public office).[6] The separate types of involvement group themselves into three classes of activities: "spectator," "transitional," and "gladiatorial."

Most people participate in politics on the spectator or transitional levels. In some sections of the country over 80 percent of the voting-age population may vote in national elections. However, as little as 30 percent may talk to others about their voting preferences; less than 20 percent may wear a campaign button or put a sticker on their car; and less than 5 percent may join a political club or work actively for a candidate.[7]

Variations in involvement occur from one kind of political event to another; among communities, states, and regions; and between individuals of different social and economic groups. More people vote in presidential elections than in "off-year" congressional, state, or local elections. More than 60 percent of the voting-age population generally casts ballots in presidential elections, but rates of less than 45 percent are common in off-year congressional campaigns.[8] More individuals are concerned with national affairs than with politics at the local, state, or international level. One survey found that 32 percent of the population

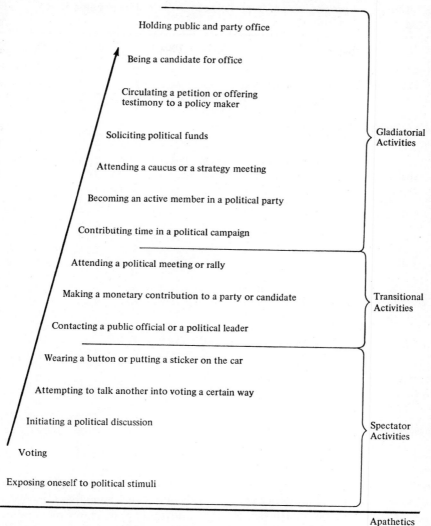

Figure 4-1 Hierarchy of political involvement. [Adapted from Lester W. Milbrath, *Political Participation*: (Chicago, Rand McNally & Company, 1965,) p. 18, with the addition of activities pertaining to policy making]

follows national affairs most closely, while only 17 percent gives primary attention to state affairs.[9]

Voter participation is generally higher in states and communities with intense political competition than in uncontested one-party areas. Also,

Table 4-2　Percentage of Voter Turnout in Selected Presidential Elections 1920–1972

State	1972	1968	1964	1960	1956	1944	1932	1920
South Dakota	70.8	70.8	72.6	78.3	73.5	70.8	73.4	52.8
North Dakota	69.8	65.5	72.2	78.5	70.6	71.0	71.4	63.7
Utah	69.4	76.9	76.9	80.1	75.2	76.2	75.1	63.8
Montana	69.0	65.0	69.8	71.4	71.0	70.8	67.4	55.8
Minnesota	68.0	71.8	76.8	77.0	67.7	70.2	62.7	53.3
Connecticut	65.7	68.5	71.8	76.8	76.6	70.2	58.3	43.6
Idaho	64.8	72.8	75.8	80.7	77.6	76.3	73.4	57.9
Wyoming	64.7	69.3	73.2	74.0	67.8	75.6	71.3	45.4
West Virginia	64.5	70.0	75.2	77.3	75.2	74.1	78.5	67.8
Iowa	64.2	71.6	72.3	76.5	73.2	72.0	67.8	62.7
New Hampshire	64.1	70.9	72.3	79.4	75.2	78.1	68.5	56.6
Delaware	63.5	71.7	71.1	73.6	72.1	68.9	72.8	69.5
Wisconsin	62.7	68.0	70.8	73.4	67.4	71.2	60.7	45.9
Illinois	62.6	69.3	74.0	75.7	73.2	79.4	68.6	53.1
Maine	62.6	67.5	65.6	72.6	62.8	60.5	60.2	41.6
Massachusetts	62.2	67.8	71.3	76.1	75.7	73.0	58.0	41.2
Washington	62.0	65.0	71.5	72.3	70.8	65.6	59.9	46.5
Oregon	61.9	64.4	69.6	72.3	68.2	59.7	57.5	48.2
Rhode Island	61.8	68.2	68.7	75.1	73.7	65.3	62.9	47.3
Colorado	61.2	70.2	68.0	71.4	67.6	76.2	71.5	51.7
New Mexico	60.7	63.3	63.9	62.1	59.6	59.0	66.2	56.9
Indiana	60.6	71.5	74.0	76.9	71.8	76.2	76.4	71.0
Vermont	60.5	65.5	68.0	62.5	67.4	63.6	62.0	41.4
California	60.0	61.0	64.7	67.4	63.8	62.9	55.9	40.7
New Jersey	59.6	65.1	68.6	71.8	69.0	70.9	62.3	48.0
Kansas	59.4	63.5	64.8	70.3	67.2	68.3	68.9	55.7
Michigan	59.4	64.9	68.9	72.4	68.1	63.7	56.6	47.3
Ohio	57.0	63.6	66.6	71.3	65.0	69.5	61.3	56.8
Missouri	56.8	63.1	67.4	71.8	67.8	68.9	68.7	65.4
Oklahoma	56.8	62.9	62.5	63.8	63.6	62.0	53.7	47.6
Nebraska	56.4	59.9	66.6	71.4	67.1	75.9	69.1	51.8

participation is highest among people who are over 30 and who have higher than average levels of education and income, have lived for several years in their community, and have middle- and upper-status occupations. Regional comparisons of voting rates reveal that voting turnout is lowest in the South, whether the contest is for national or state office.[10] Table 4-2 shows that turnouts for presidential elections have ranged from 80 percent in Idaho and Utah to less than 30 percent in Southern states. Since 1956, however, this gap has narrowed considerably. The more lively political scene in the South today appears to be due to the following factors: increased economic prosperity, urbanization, and industrialization; improved education, communication, and transportation; more

Table 4-2 (Continued)

State	1972	1968	1964	1960	1956	1944	1932	1920
Pennsylvania	56.3	63.2	68.1	70.5	65.7	64.1	48.8	36.7
New York	56.1	57.3	63.2	67.0	66.0	74.1	56.0	44.5
Nevada	52.2	54.2	55.5	61.2	62.8	62.3	63.7	52.1
Hawaii	50.9	62.7	52.5	51.3	—	—	—	—
Florida	50.6	58.2	52.7	50.0	45.9	36.3	30.2	36.0
Maryland	50.4	57.7	56.0	57.2	54.5	47.5	49.1	49.7
Arizona	50.3	43.6	54.7	54.5	50.8	43.4	46.6	35.4
Arkansas	49.7	52.5	49.9	41.1	39.9	22.0	22.5	21.2
Kentucky	48.4	46.8	52.9	59.2	58.8	59.7	67.4	71.2
Alaska	47.6	56.4	48.7	45.5	—	—	—	—
Mississippi	46.0	51.6	32.9	25.5	21.7	16.8	13.8	9.4
Virginia	45.6	53.1	41.0	33.4	33.5	23.9	21.7	19.1
Texas	45.2	51.6	44.4	41.8	37.9	30.5	25.8	19.8
Louisiana	45.0	55.6	47.3	44.8	36.4	26.3	22.5	13.6
Tennessee	44.3	53.0	51.1	50.3	46.3	31.0	26.1	35.3
Alabama	44.2	51.5	36.0	31.1	28.3	16.4	17.6	20.8
North Carolina	43.9	54.7	51.8	53.5	48.2	43.1	43.7	44.5
South Carolina	39.5	48.0	38.0	30.5	25.2	11.0	12.1	8.6
Georgia	37.8	41.6	44.9	30.4	29.7	18.2	16.4	10.4
District of Columbia	31.5	33.5	40.2	—	—	—	—	—
U.S. Average	55.7	60.6	61.8	63.8	60.1	56.3	52.9	44.2

*States are ranked by percentage turnout in the 1972 election, and the vote is a percentage of the civilian population of voting age.

Sources: United States Bureau of the Census, *Statistical Abstract of the United States: 1962*, 83d ed., (Washington D.C.: United States Government Printing Office, 1962) for civilian population of voting age figures, 1920, 1940, 1960; Population Division, United States Bureau of the Census for estimates of civilian population of voting age, 1924–1936, 1944–1956; Richard M. Scammon ed.), *American Votes*, vol. IV (Pittsburgh: University of Pittsburgh Press, 1962), for votes cast in presidential elections, 1948–1960; *Statistics of Presidential and Congressional Elections, 1920–1958*, compiled under direction of the Clerk of the House of Representatives, for votes cast in presidential elections, 1920–1924. Reproduced from the Report of the President's Commission on Registration and Voting Participation, November 1963. Figures for 1964 and 1968 were compiled by Walter Dean Burnham and taken from a table in *That All May Vote*, a report by The Freedom to Vote Task Force of the Democratic National Committee, December 1969. Figures for 1972 were taken from United States Bureau of the Census, *Statistical Abstract of the United States 1973* (Washington, D.C.: United States Government Printing Office, 1973).

intense competition between Democrats and Republicans; and less coercion of blacks intending to vote.

The policies of state and local governments can make or break citizen politics. Officials can make the task of the prospective voter easy or difficult through procedures for voter registration, residence requirements, literacy tests, poll taxes, the opening and closing hours of the polls, and the ease of qualifying for absentee ballots. The poll tax and literacy requirements are now limited by the Twenty-fourth Amendment to the Constitution and various federal statutes. Low-income blacks and whites are no longer barred from the polls because they have failed to pay poll taxes, which have added up to considerable sums from one unpaid year to the next. And voter registrars cannot impose arbitrary tests of a black person's "understanding" of a written passage while accepting even a mumbled reading by a white. Beginning in 1972, the Twenty-sixth Amendment lowered the voting age to eighteen in all local, state, and national elections. However, there remain state-to-state variations in other provisions that complicate the voter's task.

Beyond these now uniform requirements, and despite considerable progress in extending the vote to all persons,

> Generally, the higher the percentage of blacks in an area, the greater the local pressure to prevent them from voting, especially in the rural south. . . . Some of these pressures are social, such as ostracism and verbal abuse. Some take the form of economic reprisals, such as being fired from a job or evicted from rented quarters. Some pressures are unabashedly violent, such as beatings and killings. These pressures inescapably depress turnout.[11]

Linkages between Citizens and Official Policy Makers

It is not enough to describe grass-roots political involvement. Our policy-making focus requires us to explore linkages between the activities and preferences of ordinary citizens and the decisions of policy makers. In this section we consider three devices that may help form public opinion or transmit citizen demands to policy makers: the mass media, public opinion polls, and elections. As we will see, each device helps transmit citizen demands, but they are less than perfect channels of communication.

The Mass Media   The mass media include newspapers, popular journals, radio, and television. They provide the public with information about public affairs and influence attitudes about many issues. Most people identify television as their primary source of information, although magazines and newspapers are the most important sources for people who are active in politics.[12]

There are limits to the political role of the mass media. Many people view them as less reliable sources of political information than friends, family members, or coworkers. Many newspapers and broadcasting stations offer little useful information about politics or policy, concentrating instead on sports, social events, music, and advertisements. The major television networks offer few documentary or public affairs programs, and when they do, most viewers prefer a movie or football game on another network. When CBS aired *The Selling of the Pentagon* in 1970, it was seen by less than one-fifth of the television audience.[13] Wire-service copy provides the bulk of national or international news, with the coverage of local politics especially thin—except for a brief spurt around election time or in response to a crisis.

The mass media have only limited influence on public opinion. It is seldom that they actually *change* opinions or cause people to *switch* from one candidate to another. It is somewhat more common for the media to create opinions about issues which previously received little notice, or to strengthen existing attitudes by providing evidence for their support. Most commonly, the media "activate" individuals (by convincing them of the correctness of their position and by leading them to vote, talk with others, attend a political meeting, or work in a political campaign).

Professor Michael Robinson has found that television can shape public opinion. He conducted a series of experiments to assess the impact of *The Selling of the Pentagon* upon individual opinions about the military, the government in Washington, and the media. In this controversial documentary, CBS asserted that the military had deceived the American people and that it was deeply involved in politics. In response, military spokesmen and administration officials accused the network of knowingly misrepresenting the facts. After viewing the documentary, subjects in Robinson's experiment saw the military as more likely to lie about the war in Southeast Asia, to get involved in politics, and to seek special political advantage than they had previously believed. The program also produced a decline in the subjects' political efficacy and self-confidence, and a heightened sense of frustration.

It has been charged that television, *by its very presence,* constitutes a self-fulfilling prophecy by creating a situation or by inflaming one which already exists. How much of the "riots" in the 1960s were real, and how much staged for the TV camera? No one knows. Further, the fifteen- or thirty-minute time limit for newscasts requires film to be edited. In the process of editing, certain segments wind up on the cutting room floor. The public, which knows nothing of this, thus receives part of the story—often the most sensational part—with nuances and mitigating influences frequently left out. Such subtle distortions of the "news" take place every day. Discussing the effect of television journalism, Robinson writes:

> Events get conveyed and given the credibility of the network news program, . . . but events are frequently conveyed by television news through an *inferential structure* that often injects a negativistic or anti-institutional bias. These biases, frequently dramatized by film portrayals of violence and aggression, evoke images of American politics and social life which are inordinately sinister and contentious. The less sophisticated viewer (the most frequent TV dependent) witnesses the conflicts within the society and sees

them as evils. This unsophisticate, unable or unwilling to reject the network reports, turns against (1) the group most directly responsible; (2) against the social and political institutions involved in the conflict; or (3) against himself as a political entity, regarding himself as simply unable to cope with or get response from a political system "like this."[14]

We actually know little about the effectiveness of mass media in transmitting citizens' preferences to public officials. The media do help to shape the agenda of public debate by emphasizing some issues and making them more noticeable than others. Occasionally, the media originate issues with "campaigns" against social problems, the failure of government programs, or the corruption of certain officials. In recent years the efforts of investigative reporters have led to revelations about atrocities committed by American soldiers in Vietnam and the involvement of high Nixon appointees in the series of events known as Watergate.

Public Opinion Polls   There is an abundance of polls used to assist officials in gauging public opinion; to aid candidates in identifying popular campaign positions; to serve as instruments of propaganda by individuals and groups seeking to dramatize their causes; and to help political scientists analyze the formation, character, and effects of public attitudes.[15]

Polls explore a wide variety of subjects: support for political candidates and incumbent officeholders; support for government institutions and procedures; and public preferences on policy questions. However, poll results do not guarantee influence over policy decisions. Most issues do not present clear and simple alternatives that lend themselves to polling. News that the public opposes an increase in taxes, for example, does not mean that it will support or oppose a limited increase if the additional revenues are needed for certain programs. Likewise, public support for a politician does not identify which of his programs is popular.

Further, most surveys do not indicate how *seriously* people stand by their opinions. Respondents may never have thought about day-care centers when faced with the question: "Do you think that additional federally-financed day-care centers should be opened in your city?" With only superficial thought being given to the question, answers are uninformed and subject to change. Finally, the form in which a question is asked may affect the answer:

In June, 1969, the Gallup poll told respondents that the President had "ordered the withdrawal of 25,000 troops from Vietnam in the next three months" and asked for opinions on whether troops should be withdrawn at a faster or a slower rate. "Faster" won over "Slower" by 42 percent to 16 percent, with 29 percent refusing the alternatives presented and instead spontaneously declaring agreement with the President. Scarcely three months later the Harris poll asked a similar question but presented three choices: "In general, do you feel the pace at which the president is withdrawing troops is too fast, too slow, or about right?" Again the equivalent of "faster" won over "slower," by 29 percent to 6 percent, but this time 49 percent approved the current rate. The key to the difference in the two results is that the Gallup format made it easier for respondents to disagree with the existing rate of withdrawal.[16]

The question here is: Which of these sets of responses best portrays the preferences of the American people? In one instance 29 percent of the respondents and in the other 49 percent endorsed the President's rate of withdrawal. This is only one illustration of the problems encountered by those who try to make sense out of public opinion polls.

Elections Elections give citizens their major chance to control public officials. Executives, legislators, most state judges, and the heads of some administrative departments win office by means of election. Even those localities that employ an appointed city manager as their chief executive make him subordinate to an elected council. Yet elections have only limited value in allowing private citizens to determine public policy.

Elections allow voters to choose officials. In most instances, however, a voter does not show his support for or opposition to a government program by his vote for a person. "To choose a government is not to choose governmental policies. Whereas the voters largely do determine the players . . . they have far less control over the signals the players will call, the strategies they will employ, or the final score. The popular will, as represented by a majority of voters, does not determine public policy."[17]

Several factors contribute to this situation. First, American political parties are not so tightly organized that they can discipline individual candidates for failing to support a party program. Thus, a voter cannot be sure by a candidate's party label alone which policies he will support once in office. In a primary, of course, the party label provides no policy guidance. Candidates run as individuals or as the head of their own organizations, with party labels not helping voters choose between Democrats or Republicans.

Second, the complexity of most campaigns makes it impossible to view elections as mandates for specific policies. The presidential campaign of 1972 was unusually clear in terms of the policy choices given to the voters. Voters could choose, for example, between Richard Nixon and George McGovern on the issues of busing, the war in Vietnam, and tax policies. Most observers agree that McGovern took more liberal positions on busing and taxation, and urged more rapid withdrawal from Vietnam. Despite the overwhelming size of Nixon's victory, the election results do not indicate which of his policies were supported by a majority of the voters. It is possible that only a minority of Nixon's supporters agreed with any one of his positions. Many people could have agreed with McGovern on particular issues but voted for Nixon because they believed that he took the better position on other issues felt to be more important, or that he was a more reliable person. When dealing with a presidential election, we usually have a large number of poll results to compare with the election outcome in order to gain some insight into the voters' preferences. However, these are not available for most state and local elections; the winner can read into his victory any combination of policy preferences, and the loser cannot present substantial evidence to the contrary.

Third, even when election campaigns seem to offer clear choices, they may not remain relevant beyond the first crisis faced by the new government. Although Lyndon Johnson strongly opposed expanded American participation in Vietnam during the 1964 campaign, developments after the election allowed him to reverse his position. Many of the President's critics felt that he had betrayed the will of the people; his defenders argued that new conditions justified and made necessary new war policies. Likewise, as a candidate in 1968, Richard Nixon rejected government controls as a means of limiting inflation. By 1971, he admitted the failure of voluntary actions and initiated stringent wage-price controls in the face of heightened inflationary pressures.

Although elections do not allow the people to control public policy, they do limit the power and the options of elected officials. Voters can influence the actions of politicians through *retroactive* judgment. "Governments must worry, not about the meaning of past elections, but about their fate at future elections."[18] Another way of putting it is that "government officials act in anticipation of certain consequences if they do not so act. They believe that if they do not act to benefit a group, that group will at some point in the future withdraw its support or its vote."[19]

THE POLICY MAKERS' DILEMMA: WHAT DO THE PEOPLE WANT?

American officials enjoy wide discretion as policy makers. While their options can be limited and their actions influenced by the demands of private citizens, they are seldom subject to direct popular control. If private citizens are to affect the actions of government, even indirectly, two conditions must be satisfied. First, people must use the channels of communication available to them. If no message is received, policy makers can hardly respond to popular demands. Second, people must be sufficiently informed about government personnel, procedure, and policy issues to transmit a useful message that clearly specifies the action desired.

Nearly three decades of research has shown that the American people have considerable trouble measuring up to these standards. Large numbers of people do not bother to vote in national elections; and even larger numbers fail to vote in state and local elections, devote time or money to a political campaign, attend a political meeting, or circulate a petition.

The lack of vital information appears in several ways: more than half the population does not know the number of United States Senators elected from their state; nearly half does not know the length of a legislator's term in office; and less than a quarter can identify a single provision of the Bill of Rights.[20] A survey conducted during the 1964 presidential campaign found that 26 percent of the respondents could not name the Republican vice presidential candidate, William E. Miller; and 21 percent did not know that Hubert Humphrey was the Democratic vice presidential nominee.[21]

At the local level we see the same dismal picture. Most people do not know who their state assemblyman or local councilman is. Moreover, unlike the national elections, in which information on the candidates is broadcast every day, at the local level there is often a real information gap. Many local officials stay out of public sight between elections so that the voter finds it impossible to choose between them. Aside from campaign literature, little information on local candidates exists, and the onus is put on the exasperated voter. In New York, the League of Women Voters is one of the few organizations that collects and distributes objective information on the candidates. In general, confusion reigns.

People's familiarity with political issues is no better. In September 1963, "at the height of the great debate over the ratification of the nuclear test ban treaty, the Gallup poll found that 22 percent of the electorate had not heard of the issues."[22] Twenty-eight percent of the respondents in a 1964 survey had not heard or read of the North Atlantic Treaty Organization (NATO).[23]

A striking example of the public's lack of concern for policy issues is found in two Gallup surveys conducted nearly twenty years apart. In November 1952 a sample of Americans was asked: "What do you, yourself, think we should do next in the Korean war?" No less than 25 percent of the respondents indicated that they had no opinion on the matter. When faced with the same question in March 1969—this time in

Table 4-3 The Distribution of Party Identification in the United States, 1952–1972

Question: "Generally speaking, do you usually think of yourself as a Republican, a Democrat, an Independent, or what? (IF REPUBLICAN OR DEMOCRAT) Would you

	Oct. 1952	Oct. 1954	Oct. 1956	Oct. 1958	Oct. 1960
Democrat					
Strong	22%	22%	21%	23%	21%
Weak	25	25	23	24	25
Independent					
Democrat	10	9	7	7	8
Independent	5	7	9	8	8
Republican	7	6	8	4	7
Republican					
Weak	14	14	14	16	13
Strong	13	13	15	13	14
Apolitical,					
Don't know	4	4	3	5	4
Total	100%	100%	100%	100%	100%
Number of Cases	1614	1139	1772	1269	3021

reference to the Vietnam war—21 percent offered no opinion. Also, in both instances, we cannot be sure that those who did express an opinion had any substantial knowledge about the issues involved.[24]

Given this picture, political scientists have tried to identify the bases for people's votes. If, in fact, many people have no clear issue preferences in mind, why do they vote as they do? Three factors appear to be most crucial: the voters' party identification, candidate orientation, and issue orientation.

Party Identification

Party identification is the "sense of general attachment" to a party.[25] This psychological tie is generally the most significant factor influencing a vote. One study found two-thirds of its sample still identifying with the same party for which they had cast their first presidential vote. Fifty-six percent claimed they *never* deviated from the support of presidential candidates belonging to their initial party.[26] Later we will consider the sources of these partisan attachments.

Party identification shows considerable stability. Table 4-3 shows the distribution of Democrats and Republicans fluctuating little since 1952. The two most pronounced shifts occurred in 1964 and 1972. During the Goldwater candidacy the proportion of Democrats jumped 5 percent. Eight years later, when George McGovern was their candidate, the call yourself a strong (R) (D) or a not very strong (R) (D)? (IF INDEPENDENT) Do you think of yourself as closer to the Republican or Democratic party?"

Nov. 1962	Oct. 1964	Nov. 1966	Nov. 1968	Nov. 1970	Nov. 1972
23%	26%	18%	20%	20%	15%
23	25	27	25	23	25
8	9	9	10	10	11
8	8	12	11	13	13
6	6	7	9	8	10
16	13	15	14	15	13
12	11	10	10	10	10
4	2	2	1	1	3
100%	100%	100%	100%	100%	100%
1289	1571	1291	1553	1802	2705

Source: Center for Political Studies, Institute for Social Research, University of Michigan, 1973.

proportion of "strong Democrats" declined 5 percent. Yet, even when overwhelming majorities cast ballots for one candidate, as they did in 1964 and 1972, party loyalties did not change radically. Large numbers of people voted for Johnson in 1964 and for Nixon in 1972 while still thinking of themselves as Republicans or Democrats. The number of independent voters has grown gradually since 1958, with more than a third of the electorate taking such a position in 1972.

Most often, an individual's vote does reflect his party label. Table 4-4 shows that in 1964, 1968, and 1972, Democratic identifiers tended to vote for their own party's candidate. Barry Goldwater's crushing defeat in 1964 can be attributed to the minority status of the Republican party (see Table 4-3) and the rush of Republicans (especially "weak" Republicans) to Johnson. Richard Nixon's victory in 1968 resulted from the number of votes he received from Democratic identifiers and his considerable support among independent voters. His 1972 landslide is discussed on pages 88–92.

Candidate Orientation

Quite often a voter finds himself attracted to a candidate not because he or she is a Republican or Democrat but because the candidate has desirable personal qualities. In some cases, the candidate is a member of

Table 4-4   Voting Behavior of Party Identifiers, 1964, 1968, and 1972

	1964		1968			1972	
	Johnson	Goldwater	Humphrey	Nixon	Wallace	McGovern	Nixon
Strong Democrat	95%	4%	85%	8%	8%	76%	24%
Weak Democrat	81	18	58	27	15	45	55
Independent Democrat	89	10	53	30	17	56	44
Independent	72	22	24	55	21	18	82
Independent Republican	25	75	4	82	14	4	96
Weak Republican	42	56	10	82	8	4	96
Strong Republican	10	90	2	96	2	2	98

Source: Center for Political Studies, Institute for Social Research, University of Michigan.

the voter's party, reinforcing the voter's partisan attachments; in other instances, a voter may like a candidate so much that he or she crosses party lines.

In 1952 and 1956, Adlai Stevenson found himself pitted against the highly popular and respected Dwight D. Eisenhower, who appealed to many Democrats. While it is popular mythology to credit John Kennedy's victory in 1960 to his personal attractiveness, surveys actually show that Richard Nixon's "appeal to the electorate, especially the sense of his broad experience," won him many votes and contributed to the closeness of the final outcome.[27] Negative responses to Barry Goldwater's erratic campaign in 1964 generally added to the size of Lyndon Johnson's victory, while voter assessments in 1968 gave Nixon a slight advantage over Hubert Humphrey. As our discussion of the 1972 election points out, Nixon, when running against McGovern rather than Humphrey, looked even better to the voters the second time around.

Issue Orientation

A third influence on a voter's decision is his stand on public issues and his judgment that one candidate is more likely to support the programs he himself favors. We have already stated that the decisions of *most* voters do not rest upon such considerations. Voters are frequently unaware of basic political issues or have not formed opinions about them. And many voters who *are* aware of the issues may not be sufficiently concerned to let the candidate's stand affect their decision. In still other cases, the voters are offered a choice between Tweedledum and Tweedledee, with the "differences" impossible to see.

There are many examples of the first case, voter ignorance. One issue given primary attention by both the Republican and Democratic candidates in 1948 was the Taft-Hartley Act, but fully 70 percent of the electorate could not identify the content of this law, express an opinion about it, or see any difference between the positions of the two nominees.[28] Early in the 1968 campaign, 54 percent of the respondents could not identify Eugene McCarthy's position on the Vietnam war, and another 17 percent identified him as a "hawk" or supporter of the war—all in spite of considerable publicity given to McCarthy's opposition to it.[29] A plurality of those Democrats who supported McCarthy in the spring of 1968 ended up as backers of George Wallace in November—surely a shift that could not be explained in terms of issue orientation.[30]

This is not meant to suggest that issues have *no* consequence. The fact is that for some elections, and for some voters, issues have central importance. However, many voters' concern with issues is a general one; they cast their ballots in response to the "nature of the times"—that is, they vote for the party in power when times are "good" and throw the rascals out when times are "bad." Thus, public frustrations with the Korean war and corruption in government contributed to Eisenhower's victory in 1952 after twenty years of Democratic rule. Lyndon Johnson's election reflected, in part, the voters' sense that the Democratic party would be more able to deal with the nation's domestic and foreign affairs. More recently, issues of law and order, Vietnam, and civil rights and feelings of respondents' general competence had significant effects on the 1968 presidential elections.

Political scientists continue to debate the importance of issues. While many feel that most Americans are generally incapable of consciously voting on the issues, others argue that the importance of issues is actually greater than indicated. Those who see much "issue voting" point to the electorate's growing ability to understand political events. The proportion of the voters able to use such ideological terms as "liberal" and "conservative" in a meaningful way doubled between 1956 and 1964.[31] During the past decade, voters seem to have become more concerned with issues, with 42 percent of them showing an interest in policy in 1968.[32]

The George Wallace candidacy in 1968 further indicates the importance of political issues. To a large extent, the public responded to Wallace as an issue candidate. Since Wallace did not run as a Republican or as a Democrat, voters could not be attracted to him by traditional party loyalties. The University of Michigan's Institute for Social Research reports that approximately half of the favorable comments it received about Wallace in its 1968 election survey had to do with his position on such issues as racial segregation, law and order, and Vietnam. The typical Wallace voter was angry about one or more of these issues. In contrast, only 25 percent of the favorable feelings toward the other candidates reflected agreement with their issue positions. "Wallace was a 'backlash' candidate, and there is no question but that the positions communicated to the public accounted for his electoral support in a very primary sense."[33]

The power of the Wallace vote could be seen in the positions taken by many of those who sought the 1972 Democratic presidential nomination. In 1972, both Nixon and McGovern tried to appeal to the Wallace voters. Nixon's concern was reflected in his "Southern Strategy," which actually dated from his 1968 election. Nixon owed a great debt to Southern Republicans for his 1968 nomination and victory. His aim was to retain his 1968 constituency and draw as many Wallacites to him as possible in 1972. His policies for achieving this consisted of going slow on integration, opposing busing, and attempting to appoint a conservative white Southerner to the Supreme Court. While Governor Wallace's political future is still not clear, he can be expected to talk in terms of a bid for the Presidency in 1976, all the while trying to persuade both Democratic and Republican politicians to take his policy views—and those of his supporters—seriously.

THE 1972 PRESIDENTIAL ELECTION

Only 54.5 percent of eligible voters cast ballots in the 1972 election, the lowest turnout since 1948. The growing distrust and cynicism about politics, the widespread dislike for both candidates, and the anticipated size of Nixon's victory may explain some of the drop in participation. Another factor was the eighteen-year-old vote. These newcomers, as political scientists predicted, showed lower rates of participation than older voters.[34] The eighteen-year-olds showed the same traits that worked to keep the youngest voters before 1972 (the twenty-one- to thirty-year-olds) relatively inactive: ignorance of registration procedures; ignorance of issues; apathy toward their community of residence; lack of perceived stake in the outcome; relatively less income, property, education, and occupational status than older voters; and an inadequate period of residence.

In the aftermath of Nixon's landslide victory, numerous commentators talked about a "new Republican majority." This assertion is difficult to defend. Richard Nixon may have received 61.8 percent of the vote, but—as we saw in Table 4-3—the American people did not shift their loyalties to the Republican party. In fact, the slight decline in Democratic identifiers was not accompanied by a corresponding increase in Republicans; rather, the proportion of Republican identifiers fell to its lowest point since 1952.

If the voters' party identification cannot account for Nixon's reelection, how can it be explained? The electorate's candidate orientation (i.e., how they evaluated the candidates' personal qualities) provides a partial answer. Figure 4-2 shows a consistently more positive response to Richard Nixon than to George McGovern. Fifty-five percent of the

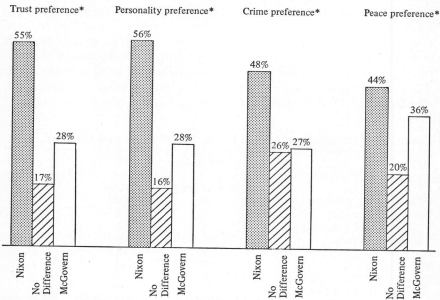

Figure 4-2 Voter assessments of presidential candidates, 1972. Center for Political Studies, Institute for Social Research, University of Michigan. *Respondents were asked to use a 7-point scale to indicate their agreement or disagreement with a series of questions about the personalities and capabilities of the two candidates. These data reflect their relative ratings of Nixon and McGovern on the following questions:

Trust Preference. Nixon (McGovern), as President, could be trusted.

Personality Preference. Nixon (McGovern) has the kind of personality a President ought to have.

Crime Preference. Nixon (McGovern), as President, could control crime.

Peace Preference. Nixon (McGovern), as President, would bring peace to Vietnam.

respondents felt that Nixon, as President, could be trusted more than McGovern, while only 28 percent saw McGovern as more trustworthy. There were similar responses about the candidates' personalities, and about their capacity to control crime and bring peace in Vietnam.

The significance of the voters' candidate orientation is obvious. An overwhelming majority of people interviewed said they would vote for the candidate whose personal qualities attracted them most.

Issue orientation was also important in 1972. Unlike many presidential elections, this was not a contest between two candidates seeking to conceal their policy conflicts. Nixon and McGovern voiced different positions on a range of issues, which were quickly picked up by the voters. For each of these issues, shown in Table 4-5, respondents were asked to place themselves and each of the candidates on a 7-point scale ranging from "extreme liberal" to "extreme conservative." In each instance, Nixon was seen by most respondents as being more conservative than McGovern. Also, Nixon's positions tended to be very similar to those of the persons interviewed. Most people opposed busing and the elimination of the neighborhood school, and saw Nixon as sharing their

Table 4-5   Perceptions of Issues in the 1972 Presidential Election

Standard of living			
	Respondent*	Nixon†	McGovern†
1 (Government should see to	14%	8%	43%
2 it that every person	7	6	24
3 has a job and a good	9	10	12
4 standard of living.)	24	29	10
5	15	18	5
6	9	14	4
7 (Government should let each person get ahead on his own.)	22	16	3

Marijuana			
	Respondent	Nixon	McGovern
1 (Marijuana should be	11%	2%	21%
2 made legal.)	5	1	16
3	7	4	14
4	11	20	18
5	7	19	8
6	7	16	8
7 (Penalties for using marijuana should be set higher than they are now.)	53	38	15

views. Likewise, most respondents saw Nixon supporting their preference for a moderate policy in Vietnam. In these and other instances, McGovern was seen as taking an extreme and unpopular position.

The 1972 election, like most of those before it, points to the fact that Americans disagree about the proper goals for public policy. However, most do tend to be centrists, avoiding the extreme right or left. It was George McGovern's dilemma that many voters saw him as an extremist, and therefore doubted his personal qualities. Barry Goldwater's crushing defeat eight years earlier reflected a similar set of circumstances.

A book that summarizes what many Americans want from the policy delivery system is Richard Scammon and Ben Wattenberg's *The Real Majority.* The authors see moderation as the dominant feature of American politics, even though we are now in the midst of a conservative drift. More people today think of themselves as "conservatives," in contrast

Table 4-5 (Continued)

Vietnam			
	Respondent	Nixon	McGovern
1 (Immediate withdrawal.)	20%	4%	68%
2	11	5	14
3	13	13	6
4	25	29	2
5	13	17	2
6	6	15	2
7 (Do everything necessary to win a complete military victory.)	12	18	3

School busing			
	Respondent	Nixon	McGovern
1 (Busing is justified	5%	9%	23%
2 by the importance	3	5	16
3 of achieving racial	3	6	16
4 integration in the	5	13	18
5 schools.)	4	14	9
6	8	16	5
7 (Letting children go to their neighborhood school is so important that busing must be opposed.)	73	36	12

*In each instance, the respondent was given the extreme positions on the 7-point scales and was then asked: "Where would you place yourself on this scale, or haven't you thought much about this?"

†After the extreme positions were identified, each respondent was asked to rate Nixon and McGovern on the four scales.

Source: Center for Political Studies, Institute for Social Research, University of Michigan.

to the early 1960s, when "liberal" was a more common choice. Scammon and Wattenberg point out, however, that a large proportion of conservatives qualify their label by calling themselves "moderate conservatives."

The conservative drift is most pronounced on a series of social issues: student disorders, racial unrest, the crime wave, obscenity and pornography, and marijuana. There is continued support for liberal policies on such economic issues as programs for education, poverty, medical care, and the aged.[35] According to Scammon and Wattenberg:

> The winning coalition in America is the one that holds the center ground on an attitudinal battlefield. In the years until the election of 1968, the battlefield had been mostly an economic battlefield, and the Democrats held the ideological allegiance of . . . middle-income, middle-aged voters who wanted a high minimum wage, Social Security, Medicare, union protection, and so on. That seems to be changing. For the seventies, the battlefield shows signs of splitting into two battlefields: the old economic one and the new social one that deals with crime, drugs, racial pressure, and disruption. To the extent that this transformation occurs, then the party and the candidate that can best occupy the center ground of the two battlefields will win the Presidency.[36]

It is too early to tell what changes in liberal, conservative, or middle-of-the-road thinking will emerge from the scandals of the Nixon Presidency and the Agnew Vice Presidency. Yet the investigations and revelations have so occupied the government, the media, and the public that the trends noticed by Scammon and Wattenberg prior to 1972 may shift by 1976.

POLITICAL PARTIES

The role of political parties in American politics has long been a concern of political scientists. Some credit parties with the creation of democracy and assert that democratic government could not survive without them. It is through political parties, they maintain, that the individual citizen can control government officials and influence their policies. "It should be stated flatly . . . that the political parties created democracy and that modern democracy is unthinkable save in terms of the parties."[37]

There is nothing modest in this claim. However, while this position may be overstated, we should not reject it altogether. Remember, most people feel a psychological tie to one of the major parties and use this attachment to guide many voting decisions, and it is the parties that nominate and campaign for public officials who become policy makers.

There are nonpartisan elections for statewide contests in Minnesota and Nebraska and for council and mayoralty races in many localities, but these are exceptions when viewed against the importance of partisan elections in all national and almost all state contests. The mythology is that parties can shape policy by controlling their nominees once they have been elected; but in this task, parties have proved most inadequate.

While some writers praise the contribution of political parties to the American political system, others view them with scorn and ridicule. For many, party politics means dirty politics, whereby politicians place their personal interests and those of their party above the so-called public interest. Political parties are often seen as boss-dominated machines which promote and thrive upon graft and corruption. Less cynical observers see parties as fragmented, ineffective structures unable to help solve public problems.

Disciplined party organizations dominated by a few activists *can* be found in some states and localities, but the days of these monolithic political machines appear to be over. Even Richard J. Daley's long-successful Democratic organization in Chicago has fallen on bad times and now finds itself fighting for its life. At the national level, both parties have instituted reforms aimed at lessening the power of party professionals and ensuring that private citizens can influence the selection of candidates and programs. The most striking of these reforms took place at the 1972 Democratic National Convention. Following its chaotic convention in 1968, the Democratic party established a Commission on Party Structure and Delegate Selection. The recommendations of this commission were adopted, in large part, by the full convention four years later. The new rules required that a state Democratic party ensure that delegates to the National Convention be chosen and certified through a process "in which all Democratic voters have had full and timely opportunity to participate." Furthermore, the rules require that "(1) the unit rules not be used in any stages of the delegate selection process, and (2) all feasible efforts have been made to assure that delegates are selected through party primary, convention or committee procedures open to public participation within the calender year of the National Convention."[38]

Two consequences of these reforms can be identified. First, the Democratic Convention of 1972 was more *representative* in the sense that demographic groups that had long been discriminated against in delegate selection (women, youth, minorities) were present in considerably larger numbers. In this respect, the reforms "worked splendidly and defied all efforts by the professionals, including those in McGovern's organization, to make them serve the old purposes."[39] On the other hand, reform weakened the party's effort to win the November election. In a number of states, particularly California, the victorious McGovern delegations largely ignored organized labor. Therefore, the support that the Democratic candidate has traditionally received from this group did not go to McGovern.

To date, the reforms initiated by the Republican party have not been as striking as those of the Democrats. It is likely, however, that additional changes will be made before the two parties stage their 1976 national conventions. A Democratic party commission has already recommended that the party drop its system of demographic quotas, which aroused great controversy in 1972, and that a larger number of party notables—that is, elected officials and party professionals—be included as convention delegates. On the Republican side, it is likely that larger numbers of women, youth, and minority delegates will attend the party's 1976 nominating convention.

American parties are fragmented and divided, and have great difficulty in developing a coherent set of policies that their nominees and officeholders—not to mention the voters—will accept. Perhaps because only two major parties attempt to accommodate all the major interests in this country, they cannot function without internal disturbance. As loosely knit coalitions, they reveal the conflicts inherent in our diverse culture and economy. Factions of each major party display the parochial interest of regions, communities, subcultures, and economic groups; they show the problems in defining an overriding national interest at all but the highest level of abstraction (e.g., patriotic support for the country in the most general terms) or except in those rare times when most groups in the nation pull together when threatened by a common enemy. (The last time this happened was during World War II.)

The fact that it is difficult to talk about any political party in the United States as a single entity underscores this fragmentation. American parties are actually "three-headed political giants," which attempt to mesh the separate interests of politicians, citizens, and government officials:[40]

1 An organization of candidates, potential candidates, and professional and amateur party workers whose primary concerns are to get out the vote and win elections.

2 Voters who identify with the party, may be casually and infrequently involved in its activities, and vote for its candidates with varying enthusiasm.

3 Incumbent officeholders who identify themselves as party members, share some policy goals, and work together (often or sometimes) to produce some cooperation among the different branches and levels of government.

A common criticism of American parties is their inability to mobilize voters, party activists, and officeholders behind a set of programs. This inability "constitutes the most important single fact concerning the American parties. He who knows this fact, and knows nothing else, knows more about American parties than he who knows everything except this fact. What kind of party is it that, having won control of government, is unable to govern?"[41] Why are the political parties unable to mobilize their members and simply run the government? To answer this question, we must consider the three components of American parties outlined above.

Party as Organization

Few Americans can be described as actual "members" of political parties. Most of them are linked only by the support they feel for the party's candidates and programs. Grass-roots party organizations do exist in some states, but there are few dues-paying, card-carrying members. The party as organization consists generally of those individuals, both leaders and followers, who make irregular and sporadic contributions of their time, money, and skill.

The primary goal of most party supporters is to elect candidates. They are less concerned with promoting a common set of values, programs, or objectives. Candidates and their supporters are generally willing to compromise on matters of program in order to broaden their appeal to independents and supporters of the other party. State and local activists may be concerned more about candidates at their own level than with the national party. In 1964, many Republican organizations concentrated on the election of state and local candidates, making little effort to campaign for the seemingly hopeless presidential candidacy of Barry Goldwater. At the same time, many Democratic party members throughout the South promoted the Goldwater candidacy even while working for state and local Democratic nominees. In 1972, some local Democratic organizations concentrated on their own contests and hoped to isolate their candidates from George McGovern's losing national ticket.

Because American parties are concerned primarily with victories in elections, we sometimes see organizations and candidates within the same party assuming very different positions on public issues. Democratic candidates in Massachusetts and New York may back a national lettuce boycott because local voters sympathize with Cesar Chavez's National Farm Workers Organization, while Midwestern Democrats oppose the boycott in hopes of gaining the votes of farmers. Republicans campaigning in urban areas may advocate more federal dollars for mass transit, while rural Republicans oppose such efforts if they would limit funds for highway programs.

State laws contribute to this inconsistency. Laws give voters a primary role in selecting local committeemen and other party officers, as well as nominees for office. The problem with this is that many voters identify with the party only sporadically and have little concern for traditional party policies. As laws have sought increasingly to "democratize" political parties, they have made it easier for candidates with current and short-lived popularity to gain control of parties, and have inhibited the development of professional staffs that could discipline candidates and make incumbent elected officials support the party's program.

Related to the two parties' lack of discipline is their decentralized structure. The national parties are composed of fifty state parties which, in turn, consist of parties based in counties, municipalities, or legislative districts. Nominations and financial support for state and local offices come from state or local party organizations. Presidential hopefuls must pay homage to the state or local party officials who control votes at the national party convention. The national party offers few tangible incentives for state or local cooperation and has no formal way of keeping dissidents in line. Some congressmen and governors campaign in open opposition to their party's presidential nominee. At one time this problem was peculiarly Democratic, with liberal presidential nominees expecting to write off the support of conservative Southerners. The latest example has been George McGovern's 1972 presidential campaign. But the 1964 presidential contest showed that Republicans can also have a major problem with party discipline. Governors Nelson Rockefeller and George Romney, Senator Jacob Javits, and New York City's Mayor John Lindsay were noticeably absent from the list of those who supported Barry Goldwater.

Ideological diversity is accepted as a virtue and perpetuated by many party leaders, who view the voters as "middle of the roaders" and who make their platforms ambiguous in order to broaden their appeal. This "umbrella effect" lessens whatever chance the parties have to make their members, officers, and candidates support the party line—if they can figure out what it is. Candidates are pragmatists who put a premium on flexibility; there are many stories of "the Speech" that varies in detail from state to state and from region to region in order to ensure a winning ticket in November.

Party as Voters

As our discussion of voting patterns pointed out, most Americans identify with one of the two major parties and tend to keep a loyalty over a period of time. However, we also noted that party identification is only one of several factors that influence the voters' choice of candidate. The lack of strong party discipline means that a voter's party loyalty must compete with his view of the candidates and prominent issues, and with his sense of economic well-being. "Deviating elections," those in which the minority-party candidate wins many temporary supporters from the other party, generally indicate that party loyalty has, for the moment, lost out. These elections, such as the Eisenhower victories in 1952 and 1956, and Nixon's successful campaigns in 1968 and 1972,[42] signaled fundamental shifts of public mood that have caused voters to cross party lines.

The history of the Democratic and Republican parties predates that of almost all the major foreign governments. For more than one hundred years, Americans have been able to think of themselves as Republicans or Democrats. In that time the British have had to accustom themselves to a mass electorate; the French have experienced three military defeats and foreign occupations, plus three Republics; and the Germans, Italians, Russians, Mexicans, and Japanese have deposed or severely modified their monarchies. The American political parties, as continuing viable institutions, have outlasted their identification with any particular personalities or events. Each party has its memories of great men and great causes, but neither party is fixated on the past. Indeed, they have both tried to recruit the newcomers to politics since the nineteenth century, and in so doing have broadened their positions. In fact, a major criticism today is that the Republicans and Democrats have become too much alike, a claim that has fueled George Wallace's campaigns.

The continuity of American parties facilitates the learning of political roles. Children acquire the party affiliations of their parents, along with numerous other traits of the family, and since there are only two major parties to choose from, the problem of choice is minimized. A 1968 study found that 59 percent of high school seniors held the same party loyalties as their parents; only 7 percent of the students crossed over to the opposition party, and the remainder claimed independence or were the offspring of independent identifiers.[43]

Children's opinions on candidates and issues also tend to resemble those of their parents—but less so than on party identification. A party label, requiring little thought, is easier to acquire and is less confining than an opinion about a candidate or program. Party affiliation is one of the first-learned of a child's political traits. Because of this, it may help to condition his or her later attitudes toward political issues and gain reinforcement from the more complex attitudes picked up from family and friends. Democrats tend to be more liberal on economic issues than Republicans, regardless of income level. This may reflect the Democrats' identification with the "little man" since the 1930s and the success of Democratic parents in preparing their children to take a liberal position on certain kinds of issues.

Even though the family is important in teaching party affiliation and other political traits, its influence is subject to erosion; some families are not successful propagandists. In other cases, when the father and mother express contrasting party loyalties, the child is subject to differing influences; he or she will probably absorb a little of both. Even when both parents are united politically, the child is exposed from early school years to political messages that differ from those of the family. The child who is mobile socially or economically is especially likely to absorb contrasting political messages. When leaving home for a school, job, or marriage, he or she acquires new contacts who can change the political identity learned from parents. The political environment of an era can also affect the resilience of the family's political traits. A 1952 study indicated that respondents under the age of fifty-five from Democratic families were more likely to retain their parents' party loyalty than were Republicans. The longevity of the Roosevelt and Truman administrations made it more likely that Republican offspring would encounter Democratic influences to change their early loyalties.[44]

This transmission of party identification and other political values from one generation to the next has serious implications for the character of political parties. The ease in acquiring a party label spells trouble for the party. With voters' identification with the party open to all who would emulate their parents, there is no screening of members for their loyalty to party traditions. All can enter, and are welcome to stay and pass on the loyalty to their children, whether they are liberal or conservative, hawk or dove, internationalist or isolationist—or, as is most often the case, not concerned with issues consistently.

Party in Government

In looking at the operation of politicians in government, we find some of the same traits as among voters: government officials usually vote with their party colleagues but occasionally deviate on important issues. The political scientist wants to know: How often, and under what conditions, do government officials adhere to and deviate from the party line? If we can answer this question, we can determine the extent of party unity and define the contribution that parties make to the formulation and implementation of public policy. By knowing when officials act as partisans and when they act independently, we can make some statements about how party identification links officials and voters, and the types of issues that are likely to be resolved by elected Democrats and Republicans acting together.

Such diverse critics as Eugene McCarthy and George Wallace, as well as numerous political scientists, have argued that Democratic and Republican officeholders do not differ on important policy questions.

They point out that Republican Senators like Clifford Case (N.J.) and Edward Brooke (Mass.) vote with Democrats such as Hubert Humphrey (Minn.) and Abraham Ribicoff (Conn.) more often than they do with their fellow Republicans. Similarly, Democratic Senators John Stennis (Miss.) and Russell Long (La.) vote with the Republicans more frequently on key issues than with their own party.

Numerous studies have revealed, however, that such anti-party behavior is atypical. During the past twenty years, on approximately half the congressional votes at least 50 percent of the Republicans were opposed by at least 50 percent of the Democrats. Party loyalty is usually influential on important issues. Democrats have been much more likely than Republicans to support a low tariff, agricultural subsidies, expanded health and welfare programs, legislation benefiting labor and the poor, government regulation of business, and a larger role for the federal government.[45] Democrats in Congress are more likely to vote together than Republicans. To be sure, there are North-South differences among Democratic congressmen, but on issues that affect the interests of cities, labor, and Westerners, Democrats from all over the country tend to unite. Theirs is the party of vote-trading among members, or "logrolling," from one issue to another. Republicans, in contrast, are more likely to find themselves alone or voting with the Democrats when the needs of their own district are at stake.[46]

Party-line voting in state legislatures varies a great deal from one state to another. All roll calls during 1959 and 1960 in the Rhode Island Senate found party majorities arrayed against each other; in Pennsylvania, Massachusetts, and New York, party-line votes occurred more than 70 percent of the time. On the other hand, in California party-line votes occurred only 17 percent of the time, while less than 30 percent of the controversial roll calls found party majorities opposing each other in Utah, Nevada, and Oregon.[47]

In Congress and the state legislatures, party loyalty is greatest when the legislature is being organized. The selection of presiding officers, committee chairmen, and committee members directly influences the parties' capacity to function and leads all members to vote along party lines. Likewise, state legislators vote as partisans on patronage, the organization of local and state governments, and election laws. Party members in Congress and state legislatures also tend to vote together on issues that command great public attention and will be useful at the next election: taxation and budgeting, education, welfare, regulation of business and labor, and the control of natural resources.[48]

Partisanship has a significant influence on the staffing of executive and judicial institutions. In the administrations of Franklin Roosevelt through Lyndon Johnson, almost 75 percent of upper-level administrative and judicial appointments went to the president's party colleagues.[49] All but two Presidents in the twentieth century have appointed supporters of their own party to at least *90 percent* of the available judgeships (see Table 4-6). This has great significance for the nature of public policy, since a judge's party affiliation influences the decisions he makes:

> The Democrats on the bench tend to decide more frequently for the defendent in criminal cases, for the government in taxation cases, for the regulatory agency in cases involving the regulation of business, and for the claimants in workmen's compensation, unemployment compensation, and auto accident cases.[50]

VARIATIONS IN STATE PARTIES AND POLITICAL PARTICIPATION

In discussing the nature of party organizations, we noted their basis in the fifty states. The diversity of state parties is one factor that keeps the national party organs from counting on support from all their voters, or on the consistency of the party's President and congressmen once in office. State parties vary markedly in their strength and competitiveness. The Republican party is only an occasional threat in state and local elections throughout the South, though its strength has increased somewhat in recent years. In some of the New England and Great Plains states, the Republicans almost always run state and local affairs and usually capture their states' electoral votes for the Presidency. John Kennedy once commented during a senatorial campaign in western Massachusetts that in some communities of his own state the only Democrat was the town drunk!

The competitiveness of state parties tends to influence the amount of

Table 4-6 Proportion of Judicial Appointments from the Party of the President: Cleveland through Nixon

Cleveland	97.3%		Hoover	85.7%
Harrison	87.9		F. Roosevelt	96.4
McKinley	95.7		Truman	90.1
T. Roosevelt	95.8		Eisenhower	94.1
Taft	82.2		Kennedy	90.1
Wilson	98.6		Johnson	94.6
Harding	97.7		Nixon*	93.2
Coolidge	94.1			

*First term only.
Source: Data from Evan A. Evans, "Political Influences in the Selection of Federal Judges," *Wisconsin Law Review* (May 1948), pp. 300–351; Hugh A. Bone, *American Politics and the Party System*, 4th ed. (New York: McGraw-Hill, 1971), p. 248; Frank J. Sorauf, *Party Politics in America*, 2d ed. (Boston: Little, Brown, 1972), p. 378; and *Congressional Quarterly Weekly Report*, vol. XXX (December, 1972), p. 3158.

Table 4-7   Ranking of the States on Measures of Voter Turnout and Party Competition*

1	Utah	25	New Hampshire
2	Nebraska	26	Rhode Island
3	Minnesota	27	Massachusetts
4	Idaho	28	Maine
5	Montana	29	South Dakota
6	Indiana	30	Arizona
7	Illinois	31	Nevada
8	Wisconsin	32	North Carolina
9	Oregon	33	Oklahoma
10	New Jersey	34	Kentucky
11	North Dakota	35	Maryland
12	Washington	36	Vermont
13	Colorado	37	Tennessee
14	Michigan	38	Florida
15	Connecticut	39	Texas
16	Wyoming	40	New Mexico
17	California	41	New York
18	Kansas	42	Virginia
19	Iowa	43	Louisiana
20	Missouri	44	Arkansas
21	West Virginia	45	Mississippi
22	Ohio	46	Alabama
23	Pennsylvania	47	Georgia
24	Delaware	48	South Carolina

*Alaska and Hawaii were excluded from the analysis.
Source: Ira Sharkansky and Richard I. Hofferbert, "Dimensions of State Policy," in Politics in the American States, 2d ed., edited by Herbert Jacob and Kenneth Vines (Boston: Little, Brown, 1972), p. 336.

public participation in state politics: the more competition, the more voting. Perhaps the competition makes politics seem interesting and important; the prospect of resolving real conflicts may lead more people to the polls. At the same time, the activity of all those voters gives the candidates of each party plenty of targets for their campaigns. Thus, the process is circular. Table 4-7 ranks the states according to the combined measure of voter turnout and competition for state offices. Utah, Nebraska, Minnesota, and Idaho score at the top; at the bottom are the one-party, low-competition states of South Carolina, Georgia, Alabama, and Mississippi.[51]

The economic and social characteristics of the states have something to do with party competitiveness and voter turnout. The states that rank high on Table 4-7 tend to have high levels of per capita income and education. High education and income levels support an interest in politics. These same traits also affect public resources. Many of the states that score high on Table 4-7 can support generous levels of public service.

Party leaders are spurred to compete, perhaps, for the opportunity to decide how the funds will be spent.

Habit and tradition also influence voter turnout and party competition. Chapter 7 discusses the regional patterns in state politics, some of which exert stronger influence on turnout and competition than the economic or social traits of the individual states. Nebraska, Utah, and Idaho are not so wealthy as to achieve their high rates of competition and turnout on an economic basis alone: these traits of competition and turnout reflect patterns evident among all their regional neighbors.[52]

The states that score high on competition and turnout also tend to score high on some measures of public policy. Welfare and education programs, in particular, prosper under these political conditions.[53] Party leaders may compete with their adversaries by promising more generous services. However, the web of cause-and-effect that connects competition, turnout, welfare, and education programs is not entirely clear.

PRIVATE INTEREST GROUPS

Interest groups (also called lobbies and pressure groups) join political parties in helping to link citizens with their governments. Like the parties, the interest groups have a mixed reputation. From a positive perspective, they reflect our diverse interests and serve as the spokesman of economic groups, cultural communities, and points of view. James Madison, a framer of the Constitution and later President, approved of the clash of interest groups, which he saw as the basic stuff of American politics: the compromises among these groups become the policies of government.[54] The play of groups takes place most visibly in the legislature but also is an integral feature of policy making in the executive, administrative, and judicial areas.[55]

The negative reputation of interest groups focuses on their pursuit of selfish goals. Several generations of muckrakers, including Ralph Nader on the consumer front and the peace spokesmen who tilt with the "military-industrial complex," have exposed the shady dealings of business, professional, and labor groups to secure the passage of favored legislation, or to block measures that threaten their positions.[56]

Some Recent Scandals

These illegal or questionable dealings have received great attention in the wake of the Watergate scandals. Numerous groups, including International Telephone and Telegraph, Associated Milk Producers, Inc., Braniff Airlines, The American Shipbuilding Company, the oil industry, and the Teamsters Union, have been investigated and/or indicted for making illegal contributions to President Nixon's 1972 reelection campaign. Pointing out that 413 company officers and principal stockholders in the oil industry contributed almost $5 million to the President's 1972 reelection, Representative Les Aspin (D., Wis.) made a charge that President Nixon's "hands are tied, preventing him from dealing with the current energy crisis." According to Aspin, the oil companies "have Mr. Nixon in a double hammerlock—after their massive contributions there is little he can do to control them."[57]

The political activities of the nation's largest dairy cooperative, Associated Milk Producers, Inc., (AMPI), are even more revealing. AMPI's contributions to the Nixon campaign have been under investigation for more than a year, and associates of Ralph Nader have charged that these funds were used to "buy" administration support for an increase in milk price supports in 1971. Responding to these charges, AMPI reported that its contributions had gone to support many candidates, both Republican and Democratic. In 1968, AMPI gave more than $91,000 to Hubert Humphrey's presidential campaign. In 1972, AMPI paid the salary and apartment rent of a full-time campaign worker in Representative Wilbur Mills's (D., Ark.) organization. The AMPI report also revealed numerous contributions to support the political activities of the late President Lyndon B. Johnson.

Identifying Interest Groups

Interest groups come in a variety of forms and represent virtually every kind of citizen and goal. Economic groups include various segments of commerce, manufacturing, finance, labor, agriculture, and the professions. The character of many of these economic interests is not clear, in part because they have "hidden behind vague, institutional titles like the Sugar Lobby, the Tobacco Lobby, the Highway Lobby, etc."[58] The Ralph Nader Congress Project reported that the oil lobby is the most influential of all. It can usually "send into action lawyers from the most respectable law firms, public relations consultants, numerous ex-government officials, newsmen who serve as 'advisers,' company executives, corporate legal departments, government officials in several of the executive departments, trade association representatives, and—though only a small fraction of the total—men who actually register as lobbyists."[59] Given this array of manpower, it is not surprising that the oil industry has profited from tax bonanzas (e.g., the 27½ percent depletion allowance) and special import benefits.

Other groups seek to realize ideological goals, ranging from the left-wing Weathermen to the right-wing American Nazi party. All ethnic and religious groups have their lobbies; most have several organizations

that represent different wings of the community (e.g., the more conservative, legalistic National Association for the Advancement of Colored
People and the radical Black Panthers). Most groups claim to represent
the needs of the total population—e.g., "what is good for business (labor,
consumers, or the environment) is good for America." Some groups
represent government officials (see pages 106–108). Public employees'
unions seek to improve salaries and working conditions. Other government interest groups pursue general policy goals. The National Governors' Conference is the most visible association of elected officials and
administrators that lobbies for measures in Congress and state legislatures. Some lobbies of government employees get their support from the
voluntary donations of their members; others are unofficial extensions of
government agencies that seek to enhance their clout in the policy
delivery system. Some government lobbyists work the legislative branch
as spokesmen for the administrative or executive branches. These are the
"legislative liaisons" who line up support among key lawmakers to obtain
the passage of administration programs.

The following features of interest groups give them great leverage in
the policy delivery system: membership size, prestige, and wealth; the
"legitimacy" of the groups' objectives; the groups' tendency to stand
behind a clear set of policy goals; and the skills of their leaders. These
"resources" are most often found in commercial and professional groups,
and in organizations seeking to further the interests of the rich. Wealthy,
prestigious persons tend to be the most active in organizations; thus,
pressure group politics has an upper-class bias. This does not mean that
less favored, low-prestige groups are powerless. Such groups use atten-
tion-getting tactics to rally more established organizations behind their
demands. Rent strikers and ghetto rioters fit this pattern. Their protests
and unrest may elicit support from civic groups, the mass media, or public
officials—with improvements in public services as a possible consequence. What these groups risk, however, is the "backlash" of reaction
by some of the groups they wish to attract.[60]

How Successful Are Interest Groups?

Any effort to understand the success of interest groups must also reckon
with several elements that limit them. The most obvious limitation is the
greater power of government officials in their relationships with interest
groups.

> Analysts of the political process often overlook the fact that the elected
> officials have the upper hand in setting up and enforcing the rules. This is
> especially true in the relationship between lobbyists and officials. Officials

can make decisions without consulting or depending on anyone else—except the voters at the next election. They can neutralize the lobbyists by cutting off access or neglecting to listen. They have many alternative sources for the information they seek. Lobbyists have much less power; they can accomplish their ends only by reaching officials; they have no alternative target. It is the officials who admit the lobbyists to the trust relationship—not vice versa.[61]

The goals of some interest groups are easier to achieve than others. American policy delivery systems, as we have said, show a fragmentation of power. No single official can implement major policy decisions alone, and major ventures require cooperation among several institutions. Thus, if a lobbyist desires to *block* action on a new proposal, he may have little trouble finding one institution to cooperate with him. If he wishes to *promote* a change in policy, however, he must earn the cooperation of many officials, any one of whom may shut off his access and frustrate his program.

Even when he approaches a sympathetic official, a lobbyist might not receive a fair hearing of his case. Officials suffer from an *information overload*, created by the surplus of individuals and groups who seek their attention.

> It is physically impossible for any government official to attend to all the communications directed to him. Officials use their personal perceptual screen to protect themselves from some of this overload. They also have devised some institutional means, such as staff assistants and data coding, to help them sort, condense, and comprehend as much of the incoming information as possible. In the scramble for limited attention, the lobbyist must plan carefully and seize a rare moment of receptivity to drive home a communication.[62]

To be sure, large campaign contributions may assure a group's access to key elected officials. But major policy changes require the cooperation of many officials, including selected—not elected—administrators who are *not* subject to reelection pressure. (This bias in favor of the status quo is one of the factors that adds to the frustration of the poor, black, and other minorities that seek radical changes in policy.) The *communications overload*, another problem of lobbyists, is evident at legislative hearings. Witnesses typically address a limited number of committee members, and even those present may be distracted by some other business. Legislators "read over" the fat volumes of transcripts that report the hearings, but they may not perceive a spoken or written message that is sent in their direction.

Even after the interest group's message is received by the government, it must still survive an official decision before it can influence public policy. The crucial obstacles include the official's personal convictions; his or her view of the constituency's desires and potential opposition; the party's position, if any, on the policy; the advice and information given by the official's professional staff; and the recommendations made by trusted colleagues. Since officials give varying weight to these factors in making decisions, lobbyists cannot be sure of what competition they face for the officials' support. Often the lobbyist is reduced to guesswork about the particular strategies that will accomplish his goals.

GOVERNMENT INTEREST GROUPS

Government officials have their own lobbyists who compete with those of the private sector to shape public decisions. Given the governmental focus of this book, it is fitting to close this chapter on citizens, parties, and interest groups with a discussion of governmental efforts to mobilize support from the public—the environment—and to minimize any hostile demands.

Among government interest groups are the unions of government employees. The lobbies of high-level policy makers include the National League of Cities and the U.S. Conference of Mayors. They frequently support new legislation that would establish or enlarge federal aid, and they testify before legislative subcommittees to support funding for existing programs. There are separate organizations for social workers, public health physicians, highway administrators, state departments of agriculture, and public safety officials. Although local and state boards of education may protest their employees' lobbying, school boards themselves (along with educational associations and teachers' unions) have their spokesmen in state capitols and Washington. Individual states and municipalities maintain representatives in Washington, as well as support the variety of groups that represent separate officials and departments.

The federal agencies should not be slighted in any description of government lobbying. Their principal targets are the committees that handle their legislation and appropriations. Although the U.S. Congress has objected and even outlawed the spending of public money for lobbying activities, an aide of President Johnson counted about forty "congressional relations people" in high administrative positions. They carry their department's message directly to important legislators and enlist additional support from nongovernment interest groups.[63]

When government officials are not supporting their own interest groups, they may be giving covert aid to private sector groups that serve as allies.

A first and fundamental source of power for administrative agencies in American society is their ability to attract outside support. Strength in a constituency is no less an asset for an American administrator than it is for a politician, and some agencies have succeeded in building outside support as formidable as that of any political organization.[64]

Administrative agencies use several techniques to develop and nourish a constituency of interest groups. They keep the mass media informed about activities that have widespread public interest, and they maintain frequent contacts with groups affected by their programs.

An interest group ally can help an agency in several ways. First, the group can align itself with a position held by administrators, but which the administrators cannot take publicly because it would offend the President or important legislators. Second, interest groups can support an agency's requests for funds and greater authority or help the agency resist undesirable directives from the President or Congress. An interest group can also make an argument and build public support for an administrator who is currently the target of executive or legislative hostility.

Some agencies have such strong support from interest groups and private citizens that they seem to be a law unto themselves; the President and Congress tread carefully when dealing with them. The Federal Bureau of Investigation, especially during the "reign" of J. Edgar Hoover, had an enormous reservoir of good will among associations of local police departments (whose members are trained at FBI academies and whose analyses are done in FBI laboratories) and among many private citizens (long accustomed to watching the FBI on television shows put together with agency cooperation). Hoover was Director of the FBI from 1924 until his death in 1972; his personal rule was so strong that Presidents Kennedy, Johnson, and Nixon kept him in office long beyond the mandatory retirement age for federal personnel.

Some alliances between interest groups and government officials are so strong that they are labeled *subgovernments*. The term is applied to the military-industrial complex: a network of military and civilian personnel in the Department of Defense, defense contractors and the interest groups that represent them, and legislators who seek to improve the military posture of the United States or to land lucrative defense contracts for their districts. For example, Senator Henry Jackson (D., Wash.) has long been known for his support of Seattle's Boeing Aircraft. Former Deputy Assistant Secretary of Defense Adam Yarmolinsky has written that Representative John Brademas (D., Ind.) "spends many hours promoting defense contracts for Studebaker and Bendix Corporation and frankly contends, 'anyone who didn't do it wouldn't be here very long.'" He also points to a Senate debate on an Air Force appropriations bill in which Senator J. Glenn Beall (R., Md.) "begged his colleagues to add money for the purchase of transport planes from Fairchild Aircraft Company in Hagerstown, Maryland. 'All we ask for Fairchild is $11,000,000,' said Beall."[65]

The pressures of this alliance have implications for the size of the military budget and for the flexibility of United States foreign policy. Can the military-industrial complex block the deescalation of international tension? It is difficult to answer this question. Although there are complementary interests linking the military, defense contractors, and certain legislators, there is no clear indication that major actions in recent military or foreign policy have been motivated primarily by the need to provide economic support for defense contractors.[66]

SUMMARY

While the following chapters concentrate on government officials who take the formal steps in making and implementing policy, we have begun our discussion with the activities of citizens, political parties, and interest groups. Private citizens are the constitutional basis of the American system and help to shape the perceptions and behaviors of officials at all levels of government. Yet, American citizens do not involve themselves persistently or intimately in government. Most people take part only sporadically, and then more typically as "spectators" than as "gladiators." When they do participate, it is usually as members of interest groups or political parties. The lone individual has extensive political rights but few genuine opportunities to shape policy.

Several channels transmit policy information to citizens and citizen preferences to policy makers. The most prominent are the mass media, public opinion polls, and elections. The campaign and the election constitute the formal link between citizens and public officials, but they do not serve to keep the mass of voters and officials informed about one another's desires or actions.

The interpretation of election outcomes is a formidable task. The American voter is noted for lack of interest in and knowledge about political issues. In general, election results are not clear indicators of voters' preferences on matters of policy. Rather, they reflect voters' feelings of party identification and assessments of the personal qualities of candidates, as well as attitudes on selected issues. In the 1972 campaign, voters paid more attention to issues than in earlier years.

Between elections, political parties and interest groups help to inject citizen demands into the policy delivery system in a more-or-less formal way. However, American political parties are undisciplined coalitions of voters, candidates, organization activists, and officeholders. Despite the apparent simplicity of the two-party system, neither party has much discipline over its "members." While party loyalty exists, there is no assurance that it will prevail at crucial points when other influences compete with it. Interest groups have their fingers in every government pie, but they resemble the parties in being unable to dominate. Government officials often use the information provided by interest groups, but without assuring these groups of their support. It is always difficult to assess the influence of interest groups, especially those that represent some of the government officials who themselves help make the decisions the interest groups wish to influence.

REFERENCES

1 For a more extensive discussion of this issue, see Kenneth M. Dolbeare and Murray J. Edelman, *American Politics: Policies, Power, and Change*, 2d ed. (Lexington, Mass.: D. C. Heath and Company, 1974), pp. 183–190.
2 *Gideon v. Wainwright* (1963); *Escobedo v. Illinois* (1964).
3 Arthur Miller, "Political Issues and Trust in Government: 1964–1970," *The American Political Science Review*, vol. 68 (September 1974), p. 951.
4 See Gabriel Almond and Sidney Verba, *The Civic Culture* (Princeton: Princeton University Press, 1963); Jack Dennis, "Support for the Party System by the Mass Public," *The American Political Science Review*, vol. 60 (September 1966), pp. 600–615; and Robert Lane, "The Politics of Consensus in an Age of Affluence," *The American Political Science Review*, 59 (December 1965), pp. 874–895.
5 Miller, op. cit.
6 Lester W. Milbrath, *Political Participation* (Chicago: Rand McNally & Company, 1965).
7 Ibid., p. 19.
8 Hugh Bone and Austin Ranney, *Politics and Voters*, 2d ed. (New York: McGraw-Hill Book Company, 1967), p. 44.
9 M. Kent Jennings and Harmon Zeigler, "The Salience of American State Politics," *The American Political Science Review*, vol. 64 (June 1970), pp. 523–535.
10 See Lester Milbrath, "Political Participation in the States," in Herbert Jacob and Kenneth Vines (ed.), *Politics in the American States*, 2d ed. (Boston: Little, Brown and Company, 1972), p. 36.
11 Ibid., pp. 42–43. See also Donald R. Matthews and James W. Prothro, *Negroes and the New Southern Politics* (New York: Harcourt Brace Jovanovich, Inc., 1966).
12 V. O. Key, Jr., *Public Opinion and American Democracy* (New York: Alfred A. Knopf, Inc., 1964), pp. 344–369.
13 The Nielsen rating for this program is reported in Michael J. Robinson,

"Public Affairs Television and the Growth of Political Malaise: The Case of *The Selling of the Pentagon*," Catholic University of America, 1973, p. 13. (Mimeographed)

14 Ibid., pp. 42–43.

15 For a more detailed discussion of the nature of public opinion polls, see Charles H. Backstrom and Gerald D. Hursh, *Survey Research* (Evanston, Ill.: Northwestern University Press, 1963) and Harold Mendelsohn and Irving Crespi, *Polls, Television, and the New Politics* (Scranton: Chandler Publishing Company, 1970).

16 Philip E. Converse and Howard Schuman, "Silent Majorities and the Vietnam War," *Scientific American* (June 1970), pp. 18–19.

17 Gerald M. Pomper, *Elections in America* (New York: Dodd, Mead & Company, 1968), p. 51.

18 V. O. Key, Jr., *The Responsible Electorate* (Cambridge, Mass.: Harvard University Press, 1966), pp. 76–77.

19 Pomper, op. cit., p. 3.

20 Fred I. Greenstein, *The American Party System and the American People*, 2d ed. (Englewood Cliffs, N.J.: Prentice-Hall, Inc., 1970), pp. 12–13.

21 Lloyd A. Free and Hadley Cantril, *The Political Beliefs of Americans: A Study of Public Opinion* (New York: Simon and Schuster, 1968), p. 206.

22 Leonard Freedman, *Power and Politics in America* (Belmont, Calif.: Duxbury Press, 1971), p. 168.

23 Free and Cantril, op. cit., p. 199.

24 John E. Mueller, *War, Presidents, and Public Opinion* (New York: John Wiley & Sons, Inc., 1973), pp. 80, 92.

25 Angus Campbell and Henry Valen, "Party Identification in Norway and the United States," *Public Opinion Quarterly*, vol. 25 (Winter 1961), p. 505.

26 Angus Campbell et al., *The American Voter* (New York: John Wiley & Sons, Inc., 1960), p. 148.

27 Donald Stokes, "Some Dynamic Elements of Contests for the Presidency," *The American Political Science Review*, vol. 60 (March 1966), p. 22.

28 Campbell et al., op. cit., p. 172.

29 Milton J. Rosenberg, Sidney Verba, and Philip E. Converse, *Vietnam and the Silent Majority* (New York: Harper and Row, Publishers, Incorporated, 1970), p. 49.

30 Philip E. Converse et al., "Continuity and Change in American Politics: Parties and Issues in the 1968 Election," *The American Political Science Review*, vol. 63 (December 1969), p. 1093.

31 John C. Pierce, "Party Identification and the Changing Role of Ideology in American Politics," *The Midwest Journal of Political Science* (February 1970), pp. 25–42.

32 Peter B. Natchez and Irvin C. Bupp, "Candidates, Issues, and Voters," *Public Policy* (1968), pp. 409–437.

33 Converse et al., op. cit., 1097.

34 Ibid., p. 1099.

35 Richard M. Scammon and Ben J. Wattenberg, *The Real Majority* (New York: Coward-McCann, Inc., 1970), pp. 72–75.

36 Ibid., pp. 80–81.

37 E. E. Schattschneider, *Party Government* (New York: Holt, Rinehart and Winston, Inc., 1942), p. 1.

38 Quoted in William Cavala, "Changing the Rules Changes the Game: Party Reforms and the 1972 California Delegation to the Democratic National Convention," *The American Political Science Review*, vol. 68 (March 1974), p. 27.

39 Austin Ranney, "Comment on 'Changing the Rules of the Game,'" *The American Political Science Review*, vol. 68 (March 1974), p. 44. For a discussion of the character and consequences of these Democratic party reforms, see Commission on Party Structure and Delegate Selection, *Mandate for Reform* (Washington: Democratic National Committee, 1970); and Dennis G. Sullivan et al., *The Politics of Representation: The Democratic Convention of 1972* (New York: St. Martin's Press, Inc., 1974).

40 Frank Sorauf, *Party Politics in America*, 2d ed. (Boston: Little, Brown and Company, 1972), pp. 9–10.

41 Schattschneider, op. cit., pp. 131–132.

42 Campbell et al., op. cit., p. 124.

43 M. Kent Jennings and Richard G. Niemi, "The Transmission of Political Values from Parent to Child," *The American Political Science Review*, vol. 62 (March 1968), pp. 169–184. Also see Fred I. Greenstein, *Children and Politics* (New Haven, Conn.: Yale University Press, 1965), p. 306.

44 Key, *Public Opinion and American Democracy*, p. 301.

45 William J. Keefe, *Parties, Politics, and Public Policy in America* (New York: Holt, Rinehart and Winston, Inc., 1972), p. 116.

46 See David R. Mayhew, *Party Loyalty among Congressmen: The Differences between Democrats and Republicans, 1947–1962* (Cambridge, Mass.: Harvard University Press, 1966).

47 Hugh L. Le Blanc, "Voting in State Senates: Party and Constituency Influences," *Midwest Journal of Political Science*, vol. 13 (February 1969), pp. 35–37.

48 Thomas R. Dye, "State Legislative Politics," in Herbert Jacob and Kenneth N. Vines (ed.) *Politics in the American States*, 2d ed. (Boston: Little, Brown and Company, 1971), p. 196.

49 See David T. Stanley et al., *Men Who Govern* (Washington: The Brookings Institution, 1967), chaps. 2 and 3.

50 Sorauf, op. cit., p. 376.

51 See Ira Sharkansky and Richard I. Hofferbert, "Dimensions of State Policy," in Herbert Jacob and Kenneth N. Vines (ed.), *Politics in the American States*, 2d ed., pp. 315–353.

52 See Ira Sharkansky, *Regionalism in American Politics* (Indianapolis: The Bobbs-Merrill Company, Inc., 1970), chap. 5.

53 Sharkansky and Hofferbert, op. cit.

54 *The Federalist Papers* (New York: Mentor Books, New American Library, Inc., 1961), number 10, p. 79.

55 See David B. Truman, *The Governmental Process* (New York: Alfred A. Knopf, Inc., 1951).

56 See Mancur Olson, Jr., *The Logic of Collective Action* (Cambridge, Mass.: Harvard University Press, 1965) and Robert H. Salisbury (ed.), *Interest Group Politics in America* (New York: Harper and Row, Publishers, Incorporated, 1970).

57 *Congressional Quarterly Weekly Reports*, vol. 32 (Jan. 19, 1974), p. 113.

58 Mark J. Green, James M. Fallows, and David R. Zwick, *Who Runs Congress?* (New York: Bantam Books, Inc., 1972), p. 32.

59 Ibid., p. 33.

60 See Michael Lipsky, *Protest in City Politics: Rent Strikes, Housing and the Power of the Poor* (Chicago: Rand McNally & Company, 1970).

61 Lester W. Milbrath, *The Washington Lobbyists* (Chicago: Rand McNally & Company, 1963), p. 288. This section relies on Ira Sharkansky, *The Routines of Politics* (New York: Van Nostrand Reinhold, 1970), chap. 9.

62 Ibid., p. 210.

63 See *Legislators and the Lobbyists* (Washington, D.C.: Congressional Quarterly Service, 1968, pp. 63–72.

64 Francis E. Rourke, *Bureaucracy, Politics, and Public Policy* (Boston: Little, Brown and Company, 1969), p. 11.

65 Adam Yarmolinsky, *The Military Establishment* (New York: Harper and Row, Publishers, Incorporated, 1971), p. 40.

66 See Bruce M. Russett, *What Price Vigilance?* (New Haven, Conn.: Yale University Press, 1970).

Chapter 5

Intergovernmental Relations in America

In this first chapter that deals systematically with policy making in American governments, it is fitting to begin with intergovernmental relations. This is a feature of American government that has been with us since the eighteenth century and remains an important part of policy systems. *Intergovernmental relations*, or the transactions among national, state, and local governments, reflects the founding fathers' desire to write a Constitution that would separate powers between different units of government in order to prevent tyranny. One product of these efforts was federalism: the creation of a national government and separate state governments, each partly independent of and capable of resisting encroachment from the other. Another feature of the separation of powers was the division of the national government into legislative, executive, and judicial branches, a topic we discuss in Chapters 8 through 11.

We see in the federal nature of American government and separation of powers among legislative, executive, and judicial branches the same fragmentation of power already seen in American political parties. As loosely knit coalitions, parties reveal the conflicts inherent in our diverse society—conflicts which hinder them in identifying or promoting any coherent set of policies or programs. In this and succeeding chapters, we will see that the fragmentation of government likewise hinders any simple, coherent attack on our social problems. With this fragmentation of power, we find that coalition formation is an essential ingredient of American politics. To realize policy objectives, any one actor must have the support of others. The success of national programs requires the support of state and local officials.

It is not sufficient to ask questions about one actor's control over others. It is an individual's skill at making alliances—not his ability to issue orders—that most often determines his success in the policy delivery system. Our discussion of policy making in American government must recognize the different government units and the give and take that are at the heart of policy making.

THE DYNAMICS OF AMERICAN FEDERALISM

Federalism, one example of the fragmentation of our policy delivery systems, must be seen as a means, not as an end. It serves, according to its defenders, as a check on those who would threaten the existence of limited, democratic government. Federalism distributes power between national and state governments in a manner designed to protect the authority of both.[1] The American national government may therefore have less strength than a central government whose subdivisions are totally dependent upon it for authority. Our Constitution assures the states their continued existence, plus certain powers over their own affairs and those of the national government. The American states themselves are systems divided into cities, counties, and other local units; these units have no powers other than those given them by the states.

The Articles of Confederation

In creating a federal system, the framers of the Constitution responded to their own experiences. Years of struggle against an unresponsive, oligarchical British government had alerted them to the injustices of tyrannical rule. Bitter experiences with British rule fostered a strong sense of individualism, and a concern with the rights of individuals strengthened demands for limited government. The Articles of Confederation that were adopted by the Continental Congress in 1776 reflected these concerns, giving the central government few real powers. As with other confederate systems, the states retained their sovereignty and the central government had to depend on them for voluntary and unreliable contributions of soldiers and money.

The Constitutional Convention

When the founding fathers met in Philadelphia more than a decade later, the serious shortcomings of the confederation had become obvious. Yet delegates to the Constitutional Convention were not agreed on the nature of the problems or the proper remedies. A minority opposed any plan that would weaken state sovereignty. As one delegate from Maryland argued, "the General Government was meant merely to preserve the State Governments; not to govern individuals; that its powers ought to be kept within narrow limits; . . . that the states like individuals were in a State of nature equally sovereign and free."[2]

Under the Articles of Confederation, the central government was wholly dependent on states for the implementation of its decisions. A somewhat larger number of delegates disagreed with this, calling for the creation of a strong national government with direct legal authority over individual citizens. They felt it was essential that Congress, and other elements of the central government, be permitted to compel individuals to obey the national laws.

While the decisions of the Constitutional Convention reflect a series of compromises between these two groups, those favoring a stronger central government gained the best of the bargain. The new national government was granted broad powers, including the power to tax, regulate interstate commerce, coin money, and conduct foreign affairs. The power of the national government was reinforced by "implied powers" appearing in the constitutional language, which gave Congress the power "to make all Laws which shall be necessary and proper for carrying into Execution the foregoing Powers, and all other Powers vested by this Constitution in the Government of the United States, or in any Department or Officer thereof."[3]

The victory achieved by the proponents of a strong national government is also reflected in the *legal* superiority of the national government. As Article VI states:

> This Constitution and the Laws of the United States which shall be made in Pursuance thereof; and all Treaties made, or which shall be made, under the Authority of the United States, shall be the supreme Law of the Land; and the Judges in every State shall be bound thereby, any Thing in the Constitution or Laws of any State to the Contrary notwithstanding.

While the central government established by the Articles of Confederation had been composed of representatives from state governments—who owed their salaries and loyalties to the states—the new national government would permit the direct representation of private citizens. As Article I, Section 2, of the Constitution stipulates:

> The House of Representatives shall be composed of Members chosen every second Year by the People of the several States, and the Electors in each State shall have the Qualifications requisite for Electors of the most numerous Branch of the State Legislature.

THE EVOLUTION OF AMERICAN FEDERALISM

The nature of American federalism has changed much since 1787. While the Constitution made the national government supreme, state governments were given numerous checks and balances to protect themselves against Washington. Most notably, the Tenth Amendment to the Constitution declares that those powers not delegated to the national government, nor prohibited to the states, are reserved to the states. Yet, this statement did not prevent jurisdictional disputes between national and state governments. In a classic confrontation, the state of Maryland sought to tax the Bank of the United States, which had been chartered by Congress in 1816. At issue in this conflict was the national government's right to establish the bank and the state's right to tax it. Although the Constitution did not explicitly give any bank-chartering authority to the national government, the Supreme Court held in *McCulloch v. Maryland* (1819) that this authority was implied as an appropriate means of carrying out other specifically delegated powers. As Chief Justice John Marshall argued:

> We admit, as all must admit, that the powers of the government are limited, and that its limits are not to be transcended. But we think the sound construction of the Constitution must allow to the national legislature that discretion, with respect to the means by which the powers it confers are to be carried into execution, which will enable that body to perform the high duties assigned to it, in the manner most beneficial to the people. Let the end be legitimate, let it be within the scope of the Constitution, and all means which are appropriate, which are plainly adapted to that end, which are not prohibited, but consistent with the letter and the spirit of the Constitution, are constitutional.[4]

Hence, the constitutionality of the bank was upheld, and Maryland's tax was invalidated since "the power to tax involved the power to destroy."

In defending the "implied powers" of the national government, the

Court provided the legal setting for further growth of national powers. Through much of the nineteenth century, however, there was still a distinction between national and state matters. Defense was a responsibility of the national government and the states took care of education, health, and social welfare. Underlying this division was the assumption that some matters required a single, national policy. In other kinds of policy, variations to meet state conditions were tolerable or even necessary. As the nineteenth century drew to a close, however, the once-clear distinction between national and state roles became increasingly foggy.

While the twentieth century has seen the massive expansion of national programs, there has been no corresponding decline of state programs. The activities of national, state, *and* local governments have all expanded greatly in recent decades; it is difficult to determine just which government's powers have grown the most. In terms of federalism, the most significant feature of expanding activity is the increased interdependence of the national and state governments. Areas that once were the domain of states and localities are now of national concern (e.g., education, health, public safety). Yet state and local initiatives have continued to grow. And most recently, national officials have begun to return many policy initiatives to state and local officials, as illustrated by the new ventures in revenue-sharing.

THE POLITICS OF CONFLICT AND COOPERATION

Although federalism is generally viewed as a system of shared functions, there is little agreement as to what best characterizes intergovermental relations: *conflict* or *cooperation*. No one questions that such problems as energy, transportation, education, environmental pollution, and urban revitalization receive the attention of national, state, and local governments. But it is not clear whether these governments compete with one another or work cooperatively together.

Since the 1950s, prevailing theories have emphasized *cooperation*. Rejecting the notion that American governments function within distinct and separate spheres of influence. Morton Grodzins describes our policy delivery system as a blending of governments, resembling a "rainbow or marble cake, characterized by an inseparable mingling of differently colored ingredients, the colors appearing in vertical and diagonal strands and unexpected swirls. As colors are mixed in a marble cake, so functions are mixed in the American federal system."[5] Seeking to bring greater realism to our conception of federalism, Grodzins points to federal land grants that have enabled states to promote elementary, secondary, and higher education programs; collaborative efforts of national and state health officials in the area of communicable diseases; and myriad other programs that have grown from joint federal-state efforts.

The War on Poverty and the Model Cities Program

In the 1960s, the development of direct federal-city relationships added a new dimension to cooperative federalism. Some earlier programs had included ties with urban governments, but not to the extent of federal-state programs. Several programs of the Johnson administration added a new dimension of federal aid to private organizations, as well as to cities and states. "Creative federalism" became a label for this era.[6]

Two striking illustrations of creative federalism were the War on Poverty, administered by the Office of Economic Opportunity, and the Model Cities Program, directed by the Department of Housing and Urban Development. The War on Poverty included a variety of programs, such as the Job Corps, the Head Start Program for preschool children, and the Community Action Agencies. In their original form, these programs provided resources to local organizations which operated independently of state officials, and often of local officials as well. We will discuss these programs in greater detail elsewhere (see pages 197–199). Here, it is important to note that Congress stipulated that representatives of client groups would be included in the programs to make policy decisions. This allowed the poor to participate directly in the design of the programs that—with government money—were directed at their own social and economic problems.

State and Local Reactions

State and local reactions to these innovative programs were not always positive. Local authorities objected to giving public funds to community organizations beyond their control. State officials questioned the propriety of Washington's funding private programs that ran counter to other programs within their states. State and local officeholders successfully lobbied for changes in federally-financed community action programs, and thus acquired greater control over policy matters within their jurisdictions.[7]

The inauguration of Richard M. Nixon in 1969 marked the most recent phase in American federalism. In an address to the National Governors Conference on August 8, 1969, President Nixon called for a "new federalism" which would rechannel "power, funds and authority ... increasingly to those governments closest to the people ... to help regain control of our national destiny by returning a greater share of control to state and local authorities."[8] Nixon's speech called for "responsible decentralization": the federal government would provide much-needed resources to state and local governments without dictating specific policies or programs. "Washington will no longer try to go it alone," the President stated; it will "refrain from telling states and localities how to conduct their affairs and will seek to transfer ever-greater responsibilities to the state level."[9]

It is still too early to determine for certain whether the "new federalism" represents a basic change in intergovernmental relations or is merely an exercise in political rhetoric. Like "creative federalism," this new term emphasizes cooperation among national, state, and local jurisdictions; but unlike earlier cooperative approaches, the federal government would take only a limited role in this partnership. One critical observer has written:

> . . . the essence of the so-called New Federalism is in fact the reactionary (in the literal sense) notion of moving back toward a day when there were no national priorities, . . . when to speak of one's "community" usually meant one's hometown, and perhaps sometimes one's state, but never the United States as an integrated national entity.[10]

Actually, the numerous programs to provide money for state and local governments represent only one aspect of federalism today. Even more important may be the work of the federal judiciary in the field of civil rights—resulting in imposing national standards on state authorities for racial justice, the equal representation of urban and rural voters in state legislatures, freedom of expression, and the fair treatment of suspects by the police. We address these issues of federalism more fully in Chapters 2 and 11. Here we continue the discussion of changing modes of federalism in the financial relationships among the national, state, and local governments.

FISCAL FEDERALISM

Federal funds support state and local programs in vocational education, mass transportation, air pollution control and prevention, urban renewal, airport construction, medical assistance and welfare payments, adult work training, health services, and land and water conservation. Observers have long debated the extent of federal financing in these programs and the methods used to control them. Now the debate takes new form as revenue-sharing becomes a national issue.

Federal aid to state and local governments comes as: (1) loans and financial guarantees, (2) grants-in-aid, or (3) revenue-sharing.[11] Until fiscal year 1972, most federal aid fell into the second category of grants-in-aid, accounting for all but $700 million out of a total of $30.7 billion. Most grants-in-aid are so-called categorical grants. They are "conditional" aids whereby states or localities agree to perform certain activities, as defined by the statutes creating the programs, and the contracts approved by the federal agency in charge of the program.

The History of Federal Aid

The first grants-in-aid from the federal government were authorized in 1887 to help states develop agricultural experiment stations. Since that time, programs have expanded to include, by 1971, "175 major programs, over 500 specific sub-authorizations, and approximately 1300 federal assistance activities that provide money figures, application deadlines, precise contacts, and use restrictions."[12] While virtually no area of public policy has escaped the influence of grants-in-aid, the federal government has shown more interest in some fields than in others. As Figure 5-1 reveals, the bulk of the grants-in-aid are for health, welfare, and labor programs that trace their origins to the New Deal. Not surprisingly, grants for veterans' service and benefits expanded greatly at the end of World War II. During the Eisenhower years, the greatest increases occurred in the area of transportation with the advent of the Interstate Highway Program. Between 1955 and 1971, total federal grants-in-aid increased more than tenfold, with the largest sums going for economic and human resources development.

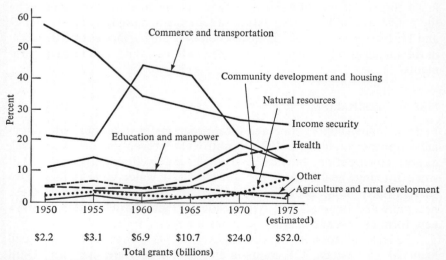

Figure 5-1 Distribution of federal grants-in-aid to state and local governments, by program, 1950–1975.

Who Benefits and Why

Just as some programs have benefited more than others by federal aid, so have some states. In 1968, nearly half of Alaska's revenue came from the federal government, as did more than 25 percent of state revenue in Wyoming, New Mexico, Arkansas, Vermont, Kentucky, West Virginia, Oklahoma, and Utah. In contrast, New York derived only 11.5 percent of its revenue from Washington; New Jersey, Indiana, Wisconsin, Michigan, Ohio, Maryland, Florida, and Massachusetts less than 15 percent.

Many factors explain these variations. Not all states respond with equal enthusiasm to each new program. About half the states choose to avoid participation in a segment of the Aid to Families with Dependent Children Program that would extend aid to children of unemployed parents.[13] Some states find it difficult to meet the "matching requirements" of federal programs (i.e., those provisions calling for a certain state expenditure along with the federal money).

Another reason for this state-to-state variation is the intent of programs to aid most of the poor states. During 1970, federal funds accounted for more than three-fourths of the aid to families with dependent children in Mississippi, Arkansas, Louisiana, Alabama, South Carolina, Florida, West Virginia, and Georgia, but less than half the program's costs in New Jersey, Connecticut, Illinois, and Massachusetts.

Source of Federal Aid: The Income Tax

The direction of federal aid is upward: from $6.7 billion in 1959 to some $48 billion in 1974. Expressed in other terms, federal aid provided 14 percent of state and local expenditures in 1959 and 23 percent in 1974. How can we explain this increased reliance upon federal revenue? Part of the story lies in the curious distribution of resources among American governments. There is a fiscal mismatch whereby "affluence lies with the national government, while the effluents are the responsibility of the states and cities."[14] The simple fact is that the federal government has the money. In 1971, Washington collected 59 percent of all tax revenues in the United States. This is largely a result of the federal government's near monopoly on the single greatest source of revenue—the progressive income tax. In contrast, state and local governments rely upon sales and property taxes for the bulk of their revenue; and these forms of taxation are regressive—that is, not correlated with income changes—and therefore, less effective than the federal income tax as producers of money.

The strength of the federal income tax lies in its progressivity: rates increase along with income. As the taxpayer goes from a taxable income of $10,000 to $20,000, for example, the percentage of each additional dollar paid in taxes increases from 22 to 32. As the whole population moves upward in income, because of inflation, federal tax rates move upward along with inflation. But for the typical state and local sales and property taxes, whose rates do not move up automatically, there is no such keeping abreast of inflation. The result is that the federal government has money to distribute, while state and local governments need help.

Fiscal Mismatch

While Washington has the money, the delivery of public services rests with states and localities. The services coming directly from the federal government (e.g., social security, agricultural subsidies, postal services) cost less than the sums for education, public welfare, health, public safety, and highway construction, which are handled by states and localities.

Added to this fiscal mismatch is another factor that has contributed to the expansion of federal aid. The complex, expensive problems of society (e.g., the decay of urban areas, the shortcomings of public education, and environmental pollution) are national in character. They transcend state and local boundaries, and require the coordinated attention of public officials at all levels of government. They are also common to all parts of the nation, and it is in the national interest to deal with them. Finally, these problems result partly from the movement of people and industry across state lines, and cannot be dealt with by even the most affluent states working alone. Therefore, the expansion of federal grant programs reflects Washington's efforts to achieve *its* objectives through partnerships with state and local governments.

Federal Control: Fact or Fiction?

It is often said that federal aid permits Washington to control state and local governments. "The States are today, for those programs involving national financing, largely administrative subdivisions of the national government . . . more susceptible to national control than ever before in our history."[15] However, allegations about federal control are more easily stated than demonstrated. To determine the extent of federal control, we must take account of several features that may affect its influence over state and local programs. First, before a federal program can have an impact, it must be adopted. We have already observed that some programs (e.g., the optional unemployed parent segment of the Aid to Families with Dependent Children Program) are not adopted in many states. Also, one study found that states with well-established, generous programs in the fields of welfare, health, and education were the most likely to make early use of Office of Economic Opportunity programs.[16] This finding suggests a process that minimizes the threat of federal control: among new programs, it is those which represent little departure from established activities that are most readily adopted.

Second, there are numerous options for both the recipients and the grantors of aid that minimize federal control. State officials were notorious for evading compliance with federal regulations for unemployment and welfare programs during the early days of the New Deal. According to one federal agent sent to check on state administrators in Oklahoma, there was "thieving and favoritism on all sides. I found that every Tom, Dick, and Harry in the state was getting relief whether they were unemployed or not." Federal officials prevailed upon Oklahoma's governor to dismiss some ineffective county administrators. But soon after the federal official left the state, the governor appointed another group of his cronies to the program and blamed Washington for the earlier removals.[17]

Existing prejudices within states and regions have been found to exist years after federal programs have been initiated. Welfare payments are generally lower than average in those states and regions that have a conservative attitude toward social services, and are markedly higher than average in more progressive states and regions.[18] The availability of federal funds may have narrowed the gap somewhat between progressive and conservative states, but the differences still remain large. Citing only one example, in 1971 monthly payments for recipients of Old Age Assistance averaged $95.15 in Massachusetts and $48.50 in South Carolina. Moreover, in Massachusetts the highest grants went to people in the poorest counties, while in South Carolina the wealthiest counties benefited most.

These illustrations warn us to tread carefully when speaking about the federal control that comes with federal aid. Yet officials at all levels of government remain sensitive about this issue. Mayors complain about local bureaucracies that are more responsive to their counterparts in Washington than to local officials; governors charge that they are forced to live with programs designed by federal officials unfamiliar with the particular problems of their states. In an address before the National Governors Conference in 1969, President Nixon called for a new system of intergovernmental relations in which Washington would no longer tell state and local governments how to conduct their affairs; it would merely provide the necessary resources, leaving states and localities free to design programs that would best serve their particular needs.[19] At the core of the "new federalism" was *revenue-sharing*.

REVENUE-SHARING

Although it was first proposed in 1958 and was discussed throughout much of the 1960s, revenue-sharing did not become a reality until October 1972. In proposing this new type of fiscal federalism in 1971, President Nixon identified two forms. First, *general revenue-sharing* would involve the federal government's sharing of its money with state and local governments. New funds, in addition to the existing grants, would be distributed among the states according to population and tax effort. States would be permitted to spend as they saw fit, with each state deciding for itself how, and if, to share its funds with local governments.

Special revenue-sharing was the second form proposed by the President. These funds would replace existing grants-in-aid programs, and would be used by states in such policy areas as law enforcement, manpower training, urban and rural community development, transportation, and education. Special revenue-sharing would not permit states and localities the same freedom as general revenue sharing, but it would provide greater flexibility than that allowed by existing grants-in-aid programs.

To date, the President's proposed special revenue-sharing has not passed Congress. General revenue-sharing was approved by Congress in October 1972, but with final provisions differing from those proposed by the President. For one thing, the distribution formulas are more complex, including such factors as population, total tax effort, state income tax effort, level of urbanization, and per capita income (with the poorest states being favored). A second change allocates only one-third of each state's funds to the state government and requires that the remaining two-thirds be distributed to the local governments. In 1974, revenue-sharing provided $6.1 billion to state and local governments. The more traditional grants-in-aid accounted for $42.1 billion.

Pros and Cons of Revenue-Sharing

Proponents of revenue-sharing cite the following arguments in its favor. First, the automatic transfer of funds is seen as an effective means of correcting the fiscal mismatch between national revenues and state and local responsibilities. Not only will this device give state and local governments much needed revenue, it will also take some of the pressure off state and local sales and property taxes. Second, revenue-sharing offers political advantages by reducing federal controls over state and local activities. Revenue-sharing contains few strings; it requires that funds be distributed between state and local jurisdictions on a one-third to two-thirds ratio; that federal minimum wage standards apply to jobs and projects financed by revenue-sharing money; that the money be used for certain broadly defined activities; and that there be no discrimination by race, color, national origin, or sex in any activity funded by revenue-sharing. Finally, proponents of revenue-sharing point to public support. In three surveys from 1967 to 1971, the Gallup poll found between 70 and 77 percent of respondents favoring plans like the one currently in operation.[20]

Critics of revenue-sharing also make several arguments. Michael Reagan sees it as "a facade behind which the national government is to abrogate its domestic role," meaning its failure to require certain programs from state and local governments.[21] President Nixon's 1969 revenue-sharing message gives weight to Reagan's observation. The President asserted that "a majority of Americans no longer support the continued extension of Federal services. The momentum for Federal expansion has passed its peak; a process of deceleration is setting in."[22] These comments indicate that national priorities will become less important. It may well be that national efforts to attack poverty, ignorance, discrimination, disease, hunger, and pollution will suffer in the hands of those state and local officials considered backward or irresponsible, who will not use their revenue shares for progressive social programs.

The early reports from the Treasury Department's Office of Revenue Sharing dealt with the general allocation of money. During the first eighteen months of operation, 70 percent of the states' money from revenue-sharing went for educational programs, with recreation and social services receiving 6 percent each. Local governments divided their funds among more categories, with 35 percent going for public safety, 20 percent for transportation, 10 percent for environment and general government, 8 percent for health, and 6 percent for recreation.

Revenue-sharing does mark the beginning of a new, yet still undefined phase of intergovernmental relations. At present, intergovernmental relations can be described best as a "nationally dominated system of shared power and shared functions."[23] Defenders of the "new federalism" see revenue-sharing as a means of cutting into the dominance of the federal government; most critics of this new system anticipate similar consequences, though they do not share the enthusiasm of the supporters. But on one point groups agree: the essential relationship between national, state, and local governments is one of neither independence nor conflict; rather, it is one of interdependence, with much cooperation and occasional disagreement.

SUMMARY

Fragmentation of power pervades the policy delivery systems of the United States. Government authority is scattered among legislative, executive, administrative, and judicial institutions, and further among national, state, and local governments. This federal character of the policy delivery system, reflecting a series of compromises worked out at the Constitutional Convention of 1787, remains a basic feature of American politics.

While American federalism traditionally pictured national and state governments as competitive and distinct from one another, the prevailing view today emphasizes their efforts at collaboration. Washington is not a controlling partner. It contributes vast and increasing revenues, establishes rules that determine the scope and character of programs, and can deny funds to states and localities that fail to meet its standards. Yet several features keep Washington from controlling state and local officials: potential recipients may choose not to accept federal resources; once funds have been accepted, recipients may evade federal requirements; and federal officials may fail to monitor the results of programs or to enforce the requirements on which grants depend. Each federal grant requires state agencies to hire personnel according to federally-approved merit criteria. Yet for many years the Indiana and Ohio Highway Departments, for example, used older styles of party patronage, with federal authorities unwilling to use their powers in a meddling fashion. The politics of intergovernmental relations, with each state having its spokesmen in the House and Senate, keeps the federal government from pushing the states too emphatically. Overly strict enforcement of federal guidelines may bring congressional pressure on federal agencies.

The fiscal relations between national, state, and local governments are subjects of continuing controversy. In the twentieth century, states and localities have become more dependent upon the federal government for revenue. As government programs have expanded at all levels, however, most of the burden of delivering services has fallen on the states and localities. Until 1972, federal grants-in-aid were virtually the only means of redressing the revenue imbalance. Revenue-sharing, a significant new tool, may have extensive policy implications.

Finally, it is important to remember that political fragmentation generally, and federalism in particular, have an important effect on policy. The *manner* in which policy decisions are made influences the *kinds* of decisions made. Fragmentation of power means that no one person or group rules. Fragmentation requires the building of coalitions, with the inevitable loss of any one actor's capacity to control outcomes.

In the next two chapters, we explore the structures of procedures within national, state, and local governments. In so doing, we should remember that programs and activities at one level of government provide both opportunities and limits for the others. Federal funds may create vast opportunities for states and localities, but federal standards may limit state and local options. In providing money for local education programs, for example, Congress stipulates that no funds can be used to support racially segregated schools. State and local governments, in turn, constrain the federal government. The rule that two-thirds of the revenue-sharing funds must go to local governments was a condition laid down by local officials in exchange for their support of this new program in Congress. The earlier success of state and local officials in lobbying for changes in federally-aided community action programs should give more power to states and localities.

REFERENCES

1 Daniel J. Elazar, *American Federalism: A View from the States*, 2d ed. (New York: Thomas Y. Crowell Company, 1972), p. 2.
2 From "Debates in the Federal Convention of 1787 as Reported by James Madison," in *Documents Illustrative of the Formation of the Union of the American States*, selected, arranged, and indexed by Charles C. Tansill (Washington, D.C.: Government Printing Office, 1927), pp. 287–288.
3 U.S. Constitution, Art. I, sec. 8.
4 *McCulloch v. Maryland* [4 Wheat. 316 U.S. (1819)].
5 Morton Grodzins, "The Federal System," in *Goals for Americans*, The American Assembly (Englewood Cliffs, N.J.: Prentice-Hall, Inc., 1960), pp. 265–266.
6 The term *creative federalism* was first used by Governor Nelson Rockefeller in 1962. See his *The Future of Federalism* (Cambridge, Mass.: Harvard University Press, 1962).
7 See John C. Donovan, *The Politics of Poverty*, 2d ed. (Indianapolis: Pegasus, 1973).
8 President Nixon before the National Governors Conference, reprinted in *Congressional Record* 115: H7533 (Sept. 4, 1969).
9 Quoted in *The New York Times*, Sept. 3, 1969, p. 1.
10 Michael Reagan, *The New Federalism* (New York: Oxford University Press, 1970), p. 161.
11 For a more detailed discussion of these three forms of federal aid, see Deil S. Wright, "Policy Control: The Hidden Issue in Revenue Sharing," *Politics 1972* (Greenville, N.C.: East Carolina University Publications, 1972), pp. 47–60.
12 Ibid., p. 47.
13 Gilbert Y. Steiner, *The State of Welfare* (Washington, D.C.: The Brookings Institution, 1971), p. 34.
14 Reagan, op. cit., pp. 33–34.
15 William H. Young, *Ogg and Ray's Introduction to American Government*, 13th ed. (New York: Appleton-Century-Crofts, 1966), p. 65.
16 Andrew T. Cowart, "Anti-Poverty Expenditures in the American States: A Comparative Analysis," *Midwest Journal of Political Science*, vol. 13 (May 1969), pp. 219–236.

17 James T. Patterson, *The New Deal and the States: Federalism in Transition* (Princeton, N.J.: Princeton University Press, 1969), p. 54.

18 These differences in policy remain even after allowing for economic differences between conservative and progressive states. See Ira Sharkansky, *Regionalism in American Politics* (Indianapolis: Bobbs-Merrill, 1970), chaps. 3 and 6.

19 President Nixon before the National Governors Conference, reprinted in *Congressional Record*, op. cit.

20 Wright, op. cit., p. 52.

21 Reagan, op. cit., p. 163.

22 Quoted in ibid., p. 97.

23 Ibid., p. 145.

The National Government and Public Policy

As we enter the last quarter of the twentieth century, the United States is confronted by a variety of problems: poverty, racial unrest, environmental pollution, urban decay, widespread crime, inequalities in educational opportunities, and energy shortages. In the face of these problems, most Americans agree that remedies must be sought through public action: public service must be made more effective; poverty and inequality must be reduced if not eliminated; our economy must be made secure; and our physical environment must be protected and made more attractive. For most people, these are desirable goals that deserve serious attention at all levels of government, but particularly at the national level.

This has not always been the case; no more than a generation ago, federal activity in these areas would have met with intense opposition.

Before the 1930s the existence of poverty, the quality of education or police protection, or the deterioration of the environment were generally considered no business of the central government. But in the last forty years that attitude has changed dramatically. Presidential candidates of both major parties now make speeches about the need to reduce poverty, improve education and health care, clean up pollution, rebuild cities, and reduce crime. Recent political debate has not been over whether the federal government should be concerned with these objectives, but over what it should and how much.[1]

Recent decades have witnessed a massive change in the size and scope of the national government. In 1950, federal revenues barely surpassed $40 billion; in 1975 they exceeded $300 billion. The national government scores high in the amount of revenue it raises and spends; the number and variety of people it employs; the number of citizens it affects; and the resources, services, and leadership it provides to states and localities.

THE ECONOMIC ENVIRONMENT OF THE NATIONAL GOVERNMENT
Income Taxes

Economically, the national government draws strength from a series of programs designed to maintain stability and growth. It also relies on a program that extracts vast sums from the economy with relatively little effort. Anyone working his way through Internal Revenue Service Form 1040 can discover the reason for this. There are numerous steps in tax rates from the $500- to the $100,000-income categories. In 1972, the family with $1,000 in taxable income paid $140 (14 percent) in taxes; the family with $10,000 in taxable income paid $1,820 (18.2 percent) in taxes; and the family with $100,000 in taxable income paid $45,180 (45.2 percent) in taxes. In other words, federal tax laws can stay the same, yet produce considerable increases in revenue. As individuals and business firms move to higher income levels, as a result of either prosperity or inflation, their federal income tax increases *progressively*. In contrast, the *regressive* tax systems of state and local governments—which rely mainly on sales and real estate taxes—cannot produce as much money as the federal tax during periods of economic growth. For this reason among others, the national government is an important source of financial aid for state and local governments (see pages 121–122).

In recent years, federal income tax rates have either stayed the same or declined. Changes in personal exemptions and tax rates for the individual income tax since its modern inception in 1913 are shown in Table 6-1. After the rate increases (and reductions in personal exemptions) that came during World War II (1940–1945), the trend has been toward lower rates and greater exemptions. The only exceptions occurred during the Korean and Vietnam wars. Each of the wartime tax increases (particularly the most recent) was temporary, and served not only to raise revenues but also to decrease private purchasing power and put a brake on inflation.

Borrowing

The national government's economic advantage is also reflected in the fact that it can borrow funds with relative ease—an opportunity generally denied to state and local governments. Congress can authorize an increase in the national debt with little difficulty. Most state and local governments, in contrast, are kept to strict debt limitations by their constitutions or charters. Budget-makers in states and localities typically keep their total requests to the sum that will be raised by taxes or constitutionally permitted borrowing within the fiscal year. No such procedures confine policy makers in Washington. As a result, while the combined debt of state and local governments was $175 billion in 1972, the national debt approached $430 billion, with continuing pressure to push it even higher.

The Gross National Product

Our society and economy contain both the resources that fuel government activity and the demands for public services that motivate policy makers. In terms of population, ours is the fourth largest country in the world. Our Gross National Product (the most widely used indicator of a country's wealth) far surpasses that of any other nation. When we examine our national wealth relative to population, we find that our Gross National Product per person averaged $5,515 in 1972, while Western Europe averages $2,759, and Africa, Asia, and Latin America $100 to $500.[2]

However, these indicators of wealth can be misleading, since they hide the great diversity found in the national environment. Some of this diversity shows itself in data on nonwhites, the foreign-born, and the offspring of foreign-born. Other diversity appears in the distribution of families in metropolitan, urban, rural, and farm settlements, and the distribution of employees in various sectors of the economy. Differences in background and economic position lead to differences in political perspective and in the kinds of demands that individuals make on government. Although the national government commands vast resources, it must also cope with an enormous range of demands, complaints, and protests. In the pages that follow, we deal with the demands and resources which derive from the national government's economic and political environments.

Table 6-1   United States Individual Income Tax Rates and Personal Exemptions, from 1913

| Income year | Personal exemptions[1] | | | Tax rates[2] | | | |
| | Single persons | Married couples | Dependents | First bracket | | Top bracket | |
				Rate (percentages)	Income up to	Rate (percentages)	Income over
1913–15	$3,000	$4,000	—	1	$20,000	7	$ 500,000
1916	3,000	4,000	—	2	20,000	15	2,000,000
1917	1,000	2,000	$200	2	2,000	67	2,000,000
1918	1,000	2,000	200	6	4,000	77	1,000,000
1919–20	1,000	2,000	200	4	4,000	73	1,000,000
1921	1,000	2,500[3]	400	4	4,000	73	1,000,000
1922	1,000	2,500[3]	400	4	4,000	56	200,000
1923	1,000	2,500[3]	400	3	4,000	56	200,000
1924	1,000	2,500	400	$1^{1}/_{2}$[4]	4,000	46	500,000
1925–28	1,500	3,500	400	$1^{1}/_{8}$[4]	4,000	25	100,000
1929	1,500	3,500	400	$^{3}/_{8}$[4]	4,000	24	100,000
1930–31	1,500	3,500	400	$1^{1}/_{8}$[4]	4,000	25	100,000
1932–33	1,000	2,500	400	4	4,000	63	1,000,000
1934–35	1,000	2,500	400	4[5]	4,000	63	1,000,000
1936–39	1,000	2,500	400	4[5]	4,000	79	5,000,000
1940	800	2,000	400	4.4[5]	4,000	81.1	5,000,000
1941	750	1,500	400	10[5]	2,000	81	5,000,000
1942–43[6]	500	1,200	350	19[5]	2,000	88	200,000
1944–45[7]	500	1,000	500	23	2,000	94[8]	200,000

1946–47	500	1,000	500	19	2,000	86.45[8]	200,000
1948–49	600	1,200	600	16.6	2,000	82.13[8]	200,000
1950	600	1,200	600	17.4	2,000	91[8]	200,000
1951	600	1,200	600	20.4	2,000	91[8]	200,000
1952–53	600	1,200	600	22.2	2,000	92[8]	200,000
1954–63	600	1,200	600	20	2,000	91[8]	200,000
1964	600	1,200	600	16	500	77	200,000
1965–67	600	1,200	600	14	500	70	100,000
1968	600	1,200	600	14	500	75.25[9]	100,000
1969	600	1,200	600	14	500	77[9]	100,000
1970	625	1,250	625	14	500	71.75[9,10]	100,000
1971	650	1,300	650	14	500	70[10,11]	100,000
1972	700	1,400	700	14	500	70[10,11]	100,000
1973 and later	750	1,500	750	14	500	70[10,11]	100,000

[1] Beginning in 1948, additional exemptions are allowed to taxpayers and their spouses on account of blindness and/or age over 65.

[2] Beginning in 1922, lower rates apply to long-term capital gains.

[3] If net income exceeded $5,000, married person's exemption was $2,000.

[4] After earned income credit equal to 25 percent of tax on earned income.

[5] Before earned income credit allowed as a deduction equal to 10 percent of earned net income.

[6] Exclusive of Victory tax.

[7] Exemptions shown were for surtax only. Normal tax exemption was $500 per tax return plus earned income of wife up to $500 on joint return.

[8] Subject to the following maximum effective rate limitations:

Year	Maximum effective rate	Year	Maximum effective rate
1944–45	90.0%	1951	87.2%
1946–47	85.5	1952–53	88.0
1948–49	77.0	1954–63	87.0
1950	87.0		

[9] Included surcharge of 7.8 percent in 1968, 10 percent in 1969, and 2.5 percent in 1970.

[10] Does not include 10 percent tax on tax preference items beginning in 1970.

[11] Earned income subject to maximum marginal rates of 60 percent in 1971 and 50 percent beginning in 1972.

Source: Joseph A. Pechman, Federal Tax Policy (New York: Norton, 1971), p. 255. © 1971 The Brookings Institution, 1775 Massachusetts Avenue N.W., Washington, D.C. 20036.

HOW THE FEDERAL GOVERNMENT INFLUENCES THE ECONOMY

Redistributing Resources

The national government's easy and productive measures for taxation and borrowing reflect an enviable economic position. Washington sits astride the entire resources of the richest economy in the world. If one industry or geographic region is affected by temporary or chronic low productivity, then resources can be raised elsewhere and redistributed to help where conditions are poor. The national government is the chief mechanism for redistribution in the country, taking from "have" sectors to support programs that stimulate economic growth among the "have-nots." The state and local governments do not have such a wide distribution of resources; their economies are more homogeneous. If economic conditions are poor in one area of a state, it is difficult to raise sufficient resources elsewhere in the state to support the needs of the have-nots. Moreover, some low-income states and localities have a record of financial failure in hard times. Even if their constitutions or charters permitted unlimited borrowing, the sources of private capital would not meet their demands at low rates of interest.

Economic Policies and Projects

While the states and localities must contend with limited resources and fluctuating credit ratings, the United States government has important controls over the economy that provides its funds. The economy's health depends partly on the availability of funds that banks lend to private citizens and business firms, and bank policies depend on the actions of the Federal Reserve Board. The economy reflects the employment provided by construction and other heavy industries that depend greatly on federally-financed building and procurement programs. The economy also depends on a wide range of federally-aided programs to train workers; inform them of job openings; and insure them against unemployment, disability, and old age. Moreover, federal taxes provide important economic leverage that can affect investments and consumer funds in the private sector. One of the great economic events of the 1960s was the demonstration that, under favorable economic conditions, a *reduction* in federal tax rates could stimulate enough economic activity to *increase* federal tax revenues.

Braking the Economy

To be sure, federal spending is not without important checks. President Nixon vetoed numerous programs approved by Congress, often arguing that increased federal spending would merely intensify inflation. Where formal vetoes were either impossible or politically unwise, Nixon impounded funds, refusing to spend money appropriated by Congress. As we shall see later, impoundment created widespread political and legal controversy. Another nemesis of bureaucrats and legislators who advocate major spending programs with unconvincing justifications is Senator William Proxmire (D., Wis.). As the senior Senator on the Joint (House-Senate) Economic Committee, Senator Proxmire has the status to make his conservative views on spending widely heard. Among the tasks of the Joint Committee is the review of the annual Economic Report of the President and the general control of government spending on behalf of Congress.

However, the major opposition to federal spending comes from personnel within the national government itself. President Ford, Senator Proxmire, and other critics of spending could be persuaded from their opposition to individual projects. This is important, since it is easier to spend money in Washington than in a state or local community; the restraints are much more flexible. More than any other policy makers in the country, those in the national government can, as yet, make their decisions without undue concern for the source of their next dollar.

THE POLITICAL ENVIRONMENT OF THE NATIONAL GOVERNMENT

The environment of the national government includes political as well as economic stimuli. The political element includes (1) a wide range of expectations about national policy, (2) demands from state and local governments, and (3) demands from private citizens and interest groups. Requests also come from governments throughout the world. Federal officials serve as promoters of American interests abroad; as treasurers and program developers for state and local governments at home; as patrons for science, the arts, and ecology: as providers of health care and welfare benefits; and as regulators of business practices. Our foreign involvements are reflected in a foreign aid budget of $3.5 billion and a defense budget of $81 billion for 1974. In order to meet the demands of state and local governments, the national government provided $48 billion in grants for 1974, and additional sums as loans, loan guarantees, and federal tax deductions for taxes paid to states and localities.

Conflicting Imperatives

In honoring demands for help, the national government sometimes pursues objectives that are contradictory and counterproductive. Antagonists on both sides of the Jordan River have attacked one another with arms supplied by the United States. Closer to home, the loan programs of the Federal Housing Administration and the Veterans Administration have produced suburban sprawls that create headaches for the Bureau of Public Roads, the Environmental Protection Agency, and other agencies that deal with urban renewal and development. The national government's tendency to work against itself also appears in other housing policies. While some agencies were trying to eliminate racial segregation in housing in the early 1960s, the Federal Housing Authority pursued programs which helped to perpetuate discrimination:

> Not only was Federal financing used to perpetuate segregation, housing policy-makers did not pay even lip service to the precept of separate but equal treatment. Only a tiny percentage of Federal loan guarantees found their way to black homeowners. During FHA's first quarter century 5.8 million dwelling units were constructed under its auspices. Of these, approximately 200,000 were for blacks and most of these were in segregated developments in the South. Evidence such as this has prompted the Civil Rights Commission to the following accusation: "FHA was a major factor in the development of segregated housing patterns that exist today."[3]

State and Local Demands: A Cornucopia

As we have seen in Chapter 5, interactions with state and local officials are a crucial feature of the national government's environment. Much of the work that goes on in the Departments of Health, Education, and Welfare; Housing and Urban Development; and Transportation produces a steady flow of dollars from federal officials to state capitols and city halls, plus constant communications with state and local officials seeking more money or more freedom in the use of presently available funds.

With so many public services provided ultimately by state and local officials, but with much of the money coming from Washington, citizens' demands for improved service often result in changes in intergovernmental relations. Where citizens find themselves at odds with state and local officials, they often bring their complaints to Washington. In response to demands, the federal courts and agencies have enforced social progress on lax state and local governments. Grants in the fields of public welfare, education, health, transportation, and housing frequently serve to promote racial integration; and federal standards have become prominent in the fields of criminal justice, voting rights, abortion, and in requiring the equal apportionment of urban, suburban, and rural voters in state legislatures.

Other demands involve services from the national government directly to private citizens. Social security payments are vital for about 30 million recipients of old age, survivors', disability, and health-care benefits, plus countless relatives who would be called upon to support them if these payments were decreased or eliminated. Washington's public works activities include the construction of dams, power-generating stations, canals, harbors, and recreation facilities; and they stir lasting commotions among those individuals, business firms, and communities that seek to maintain or expand their present benefits or to keep others' benefits from spoiling the physical environment. The Department of Defense represents a treasure house of demand-generating activities. These include not only contracts to whet the appetites of businessmen, labor unions, and antimilitary protesters, but also promotions, transfers, and salary increases that affect the lives of millions of servicemen and civilian employees, not to mention their families and communities.

Too Much or Too Little?

Some people believe that the national government already does too much, and that the scope of its activities should be drastically cut; others feel that federal programs must expand. Our affluent and growing economy has stresses, such as inflation, that suggest the need for government regulation. Because of earlier changes in national policy or private enterprise (such as technology), large numbers of people are unemployed. They demand both short-term financial help and long-range programs to support and retrain them. Some people believe that the ills of urban America require massive new programs, including mass transportation, improved police training, better housing, job training, and/or greater attention to preschool, elementary, and secondary education. They look to the national treasury for the dollars to pay for these programs and for the people and research funds to develop needed technologies. Others maintain that Washington must intensify its efforts to protect consumers from new drugs, prepared foods, and other products that are marketed before tests have fully identified and eliminated their harmful effects.

CONVERSIONS PROCESSES IN THE NATIONAL GOVERNMENT

The Primacy of the National Government

The national government's structures and procedures, like its economy and current events, dominate those of the individual states. This dominance is evident in the way Washington's institutions and procedures are copied by states and localities, and in the legal supremacy of national policies when they conflict with those of state or local governments. We have already cited the "supremacy clause" in the U.S. Constitution. It provides the clout for the United States Supreme Court when it defines the meaning of other clauses in the Constitution and uses them as standards for judging activities of state and local governments (see pages 115–116). The supremacy of the Fourteenth Amendment allows the Supreme Court to invalidate state and local statutes and practices that produce racial segregation, plus other state actions that deny equal representation of city and suburban voters in state legislatures. The crucial language of the Fourteenth Amendment reads:

> No State shall make or enforce any law which shall abridge the privileges or immunities of citizens of the United States; nor shall any State deprive any person of life, liberty, or property, without due process of law; nor deny to any person within its jurisdiction the equal protection of the laws.[4]

Other provisions of the Constitution give the national government control over interstate commerce, international affairs, and war. In contrast to the situation that prevailed under the Articles of Confederation, it is not necessary for the President or members of Congress to have the states approve foreign policy. During the war in Vietnam, the Massachusetts legislature passed a resolution that would allow its young men to refuse service in the Armed Forces. Yet, this action met its doom against such constitutional language as:

> The Congress shall have Power to lay and collect Taxes, Duties, Imports and Excises, to pay the debts and provide for the common Defense. . . .
> The President should be Commander in Chief of the Army and Navy of the United States and of the Militias of the several States, when called into the actual Service of the United States. . . .

We explore the structures of the national, state, and local governments in Chapters 8 through 11. Here we identify briefly those features of the national government that reflect widely held political values, and which occur extensively in state and local governments. Also, by exploring controversy over the President's right to impound funds, we can gain a better understanding of the conversions processes in the national government.

Limitations of the National Government

While there can be little question about the dominance of the national government, it is wrong to think of Washington's power as unlimited. The U.S. Constitution restricts the federal government's powers over both private citizens and state governments, defining Washington's area of authority and prescribing "the matters with which the government may (or may not) deal, the specific agencies that are to deal with them, the procedures that those agencies must follow, and the processes by which members of the various agencies are selected."[5]

One political scientist has identified three kinds of restrictions on the national government.[6] First, there are limits on its authority over the political rights of individuals. It cannot abridge a citizen's voting rights because of race, creed, color, or sex; nor can it violate an individual's right to speak, publish, or assemble in an attempt to express his political views. While these limits may seem straightforward, they have caused great controversy. In defining the limits of free speech, for example, courts have held that the burning of draft cards does not constitute a form of "speech" deserving constitutional protection. But they have ruled that arresting persons with the American flag sewn to the seat of their pants constitutes a violation of political freedom.

A second group of limitations on the powers of government seems to guarantee citizens the right to pursue certain preferences (e.g., the right to worship, attend school, live where they desire, and read what they prefer). Despite these assumptions of freedom, there have been disputes about the public financing of parochial education, the use of public school facilities for religious activities, the refusal by members of some religious groups to salute the flag or serve in the Armed Forces, as well as racial and sexual discrimination, and the publication of pornography.

Finally, the government faces certain constraints in the area of crime and punishment. This is done by limiting the procedures that can be used in dealing with suspected criminals.[7] The national government must conduct speedy, public, and impartial trials by jury; it must inform those accused of crimes of the charges against them, and of their right to counsel, to remain silent if they desire, and to question witnesses against them. We return to these limits in Chapter 11, which discusses the judicial branch of government.

Democratic Government via Political Accountability

The Traditional Approach Democracy is best reflected in the principle of *political accountability*, which has been approached in two ways by the national government. One approach, which has been termed "traditional" because of its long history, maintains that elected officials should have authority over appointed officials. This means that agency programs and actions are defined by laws which must be approved by officials elected by and responsible to the people (i.e., Congress and the President). Annual budget requests are subject to similar law-making procedures and require the approval of Congress and the President. Political accountability sometimes involves executive and legislative control over agency personnel. At the extreme, this has meant that elected political officials control individual appointments and that appointees must be contributing members of the party in power. This "spoils system," with its partisan bias in political appointments, is identified with President Andrew Jackson. In recent decades the excesses of Jacksonian patronage have diminished, but there is some turnover in bureaucracy whenever a President of the opposite party is elected. Although Jacksonianism is often equated with corruption for the sake of maintaining party strength, it was first justified on the grounds of democratic political theory. President Jackson felt the administration had become the possession of an elite class, and he sought to bring it within reach of the common man (i.e., those who had voted for him).

The theme of political accountability remains strong in national government. While most bureaucratic jobs are now covered by civil service regulations, many senior positions are filled by the President's appointment of an "outsider" brought in from private life rather than by a person who has devoted his career to the agency. In this way, the administration is thought to be responsive to the wishes of the "people," either because the elected Chief Executive makes the top appointments or because the appointee is a private citizen rather than a professional bureaucrat.

The Progressive Approach A second approach to political accountability is the direct participation of clients in agency policy making. As we have seen elsewhere, this feature has recently attracted considerable attention when implemented through community action programs funded by the U.S. Office of Economic Opportunity. As these efforts began, there were direct clashes between the two forms of political accountability. Elected officials—particularly governors and mayors—felt their own control over program administration would be undercut by citizen control over appointees. In such cities as Newark, Syracuse, and San Francisco, the struggle evolved into almost warlike confrontations between proponents of community action and city hall. Criticizing the OEO program, the mayor of Durham, North Carolina, remarked: "It's the federal government challenging local government—the whole thing's designed to bypass or challenge local authorities."[8] In San Francisco, the struggle over OEO "evolved from a contest between the mayor and minority group spokesmen for control of the program into a succession of power struggles within the target areas and between them and the central administration."[9] In such programs as child development, Head Start, health services, and social services, this issue caused little difficulty. But the OEO's legal aid and neighborhood organization activities led to intense and occasionally violent confrontations.

This was a clear instance of intense political conflict over the design of the conversions process in a policy delivery system, and reflected the unwillingness of some state and local officials to accept the national government's structures. Opponents charged that "extremes" of citizen participation would undermine public officials' supervision and control of government activities, and would put untrained and irresponsible persons in charge of public resources. They predicted that huge sums would be siphoned off for the support of new "political organizations," that untrained supervisors would waste money in ill-conceived and poorly managed programs, and that revolutionaries would gain control of these programs and use them to challenge the establishment. From the other side, those in favor of citizen participation alleged that traditional programs for public welfare, health, and education were poorly designed, and that the recipients were the people best qualified to know what they needed and to make policies for their own benefit.

When the Office of Economic Opportunity was funded for another two years in 1967, Congress modified the original statutes to assure governors and mayors some influence over federally-funded community action programs in their jurisdictions. These amendments, requiring that all community action agencies be controlled or approved by local governments, reduced the friction with city hall, but they also limited the effectiveness of such agencies. Still not satisfied, critics of community action tried to further restrict both the authority and the appropriations of OEO for the next six years. By 1974, it seemed only a matter of time before OEO's critics would bring about its demise. And yet, the controversy about the "proper" approach to political accountability rages on, and the contributions made by OEO programs to lessen the social, economic, and political problems in American cities remain unclear.[10]

Fragmentation of Political Power

The framers of the U.S. Constitution set a pattern of separation of powers with the creation of a two-house legislature, a separately elected President, and an independent judiciary. Each of these structures was given checks and balances to protect itself against the others: the President was given a veto over actions of the legislature; the legislature was given the opportunity to override the President's veto with a two-thirds majority in both the House and the Senate; the Senate was permitted to review major presidential appointments; and the judiciary was given a vague grant of authority, which it interpreted [*Marbury v. Madison* (1803)] as the right to determine the constitutionality of executive and legislative actions. Finally, the President, Vice President, and federal judges face the threat of impeachment and conviction by Congress if they violate certain limits in their actions. The procedures of impeachment have become vague with their lack of use. As one contribution of his presidency, however, Richard Nixon helped to clarify the debate over what constitutes "an impeachable offense." Even if the Nixon administration did end with a resignation, the end came with the impeachment process well underway and its results predictable. As we shall see in the next chapter, fragmentation is a basic feature of each state government and many localities as well, and it appears in the divisions among the national, state, and local governments examined in Chapter 5.

The attachment of American constitution makers to the separation of powers and to checks and balances has several implications. First, control of programs is not given entirely to any one branch of government. Second, with a divided leadership, there can be no simple hierarchy with well-defined, superior-subordinate roles. For example, the control of bureaucrats is not the sole responsibility of the President; he must share it with the legislature and the judiciary. The judiciary hears cases on appeal and may void or restrict certain program features. The courts have intervened in behalf of accused citizens to limit the actions of the police and public prosecutors; and in behalf of parents to order or to stop busing programs designed to integrate schools. The legislature has many opportunities to affect program structures and procedures: review of new program proposals; periodic review of budgets; the approval of key personnel appointments; special investigations into program operations; the ability to initiate (and to pass, over the President's veto) new programs or to make changes in existing programs; and the review of certain decisions made by administrators. Third, bureaucrats in charge of particular programs may receive conflicting demands from competing superiors. A House committee, a Senate committee, or the President may issue contrasting directives. Each potential superior may have his spokesman within an agency. Multiple loyalties within a department can upset the department head's control over his own agency at the same time that they inhibit clear control by either the President or one house of the Congress. The busing controversy pitted congressional statutes against presidential directives and an ambiguous record of court decisions, with bureaucrats in the Department of Health, Education and Welfare having to decide which "instruction" fit a particular case.

The Dynamics of Fragmentation: The Case of Impoundment

A Brief History *Impoundment*, as we have said, is the withholding of funds voted for a specific purpose. Contrary to what many people believe, presidential impoundment of funds did not begin with the Nixon administration. In 1803, President Thomas Jefferson informed Congress of his refusal to spend $50,000 that has been appropriated for gunboats to patrol the Mississippi River. In defense of his action, he argued that "the favorable and peaceful turn of affairs on the Mississippi rendered an immediate execution of that law unnecessary, . . ."[11] While impoundment occurred sporadically during the nineteenth century, it was not until the 1940s that a President made extensive use of it. During the early years of World War II, Franklin D. Roosevelt sought to control inflation by withholding funds from several programs not related to the war effort. In general, these actions caused little opposition, though some supporters of the affected programs raised the question of constitutionality.

In 1948, Harry S. Truman impounded $735 million that had been appropriated to increase the size of the Air Force from forty-eight to fifty-eight groups. Truman maintained that the end of the war eliminated the need for an expanded Air Force, and that he would lessen the strain on the domestic economy by limiting defense spending. President Dwight D. Eisenhower impounded $137 million which had been appropriated for the development of the Nike-Zeus antimissile system, with the argument that additional tests were necessary.

A major executive-legislative squabble occurred in 1961, when President John F. Kennedy refused to spend $180 million that Congress had added to his request for the B-70 bomber. The administration argued that added funding was not justified since the United States already had an advantage over the Soviet Union in bombers, in addition to the American missile system. Congress threatened to "direct" the President to spend the added funds, but an impasse was averted when the House Armed Services Committee backed off from the conflict. President Lyndon B. Johnson also impounded funds in an attempt to curb the inflationary pressures generated by the escalation of the Vietnam war. In 1966, he withheld $5.3 billion, the majority of which had been appropriated for highway, housing and urban development, education, agriculture, and health and public welfare programs.

The Nixon Administration   In Spring 1971, the Nixon administration announced that it was withholding some $12 billion, most of which had been appropriated by Congress to support highway and urban programs. Administration spokesmen defended this action by arguing that since the programs were "scheduled for termination," it was pointless to pour more money into them. Congressional critics were quick to oppose these actions, frequently charging that impoundment posed a threat to the spirit, if not the letter, of separation of powers. According to one writer,

By refusing to spend appropriated funds, the President provokes the charge that he is obligated under the Constitution to execute the laws, not hold them in defiance—obligated to interpret appropriation bills not as mere permission to spend but as a mandate to spend as Congress directed. Otherwise, the argument runs, he encroaches upon the spending prerogatives of Congress, violates the doctrine of separated powers, and assumes unto himself a power of item veto that is neither sanctioned by the Constitution nor granted by Congress.[12]

While the impoundment controversy is not Richard Nixon's creation, his administration introduced two new elements to the issue. First, President Nixon impounded more funds than his predecessors—an estimated $12 billion in 1972 alone. Nearly half of this amount had been intended for water pollution abatement and sewage treatment programs administered by the Environmental Protection Agency; and the President's refusal to spend these funds was particularly controversial since the Congress had overriden his earlier veto of this program.

The second aspect of the impoundment controversy is that unlike his predecessors, who withheld funds simply as an anti-inflationary technique, President Nixon used impoundment to promote his own domestic priorities over those of Congress. As Louis Fisher has pointed out, the Nixon administration withheld spending "from domestic programs because the President considered those programs incompatible with his own set of budget priorities. Priorities and impoundments were at issue in 1969 when President Nixon announced plans to reduce research health grants, defer Model Cities funds, and reduce grants for urban renewal. During that same period he proceeded with his own preferences, such as the supersonic transport, a new manned bomber, a larger merchant marine fleet, and the Safeguard ABM system."[13]

The Case for Impoundment   The impoundment controversy shows many of the tensions inherent in a system of fragmented power. Both proponents and opponents of impoundment defend their positions on constitutional and statutory grounds. Consider, for example, the testimony of the former director of the Office of Management and Budget, Casper W. Weinberger, before a congressional committee in 1971:

Although the Constitution provides that no money can be drawn from the Treasury unless appropriated by law, it does not follow . . . that the expenditure of government funds involves an exclusively legislative function; in fact, the provision . . . seems to assume that the expenditure of funds—as distinguished from the granting of authority to withdraw them from the Treasury—is an executive function. In any event, it has always been so regarded. . . . Authority for the President to establish reserves is derived basically from the constitutional provisions which vest the executive power in the President. . . . We believe the power to withhold appropriated funds is implicit in them. . . .[14]

In a 1972 press release, the Office of Management and Budget provided a further defense for the practice of impoundment:

The reasons for withholding or deferring the apportionment of available funds usually are concerned with routine financial administration. They have to do with the effective and prudent use of the financial resources made available by the Congress. The provisions of the Anti-deficiency Act require the President to establish reserves of appropriated funds for such reasons as a change in conditions since they were appropriated or to take advantage of previously unforeseen opportunities for savings. . . .[15]

The Case against Impoundment   Opponents of impoundment are equally emphatic. As Senator Sam Ervin, Jr., (D., N.C.) has argued:

Reserving of appropriated funds is not a new concept, and when undertaken pursuant to Congressional dictate it may be quite useful in effecting economy. Unfortunately, however, impoundment most frequently occurs under circumstances where the executive branch, for reasons of its own, desires to avoid expending funds which the Congress has explicitly directed to be spent for some particular purpose. It is this situation which poses a threat to our system of government and which so patently violates the separation-of-powers doctrine. . . .

By impounding appropriated funds, the President is able to modify, re-shape, or nullify complete laws passed by the legislative branch, thereby making legislative policy—a power reserved exclusively to the Congress. Such an illegal exercise of the power of his office violates clear constitutional provisions.[16]

In a memorandum written before President Nixon appointed him to the U.S. Supreme Court, then Assistant Attorney General William H. Rehnquist asserted that he could find no constitutional or statutory justification for the practice of impoundment: "It is in our view extremely difficult to formulate a constitutional theory to justify a refusal by the President to comply with a congressional directive to spend."[17]

While the merits of impoundment are usually phrased in constitutional or statutory terms, many observers have evaluated the practice in terms of their own preferences: those who share the President's policy goals support impoundment, while those who reject these priorities find reasons to oppose it. As Harry Truman's Secretary of the Air Force, Stuart Symington was quick to defend the President's refusal to spend funds appropriated by Congress. In 1972, Senator Stuart Symington (D., Mo.) was an outspoken critic of President Nixon's impoundment policy, particularly as it resulted in the withholding of funds earmarked for highway construction in Missouri.

The Position of the Federal Courts The hesitancy of federal courts to tackle the impoundment controversy is a further example of our political fragmentation. Judges have a doctrinal excuse for cases they want to avoid, calling them "political" matters. With this rationale, federal courts refused for many years to hear cases involving legislative reapportionment, and the constitutionality of military actions in Southeast Asia. To date, the Supreme Court has avoided the impoundment controversy, although many impoundment suits have reached the lower federal courts. In most cases, federal courts have ruled against the administration, calling upon federal officials to release impounded funds. The Department of Transportation has been ordered to release approximately $26 million to the Missouri Highway Commission, and the Environmental Protection Agency has been instructed to allocate $11 billion among the states for the control of water pollution. In October 1973, the Justice Department's Civil Division was working on about forty impoundment suits, including several cases the federal government was appealing in higher federal courts.[18]

The Position of Congress The Supreme Court may eventually rule that impoundment is a "political" question over which courts have no control. In any event, the President's critics need not rely solely upon judicial remedies. Congress can "direct" the President to spend appropriated funds; it can define minimum levels of service below which his agencies cannot fall; and it can exert pressure through investigations of the President's constitutional authority to withhold funds. In addition, Congress may insist on being promptly informed by the President when funds are to be impounded; congressmen may encourage private interest groups to exert pressure on the President to release funds. Congress can also threaten to block programs favored by the President if impounded funds are not released. Arguing that this final approach may well be Congress's strongest tool, the late Senator Allen Ellender (D., La.) observed that "members of Congress, individually and as a body," can force the release of impounded funds by saying "no" to other programs whose support the President is seeking.[19]

THE POLICIES OF THE NATIONAL GOVERNMENT
The Federal Budget

The priorities of the national government have been the subject of much discussion in recent years. Virtually all the policies mentioned in this book come in part from the national government—even those which are delivered ultimately by states and localities. In order to summarize the magnitude of national policies, let us look briefly at a hotly debated document—the budget. The decisions behind it tell us where the national government's resources come from and how they are spent.

> National life is profoundly affected by decisions to spend more federal resources for health care and less for highways, or more for strategic submarines and less for day care centers; to increase aid to old people and decrease that for children or farmers or Indians; to shift tax burdens from corporations to individuals or from the poor to the rich; to change the locus of decision making from Washington to state and local authorities or from government to individuals. All these types of decisions are reflected in the budget.[20]

One way to appreciate the size of the federal budget is to examine the growth in money spent over recent decades. Much of the increase in federal spending has occurred in areas Washington serves *alone*, independent of state and local governments. Thus, spending for defense, international affairs, space exploration, and interest on the national debt increased from 30 percent of the national government's total in 1932 to 51 percent in 1972.[21]

We can also view the national budget in terms of current spending. For fiscal year 1975, national government activities are estimated to cost $304 billion. These outlays are shown in Table 6-2, classified by major types of activities and compared to the amount spent a decade earlier. National defense is a great consumer of federal money: $88 billion and 29 percent of the total. In percentage terms, however, this represents a rather significant decrease from the 44 percent of 1967. Other sectors that have shown a percentage decline over the last decade are international affairs and finance, agriculture and rural development, and natural resources and environment. The big gainers have been community development and housing, education and manpower, health, and income security. These comparisons point to an important trend in national policy: the proportion of federal spending for national defense and its related activities (i.e., international affairs and space programs) has declined during the past decade, while spending on human resources (i.e.,

Table 6-2 Summary of Budget Outlays by Function, 1961 through 1975
(In Billions of Dollars)

Function	1961	1964	1967	1970	1973	1975 (estimate)
National defense	$47.4	$ 53.6	$ 70.1	$ 80.3	$ 76.0	$ 87.7
International affairs and finance	3.4	4.1	4.6	3.6	3.0	4.1
Space research and technology	0.7	4.2	5.4	3.7	3.3	3.3
Agriculture and rural development	3.3	5.2	4.4	6.2	6.2	2.7
Natural resources and environment	1.6	2.0	1.9	2.6	0.6	3.1
Commerce and transportation	5.1	6.5	7.6	9.5	13.1	13.4
Community development and housing	0.2	−0.2	2.6	3.0	4.1	5.7
Education and manpower	1.5	2.0	6.1	7.3	10.2	11.5
Health	0.9	1.7	6.7	12.9	18.4	26.3
Income security	21.0	24.8	30.9	43.7	73.1	100.1
Veterans' benefits and services	5.7	5.7	6.9	8.7	12.0	13.6
Interest	8.1	9.8	12.6	18.3	22.8	29.1
General government	1.5	2.0	2.5	3.3	5.5	6.8
General revenue-sharing	0	0	0	0	6.6	6.2
Allowances*	0	0	0	0	0	1.1
Undistributed intragovernmental transactions	−2.5	−2.9	−3.9	−6.4	−8.3	−10.7
Total budget outlays	97.8	118.6	158.3	196.6	246.5	304.4

*Includes allowances for acceleration of energy research and development, and for civilian pay.

most of the HEW, HUD, plus veterans' and manpower programs) has shown a steady growth, from 34 to 52 percent of outlays.

Federal Tax Policies

In addition to the magnitude and distribution of federal spending, we should also take account of revenue sources. Tax policies determine who will pay the bills for government services. The individual income tax is presently the major source of federal revenue. From the introduction of this form of taxation in 1913 until 1960, it produced an ever-increasing proportion of federal revenue; during the last fifteen years its revenue contribution has remained fairly stable. As shown in Table 6-3 and Figure 6-1, it accounted for $129 billion, or 42 percent of all federal revenues in 1975. Customs duties and sales and excise taxes have declined in importance since the beginning of the twentieth century. They accounted for 75 percent of all federal revenue collected in 1902, but only about 7 percent in 1975. Since World War II, the federal government has come to rely more and more on social insurance taxes. These include money withheld from workers for social security and unemployment insurance, employee contributions for federal retirement, and contributions for supplementary medical insurance. In 1950, such taxes accounted for less than 10 percent of all federal revenues; in 1975, they were approximately 29 percent. A result of this increasing prominence of social insurance taxes is a change in the distribution of tax burdens. Whereas personal and corporate income taxes are distributed in a "progressive" manner (the wealthy pay a higher percentage of their income than the poor), social insurance taxes are "regressive" (the higher one's income, the smaller the percentage taken for these taxes). With social insurance taxes showing the sharpest increases of all federal levies, this has the effect of making the whole federal tax system less progressive.

ASSESSING THE SERVICE PERFORMANCE OF THE NATIONAL GOVERNMENT

As we noted in Chapter 1, there is no guarantee that public services will be delivered in ways that match the hopes, intentions, or statements of policy makers. Different programs may work at cross purposes; funds may not be sufficient to meet the needs of a situation; the money allocated to a program may not be distributed among its components in the manner necessary to produce the service intended; the statutes or regulations that govern a program may not be up to their task; or competing interests in the legislature and the administration may so limit or weaken a program as to leave it in a state of confusion.

Table 6-3 Federal Revenue Sources, 1961 through 1975
(In Billions of Dollars)

Source	1961	1964	1967	1970	1973	1975 (estimate)
Individual income taxes	$41.3	$ 48.7	$ 61.5	$ 90.4	$103.2	$129.0
Corporation income taxes	21.0	23.5	34.0	32.8	36.2	48.0
Social insurance taxes and contri- butions (trust funds)*	12.7	17.0	27.8	45.3	64.5	85.6
Excise taxes†	11.8	13.7	13.7	15.7	16.3	17.4
Estate and gift taxes	1.9	2.4	3.0	3.6	4.9	6.0
Customs duties	1.0	1.3	1.9	2.4	3.2	3.8
Miscellaneous receipts†	0.9	1.1	2.1	3.4	3.9	5.2
Total budget receipts	94.4	112.7	149.6	193.7	232.2	295.0

*Includes employment taxes, unemployment insurance, and other contributions.
†Includes both federal funds and trust funds.

150

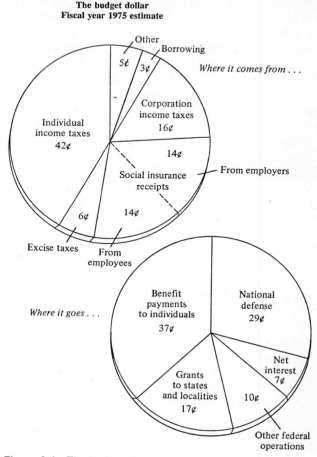

The budget dollar
Fiscal year 1975 estimate

Where it comes from . . .

Other

Borrowing

5¢   3¢

Corporation
income taxes
16¢

Individual
income taxes
42¢

14¢

Social insurance
receipts

From employers

6¢   14¢

Excise taxes   From
employees

Where it goes . . .

Benefit
payments
to individuals
37¢

National
defense
29¢

Net
interest
7¢

Grants
to states
and localities
17¢

10¢

Other federal
operations

Figure 6-1 The budget dollar.

Subjective Tests of Policy: Public Opinion

Presidential Popularity Polls There are several ways of assessing
the service performance of the national government. One involves
gauging the attitudes of the people being served. By seeing what the
American people think about federal officials, we can make some
inferences about their views of federal programs. We can also see what
people think about specific programs.

Americans' answers to a persistent question of the Gallup poll allow
us to gauge their overall assessment of national policy. Since the

administration of Harry S. Truman, the Gallup organization has asked: "Do you approve or disapprove of the way President _____ is handling his job as President?" The greatest range of approval and disapproval occurred during the Truman years; no other President has equaled the almost 90 percent approval that Truman enjoyed in 1945, and only President Nixon has seen his popularity fall near the 25 percent approval that Truman endured in 1952.[22] Figure 6-2 shows that the approval scores of Presidents Eisenhower and Kennedy ranged from 80 to 50 percent; President Johnson's from 80 to 37 percent; and President Nixon's (as of March 1974) from 65 to 25 percent. With the exception of Eisenhower, the trend has been generally downward, with the peak coming at the beginning of each term.

One interpretation is that a President enters at a high point of public confidence and expectation, and then suffers the inevitable alienation of interest groups that are disappointed in his failure to meet their demands. A reelection campaign (see 1948, 1956, and 1964 data in Figure 6-2) is a time for the President to rebuild his coalition and earn another "honey-moon" from the people. Soon after the second inauguration, however, the slide in popularity begins again. Another event that seems to boost the people's evaluation is an international crisis (a "rally round the flag" event). In contrast, a period of economic decline (e.g., an increase in unemployment) or a persistent war has a tendency to diminish popular approval. The aura of an individual President can overcome these general tendencies. Approval scores during the Eisenhower years held up better than the general rules would predict. "President Eisenhower's ability to maintain his popularity, especially during his first term, is striking and unparalleled among the postwar Presidents. . . . If a President wants to leave office a popular man he should either (1) be Dwight David Eisenhower, or (2) resign the day after inauguration."[23]

At best, measures of presidential popularity provide only indirect indicators of how people view federal programs. For example, it is not clear that assessments of the Nixon administration had much to do with the tremendous decline in Nixon's popularity in 1973. The President's personal slide in popularity can be traced to Watergate and its related controversies, and not to the administration's handling of Vietnam, its relations with China and the Soviet Union, or its mediating role in the Middle East.

Polls of Specific Issues More specific assessments come from surveys directed toward particular policy issues. Consider, for example, a series of Gallup questions about the wage and price controls announced in August 1971. At the time of the survey, some ten months after the

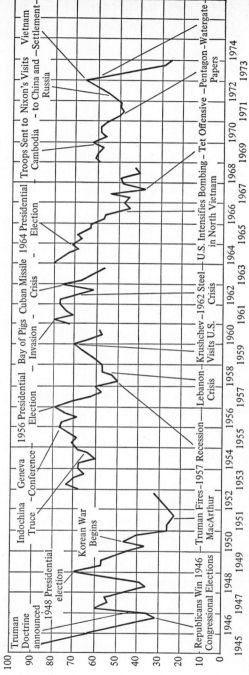

Figure 6-2 Fluctuations in presidential popularity. [*Truman and Eisenhower data from "The Polls—Presidential Popularity," Public Opinion Quarterly, 15 (1961), pp. 135–137. Kennedy data from Hazel Gaudet Erskine, "The Polls: Kennedy as President," Public Opinion Quarterly, 27, no. 2 (Summer 1964), pp. 334–335. Johnson and Nixon data from selected issues of Gallup Opinion Index.*]

153

controls began, more than half of the respondents felt that wage controls were not being fairly administered; only 36 percent supported the wage controls; nearly 60 percent perceived price controls as being unfair and unjust; and less than 25 percent supported existing price control programs.[24]

Objective Tests of Policy: Program Evaluation

An "objective" evaluation of a program's success relies not on public opinion but on a careful evaluation of how certain policy goals match up with actual accomplishments. During the past decade, evaluation of this sort has become increasingly important, to ensure that national government programs meet society's needs, both at home and abroad. Then Secretary of HEW Robert Finch told a congressional committee in 1969:

> Evaluation is a necessary foundation for effective implementation and judicious modification of our existing programs. At this point, evaluation is probably more important than the addition of new laws to an already extensive list of educational statutes. . . . Evaluation will provide the information we require to strengthen weak programs, fully support effective programs, and drop those which simply are not fulfilling the objectives intended by the Congress when the programs were originally enacted.[25]

In the final section of this chapter, we shall examine three efforts which demonstrate both the shortcomings and the successes of program evaluation. The studies focus on issues which have been the subject of considerable controversy: the reform of the draft system; the distribution of the costs and benefits resulting from programs of the national government, and various regulatory programs reviewed by Ralph Nader and his associates.

Draft Reform   After considerable debate, the national government ended in 1972, at least temporarily, its policy of drafting young men into military service. Six years earlier, the Selective Service System had undergone major reform. One possible contributory factor was an assessment of the draft system conducted by Professors James Davis and Kenneth Dolbeare. They examined the workings of local draft boards in Wisconsin during the mid-1960s, and judged their success according to the policy intentions of the Selective Service System. According to policy, local draft boards should have: (1) promoted local support for the draft; (2) been composed of local citizens who knew their communities and registrants; (3) made decisions with a regard for the nation's manpower needs by granting deferments to men in vital activities or with scarce skills; and (4) made decisions fairly so that equally eligible men (excluding those having vital or scarce skills) were given equal treatment.[26] Davis and Dolbeare discovered that there was little contact between local draft board members and their communities; board members granted deferments without considering national manpower priorities; and men from lower-income families had a much greater chance of induction than men from upper- and middle-income families. These findings helped promote draft reforms that substantially lessened the power of local boards, instituted the national lottery, and revamped the criteria for granting deferments.

Tax Costs and Benefits Other studies of the national government's performance have been made to determine who pays the bills and who gets the benefits of various programs. Studies of the national government's tax programs focus on progressive and regressive taxation. Each mode of taxation has its supporters.[27] What concerns us here is not the arguments for each, but the actual workings of the national taxes in terms of progressive or regressive criteria. The determination of tax progressivity or regressivity involves far more than an examination of the statutory tax rates. It is necessary to take account of the tendency of persons to shift their own tax burden to someone else. Thus, an automobile manufacturer initially pays the federal excise tax on each car sold, but then shifts the burden of that tax to the purchaser. A corporation is directly liable for federal taxes on its profits, but passes on some of the burden to its consumers as a cost of providing its goods or services. The difficult problem is to determine what portion of the tax is eventually passed on to the stockholders in the form of reduced dividends, and what portion is passed on to the consumer as higher prices.

Calculations of federal taxes, especially the individual income tax, show that they operate in a progressive fashion. The significant exceptions are the payroll taxes that support old age survivors, disability, and health insurance programs. As we have already noted, payroll taxes are an increasingly important source of federal revenue; but they tap only the first $13,200 of annual income (as of 1974), and thus extract smaller and smaller amounts above that level.

Assessing who gets the benefits of public services is an even stickier problem than determining who pays the tax bills. It involves some untested assumptions about how direct and secondary benefits are distributed, and how these benefits may affect different population groups. Education is one example. We all benefit indirectly from the economic vitality that comes with a highly trained population. But the people who benefit directly are those whose skills are more highly prized in today's marketplace. The analyst has the problem of assessing how much of the value of education should be counted as being enjoyed by the direct beneficiaries, and how much by the whole population. Determining who benefits from defense spending presents other problems. From one perspective, defense spending benefits all of us equally. From another perspective, however, those who work for, or profit from, defense-related industries benefit more than the rest of us.

The Tax Foundation has calculated, by income class, the distribution of service benefits resulting from activities of the national government;[28] its findings are summarized in Table 6-4. The results indicate a progressive distribution of benefits. That is, lower-income families seem to receive a higher percentage of their incomes in government benefits than upper-income families. What may be questioned in this study is the allocation of national government spending for defense and international affairs. The calculations assume that we all benefit equally; benefits are distributed to each income group according to the number of families in the group. A different calculation—which would produce a more regressive distribution of the benefits—would trace out the wages, salaries, and profits resulting from defense contracts to the individuals who receive them.[29]

Ralph Nader and Associates   The work of Ralph Nader represents another approach to evaluation.[30] Nader first became prominent when his book *Unsafe at Any Speed* exposed the dangers built into automobiles. The book was a major stimulus for the enactment of federal auto safety regulations and the demise of the Chevrolet Corvair. With the income from this book and his popular lectures and personal appearances, Nader founded the Center for Study of Responsive Law, which sponsors investigations into a wide range of regulatory activities. The Center has produced major studies about the Food and Drug Administration (FDA), the Interstate Commerce Commission (ICC), the Federal Trade Commission (FTC), and the National Air Pollution Control Administration (NAPCA).[31] Nader and his colleagues operate in the grand tradition of American muckrakers. Their exposés provide one horrible example after another, pointing to the failure of regulatory policies that should protect the public from ill-conceived products and services.

Some of the most vivid materials in the studies of Nader and his colleagues describe obvious failures in regulatory policies: the FDA permitting the unrestricted use of cyclamates and monosodium glutamate long after serious research had questioned their dangers; the plight of a family who believes the ICC will regulate the practices of moving companies that transport household belongings from one state to another; the ICC's cooperation in the decline of railroad passenger service; and the ICC's failure to protect motorists from unsafe trucks. Some findings

Table 6-4   Benefits of Federal Government Expenditures as a Percentage of Total Income

(For All Families by Income Class—1965)

				Income class					
Under $2,000	$2,000 to 2,999	$3,000 to 3,999	$4,000 to 4,999	$5,000 to 5,999	$6,000 to 7,499	$7,500 to 9,999	$10,000 to 14,999	$15,000 and over	Total
79.3	46.0	31.6	21.2	18.2	15.6	13.8	12.7	11.0	19.5

Note: There are alternative methods for computing the benefits of government expenditures as a percentage of incomes in different income classes. Consult the original source for explanations and illustrations of these alternatives.

Source: Allocating Tax Burdens and Government Benefits by Income Class (New York: Tax Foundation, Inc., 1967), p. 6.

concern the procedures of regulatory agencies (i.e., their conversions processes) that affect their capacity to implement strong policies. The FTC recruits graduates of mediocre law schools, and even within this group fails to make employment offers to the best of its applicants.[32] The FDA dismissed one noted consultant who persisted in making negative reports about some pesticides the agency had decided to approve. The National Air Pollution Control Administration concedes that auto emissions account for 60 percent of urban air pollution, but spends less than 3 percent of its budget on the problem.

Nader's findings suggest how numerous elements of a conversions process and its environment can work together in shaping performance. In writing about the ICC's failure to regulate safety in the trucking industry, he points to the similar motives of the shippers, truckers, and drivers which work to weaken regulations. The shippers and truckers want rapid, low-cost delivery of goods. The drivers want the overtime pay that comes with their violation of maximum driving hours, and with their use of dangerous stimulants to keep awake for long hours at a time.

Nader and his associates are sophisticated about the problems of government regulation. They know from the experiences of existing agencies that statutory reform is not enough. A weak administration can defeat any prospect of achieving success through new laws alone. Like other muckrakers, Nader and his group have expressed faith in the value of alert citizens, intense leadership, and public exposure of administrative shortcomings.[33] At times, however, they call for a more sweeping reform of economic and political systems.

> The main reason why citizens have no impact on the corporations which they support and which affect their lives and health is that the large corporate polluter refuses to be held accountable to the public . . . because they are

generally bigger and more powerful than government agencies making halfhearted attempts at confrontation. . . .

So long as the crucial decisions remain with a small group of mammoth corporations, there is little reason to expect anything but further deterioration.[34]

Some things are missing in the reports of Nader's Raiders. Citing horrible examples of the failure of regulations may help to arouse public attention, but it does not direct energies to targets that are most in need of destruction or most easy to reform. If we must undo entire economic and political systems to improve regulatory policies, then little reform in regulatory policies seems likely.

SUMMARY

The scope and influence of the environment and the conversions processes of the national government are central to any discussion of policy making in the United States. The national government has access to the resources of the entire country through an array of productive taxing powers, easy requirements for government borrowing, and controls over the economy that allow it to take pretty much what it needs. When the revenue powers of the national government are compared to those of states and localities, Washington appears to have virtually unlimited capacity to tax, borrow, and spend.

The enviable economic position of the national government helps to explain its pervasive role in policy delivery systems. Not only does it have a monopoly on international affairs and certain domestic policies that are reserved to it by the Constitution (e.g., control over interstate commerce), but it also has a prominent role in the financing and design of domestic programs through its grants-in-aid, loans, technical assistance, and revenue-sharing to state and local governments. The domestic role of the national government is evident in the huge sums of money that it offers to states and localities ($48 billion in 1974), and in state and local adaptations of national government structures, decision-making processes, and policies.

The principles of limited government, democracy, and the fragmentation of political power appear in the conversions processes of the national government. The separation of powers is at the heart of the conversions process, and continues to provoke struggles among executive, legislative, administrative, and judicial officials. It has generated issues over the President's war powers, "executive privilege," the Supreme Court's power of judicial review, and the impoundment of appropriated funds by the President.

This chapter includes several ways of assessing public policies. The presidential scores on the Gallup poll are indicators of the public mood. Other polls offers public evaluations of individual programs. These are "subjective" measures of policy performance. "Objective" assessments compare stated policy goals with actual accomplishments. By reviewing several efforts at objective policy assessments, we have observed some of the problems in assessing and assuring the delivery of public services. The national government may be the biggest, richest, and most influential sector of American government, but even so, it cannot always guarantee to deliver according to the hopes or claims of policy makers.

REFERENCES

1 Edward R. Fried et al., *Setting National Priorities: The 1974 Budget* (Washington: The Brookings Institution, 1973), p. 25. Copyright © 1973 by the Brookings Institution, Washington, D.C.
2 *Statistical Abstracts of the U.S., 1973* (New York: Grosset & Dunlap, Inc., 1973), pp. 812–813.
3 Harrell R. Rodgers, Jr., and Charles S. Bullock, III, *Law and Social Change* (New York: McGraw-Hill Book Company, 1972), p. 143.
4 U.S. Constitution, Amend. 14, sec. 1.
5 Austin Ranney, *The Governing of Men*, 3d ed. (New York: Holt, Rinehart and Winston, Inc., 1971), p. 114.
6 Robert H. Salisbury, *Governing America: Public Choice and Political Action* (New York: Appleton-Century-Crofts, 1973), pp. 215–227.
7 Ibid., p. 216.
8 Quoted in Richard Blumenthal, "The Bureaucracy: Anti-Poverty and the Community Action Program," in Allan P. Sindler (ed.), *American Political Institutions and Public Policy: Five Contemporary Studies* (Boston: Little, Brown and Company, 1969), p. 129.
9 Ralph M. Kramer, *Participation of the Poor* (Englewood Cliffs, N.J.: Prentice-Hall, Inc., 1969), p. 66.
10 See Milton Kotler, *Neighborhood Government: The Local Foundations of Political Life* (Indianapolis: The Bobbs-Merrill Company, Inc., 1969); Alan A. Altshuler, *Community Control: The Black Demand for Participation in Large American Cities* (Indianapolis: Pegasus, 1970); and John C. Donovan, *The Politics of Poverty*, 2d ed. (Indianapolis: Pegasus, 1973).
11 Quoted in *Congressional Quarterly* (Feb. 3, 1972), p. 213.
12 Louis Fisher, "Presidential Spending Discretion and Congressional Controls." Reprinted, with permission, from a symposium on "Administrative Discretion," appearing in *Law and Contemporary Problems* (Vol. 37, No. 1, Winter, 1972), published by the Duke University School of Law, Durham, North Carolina. Copyright, 1972, by Duke University.
13 Fisher, op. cit., p. 162.
14 Quoted in *Congressional Quarterly* (Feb. 3, 1973), p. 124.

15 Ibid.
16 U.S. Congress, Senate, Joint Hearings before the Ad Hoc Subcommittee on Impoundment of Funds of the Committee on Government Operations and the Subcommittee on Separation of Powers of the Committee on the Judiciary, *Impoundment of Appropriated Funds by the President*, 93d Cong. 1st sess., 30 and 31 January and 1, 6, and 7 February 1973, pp. 2–3.
17 Quoted in *Congressional Quarterly* (Feb. 3, 1973), p. 215.
18 *New York Times* (Oct. 7, 1973).
19 *Congressional Record*, S5429, Apr. 22, 1971.
20 Edward Fried et al., op. cit., pp. 1–2.
21 Interest on the national debt is considered to be a special responsibility of the national government insofar as the largest portion of the debt reflects spending for the military.
22 See John E. Mueller, "Presidential Popularity from Truman to Johnson," *The American Political Science Review*, vol. 64 (March 1970), pp. 18–34.
23 Ibid., pp. 27, 31.
24 William Watts and Lloyd A. Free (eds.), *State of the Nation* (New York: Universe Books, 1973).
25 Joseph S. Wholey et al., *Federal Evaluation Policy: Analyzing the Effects of Public Programs* (Washington: The Urban Institute, 1971), p. 19.
26 See James Davis, Jr., and Kenneth M. Dolbeare, *Little Groups of Neighbors: The Selective Service System* (Chicago: Markham, 1968).
27 This section relies on Ira Sharkansky, *The Politics of Taxing and Spending* (Indianapolis: Bobbs-Merrill Company, Inc., 1969), chap. 2; and on Ira Sharkansky, *Public Administration*, 2d ed. (Chicago: Markham, 1972), chap. 11.
28 See *Allocating Tax Burdens and Government Benefits by Income Class* (New York: Tax Foundation, Inc., 1967).
29 See Bruce M. Russett, *What Price Vigilance? The Burdens of National Defense* (New Haven, Conn.: Yale University Press, 1970).
30 Portions of this discussion rely on Sharkansky, *Public Administration*, chap. 4.
31 See Edward F. Cox, Robert C. Fellmeth, and John E. Schulz, *Nader's Raiders* (New York: Grove Press, 1969); John C. Esposito, *Vanishing Air* (New York: Grossman Publishers, 1970); Robert C. Fellmeth, *The Interstate Commerce Omission* (New York: Grossman Publishers, 1970); and James S. Turner, *The Chemical Feast* (New York: Grossman Publishers, 1970).
32 Cox et al., op. cit., pp. 140–161, 226–228.
33 Turner, op. cit., p. 252*ff*.
34 Fellmeth, op. cit. pp. 299–302.

Chapter 7

Policy Making in State and Local Governments

In the aftermath of the racial disorders that rocked American cities during Summer 1967, President Lyndon B. Johnson created a National Advisory Commission on Civil Disorders. In its final report to the President, the Commission asserted:

> The racial disorders of last summer in part reflect the failure of all levels of government—federal and state as well as local—to come to grips with the problems of our cities. The ghetto symbolizes the dilemma: a widening gap between human needs and public resources and a growing cynicism regarding the commitment of community institutions and leadership to meet these needs.
>
> The problem has many dimensions—financial, political and institutional. Almost all cities—and particularly the central cities of the largest metropolitan regions—are simply unable to meet the growing need for public services and facilities with traditional sources of municipal revenue. Many cities are structured politically so that great numbers of citizens—particularly minority groups—have little or no representation in the processes of government. Finally, many cities lack both the will and the capacity to use effectively the resources that are available to them.[1]

In the years since the Commission's report, its image of the "urban crisis" has gained widespread support. The crisis represents a severe gap between aspirations and achievements in the opportunities of lower-income urbanites for education, employment, housing, health facilities, and protection from crime, pollution, and racial segregation. Some critics see the urban crisis as the most serious issue of the 1970s, one which threatens the destruction of our culture.

Many observers assert that state governments also have their crises. Writing in 1967, former Governor Terry Sanford of North Carolina charged: "The states are indecisive. The states are antiquated. The states are timid and ineffective. The states are not willing to face their problems. The states are not responsive. The states are not interested in cities. These half-dozen charges are true about all of the states some of the time and some of the states all of the time."[2] The most severe critics argue that state authorities must accept much of the blame for permitting urban decay, for the poverty, ignorance, and crime that occur in the ghettos of large cities, and for the hopeless condition of the rural poor that produces migration to the cities. It is said that the states have failed to develop programs of their own to alleviate major social problems and have also restricted local governments in handling the problems that exist within their boundaries.

Not all political scientists are prepared to accept these rather gloomy images of the condition of state and local governments. Some assert that things are not as bad as they seem in urban areas; they argue that while conditions could be much better, most residents of urban areas live more comfortably than ever before.[3] And while granting that there is some truth in the criticisms of state governments, at least one writer has suggested that we pay closer attention to their accomplishments.

The states show a capacity to handle some of the most controversial issues in society. State governments have shown the greatest capacity to raise taxes over the past two decades. During 1967, before the Federal courts took any decisive stand, 23 states considered changes in their abortion laws. . . . The states administer numerous programs that operate so smoothly as to be prosaic. There seems little point in crediting the states with the effective control of sanitation in drinking water, milk, food markets, and restaurants. It is only after a trip to an exotic part of the world—or after the occasional failure in an American water system—that we think of state programs for licencing and inspection. The states also fail to get appropriate credit for the provision of higher education. According to a recent survey of graduate education, it is a state university (University of California at Berkeley), that ranks most consistently as a top institution across a wide range of academic specialties—despite Ronald Reagan's incumbency.[4]

It would be unrealistic to try to examine all these problems in the space of a few pages. However, we can explore the state and local policy systems which have dealt with these problems, or in many instances permitted them to develop uncontrolled. As we proceed, examining first state and then local governments, we should recognize that diversity is a major theme of our discussion. Ours is a nation of 50 state and 81,000 local governments. Diversity among the British colonies led the revolutionaries to create a confederation of states; responding to this diversity, the framers of the Constitution established a decentralized structure rather than a unitary state. Today the governmental distinctiveness of the states helps to perpetuate their diversity. Despite the persistent movement of people from one state to another, and the impact of nationalism on our political attitudes and behaviors, we are still a nation of different states. As we compare one part of the country with another, we find the residue of cultural traits from the first settlers, the influences of east to west migrations in the Middle West and Western sections of the country, and the political consequences of other experiences: the Civil War and Reconstruction, plus regional experiences with agriculture, industry, and transportation.

Diversity is even more pervasive among local governments. In part, this diversity is a natural part of their sheer number; the 1967 Census of Governments identified 3,049 counties, 18,048 city governments, 17,105 townships, 21,264 special districts, and nearly 22,000 school districts. The environments, governmental structures, policies, and service performance of these jurisdictions vary widely, both from each other and from the models established by the national and state governments. While the structures of almost all state governments are copies of national government structures, local institutions come in diverse and sometimes exotic forms.

POLICY MAKING IN AMERICAN STATES
The Environments of State Governments

We can see some of the diversity in the American states by examining the social, economic, and political characteristics that affect state policies and service performance. In sheer size, California's population is 67 times that of Alaska. New Jersey is the most tightly packed state, with about 950 people per square mile, while Alaska has about 1 person per 2 square miles. The range in personal income extends from Connecticut ($4,807 per capita) to Mississippi ($2,561 per capita). As of 1969, only 5.7 percent of Connecticut's citizens had incomes below the poverty level, as defined by the Social Security Administration; nearly 35 percent of

Mississippi's residents had earnings below this level. Differences in adult education vary from Utah (averaging 12.2 years of schooling) to South Carolina and Kentucky (averaging 8.7 years). When we look at white and black adults separately, the average educational range is even greater: among white adults in Alaska and Hawaii it is about 12.4 years, while among black adults in South Carolina it is about 5.9 years.

In their politics, some states show close contests between the parties, while others are overwhelmingly Republican or Democratic. Classifying the states according to political competitiveness from 1956 to 1970, one political scientist has found that Louisiana, Alabama, Mississippi, South Carolina, Texas, Georgia, and Arkansas are the most consistently Democratic, while Vermont, South Dakota, New Hampshire, Kansas, and North Dakota are the most consistently Republican. New Jersey, Pennsylvania, Oregon, Colorado, Michigan, and Utah are the most competitive states. The degree of party competition is related to the level of voter participation. Utah had the greatest turnout of voting-age citizens in the 1968 congressional elections (75.3 percent), with most of the other highly competitive states exceeding 65 percent; in contrast, Arkansas had the smallest turnout (25.5 percent), with most of the other noncompetitive Southern states having voting rates of less than 35 percent.[5]

Regional Patterns: New England and the Northeast We can summarize the diversity in environmental traits by examining *regional* differences in state economies, cultures, and politics. Even the major regions, however, are not entirely uniform within themselves.[6] In tiny New England there are differences between states in the northern and southern sections. Maine, New Hampshire, and Vermont remain relatively rural, Yankee, Protestant, and Republican. In Massachusetts, Rhode Island, and Connecticut, however, the Democratic descendants of Catholic immigrants from Ireland and French Canada, plus Southern and Eastern Europe, have replaced the Yankees. All New England shares the characteristics of early settlement; a common ethnic background; state constitutions that are relatively old, brief, and simple; a tendency to administer locally many programs that in other regions are handled by state agencies; large state legislatures that typically include at least one representative from each town; and the primacy of the town meeting in rural areas. Politicians from New England and other states in the Northeast identify candidates in ethnic terms and seek to balance party tickets with a representative of each group. Certain places on the ticket are considered the legitimate possession of a particular ethnic group. The Catholic-Protestant division joins ethnicity in its influence on politics. Birth control legislation imposed on Massachusetts and Connecticut by

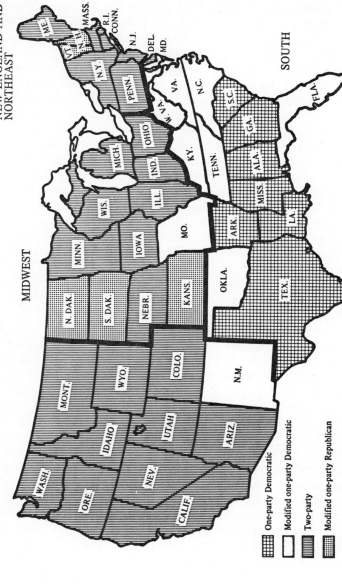

Figure 7-1 Interparty competition in the regions of the United States. *(Based on Austin Ranney, "Parties in State Politics," in Herbert Jacob and Kenneth N. Vines (eds.), Politics in the American States, 2d ed., Boston: Little, Brown, 1971)*

Alaska and Hawaii, not included in the map, are both two-party states.

One-party Democratic

Modified one-party Democratic

Two-party

Modified one-party Republican

NEW ENGLAND AND NORTHEAST

SOUTH

MIDWEST

WEST

Victorian Protestants in the nineteenth century has provoked antagonism between Catholics (who support the anti-birth control legislation) and Protestants, Jews, and other non-Catholics (who have supported more liberalized birth control legislation). Many children attend Catholic parochial schools, and public support of parochial education is another source of political friction. In Rhode Island, New Hampshire, Pennsylvania, New York, Massachusetts, and New Jersey, nearly 20 percent of the elementary and secondary pupils attend private schools. While Catholic leaders argue that public funds should supplement the private support given to parochial schools, non-Catholics point to the Bill of Rights, prohibition of state-supported religion and complain that parochial school enrollments lessen the support given to public school budgets.

The Northeast is the most congested and industrialized region of the country, and some of its political alignments and disputes draw their energy from the region's economy. More than elsewhere in the United States, Democrats represent the workers and speak out for generous social programs; and Republicans represent bankers, business management, and small-town merchants. Yet the children of ethnic Democrats who move to the suburbs encounter Republican temptations. At the same time, these migrants help to blur the traditions of the GOP. The New York Republican party shows its inner tensions most clearly, with Governor Nelson Rockefeller and Senator Jacob Javits boycotting Barry Goldwater's 1964 campaign, with the friction between Mayor John Lindsay and the state's leading Republicans (including Governor Rockefeller) resulting in Lindsay's conversion to the Democratic party, and with Republican Senator Charles Goodell being singled out by the Nixon administration (and most particularly by Vice President Spiro Agnew) to be replaced in 1970 by Conservative-Republican James Buckley.

South Throughout much of the South, state environments are characterized by: widespread poverty; low levels of education; a large black population that has felt the cultural and political disadvantages of slavery and segregation; low levels of participation in politics (by both whites and blacks); widespread conservatism, both social and political; one-party politics; governors who have strong political clout; and a relative centralization of state-local government relationships.

One-party domination of state and local politics in the South means that factions of the Democratic party do battle with each other. In some cases these factions have gained a permanence similar to that of full-fledged parties: Long and anti-Long factions in Louisiana have taken partylike positions against each other from the 1920s to the present, through two generations of the Long family. Similarly, throughout much of the twentieth century, many political campaigns in Georgia have pitted supporters and opponents of the Talmadge family against one another. In other Southern states, factions are more temporary in their identification with individual politicians. A disadvantage of factional politics is their lack of predictability. Given the shifts in ideology from faction to faction, the voter is hard pressed to know what his vote will accomplish—that is, what services he is likely to receive with the election of one faction or another. And the elected legislator lacks the cues that parties might provide to help him on a piece of legislation. Partly because there is no well-organized partisan opposition, Southern governors attain considerable political strength. They are almost solely in control of the resources that can attract support from legislators: government jobs, roads, improvements of the state institutions within a legislator's district, and government purchasing.

West Much of the politics in Western states results from topographic or economic peculiarities: population diffusion, huge empty spaces, uneven land surface, large mineral resources, and uneven distribution of water. Out of these features comes a pervasive concern for transportation and resource development. Another feature of Western politics is a high incidence of land ownership by the federal government. There is no state east of the Rocky Mountains where the federal government owns *more* than 13 percent of the land, and no state west of this line where it owns *less* than 29 percent. Several Western states approach Nevada's federal land ownership of 86 percent. Western congressmen have established the principle that federal ownership (even in marginal lands) carries federal responsibility for economic aid. As a result, Western states enjoy the highest percentages of federal aid in the country.

Western politics shows the highest levels of voter turnout and the closest contests between Democrats and Republicans of any region. The intense party competition reflects the late settlement of the West. The greatest migration occurred after the Civil War and settled the West with both Republican Northerners and Democratic southerners. Since that time no trauma like the Civil War has aligned Westerners with one party or another. The first settlers passed on their party loyalties to their children and helped to sustain close Democratic-Republican contests until the present. Along with this competition, Western states have weak party organizations. They use several electoral devices that lessen party control over officeholders: referendum and recall provisions; Washington's "blanket primary," which permits a voter to select candidates from both parties at the same time; the now-repealed California statute that allowed a candidate to file in the primary of both parties; and the extra-party "Democratic clubs" of California. The West exhibits weak party organizations along with strong party competition, whereas the South demonstrates weak party organizations and little party competition. At least in these cases, regional peculiarities appear to be more important than general principles of party organization and competition.

Middle West Finally, we turn our attention to America's heartland, the Middle West. In northern areas of the Middle West the countryside offers rich farmland and Republican loyalties, and the cities are industrial and Democratic. In southern areas, however, Democratic inclinations appear in rural areas. These patterns reflect the origin of early agricultural settlements: northern counties in the region were populated from anti-slavery Northeastern states or by German or Scandinavian immigrants; and southern counties were settled by secession-inclined elements from Maryland, Virginia, the Carolinas, Kentucky, and Tennessee. During the Civil War, these two population groups produced explosive cleavages within the Middle West. By now, their settlements and ideologies have become mixed throughout Ohio, Indiana, and Illinois, but their different origins continue to affect state politics. Each of these states produces liberal urban Democrats and some rural Republicans steeped in a progressive tradition, plus rural conservatives who are both Democrats and Republicans. Each party in Ohio, Indiana, and Illinois offers a home for present-day liberals or conservatives. Partly because of the lack of sharp policy differences between parties, the interparty competition turns on patronage jobs, personalities, and state contracts, rather than issues of policy.[7]

The Meaning of State Environments

What are the implications of these environments for policy making in the states? In what ways do these economic, social, and political characteristics affect the policies and service performance of state governments? Professor Thomas R. Dye has shown that states with high levels of family income, adult education, urbanization, and industrialization have high rates of voter turnout in state elections; intense competition between Republicans and Democrats for state offices; and high levels of state and local government spending for education, health, and public welfare. High income, industrialization, urbanization, and education seem to provide the incentives for political activity and the resources for generous social programs.[8] In contrast to these findings, however, are the patterns involving economics and policies in regard to highway construction and the use of natural resources. In those states with *low* levels of income, urbanization, and education, state and local expenditures for these programs are relatively *high*. Perhaps the long distances between population centers, wide-open spaces, and strong rural interest groups in the agricultural and fish-and-game sectors generate intense demands for these services, while federal grants help the states pay the bills.

Other relationships between environmental traits and public policy have already been suggested: the linkage between industrialization and the nature of partisan cleavages in the Northeast; the effect of ethnic-religious identifications on policy decisions in the areas of birth control, abortion, and public support for parochial education; and the relationship between the prevailing political opinions (e.g., widespread conservatism in the South) and the character of policy decisions (e.g., relatively limited public services in the South). Yet, we should not exaggerate the strength of these relationships. Many states either surpass or fail to meet the policy traits that tend to correspond with their social or economic traits.

Consider, for example, the case of Oklahoma. It is a state with a traditional culture and a conservative reputation, but generous payments for public aid. Oklahoma is not a rich state; its welfare payments do not reflect abundant resources. In 1971, its per capita welfare expenditure was $103.28, while the national average was $79.21. In the neighboring and more wealthy state of Texas, per capita spending for welfare was $58.32.

What accounts for Oklahoma's peculiarity? The easiest explanation focuses on its sales tax. When the 2 percent levy was introduced in 1933, its proceeds were earmarked for the newly devised public welfare programs. Oklahoma suffered more than average during the Depression, and one response was the dedication of its new sales tax to welfare programs. The result today is that Oklahoma's Welfare Department is guaranteed a lucrative annual revenue. The Department's budget not only supports generous payments to welfare clients but also pays for children's hospitals, prenatal care, and vocational rehabilitation.

The unusual situation of Louisiana also merits attention. Not only does Louisiana pay much higher welfare benefits than are commensurate with its relative poverty, but it makes its highest payments in the poorest counties. Louisiana's record in public welfare goes back to the administration of the *second* Governor Long (Earl, who first served in 1939). From 1928 to 1932, Governor Huey Long set the direction in public services with huge investments in free school textbooks (for both parochial and public schoolchildren); in Louisiana State University (where the football team and band, as well as academic departments and the personal funds of a corrupt president benefited from his largess); in public hospitals; and in roads and bridges.[9] Public generosity in Louisiana cannot be explained solely on the basis of altruism. While the poor do benefit from government programs far more than in other Southern states, there is also some payoff for the state's politicians. Huey Long's free spending helped other officials besides the LSU president. There is still a tendency for the number of welfare recipients to balloon in an election year.

The National Government's Influence on the States

Finally, we should remember the national government's position as a source of both resources and constraints for state governments. In 1974, the federal government disbursed more than $48 billion to state and local governments, which represented more than 23 percent of state and local expenditures. Most funds were earmarked for public welfare, education, and highway programs. Many federal grants-in-aid programs seek to redistribute resources among the states: those states with the fewest resources receive the largest amount of federal aid.[10]

The redistribution of resources also appears in the revenue-sharing program begun in 1972 (see Table 7-1). State governments whose citizens have below-average incomes generally receive larger grants. As a consequence, revenue-sharing should prove especially beneficial for the poorest Southern states. Yet, this redistributional effect is not universal. For instance, New York received more in 1972, on a per capita basis, than did three of the five poorest states. This is because a state's resources are only *one* of the factors considered in revenue-sharing. But in spite of these seeming inequities, the usual effect of federal aid is to increase the policy-making options of *all* states, from the richest to the poorest.

Conversions Processes in State Governments

Just as the states differ in their economic, cultural, and political environments, so do they vary in their governmental structures. While they all copy the structural features of the national government in some degree, their individual differences are also important. Generally speaking, the states have shown greater fascination than the national government with the fragmentation of power and such extreme forms of political accountability as having top-ranking administrators directly elected by the people (see pages 255–256).

State Executives The fragmentation of state power and political accountability is so great that most governors find it hard to lead their administrations. This is because (1) several key officials are elected rather than selected; (2) other key officials are chosen by boards or commissions over which the governor has only partial control; (3) the governor must share budget control with individuals who are not directly responsible to

Table 7-1 Revenue-Sharing Funds to State and Local Governments in 1974, by State*
(In Millions of Dollars)

State	Amount	State	Amount
Alabama	$104.1	Montana	$ 24.0
Alaska	8.1	Nebraska	45.0
Arizona	62.4	Nevada	13.6
Arkansas	63.2	New Hampshire	20.0
California	661.5	New Jersey	191.9
Colorado	64.5	New Mexico	39.3
Connecticut	76.9	New York	682.3
Delaware	18.2	North Carolina	157.2
Florida	176.7	North Dakota	25.6
Georgia	127.2	Ohio	242.4
Hawaii	27.1	Oklahoma	68.1
Idaho	25.4	Oregon	60.1
Illinois	313.5	Pennsylvania	320.1
Indiana	130.7	Rhode Island	27.7
Iowa	86.8	South Carolina	83.7
Kansas	59.6	South Dakota	27.6
Kentucky	100.3	Tennessee	114.6
Louisiana	141.1	Texas	290.7
Maine	38.9	Utah	36.6
Maryland	121.1	Vermont	17.3
Massachusetts	194.5	Virginia	120.8
Michigan	261.2	Washington	89.0
Minnesota	119.9	West Virginia	59.8
Mississippi	102.0	Wisconsin	154.4
Missouri	114.2	Wyoming	11.7
		National total	6,150.1

*Amounts shown are those the Office of Revenue Sharing expects to pay during fiscal 1974. The total amount includes $27.7 million expected to be allocated to the District of Columbia.
   Source: Department of the Treasury, *4th Entitlement Period Allocations*, Office of Revenue Sharing (July 1973).

him; and (4) several governors are weakened further by short terms. In theory, each of these restrictions limits the governor's power and gives the voters a tighter rein on their state governments. Another view, however, argues that the best guarantee of a publicly controlled government is a *strong* chief executive who is capable of putting into practice his campaign promises.

In over half the states, the following positions are held by separately elected persons: attorney general, treasurer, secretary of state, auditor, and superintendent of education.[11] Because governors have little direct control over several important department heads, there is high internal tension and discord in making and implementing state policy.

The budget powers of most governors are pitifully inferior to those of the President. Whereas the President draws up his administration's budget with the aid of the Office of Management and Budget, which is headed by his personal appointee, several governors must share budget making with persons who are politically independent of—and sometimes hostile to—his objectives. Governors in Florida and West Virginia are merely the chairmen of budgeting boards that include the separately elected secretary of state, comptroller, treasurer, attorney general, superintendent of public instruction, and commissioner of agriculture. Governors in Mississippi, South Carolina, and North Dakota act as chairmen of groups containing separately elected administrative heads, plus the chairmen of the legislature's finance committees and members of the legislature named by the presiding officers. Indiana's governor has only an indirect influence on the formulation of the budget; his appointee sits on a board with legislators appointed by the presiding officers of the House and Senate. In thirteen other states, the governor works with a chief budget officer who is either separately elected or chosen by the legislature or Civil Service Commission.

In about half the states, the governor faces restrictions on his tenure. In seventeen states the governor cannot succeed himself in office, and in six other states he can seek only one reelection before retiring. This tenure barrier may limit the expertise that the governor develops, and it certainly restricts his power in bargaining with the legislature. When it is clear that the governor will be leaving office soon, individual legislators are less amenable to his attempts at persuasion.

Some governors have substantially more or less authority than the average. Some of these differences reflect the wording of the state constitution or statutes. North Carolina's governor is alone in having no veto over the acts of his legislature. The governors of Tennessee, New Jersey, and Pennsylvania have more than the normal opportunity to appoint the administrative heads of major state departments. In our discussion of chief executives in Chapter 9 we will see that the governor's control over the budget, his appointive powers, and his legal capacity to seek reelection add some weight to his influence over state policy.

State Legislatures The formal structures that restrict most governors' powers are matched by further limits on the legislatures. State lawmakers lack several of the features that enable Congress to supervise and regulate administrative activities. Some state legislatures have no seniority system, and committees are weakened as potential sources of expertise since relatively new and inexperienced members can become chairmen. Committee assignments and chairmanships are up for grabs at the beginning of each session. Thus, the committees do not provide an opportunity for members to learn their jobs from one term to the next, and legislative decisions depend greatly upon the recommendations of administrative agencies.

The lack of a seniority system reflects the high turnover rate in legislatures, as well as the relative lack of strong legislative institutions. The prestige, salary, and perquisites of state legislators are markedly inferior to those of federal congressmen. Turnover rates of 40 percent (much of it voluntary) are not unusual. As of 1969, the average annual salary paid state legislators was less than $6,700, and fourteen states paid less than $2,500. The expense allowances and the clerical and professional staffs of legislators are similarly meager. As we will see in Chapter 8, many legislators have no office or secretary of their own, not to mention personal and committee staffs or anything comparable to the U.S. Congress's General Accounting Office.

State legislatures are limited further by the length of time they are permitted to sit and by the kinds of decisions they are allowed to make. All these limitations are discussed further in Chapter 8.

The Importance of State Government Structures While we consider the conversions processes of state governments in detail in Chapters 8 through 11, here we highlight one question vital to our understanding of policy delivery systems: *What are the policy implications of these structures and processes*? Several features of a governor's authority influence state spending. Where the governor has substantial powers of appointment, his own budget recommendations are more often honored by the legislature than where many agencies headed by separately elected executives also have their fingers in the pie. The governor's appointment powers give him some control over agency demands and administrators' tactics in the legislature. When an agency is headed by the governor's man, it is more likely to stay within his budget than an agency headed by an independent. The governor's tenure potential also strengthens his position with the agencies and in the legislature. When he is allowed by the state constitution or statutes to succeed himself in office, he offers the possibility of remaining for some time as dispenser of patronage and formulator of policy. Under these conditions, his budget is more likely to pass the legislature without substantial deletions or additions. The governor's veto power also helps him in dealing with agency requests. Where his veto power is strong (i.e., where he can veto individual items in a budget and where it takes a large majority in the legislature to override him), the governor is better able to hold down agency requests for budget expansion. This strong veto power may warn aggressive agencies that resistance to the governor's wishes may not save them from eventual control.[12]

Legislative features also influence state policy. Bodies having "professional" traits are more likely to enact generous provisions in certain fields of policy. A professional legislature is one that provides high salaries for the members and generous staff services (e.g., research and bill-drafting assistance), considers numerous bills, and remains in session throughout much of the year. These traits seem to attract more well-prepared members to the legislature and provide them with the information and the time to consider seriously the needs of state residents in such fields as public assistance, education, public safety, and workmen's compensation.[13] Still other influences on policy have come from legislative reapportionment, a topic we will discuss in the next chapter.

The Policies of State Governments

As in our discussion of the conversions process, we should consider both the general situations in state policies and important variations from one state to another. One of the most striking aspects of the general situation is the impressive growth in revenues and expenditures. From 1932 to 1972, total state expenditures increased from $65.49 to $360.87 per capita (see Table 7-2). In 1932, state outlays accounted for nearly 32 percent of all national, state, and local spending for the functions pursued in

Table 7-2   State Government Expenditures, 1902–1972

	Total expenditures per capita, constant dollars	As percentage of GNP
1972	$360.87	9.5
1967	202.10	6.7
1965	168.97	5.9
1954	113.98	4.3
1950	114.06	4.3
1946	69.73	2.5
1940	88.96	4.3
1932	65.49	4.7
1927	. . .	2.0
1902	. . .	0.7

Sources: U.S. Bureau of the Census, *Historical Statistics on Governmental Finances and Employment*, U.S. Census of Governments, 1967, Volume 6, Number 5 (1969); U.S. Bureau of the Census, *State Government Finances in 1972* (1973); and *Statistical Abstract of the United States* (New York: Grossett and Dunlap, 1973), p. 320. Grossett and Dunlap, 1973), p. 320.

Table 7-3 All Governments' Common-Function Spending, by Percentage Spent* by Each Level of Government, 1902–1972

	1972	1969	1965	1954	1950	1946
National	35.6	31.4	30.8	32.0	38.0	41.5
State	48.8	47.9	43.9	38.6	37.3	30.2
Local	52.0	52.1	60.3	58.3	44.9	52.4
		1940	1932	1922	1913	1902
National		41.8	13.6	15.2	10.9	9.9
State		30.6	31.7	22.3	16.9	16.7
Local		45.4	66.5	69.6	76.8	78.7

*Percentages sum to more than 100 because intergovernmental expenditures are counted twice: once for the granting level and once for the level of final expenditures. Presumably, each level acquires some control over the final product of the spending and thus should be credited with some of its support. Our concern in this table is not so much the position of national, state and local governments in any one year, but their changes relative to one another from one year to another.

Sources: U.S. Bureau of the Census, *Historical Statistics on Governmental Finances and Employment*, U.S. Census of Governments, 1967, Volume 6, Number 5 (Washington: GPO, 1969); U.S. Bureau of the Census, *Governmental Finances in 1968–1969* (Washington: GPO, 1970); and *Governmental Finances in 1971–1972* (Washington: GPO, 1973).

common by all governments. (This *excludes* spending for areas in which the federal government alone pays all bills: international affairs, defense, space exploration, the postal service, and interest on the national debt.) By 1972, state outlays had risen to 48.8 percent of all governments' common-function expenditures (see Table 7-3).

The periods of greatest increase in state spending were the Depression, the years immediately following World War II, and the 1964–1972 period of intense national government activity in Southeast Asia. The post–World War II years were fat years for all American governments, which had accumulated money during the war, when there was economic prosperity but a scarcity of manpower and materials. State governments had deferred construction and maintenance programs during the war, and then spent their reserves to catch up. The war-induced baby boom also made its first impact on demands for schools during the late 1940s.

The Depression and Vietnam eras provide the best indications of the states' financial strength. During the Depression, state and national governments carried the burden of public services, while many local governments joined private enterprises in bankruptcy. The states had even more of the show to themselves during the Vietnam buildup. Repeating the pattern of World War II and the Korean war, Washington withdrew federal funds from domestic programs under the necessities of military and international activities. During the late 1960s, Washington trimmed federal-state funding for highways, education, public health, and medical research. Where some effort was made to replace federal money, it was more often the work of the state than the local government. The state governments' share of the total budget for domestic services increased from 44 to about 49 percent during the late 1960s and early 1970s. Never before had the states carried as large a portion of the governmental burden.

Increasing citizen demands help to explain the growing role of the states during the late 1960s. Many demands came in areas where the states have traditionally played a dominant role, particularly in higher education. While total state budgets were going up by 68 percent between 1965 and 1969, their budgets for higher education went up by 100 percent.

The increasing demands of local governments also help to explain the growth of state budgets. The cry of "property tax relief" sounds frequently throughout the nation and influences the decisions of state officials. The tax on real estate—which is the mainstay of most local governments—comes in for more criticism than any other major source of local, state, or federal revenue. Its opponents are not limited to property owners who pay the tax directly. Tenants also pay the tax indirectly as part of their rent. Labor unions and other spokesmen for low-income renters oppose the property tax because it is regressive and weighs heavily on the poor.

In response to demands from local governments, states have sharply increased their aid to cities and have assumed added responsibility for services previously financed by local governments—such as highways, parks, and hospitals in urban areas. Since the end of World War II, the states' portion of state and local spending has increased from 47 to 58 percent.

Of the more than $89 billion spent by state governments in 1971, the bulk of funds went to support programs in education (39.4 percent), public welfare (18.3 percent), highways (16.6 percent), and health and hospitals (6.9 percent). While these policy areas accounted for more than 80 percent of all states' spending, significant variations are evident from one state to another. More than half of North Carolina's budget went to education programs, and education received more than 45 percent of state expenditures in seven other states. In contrast, Massachusetts channeled only 27.1 percent of its money into education, with California and New Jersey just behind it at over 30 percent.

Similar variations in outlay can be seen in public welfare programs. Massachusetts budgeted 32 percent of its funds for welfare, California and Rhode Island more than 25 percent. Placing a much lower priority on welfare were six states (Wyoming, Alaska, Arizona, South Carolina, Hawaii, and Indiana), which allocated it less than 10 percent.

Two areas of state policy have shown especially rapid growth: higher education and urban programs.

Higher education has consumed the greatest share of increasing state revenues since World War II. Whereas the college population approximated 4 percent of all young people in 1900, it had grown to more than 40 percent in 1970. The generation after World War II saw great developments in higher education, mainly on state campuses. In 1947, private institutions accounted for 51 percent of total enrollments; by 1970, more than 75 percent of college students were attending public institutions.[14]

In 1971–1972 state governments spent more than $13.4 billion for state university systems, as compared with about $2.6 billion spent by local governments and about $4.9 billion spent by the federal government. State spending per capita ranged from $174.32 in Alaska and $142.51 in Utah to $41.35 in Florida, $38.46 in New Jersey, and $38.11 in Pennsylvania. The public sector's role in higher education appears even stronger if we add in the increasing state subsidies to private schools. The involvement of state governments in higher education includes direct appropriations for state institutions, state aid to locally supported schools (e.g., 2-year community colleges), subsidies to private schools, and scholarships, loans, and other direct aids to students attending both public and private institutions.

State governments aid private schools in several ways. Formerly private Temple University and the University of Pittsburgh are now defined as "state-related," and received an annual state appropriation of about $80 million for operating expenses in 1969–70. Elsewhere in Pennsylvania, fourteen schools are defined as "private, state aided" and received a total of $22.4 million in 1969–70. These range from the Ivy League University of Pennsylvania to the Pennsylvania College of Optometry. In Milwaukee, Wisconsin, the Roman Catholic Marquette University divested itself of a medical college so that the state could support the college without violating a constitutional prohibition against aiding church-related institutions. In New York, the state took over the University of Buffalo. It is now the State University of New York at Buffalo and had a 1970–71 state appropriation of $61.3 million for operating expenses.

The cities, as well as the colleges and universities, have made great demands on state resources. It is widely felt that state governments are not doing enough for the cities; perhaps no government is. It is not clear, however, that any (or all) governments could cure the ills of urban America through public action. Later in this chapter we discuss the efforts of all governments to solve urban problems. At this point, we can judge state actions in a limited fashion by comparing what they are doing now with what they did in the past.

Today, state aid to cities is substantial. In 1971–1972 state governments contributed $34.6 billion, compared with the federal government's $4.5 billion. Moreover, state dollars are going in increasing amounts to cities that need help the most—that is, to the very large cities.[15] Table 7-4 shows per capita state grants of $222.51 to the largest cities (over 1 million in population) during 1972 and only $23.49 to the smallest cities (under 50,000 in population). Also, state aid accounted for a larger portion of the revenues of the bigger cities: 35.9 percent in the largest cities and 17 percent in the smallest cities.

States are paying *increasing* attention to the problems of the largest cities. From 1960 to 1971–1972 per capita state funds to cities with over 1 million population increased by almost 700 percent, and they more than doubled as a percentage of the cities' budgets. In contrast, per capita state aid to the smallest cities remained virtually unchanged as a proportion of city budgets. Since money is a fair index of concern, we can say that state governments are genuinely interested in revitalizing our largest cities.

Service Performance in State Governments: The Case of Higher Education

It is not easy to assess the linkage between state *policies* and *service performance*. In most areas of public policy—including housing, transportation, public welfare, and elementary and secondary education—the efforts of state governments are mixed with those of national and local officials. Even though state programs for urban areas are far more expensive than are federal efforts, still they constitute only 30 percent of

Table 7-4   State Aids to City Governments, 1960 and 1971–1972

	1960		1971–1972	
City size	Per capita state aid	State aid as percentage of city revenue	Per capita state aid	State aid as percentage of city revenue
1,000,000 plus	$35.95	17.8	$222.51	35.9
500,000–999,999	23.48	16.4	71.31	18.4
300,0C0–499,999	14.11	13.2	56.07	19.0
200,000–299,999	12.28	11.4	56.96	20.0
100,000–199,999	14.77	14.2	48.71	19.3
50,000– 99,999	13.91	15.0	35.14	17.4
25,000– 49,999	11.27	14.3 ⎱	23.49	17.0
Less than 25,000	8.62	17.0 ⎰		

Sources: U.S. Bureau of the Census, *Compendium of City Government Finances in 1960 and 1971–1972*, (Washington: GPO, 1961 and 1971–1972).

all the funds available to local governments. In 1970, more than 50 percent of all public assistance funds originated with the federal government, although they were distributed by states and localities. This makes it difficult in many instances to identify those services which flow from the states alone.

As one example of state service performance, we focus on a area of policy in which states have played a dominant role: higher education. Even though we are admittedly in the midst of a "new depression" in higher education, it must be granted that state budget-makers have funded education generously since World War II. Our interest here, however, is not in dollars per se; rather, we try to assess what state residents are getting for their money. As our discussion shows, however, assessing service performance is complicated by conflicting values and perspectives, and insufficient data. There are no simple measurements that tell us clearly what residents are getting for their money.

Indices of Quality Education   Measuring the quality of education is a difficult task. The problems appear in a variety of contexts: faculty committees and individual students endlessly redefine "good teaching" and try to rank instructors accordingly; deans, college presidents, and trustees seek to upgrade certain academic departments and to maintain existing high-quality departments; high school seniors and their counselors search for colleges best suited to their needs; and taxpayers question whether their tax dollars are being used wisely to develop fully the abilities of students.

According to former Secretary of Health, Education, and Welfare Wilbur J. Cohen:

> When we survey the voluminous, yet unsuitable, data now available for assessing the products of education we must conclude that practically none of it measures the output of our educational system in terms that really matter (that is, in terms of what students have learned). Amazement at the revelation of the tremendous lack of suitable indicators is almost overshadowed by the incredible fact that the nation has, year after year, been spending billions of state and local tax dollars on an enterprise without knowing how effective the expenditures are, or even if they are being directed to stated goals.[16]

Although it is difficult to quarrel seriously with Cohen's observation, we can identify some of the ingredients of quality performance in higher education. These include the qualifications and skills of the faculty, the availability of facilities, the characteristics and needs of students, and the measurement of what students have learned. Faculty skills, both in subject-matter expertise and in teaching ability, appear to be the most important area. Of lesser, though still important, concern are faculty size and accessibility to students. Sometimes these features are described as the faculty-student ratio, and sometimes as faculty interest in teaching.

But what is a "good teacher"? Can we conclude, as many have, that as the number of faculty members with advanced degrees rises, so does the quality of higher education? Both public and private institutions have upgraded their credentials in recent years, with state colleges and universities taking the lead. A 1954 study found only 37 percent of the faculty in private schools and 36 percent in public schools with doctorates. By 1966, these figures had jumped to 46 and 48 percent, respectively. In 1969, half of the faculty members in *all* institutions of higher education held doctorates or equivalent degrees.

Certain facilities also add to the quality of education: laboratories, libraries, computers, and textbooks of appropriate academic levels. However, not all ingredients of quality education can be ordered and served up by faculties and administrators. From one perspective, the instructor is only the organizer of materials and the intellectual leader who drums up enthusiasm for his or her field. Students themselves add much to one another's education. In the better schools, much learning and insight (about academic subjects as well as life in general) come from student interaction. A good school is made better by the quality of the students it attracts; they bring to it important experiences and help generate an appreciation for knowledge, truth, and beauty. Institutional prestige is an element, and not only a reflection, of educational quality. Prestige helps attract good students and thereby reinforces the other features that developed it in the first place.

Diversity, too, fosters high-quality education. The choice of faculty is controlled by administrators who must recruit teachers across a wide range of academic disciplines. The administrators' daring or timidity—apart from the salaries and perquisites they offer—determines whether the faculty will be intellectually superior and personally dynamic or competent and dull. A good mix in the student body and the cultural stimuli off-campus—concerts, museums, and theatre—add a whole dimension to learning. A university located in or near a large city offers a rewarding setting for its students.

Many assessments of quality in education conclude that "it depends on the student's needs." What is quality for one student may be a detour for another. A top-rated mathematics department offers little help or incentive to a classics major. A freshman program including a wide range of humanistic studies may bore or distract the committed engineering major. On the other hand, the humanities program will offer a rich perspective to the student who chose engineering only because an inadequate high school could not arouse his interest in arts or letters. The simple matter of an institution's size may determine its worth for various kinds of students. For some students, the large university offers anonymity and tolerance so that they can "do their thing." Others crave close personal relationships with the faculty; for them, the large university offers a poor substitute for the intimacy of a small college.

There are also great differences in evaluations of graduate training and various forms of undergraduate education. Junior colleges and state colleges recruit students from different kinds of backgrounds than do state universities and prestigious private colleges. Student interests, preparation, and needs differ among these institutions. Where some colleges should be judged on their capacity to arouse students' intellectual interests or to provide marketable skills, others should provide the most advanced and specialized faculty expertise.

Ranking the Schools   Again, we have little or no direct data that can be used to assess what students have learned. However, several studies have specified criteria for the evaluation of certain kinds of education, and have ranked institutions accordingly. One of the most highly regarded, dealing with graduate education, relies on professors' ranking of one another's universities. In 1964 and 1969 the American Council on Education asked faculty members to judge the "quality of graduate faculty" in their own field of study at each university that offered doctoral-level work. That is, historians rated the quality of history faculties, economists the quality of economics faculties, and so on.

This kind of rating system has both advantages and disadvantages. The primary advantages are that members in each field are experts on their colleagues at other institutions; they read their articles and books, and come to know one another through contacts at professional meetings. Presumably, judgments are made on the basis not of friendship but of professional standards. Also, each judgment is summary in nature; it represents an overall evaluation of separate features that make for faculty skill. The primary disadvantage is that this assessment emphasizes the highly visible features of research and publication. It does not—cannot— evaluate faculty members' accessibility to students or their teaching ability. Therefore, to determine from these findings the quality of a school in general, it is necessary to make some assumptions about the two ways that faculty reputation may affect the educational process: by attracting skilled younger members to the faculty and by attracting capable graduate students who may serve as teaching assistants in undergraduate courses.

By looking at the rankings of various institutions, we can identify the most prominent universities in the country and compare private and public institutions. Table 7-5 shows the institutions ranked as "distinguished" or "strong" by at least 50 percent of the respondents in at least two fields, and the number of fields in which each institution achieved this distinction.

The rankings of graduate faculties show the strength of three state universities. The University of California at Berkeley leads all other schools in the number of disciplines in which it enjoys high-quality

Table 7-5 Universities Having at Least Two of Their Departments Rated "Distinguished" or "Strong" by a Majority of Academic Judges, 1969

University	Number of departments rated "distinguished" or "strong"
University of California (Berkeley)*	34
Harvard University	28
Yale University	23
Stanford University	22
University of Wisconsin*	21
University of Michigan*	19
University of Chicago	18
Princeton University	17
Columbia University	14
Massachusetts Institute of Technology	14
Cornell University	13
California Institute of Technology	12
University of Illinois*	10
University of California (Los Angeles)*	9
University of Pennsylvania	9
University of Minnesota*	6
Johns Hopkins University	5
University of Rochester	4
University of Texas*	4
University of Washington*	4
University of North Carolina*	3
Bryn Mawr College	2
Duke University	2
Indiana University*	2
New York University	2
Northwestern University	2
Ohio State University*	2
Purdue University*	2

*State universities.
Source: Derived from Kenneth D. Roose and Charles J. Andersen, *A Rating of Graduate Programs* (Washington: American Council on Education, 1970).

ratings. Over half the respondents judged its faculty as distinguished or strong in thirty-four out of thirty-six of the fields considered in the study. Harvard is second, with this standing in twenty-eight fields. Yale, Chicago, Stanford, and Princeton also rank high among the private universities. Wisconsin and Michigan join Berkeley as state universities in the top group. Other state universities that rank high in at least five departments are Illinois, UCLA, and Minnesota. Six others have from two to four of their departments in the distinguished or strong categories.

In conclusion, it should be noted that several of the ingredients of quality higher education that we have identified are not tied closely to expenditures. It is not clear that salary levels are directly related to the teaching skills of faculty members, nor is there reason to believe that a state's outlays for higher education have anything to do with the diversity or needs of its students. Furthermore, the relationship between state expenditures and the quality of graduate education as reflected in the responses to the 1969 American Council on Education survey is tenuous at best: the five states whose public universities received the highest rankings—California, Wisconsin, Michigan, Illinois, and Minnesota— were not uniformly above average in their per capita expenditures for state institutions of higher education in 1970–71.[17]

POLICY MAKING IN AMERICAN CITIES

Diversity, a major theme in our discussion of state governments, applies equally to city governments. But how can we handle, in the remaining pages of this chapter, the variations in environment, government, and policy that extend from New York City to dirt-road towns with unpaid part-time officials and populations measured in the half-dozens?

The pleasant and unpleasant extremes merit equal space with diversity in any discussion of local governments. From one perspective, the cities are the new American frontier; from another, they are the garbage cans of our society. They contain our most glaring signs of wealth and decay. One irony of the urban scene is that the great private wealth of some of its residents is not available to the city fathers. There are many signs of public poverty in the midst of private plenty. The logical question is: Why can't local resources be tapped? Once we know the answers to this question, we can approach one of our toughest policy problems: how to funnel more resources to city governments.

Although we are nominally interested in all local governments, our primary concern will be with governments in large urban areas—those defined by the U.S. Bureau of the Census as Standard Metropolitan Statistical Areas (S.M.S.A.'s). For the most part, these are central cities of at least 50,000 population, including the surrounding urbanized area. There were 263 S.M.S.A.'s identified in the 1970 census, which accounted for 69 percent of the nation's people. By virtue of the people, resources, and problems they contain, the S.M.S.A.'s warrant our greatest attention.[18]

The Environments of Big-City Governments

The environments of large urban areas differ greatly from each other in important details, yet they share two things: intense demands for a variety of public services and a wholly inadequate budget to supply them. In this, the cities are not alone; however, they face the most intense and severe demands. Yet, there is irony here: the cities are the centers of wealth in our industrial, urban society. While local governments shout poverty, they lie tantalizingly close to stacks of dollars that, if not for certain problems, would finance them easily.

The Economic Environment: The Irony of Urban Wealth   Cities contain the people and facilities that process the raw materials of the fields and mines into finished goods. Equally important, cities have those specialists in medicine, law, finance, the arts, fashion, and entertainment whose work is prized in a sophisticated culture. Money flows to the cities to pay these specialists, and prospective specialists move to the cities to complete their own training and seek employment.

The cities' population growth is one sign of their economic prosperity. Yet, part of this growth consists of unskilled or semiskilled persons, often from rural areas, who have come seeking better opportunities for themselves and their families. Urban slums represent both the attraction of the city for poor people and the inability of many of them to succeed in the urban environment. One aspect of the urban irony is an abundance of wealth and talent that begets poverty even while it reproduces itself through in-migration; another aspect is the helplessness of local authorities who do not have access to enough money to satisfy the intense demands made on them.

Major problems in the urban environment result from the distribution of its wealth and poverty. Within the central city, rich neighborhoods and slums stand back to back, separated by envy and fear. Another example is the economic disparities between central cities and their surrounding suburbs. Central cities have a larger share, though not a monopoly, of the poor people in the S.M.S.A., while the suburbs contain a larger proportion of the well-to-do.

Income levels reflect both demand and supply in the urban political economy. The low incomes of the majority of central city residents suggest their needs for housing, health care, education, employment, and public safety. According to the Advisory Commission on Intergovernmental Relations, "one set of jurisdictions (usually the central city) has the problems and the other set of jurisdictions (usually the suburbs) has the resources."[19] However, the conditions differ between larger and smaller metropolitan areas. The larger the population in the metropolitan area, the more the resource gap favors the suburbs. In S.M.S.A.'s below 250,000, the pattern is reversed; the central cities contain proportionately more affluent populations than do the suburbs.

The poverty in central cities creates a vicious circle, continually adding to the disparities between them and the suburbs. It causes middle- to upper-middle-class residents, as well as shopping centers and industry, to move to the suburbs. This exodus leaves the central cities with high concentrations of costly social problems and reduces their tax base. The governments of central cities must support massive programs in adult and preschool education, counseling, job training, and housing, as well as expensive versions of the more traditional local services: education, public health, transportation, sanitation, recreation, and public safety.

Each economic group in the central city makes special demands of the local government. The poor express sharp dissatisfaction at the inadequacy of public services in their neighborhoods and have tried in recent years to upgrade them. Furthermore, the poor criticize the heavy and regressive taxes they are forced to pay. Sales taxes and real estate taxes, major sources of revenue for states and communities, take larger percentages from low-income than high-income families. In a recent period, sales and excise taxes took 4.8 percent of the annual income from families earning less than $2,000 but only 2.1 percent from families earning more than $15,000; property taxes were even more sharply regressive, taking 5.9 percent from the lowest income group and 2.1 percent from the highest.[20]

Commercial, industrial, and financial groups demand from local governments those public investments that will make them richer. They often justify their demands in terms of the community's economic gain: what is good for their private industry will "spill over" to benefit everyone. If they prosper, so will other residents.

Frequently businessmen make competing demands for urban policies. Downtown merchants, fearing the suburban shopping centers, ally themselves with other occupants of the central business district—the owners of office buildings, theaters, and restaurants—who want to maintain the commercial value of their high-priced and highly taxed properties. They demand subsidized mass transportation, traffic control, expressways, and parking facilities that permit convenient access to the downtown area. Conflicting demands come from real estate developers, who would rezone outlying land areas for shopping centers, industrial parks, and housing, and build circumferential highways in order to serve their properties. To further complicate matters, opposition to the rezoning of outlying areas comes from owners of apartment houses, especially those who already have trouble keeping their units filled to capacity, and from operators of suburban shopping centers, who fear added competition or who want to avoid industrial pollution that might deter shoppers.

One problem that troubles suburbs in the larger S.M.S.A.'s is a demand for heavy spending for schools. The suburbs have larger proportions of school-age children than the central cities, plus well-educated adults who insist on expensive facilities and well-paid teachers. The suburbs also have high growth rates. This means an active school-building program, along with generous payments for teachers' salaries, counseling, enrichment programs, and extracurricular activities. Despite higher spending for education, suburban residents escape not only many problems but also much of the tax burden of the central city. The average suburbanite pays local taxes amounting to about 5.4 percent of his income, as compared to the 7 percent of the average central city resident. It is not surprising, then, that the most common explanations for a move to the suburbs include "lower taxes" and "better schools."

Disparities in the tax and spending patterns of local jurisdictions have become a focus of demands for change, particularly as they affect support for elementary and secondary education.

> There is little doubt about the great disparities in the property tax base within every state. For example, the range of per-student property values among the school districts of New Jersey in 1971 was from $3,921 to $62,598,621, or about 1 to 16,000. Districts at such extremes are usually either rural areas with little in the way of taxable property or small manufacturing enclaves and tax havens with only a handful of students. Yet, even with a single county or metropolitan area without such anomalies, the discrepancies are considerable. . . . In Los Angeles County . . . the tax base of Beverly Hills is $50,885 per pupil, while nearby Baldwin Park's is a meager $3,706. Discrepancies such as these mean that school districts may have to impose very different local tax rates to raise equivalent amounts of money per student; Baldwin Park would have to levy a 13.7 percent property tax to generate the same amount that Beverly Hills could raise from a 1 percent tax.[21]

Disparities such as these have led to court battles against existing methods of financing public education. In the early 1970s, plaintiffs in Illinois and Virginia challenged the constitutionality of school financing on the grounds that it violated the equal protection clause of the

Fourteenth Amendment. They charged that existing arrangements allowed "wide variations in the expenditures per student from district to district, thereby providing some students with a good education and depriving others, who have equal or greater educational need."[22] Both of these challenges were rejected by federal judges. In August 1971, however, the California Supreme Court ruled that that state's method of school finances did, in fact, violate the equal protection clause of the Fourteenth Amendment since it discriminated on the basis of wealth.[23] In succeeding months, similar challenges were initiated in more than twenty states, and similar decisions were handed down in Minnesota, Texas, New Jersey, Arizona, Michigan, Kansas, and Wyoming.[24]

If upheld in the federal courts, these decisions could result in a massive overhaul of school financing. The states might eventually assume full responsibility. Or states might create equalization programs, whereby state grants to local jurisdictions are inversely related to a jurisdiction's wealth. There might be a larger federal role in school finance, which could minimize both intrastate and interstate variations in spending.

It is far too early, however, to predict how this controversy will be resolved. In 1973, the United States Supreme Court, by a 5 to 4 vote, reversed a decision handed down by a lower federal court in a case involving a Texas district (*Rodriquez v. San Antonio Independent School District*). While this decision represents a serious setback for proponents of school finance reform, the close vote of the Court and hopes for an ultimate reversal will keep the issue alive.

The Intergovernmental Environment of Localities The cities are not alone. Their environments include important resources and constraints from state and federal governments. The most important constraint is clauses in state constitutions and other statutes that restrict local authorities to certain kinds and levels of revenues. Most states restrict local governments to taxes on property; charges for water, trash removal, sewage, gas, and electricity; and limited borrowing for construction or the purchase of major equipment. Several states permit local governments to tax incomes, retail sales, automobiles, and hotel rooms. Yet these taxes make only small contributions to most local revenues.

When legal conflicts have arisen between state and local governments, most outcomes have favored the states. There is no specific provision for local governments in the U.S. Constitution. Most courts accept "Dillon's rule," which limits the power of local governments to those explicitly provided by state constitutions and statutes.

Where the state constitution restricts the powers of local governments, the state legislature must enact local laws. It must approve sites for local schools and other public facilities, condemn private property, and define city employees' salaries and working conditions. In these states the legislators from an urban area become an important adjunct to the local government. They can modify those items that city officials ask them to introduce in the state legislature and choose the proposals to steer through the legislative process.

However, the cities are not completely helpless; they do have some clout in state politics. About half the states have provisions in their constitutions designed to increase the powers of local officials. These *home rule provisions* allow cities to change their operations without first going to the state legislature for approval. Some home rule cities can change the form of their local governments, including the nature of local elections; annex fringe areas; and enact ordinances relating to public health, safety, and morality. Contemporary issues concerning the regulation of morality include pornography in libraries and local bookstores, lewd entertainment, and massage parlors. Yet state reins on local authorities remain short and can be tightened at the convenience of the state legislature.

In recent years cities have gained some ground in their competition with the states. Reapportionment has increased urban representation in state legislatures and seems to have increased the states' responsiveness to urban needs (see pages 230–233). Also, the cities' dependence upon states for money has been lessened somewhat by federal aid to cities for primary and secondary education, preschool classes, job training, mass transit, and community action, and by the recent adoption of general revenue-sharing.

State governments aid as well as restrict local authorities. During 1971–1972, the states gave more than $34.5 billion directly to local governments, while the national government contributed only $4.5 billion. This total of $39 billion means that the cities have gotten back some of the money raised from their residents by the income and sales taxes of the federal and state governments—but only some. Much urban wealth is not returned but instead goes to support national defense and international relations, plus programs and financial aids for small towns and rural areas.

Conversions Processes of Local Governments

Each of the values decribed in Chapter 6—limited government, democracy and political accountability, and fragmentation—appears in the conversions processes of many local governments. Yet local governments depart more than the states from the models established by the national government. Since many traits of local governments are described in Chapters 8 through 11, the discussion here is brief.

Limited Government Limitations abound in the structures of local governments. We have seen the subordination of local to state governments and the inability of local governments to raise enough money from the abundant private wealth in their own jurisdictions. Unlike national and state governments, localities receive no guarantees from the U.S. Constitution. States limit the nature and extent of their taxation, indebtedness, and sometimes their choice of locations for public buildings.

Democracy and Political Accountability The influence of democratic principles, as shown by a concern for political accountability, appears in partisan elections for local officials and councilmen from wards, selection of candidates with an eye to balancing the ticket, and control of departments by the elected chief executive. Partisan election campaigns clarify for the voters the lines that candidates say they will take once in office. (Whether they do so once elected is another matter.) Yet, nonpartisan elections, appearing in some two-thirds of cities over 50,000 population, blur the differences among candidates and force voters to play guessing games as to policy consequences.[25] Selection of councilmen, sometimes called aldermen, by wards is common in about one-third of the cities with more than 50,000 residents; it is designed to give each neighborhood a separate voice in city hall and thus to facilitate its demands for services.

Some kinds of political accountability are distinctively urban in nature. They include suburbanites' efforts to maintain their own governments, and the demands from some central city districts for community control of schools, welfare programs, and the police. Suburbanites want separate governments to avoid the high taxes necessary to support welfare, police, health, and schools for low-income central city neighborhoods; to keep government small and in the hands of familiar officials; and to keep residential neighborhoods exclusive—either by keeping out public housing for low-income residents or by zoning out low-cost private housing.

The desire of ghetto residents for community control springs from the same roots that lead suburbanites to opt for separation.[26] While suburbanites demand separation to be free from the costs of central city programs and to maintain high-quality education, ghetto residents demand neighborhood control to obtain education, health, welfare, and police services to fit their needs. As we shall argue in Chapter 10, this movement is neither new nor revolutionary; it is merely another movement grounded in traditional American democracy.

As we have noted, one way to achieve political accountability is through the control of hired administrators by an elected chief executive.

Yet such control is less frequent in local governments than elsewhere. Few urban chief executives have controls over personnel and funds like those of the President or most governors. And most cities in the population range of 25,000 to 100,000 employ a manager. This is a professional chief executive, not directly accountable to the voters, who controls the budget and personnel of the various departments. The use of a manager signals that a community's elite is more concerned with businesslike efficiency in government than with the principle of political accountability.

Fragmentation   The classic model of local government features a separately elected mayor and council, each with certain powers to check the other's role in policy making.[27] Yet *mayor-council* cities differ among themselves in the formal powers given to the mayor and the city council. In "weak mayor" governments, the selection of department heads and the responsibility for program design are given to boards or commissions chosen by direct election or by the mayor and the council. Weak mayors may lack a veto over the council's actions or be required to share the preparation of the budget with the entire council or a council committee. A mayor can strengthen his position by having a large, well-paid, and professional staff which can assist him in dealing with the council or administrative departments.

One form of local government, the *city commission*, departs radically from the distinctive American pattern of separate legislative and executive branches. Each elected commissioner is head of an administrative department, as well as a member of the legislature. There is no chief executive with broad responsibilities, although one member of the commission is designated the nominal head of government. In some cities, the chairman's position rotates periodically among the commissioners. This form of government was first developed in 1900 and had been adopted in 108 cities by 1910. More recently, this plan has lost its appeal to reformers, most of whom now support the *council-manager* form. The commission form is used by only thirty-seven cities with populations over 50,000, plus a smattering of smaller cities. It is said that commission cities suffer from administrative duplication and overlap. Separately elected department heads and the absence of a real central authority get in the way of coordination and complicate the task of voters who wish to change policy.

The council-manager government, like the city commission form, combines legislative and executive branches, in this case through a professional manager who is selected by and is responsible to the council. (There is also a mayor, but he is generally limited to ceremonial functions.) The typical manager appoints (and removes) the heads of administrative departments; prepares the budget for the council's consideration and allocates funds after the budget's approval; and makes investigations, reports, and policy recommendations to the council on his own initiative or at its request.

Some years ago the manager was expected to administer programs but to remain aloof from politics or policy making. He was to be the "council's man" and was expected to eliminate any marked separation between legislative and executive branches. In recent years, however, it has become evident that few managers can avoid controversial issues. Even the most careful manager encounters politics when he makes up a budget for the council's deliberation, interprets the council's preferences in funding the departments, seeks to change a department's procedures in rendering service, or expresses his professional judgment for the council.

The Significance of Local Government Structures Politicians, journalists, and political scientists have argued the merits of one or another form of local government for many years. They debate the democratic merits of governments with built-in political accountability versus the businesslike efficiency of governments dominated by professional managers. However, these elements are generally mixed in the structures of most local governments, making it almost impossible to evaluate the two "pure" forms themselves.

The form of government chosen seems to depend on the city's size.[28] Table 7-6 shows that traditional mayor-council structures dominate in both small and large cities, whereas the council-manager and commission

Table 7-6 Distribution of Government Forms by Population of Cities over 5,000

	Mayor-council	Manager	Commission	N*
1,000,000+	100.0%	. . .	. . .	5
500,000–1,000,000	73.7	26.7%	. . .	15
250,000–500,000	40.0	43.3	16.7%	30
100,000–250,000	37.5	48.8	13.8	80
50,000–100,000	35.3	50.5	14.2	190
25,000–50,000	34.0	52.8	13.1	388
10,000–25,000	49.7	40.3	10.0	1,005
5,000–10,000	66.7	28.1	5.2	1,257

*N = Number of cases.

Source: John H. Kessel, "Governmental Structure and Political Environment: A Statistical Note about American Cities," *American Political Science Review*, 56 (September 1962), p. 615.

forms together dominate the middle-sized ones; among these "reformed" institutions, council-manager forms are by far the most common.

There are two explanations for the predominance of mayor-council governments in small and large cities. First, small cities seldom have enough revenue, or enough work, to justify hiring a professional manager. Both the mayor and the council in towns under 10,000 are typically part-time officials, receiving little or no salary. Second, in the largest cities there is usually much social and economic diversity and considerable political conflict. The political accountability found in mayor-council governments works best there: the mayor and council members go directly to those groups that dominate at the polls. Competing strong factions in city politics are unlikely to accept a professional manager who might isolate some of them from influence over key officials.

There is also a regional pattern in local government structures. Mayor-council cities dominate in the Northeast; council-manager cities in the South and West; a mixture of the two forms prevails in the Middle West. Northeastern cities are generally old and have enclaves of European ethnics and blacks. The mayor-council structure has the legitimacy of tradition and responds to political competition among district communities. A number of cities in the South and West reached substantial size only during this century, and adopted council-manager or commission structures that were highly touted during their periods of urban growth. In the South, moreover, entrenched whites regarded the professional manager as a device to isolate local government from the potential black vote.

The Policies of Local Governments

By this time, two features of public policies should be evident: their mutual dependence on the activities of local, state, and national governments, and their enormous breadth and importance for the American people. The breadth and the dependence of local government policies are evident in simple financial terms: 43 percent of all governments' spending for domestic programs is funneled through local authorities, but only 66 percent of the money spent locally is raised at the local level. Thus, while the local governments are at least partly responsible for the delivery of all domestic services, they must share policy making and funding for these programs with other governments.

The financial collaborators of local governments are the state and national governments. Over 30 percent of locally spent money comes from the states, and another 4 percent comes directly from Washington. Each of these governments also shares in important program decisions with local officials (see pages 117–125, 197–199). Because of the diffuse nature of local governments in metropolitan areas, countless additional kinds of coordination are necessary between local government neighbors.

The breadth of local government policies is all-inclusive. Every domestic service available in the United States is designed and/or administered in part by local authorities. These authorities dominate activities that have been the focus of sharp controversy: welfare, police, elementary and secondary education, mass transportation, pollution control for air and water, the regulation of private housing and building of public housing, and new concerns of neighborhood decentralization and citizen involvement.

Patterns in Raising Local Revenue Local governments draw upon four major sources of revenue: locally collected taxes, intergovernmental aid, consumer charges for public services, and borrowing. These categories hide thousands of policy issues: Which kinds of taxes? How much of each? What service charges should be levied? How much and what forms of indebtedness? Some of these questions can be answered by local officials alone; others require decisions by state and national officials. Locally collected funds amount to over two-thirds of local governments' income. In all communities, important choices are constrained by state and national requirements. Table 7-7 shows the sources of the revenues of city governments for 1971–1972.

State aid includes grants for specific functions (schools, roads, welfare payments), grants to support general city government where use may be determined by local officials, and state tax money that is returned

Table 7-7   Revenues of City Governments, 1971–1972*

	Millions of dollars	Distribution
Total revenues	$42,196	
General revenues	34,937	100.0%
Intergovernmental	11,434	32.7
State	8,377	
Federal	2,503	
Other local	554	
From own sources	23,502	67.3
Taxes	17,058	
Property	10,988	
Sales	3,185	
Other	2,885	
Charges and miscellaneous	6,445	
Utility revenues	5,926	

*Note: This table refers specifically to the aid received by "city" governments—i.e., municipalities. Its figures differ from those recorded for all "local" governments, a term which includes counties, towns, school districts, and special districts, as well as municipalities.

Source: U.S. Bureau of the Census, *City Government Finances 1971–1972* (Washington, D.C., 1973), Table 1, p. 5.

to the jurisdictions in which it is collected. In comparison to state assistance, federal aids to city governments have generally been quite small, although revenue-sharing may change this pattern. At present, federal aid contributes to local programs in education, urban renewal and public housing, planning, airport construction, sanitation, health and hospitals, and highway construction.

The importance of state governments for city revenues goes beyond the transfer of funds. As we observed earlier, the whys and hows of city taxation are spelled out by state law. Most states forbid their local governments to collect sales or income taxes, and enforce upper limits on the funds they can borrow. Moreover, state legislatures require cities to perform many functions with no guarantee that the money for them will be available.

Tax equity is often a topic of discussion in local politics. Equity may concern fairness, equality, or the distribution of "appropriate" burdens. Many complaints about local taxes concern the unequal assessments of properties that appear to be equal in value. Yet, equity is not simply resolved by equalizing taxes among citizens or business firms. There is debate over progressive versus regressive taxation. The "progressives" argue that tax burdens should be equal only among those earning the same income, and that people with large incomes should pay the highest taxes in percentage and dollar terms. The "regressives" defend such things as local property taxes, which take larger percentages from the poor than the rich. They prefer to leave resources in the hands of the wealthy, whose investments will supposedly promote economic growth. Regressivity is also supported by those who claim that the poor benefit most from local government spending and should therefore "pay for what they get." Walter Heller, former chairman of the President's Council of Economic Advisors, has written that "study after study has confirmed the unmistakable pattern of substantially progressive federal taxes and expenditures, strongly regressive state-local taxes, and strongly progressive state-local expenditures"[29] (see pages 121–122).

Patterns in Spending Local Revenue   The public services supported by local governments are summarized in Table 7-8. Only education and police and law enforcement programs account for as much as 10 percent each of total city expenditures; other activities requiring relatively high spending levels include highways, public welfare, hospitals, sewage and sanitation, and fire protection. Table 7-8 provides only a rough outline of the ways in which cities allocate their budgets; the figures obscure what happens in particular communities. The states vary widely in their governments' division of labor. In some states the state governments perform functions that in other states are operated by the

Table 7-8 Public Services Supported by City Governments, 1971–1972

Function	1971–1972 expenditures (in millions of dollars)	Percentage of total expenditures	Expenditures per capita
Education	$ 5,827	16.3	$ 44.14
Police protection	3,942	11.0	29.86
Public welfare	3,031	8.5	22.96
Highways	2,768	7.8	20.97
Fire protection	2,208	6.2	16.73
Hospitals	2,089	5.9	15.82
Sewerage	1,964	5.5	14.88
Parks and recreation	1,571	4.4	11.90
Interest on general debt	1,527	4.3	11.57
Housing and urban renewal	1,475	4.1	11.17
Sanitation other than sewerage	1,334	3.7	10.11
General control	982	2.8	7.44
Financial administration	565	1.6	4.28
General public buildings	531	1.5	4.02
All other functions*	5,883	16.5	44.48
Total general expenditures	35,697	100.0	270.42

*Includes expenditures for airports, water transport and terminals, parking facilities, libraries, health, and other services.

Source: U.S. Bureau of the Census, City Government Finances in 1971–72 (Washington: GPO, 1973).

cities. In some states, for example, welfare payments are made entirely from state contributions, while elsewhere, cities contribute as well. There is also wide variation in responsibilities among different kinds of local government. Education is a good example. In some states, particularly in the East, city governments operate public schools and sometimes colleges and universities. New York City's billion-dollar school budget (which alone accounts for nearly one-third of all municipal governments' spending on education) constitutes a very large proportion of its total expenditures. But in the Midwest, South, and West, schools are typically funded by individual school districts, and their spending is not recorded in city budgets. With these wide variations in distribution of responsibility, generalizations about typical local expenditure patterns become risky. Yet, we can offer some general explanations of why some localities spend more than others.[30]

The most obvious reason is the city's size. It should surprise no one that New York City spends more money than does Kokomo, Oshkosh, or Ogden. One study of the New York metropolitan region discovered that population size accounted for most of the variations in local spending levels. Because of the obvious influence of size, most students of local government "control" their measurements for population size and analyze dollars per capita spent by local governments.

Local spending also corresponds to community wealth; the richer a community, the more it spends. The city with a large proportion of poor people possesses serious disadvantages in any effort to provide a high level of public services. State governments make some efforts to compensate for income gaps among cities. But in some states, such as Alabama, Mississippi, New Mexico, and West Virginia, there is not enough state revenue to raise local services to the levels of affluent states. Dedication, imagination, and political savvy of local officials may compensate, in part, for missing resources, and some communities tolerate far higher tax rates than others.

An economic system based upon manufacturing tends to produce higher-than-average levels of municipal spending. Industrialization brings heavy service demands for police and fire protection, roads, and public utilities. Industrial properties also provide a lucrative tax base to support the full range of local services. Conversely, a high incidence of home ownership tends to lower city spending. This may reflect homeowners' preoccupation with tax rates, plus the low population densities that occur in these neighborhoods, which results in less demand for traffic control, law enforcement, sanitation, and fire protection.

The ethnic or religious composition of a community also has something to do with spending. High per capita spending goes along with a high incidence of blacks, European ethnic groups, Jews, and Roman Catholics. Such groups may have high service demands and/or a tolerance for high taxes. These people are concentrated in localities of manufacturing, high density, or low owner occupancy, factors which also have much to do with spending levels.

There is a problem in describing the correlates of local spending one at a time. Some communities do score "high" (or "low") on all the factors contributing to higher (or lower) expenditures. More likely, however, a community will show some factors that would increase its budget and others that would lower it. One factor might take on greater importance in some communities than in other communities. The particular "mix" of influences on spending may be more important than the mere presence or absence of any one of them. In any case, it is important to know that budget-makers do not simply choose the spending pattern they want. The economic, social, and political structure of the community provides them with definite opportunities and constraints.

The Service Performance of Local Governments

It is no easy matter to assess the service performance of local governments. As we noted before, much of what they administer depends, at least partly and in some instances largely, on the funds and program requirements of state and national governments. Moreover, many problems facing our cities may be ultimately beyond the reach of public remedies. Some of them—crime, congestion, decay—may be inherent in the urban condition. Others—pollution, for example—are the almost inevitable by-products of the forces that produce urban wealth. In many cases, a solution to one problem will aggravate another. For instance, removing the pollution from the land, air, and water means that industrial firms must purify and recycle waste products in sewage treatment plants—an expensive proposition. To do this, they are often forced to pass the costs on to consumers in the form of higher prices. Ultimately, this process may lower the amount of money available for other expensive problems, such as the fight against poverty.

During the past decade, political scientists have spent much time and money to assess the activities and programs of local governments. Several of these studies focus on the antipoverty programs fostered by the 1965 Equal Opportunity Act. Since there is some question concerning the objectives of these programs, there is necessarily uncertainty about how to measure their impact. The simplest indicator—counting the number of poor in a particular city before the inception of a program and after several years of its operation—is grossly misleading, particularly since the proportion of the poor had been declining long before antipoverty programs began. Any thorough evaluation of an antipoverty program must take account of both short-range goals to make life more tolerable for the poor and long-range goals, such as a more rapid or complete reduction in poverty. And against such benefits, certain costs must be tallied. Class and racial antagonisms fostered by antipoverty programs are expensive in both human and monetary terms; how expensive is still to be determined. Every public policy contains spillover effects, and every discussion of policy impact must take account of them. Since measuring these effects is difficult, if not impossible, we must emphasize that studies of all public aid programs are both tentative and incomplete.

Nonetheless, one 1969 study suggests a way to analyze the service performance of antipoverty programs.[31] The National Opinion Research Center studied fifty randomly selected communities and their Community Action Agencies. Rather than attempting a complete analysis of program impact, the study took up a more modest and manageable goal: to determine which of four programs had been most effective in changing the institutions serving the poor.

The Community Action Agencies were classified according to four general goals: education, social service, employment, and community organization and mobilization. Eighteen measures of change in institutions serving the poor were used, including, "increased numbers of people served by social welfare agencies," "increased number of graduates of vocational programs hired by employers," "increased participation of target area residents in school policy making," and "increased participation in electoral politics by target area residents." Although not all the four strategies might register on each indicator of change, it is reasonable to assume that agencies with an educational orientation should affect school policy, agencies with an employment strategy should affect hiring practices, and so on. The most striking finding was that Community Action Agencies emphasizing community organization and mobilization have had the greatest impact in changing the policies of institutions serving the poor. The most effective antipoverty agency in terms of its own goals is the one that emphasizes organizing the poor and relies heavily upon the creation of strong neighborhood centers without being militant in its strategy.

But changing social institutions is only one goal of the war on poverty. Whether changes in these institutions will reduce the number of poor people or improve the quality of life for the poor is still unknown. Until further research gives us clearer answers, any generalizations about the service performance of antipoverty programs must be made with care.

As we suggested earlier, urban demands for community control have become a frequent rallying cry. The demand is especially strong when it concerns control of the police. In a 1973 study, Elinor Ostrom and Gordon Whitaker examined the consequences of organizing neighborhood patrol functions on a small scale under local community control.[32] Arguing that traditional records (e.g., rates of reported crimes, traffic citations, and clearance of reported cases) tell us little about how well police agencies perform, Ostrom and Whitaker surveyed public attitudes to obtain two types of information about police performance. First, respondents were asked about their *experience* with police and criminal victimization: "whether anyone in the family unit had been a victim of criminal activity, whether the police had been of assistance to the family, whether the respondent had been stopped by a policeman, and whether the respondent knew any policemen who worked in his neighborhood." Second, they were asked for an *evaluation* of neighborhood police services: how rapidly they thought police responded to calls, whether they thought local crime was increasing, how they judged police-citizen relationships, whether they thought local police accepted bribes, and how they generally evaluated the job police in their neighborhood were doing.[33]

To assess the effects of community control of police services, the authors focused on six communities or neighborhoods in the Indianapolis metropolitan area: three independent communities, each having its own locally controlled police force, and three neighborhoods in the city of Indianapolis served by the city's police department. Their findings suggest that police forces under community control provided more effective police protection than forces controlled by a citywide police department. Both in terms of experiences with police and the evaluation of police performance, citizens in the independent communities rated their police department highly. While the authors are quick to point to the need for further study in other urban areas, they found that local community control of the police does, in fact, make a difference.

SUMMARY

This chapter examines the environments, conversions processes, policies, and service performances of state and local governments. While we have identified features common to most jurisdictions, we have also noted the diversity in states and localities. The fifty states vary in ways that suggest cause-and-effect linkages among their economies, politics, government structures, and public policies. In discussing how the environment influences policy making, we find that policies in the fields of education, public welfare, and health are directly related to the availability of money; in the areas of highways and natural resources, however, the most extensive programs are found in the poorest states. Looking at the structures of state legislative and executive branches, we find that a strong governor, a well-staffed, high-quality legislature, and fair legislative apportionment also influence the kinds of policy decisions made in each state.

Not all the activities of state governments are determined by their economies or their structures. Indeed, the comparative analysis of state policy is a new field of political science, and has only begun to find the patterns that may exist. Present research necessarily leaves many examples of politics and policy unexplained. They include generous welfare programs in Oklahoma, and expensive state programs in Louisiana.

There are more than 81,000 local governments in the United States, ranging from municipalities offering a wide variety of services to 7 million people to rural towns that count their populations in the dozens. Local populations vary from the homogeneity of small towns and cities to the mixtures of race, social class, religion, and culture in the largest cities. In this chapter we concentrate on the environmental traits, governmental structures, and public policies of the large metropolitan areas. Within these areas there are sharp differences between economic resources and service demands; there is also the irony of enormous private wealth in local jurisdictions where public officials cry poverty.

While local governments sometimes copy the structures found in Washington and the states, the departures from the national model are more striking among the cities than among the states. The legal and political constraints facing local governments are more severe than are those confronting state and national officials; direct citizen participation in policy making is most typical at this level of government; and the commission and council-manager forms of government depart most radically from the doctrine of separation of power. Other oddities in local government structure, as compared to the nation and the states, are the widespread use of nonpartisan ballots for choosing public officials and the selection of legislators from at-large constituencies that cover an entire jurisdiction.

Much diversity appears in local government policies. Most localities rely on the same kinds of revenues: locally collected property taxes and service charges, plus financial aid from state and national governments. However, there are sharp variations in the amounts collected and spent by local governments, and in their allocations among different budget categories. Some of these differences reflect the actions of state governments. Other differences in local policy reflect the social and economic characteristics of urban populations: the kinds of demands they generate for local governments, and the resources they make available to public officials.

Finally, we have seen that it is no easy matter to assess the service performance of state and local governments. For one thing, the interdependence of national, state, and local governments makes it difficult to identify which services flow from each source. Also, since the objectives of programs are not always made clear, it is hard to measure what they have accomplished. We have used three examples—higher education, antipoverty programs, and community control of police services—to identify some of the ways of evaluating performance. Among other things, these illustrations point to the need for careful thought and additional research on the service performance of state and local governments.

REFERENCES

1   *Report of the National Advisory Commission on Civil Disorders* (New York: Bantam Books, Inc., 1968), p. 283.
2   Terry Sanford, *Storm over the States* (New York: McGraw-Hill Book Company, 1967), p. 1.
3   See Edward Banfield, *The Unheavenly City: The Nature and Future of Our Urban Cities* (Boston: Little, Brown and Company, 1970). For three critical reviews of Banfield's book, and Banfield's rejoinder, see Duane Lockard,

Russell D. Murphy, Arthur Naftalin, and Edward Banfield, "Banfield's Unheavenly City: A Symposium and Response," *Transaction*, vol. 8 (March–April 1971), pp. 69–78.

4   Ira Sharkansky, *The Maligned States: Policy Accomplishments, Problems, and Opportunities* (New York: McGraw-Hill Book Company, 1972), p. 13.

5   See Austin Ranney, "Parties in State Politics," and Lester W. Milbrath, "Individuals and Government," in Herbert Jacob and Kenneth N. Vines (eds)., *Politics in the American States*, 2d ed. (Boston: Little, Brown and Company, 1971), pp. 82–121, 27–81.

6   This section relies on Ira Sharkansky's *Regionalism in American Politics* (Indianapolis: The Bobbs-Merrill Company, Inc., 1970).

7   See John Fenton, *Midwest Politics* (New York: Holt, Rinehart and Winston, Inc., 1966).

8   See Thomas Dye, *Politics, Economics, and the Public: Policy Outcomes in the American States* (Chicago: Rand McNally & Company, 1966).

9   See T. Harry Williams, *Huey Long* (Boston: Little, Brown and Company, 1970).

10   James A. Maxwell, *Financing State and Local Governments*, rev. ed. (Washington: The Brookings Institution, 1969), p. 61.

11   Joseph A. Schlesinger, "The Politics of the Executive," in Herbert Jacob and Kenneth N. Vines (eds.), *Politics in the American States*, 2d ed. (Boston: Little, Brown and Company, 1971), pp. 210–237.

12   See Ira Sharkansky, "Agency Requests, Gubernatorial Support, and Budget Success in State Legislatures," *The American Political Science Review*, vol. 62 (December 1968), pp. 1220–1231.

13   John G. Grumm, "The Effects of Legislative Structure on Legislative Performance," in Richard I. Hofferbert and Ira Sharkansky (eds.), *State and Urban Politics: Readings in Comparative Public Policy*, (Boston: Little, Brown and Company, 1971), pp. 298–322.

14   The data in this chapter that deal with higher education are derived from *A Fact Book on Higher Education* (Washington: American Council on Education, 1969); M. M. Chambers, *Appropriations of State Tax Funds for Operating Expenses of Higher Education, 1970–71*, (Washington: Office of Institutional Research, National Association of State Universities and Land-Grant Colleges, 1970); and Kenneth D. Roose and Charles J. Andersen, *A Rating of Graduate Programs* (Washington: American Council on Education, 1970).

15   Not all activities conducted by local governments in urban areas are operated by cities (or municipalities). Counties, school districts, and other special districts each operate important programs. There are different findings for state aid to *local* governments than for aid to *city* governments. The information available directs attention to state aid to *city* governments. State aid to cities actually shows the weaker argument for the value of state aid; state aid accounts for 33.1 percent of all local governments' revenues, but only 24.2 percent of city governments' revenues (as of 1970–1971). Approximately 60 percent of state aid goes to school districts, many of which are

outside urban areas. To the credit of state governments, however, an increasing proportion of school aid is distributed in a manner which helps compensate for inadequate financial resources in local communities.

16 Bertram M. Gross (ed.), *Social Intelligence for America's Future* (Boston: Allyn and Bacon, Inc., 1969), p. 201. The remaining discussion of higher education relies heavily on Sharkansky, *The Maligned States*, chap. 4.

17 *Ohio Master Plan for Public Policy in Higher Education, 1971* (Columbus: Ohio Board of Regents), March 1971, p. 11.

18 Portions of this discussion rely heavily on materials developed further in Robert L. Lineberry and Ira Sharkansky, *Urban Politics and Public Policy* (New York: Harper and Row, Publishers, Incorporated, 1971).

19 See Advisory Commission on Intergovernmental Relations, *Fiscal Balance in the American Federal System*, vol. 2 (1967), p. 6.

20 See *Allocating Tax Burdens and Government Benefits by Income Source* (New York: Tax Foundation, Inc., 1967).

21 Robert D. Reischauer and Robert W. Hartman, *Reforming School Finance* (Washington: The Brookings Institution, 1973), pp. 31–32. Copyright © 1973 by the Brookings Institution, Washington, D.C.

22 Ibid., p. 58.

23 *Serrano v. Priest*, California Supreme Court 938254, L.A. 29820 (1971).

24 *Van Dusartz v. Hatfield*, Civ. 243, U.S. District Court, District of Minnesota, Third Division, Memorandum and Order 3-71 (1971); *Rodriquez v. San Antonio Independent School District*, Civil Action 68-175-SA, U.S. District Court, Western District of Texas, San Antonio Division (1971); *Robinson v. Cahill*, Docket L-18704-69, Superior Court of New Jersey, Hudson County (1972); *Hollins v. Shofstall*, Civil No. C-253652, Sup. Ct. Maricopa County (1972); *Sweetwater Planning Committee v. Hinkle*, 491 P. 2D 1234, Wyoming (1971); *Caldwell v. Kansas*, No. 50616, D.C. Johnson County (1972); and *Milliken v. Green*, No. 53809, Mich. Sup. Ct. (1972).

25 See Robert L. Lineberry and Edmund P. Fowler, "Reformism and Public Policies in American Cities," *The American Political Science Review*, vol. 61 (September 1967), pp. 701–716, plus additional literature cited in that article.

26 See Alan T. Altshuler, *Community Control* (New York: Pegasus, 1970); and Milton Kotler, *Neighborhood Government: The Local Foundations of Political Life* (Indianapolis: The Bobbs-Merrill Company, Inc., 1969).

27 This discussion of local government structures relies heavily on Lineberry and Sharkansky, op. cit., chap. 5.

28 This discussion relies on Lineberry and Fowler, op. cit.; Raymond E. Wolfinger and John O. Field, "Political Ethos and the Structure of City Government," *The American Political Science Review*, vol. 60 (June 1966), pp. 206–226; and John Kessel, "Governmental Structure and Political Environment: A Statistical Note about American Cities," *The American Political Science Review*, vol. 56 (September 1962), p. 615.

29 Walter Heller, *New Dimension of Political Economy* (New York: W. W. Norton and Company, Inc., 1967), p. 153.

30 This discussion relies upon Robert C. Wood, *1400 Governments* (Garden City, N.Y.: Anchor Books, Doubleday & Company, Inc., 1964); Harvey Brazer, *City Expenditures in the United States* (New York: National Bureau of Economic Research, 1959); Oliver P. Williams et al., *Suburban Differences and Metropolitan Policies* (Philadelphia: University of Pennsylvania Press, 1965); Alan Campbell and Seymour Sacks, *Metropolitan America* (New York: The Free Press, 1967); and Ira Sharkansky, *The Politics of Taxing and Spending* (Indianapolis: The Bobbs-Merrill Company, Inc., 1969).

31 James Vanecko, "Community Mobilization and Institutional Change: The Influence of the Community Action Program in Large Cities," *Social Science Quarterly*, vol. 50 (December 1969), pp. 609–630.

32 Elinor Ostrom and Gordon Whitaker, "Does Local Community Control of Police Make a Difference? Some Preliminary Findings," *American Journal of Political Science*, vol. 17 (February 1973), pp. 48–76.

33 Ibid., pp. 55–56.

Chapter 8

Legislative Politics and Policy Making

With this chapter, we move from a discussion of the three levels of government—and the relationships among them—to a consideration of the four branches that exist within each government. It is fitting that we start with the legislature. In the U.S. Constitution, it is the first-mentioned branch, and in the democratic theories that shape the national and state constitutions, the legislature embodies the popular will. When the Constitution was ratified in 1789, the House of Representatives was the only branch elected by the people. Members of the judiciary were to be appointed by the President, the President himself was to be selected by the Electoral College, and Senators were to be named by members of the state legislatures.

THE DYING LEGISLATURE?

Congress has been the subject of great criticism in recent years. Yet not all critics are agreed on the nature of the problem, or on the needed remedies. Most criticisms, however, center on the decline of Congress as a policy-making body. Many observers feel that Congress has become subordinated to the executive branch, and that it is incapable of functioning as an equal partner of the President. As one veteran reporter has written:

> [If] Washington is the hub of government, Congress is no longer the hub of Washington. History has left it at the center of the great original plan for citizen self-rule, but power and prestige have moved elsewhere. The Capitol is a hall of illusions, peopled by the myths that the legislative branch remains proudly coequal, that Congress continues to serve the nation well, that the old ways are sufficient to the tasks of the new day.[1]

The record of recent decades reveals the subordination of Congress: executive impoundments threaten its control over national finances (see pages 142–146); its members have felt ignored by the President in determining military policy (e.g., the Cambodian "incursion" in 1970); and when consulted, they have come to feel too dependent upon the President for the information required to make a decision. Congress passed the Tonkin Gulf Resolution in 1964, giving almost free discretion to President Johnson for the subsequent conduct of the war in Vietnam. The resolution came as the result of the President's report of North Vietnamese attacks on Navy ships operating in international waters. However, later inquiries led some congressmen to feel that the earlier reports were contrived in order to obtain strong backing from Congress. In many areas of domestic policy as well, Congress finds itself responding to the initiative of the executive branch. When it acquiesces to or accepts the President's initiatives, Congress is said to be a "rubber stamp." When it asserts its autonomy and refuses to legislate, critics charge it with obstruction.

Professor Samuel Huntington has written that Congress is suffering an "adaptation crisis."[2] American society has changed during the twentieth century with rapid urbanization; technological development; intensified international involvement; increased bureaucratization of economic, social, and political organizations; and the nationalization of public problems. These changes have altered the environment of Congress. For Huntington and others, Congress has not responded effectively. In this respect, Congress does not stand alone. Few legislative bodies have thrived during the twentieth century.

Despite their critics, it would be wrong to dismiss American legislatures as an important partner in policy-making systems. To a greater or lesser extent, all American legislatures perform at least three functions: (1) representation, (2) oversight of administration, and (3) law making. In this chapter we discuss each of these functions and the controversies surrounding them. Before dealing with these functions, however, we examine the constitutional bases and current status of American legislatures, the composition of and recruitment for legislatures, and the structures and procedures commonly found in legislative bodies.

THE CONSTITUTIONAL BASE OF
AMERICAN LEGISLATURES

Congress

The U.S. Constitution highlights Congress in several ways. Article I, which describes its powers and limitations, accounts for more than half of the original document. The description of Congress is more detailed than that of any other branch. Some items seek to limit the authority of Congress, thus reflecting the founding fathers' concern that this branch was a danger to the other two. The primary limitation was bicameralism: a Senate, whose members would be chosen by state legislatures, was expected to check the pressures toward usurpation coming from the popularly elected House of Representatives. The act of one chamber would have no force of law without the other's agreement. The President could also influence the legislature by means of his veto; unless two-thirds of each House voted to override the President, he would have the final word in halting a legislative proposal. Article I also spells out the kinds of things Congress cannot do:

> The Migration or Importation of such Persons as any of the States now existing shall think proper to admit, shall not be prohibited by the Congress prior to the Year one thousand eight hundred and eight, but a Tax or duty may be imposed on such Importation, not exceeding ten dollars for each Person.[3]
>
> The Privilege of the Writ of Habeas Corpus [requiring the government to produce an accused person in court for examination] shall not be suspended, unless when in Cases of Rebellion or Invasion the public Safety may require it.
>
> No Bill of Attainder [a legislative act declaring a person guilty of a crime] or ex post facto Law [ruling illegal certain acts committed prior to a bill's passage] shall be passed.
>
> No Capitation [head tax] or other direct, Tax shall be laid, unless in Proportion to the Census or Enumeration herein before directed to be taken.
>
> No Tax or Duty shall be laid on Articles, exported from any State.
>
> No Preference shall be given by any Regulation of Commerce or Revenue to the Ports of State over those of another; nor shall Vessels bound to, or from, one State, be obliged to enter, clear, or pay Duties in another.
>
> No Money shall be drawn from the Treasury, but in Consequence of Appropriations made by Law; and a regular Statement and Account of the

Receipts and Expenditures of all public Money shall be published from time to time.

No title of Nobility shall be granted by the United States; And no Person holding any Office of Profit or Trust under them, shall, without the Consent of the Congress, accept of any present, Emolument, Office, or Title, of any kind whatever, from any King, Prince, or foreign State.

The Constitution describes the powers of Congress as well as its limits. Of great importance is congressional control over money. The House and the Senate jointly levy and collect taxes, borrow money, regulate the value of money, and appropriate funds for "the common Defense and general Welfare." The House of Representatives has a dominant position in that it initiates all expenditure and revenue proposals. Section 8 of Article I also gives Congress the power to regulate commerce with foreign nations and among the states; establish uniform naturalization and bankruptcy laws; establish post offices; punish those found guilty of counterfeiting or violating other currency laws; create a federal judiciary subordinate to the Supreme Court; declare war; and "make all Laws which shall be necessary and proper for carrying into Execution the foregoing Powers, and all other Powers vested by this Constitution in the Government of the United States, or in any Department or Officer thereof."

Thanks to the generous interpretation of that final power by the Supreme Court (see pages 116–117), and the passage of the Sixteenth Amendment (which gives Congress the authority to tax personal and corporate incomes, thus ensuring Washington of a lucrative source of revenue), Congress today has a formidable set of powers with which to define government services and regulations across the alphabetical range from the Department of Agriculture to the National Zoological Park, and around the world. In 1975, Congress controlled the employment of some 2.5 million persons and the spending of $300 billion by the national government. For its own purposes in considering proposals and supervising the activities of other governmental bodies, Congress directly employed over 33,000 persons (only 535 of whom were elected congressmen or senators) and spent $722 million.

Congress Today   When the Constitution was ratified in 1789, it was feared that Congress and the state legislatures would usurp powers that properly belonged to other branches of government. Today, however, Congress is more often criticized for doing too little than for doing too much; it is blamed for its backwardness in formulating innovative legislation, for its dependence on the policy recommendations of bureaucrats and the White House, for the parochial concerns of its members, and for its conservative nature in comparison to other policy-making bodies. To be sure, Congress's views might be altered after the legislative-executive clashes surrounding Watergate. Before all that began, however, Congress had a reputation for dullness, often as expressed by its own members.

According to former Senator Joseph S. Clark, a liberal Democrat from Pennsylvania:

> During most of its history Congress has shown little capacity for effective action. . . . Its capacity for obstruction, however, has always been high. In frighteningly Freudian fashion, Congress compensates for its inability to act creatively by exercising its negative power to the hilt. . . . One can count on the fingers of one hand measures of importance initiated and passed to enactment by Congress in the last fifty years without Presidential prodding.[4]

Senator Clark laments the failure of Congress to take the initiative in important activities and legislation. Those measures "for which Congress must take primary responsibility, where there was no active participation of the executive in the initial recommendation" makes a dreary list of undesirable enactments. These include the Alien and Sedition Laws in John Adams' administration, the effort to renew the Charter of the Bank of the United States in President Jackson's day, the Missouri Compromise of 1819 and the Compromise of 1850, Reconstruction legislation after the Civil War, the impeachment of Andrew Johnson, the war against Spain in 1898, the Neutrality Acts of the late 1930s, the Buy American Act, the Taft-Hartley Act, and the Landrum-Griffin Act.[5] While Clark fails to specify the most undesirable items on this list, he considers most of them to be undistinguished. "[It] is not . . . unreasonable to postulate that the country would have been better off without any (or at least most) of [them]."[6]

The erosion of congressional power and prestige appears in many areas of policy. In defense and foreign affairs, Congress typically accepts presidential leadership. Congress has preserved some of its autonomy in domestic policy, although even here in limited fashion. When Congress does assert itself, it is usually to obstruct a measure. It is through blocking presidential initiatives that Congress usually makes its influence felt.

Commenting on the U.S. Senate, Taylor Branch, a prominent Washington journalist, argues that not even Watergate will allow the recovery of congressional authority.

> Senators will extract what humiliation they can from [President] Nixon and they will bluster with words and resolutions. But they will fail to restore their

powers over the purse and foreign policy because they, like everybody else in the country, remain too dependent on the office of the President.[7]

State Legislatures

State legislatures, even more than Congress, are the invisible actors in policy making. As the Citizens Conference on State Legislatures observed in a 1971 study:

> State legislatures would undoubtedly rank low on most Americans' lists of governmental institutions that make a difference in dealing with the issues and problems that bother us. The legislatures are the least visible of those institutions, commanding neither the national attention that the Congress does nor the local attention that the city council or board of supervisors gets. . . . They are hampered and hamstrung by a host of restrictions on their powers and operations. Some of these restrictions are internal, stemming from the legislature's own rules, traditions, and practices. Some of them are external, contained in the state constitution or resulting from the low popular esteem in which they are held. In their structure, size, procedures, salary level—all those aspects of organization and operation that determine how well they can or cannot work—they are all too often equally as outmoded, and not always as picturesque, as the antique chambers in which many of them assemble, or the bright brass spittoons with which those chambers are still sometimes adorned. It is not simply in their ornateness, or in the musty old odors they often exude, that many of our statehouses remind us of museums.[8]

Echoing these sentiments, the Committee for Economic Development, a reform-minded organization of prestigious businessmen, recently observed that the fifty state legislatures "are beset by crucial issues, but few are organized, equipped, qualified, or even empowered to perform their policy functions with distinction."[9]

State constitutions are filled with limits on policy making, most of which originated in attempts to curb the corrupt and foolish practices of state legislatures in the nineteenth century. The 1830s and 1840s saw extravagant commitments in behalf of roads, canals, railroads, and other "internal improvements." Legislatures authorized huge loans on their states' credit, made outright state grants to companies which then defaulted on their obligations to construct facilities, and voted funds for elaborate, unrealistic transportation schemes. The period after the Civil War featured appropriations for projects that would bring great benefits to individual legislators and their cohorts, plus the outright stealing of public funds. All over the country, states and localities shared the corruption of President Ulysses S. Grant's administration. Conditions were worst in the South, where Reconstruction governments of white carpetbaggers and untrained blacks exploited their enforced positions of control by stripping the few resources left to the states after military defeat. Under the impetus of incompetence and/or corruption in the legislatures, reformers tried to minimize the damage that could be done. They pursued a goal of "the less legislation the better."

A comparison of the U.S. Congress with state legislatures illustrates the constraints imposed on the states. One feature of Congress is the unlimited nature of its sessions. In recent years, Congress has met beginning early in January and continuing into the following December. On the state level, however, all but seven states limit their legislatures' sessions. The typical arrangement calls for one session every other year, with that session kept to forty to sixty days. There are provisions for special sessions and parliamentary devices to lengthen a session. Yet, even where these are possible, the weight of tradition—and limitations on legislators' expenses—favors short durations. Besides, the value of special sessions is limited. As one Connecticut legislator has remarked: "Let's face it. While special sessions are technically possible for any-thing, the fact is that there has to be a really extreme emergency before one is called and when we do have special sessions they are always disorderly and chaotic."[10]

The U.S. Constitution imposes few restrictions on the policy options available to Congress, outside of those designed to keep all branches of government from infringing on individual freedoms. Written into state constitutions, in contrast, is a maze of detailed provisions to limit the choices open to legislators. Many restrictions apply to finances, where reformers concentrated their efforts to minimize damage. State constitu-tions specify the kinds of taxes that can be raised, and sometimes the upper limit of tax rates; they also limit or even prohibit state borrowing. Further, certain tax revenues are earmarked for specific types of service, thereby restricting the legislature's control over the annual budget. State constitutions typically restrict the proceeds from gasoline taxes, and drivers' motor vehicle licenses to highway uses, and require that proceeds from fishing and hunting permits be used for conservation programs. The constitutions of several states prevent their legislatures from approving a higher budget than projected revenues would support. The legislatures of Maryland and West Virginia may not grant more money to an administra-tive agency than the governor has recommended in his budget, although they are free to grant less. In Nebraska, a simple majority of the legislature may reduce the governor's recommendations, but a three-fifths vote is required to increase them.

Not satisfied to merely accept the limits on their powers that appear in state constitutions, state legislators typically hem themselves in with further restrictions voted upon themselves. The statutes that create staff aides for the legislature, provide their working conditions, and pay their salaries are more stingy than is necessary under the provisions of most state constitutions. The record suggests that today's legislators hold themselves in no higher regard than did those who reformed them 100 years ago. Due to their own enactments, legislators in most states draw a salary that is laughably small; and their staff aides are pitifully unequipped to help them design and control programs. The members of some legislatures have no desk or office space other than their table on the floor of the chamber. Describing the rather typical Connecticut legislature, David Ogle has written:

> Almost all committees are forced to share a single hearing room with two or three others. Legislators have no office space other than their small desks in the Senate or House chambers. These desks are smaller than those provided to many public school children. Only the legislative leaders have anything which even remotely resembles adequate facilities at their disposal. A rank-and-file who wishes to meet with a constituent must do so at his desk in the chamber or in the hall outside since there are no rooms in the Capitol set aside for this purpose.[11]

More important than office space, many state legislators suffer from inadequate training and information in dealing with the specialists who operate the administrative agencies. United States congressmen and senators have the same problems but can solve them more easily. They provide themselves with sizable personal and committee staffs, and can call on the expertise of the Library of Congress and the General Accounting Office. The GAO alone has a staff of about 3,000 professionals and a budget of about $70 million; with these resources, it can investigate the operations of government programs on a continuing basis (see pages 225–227). Congressmen also employ a seniority system to guarantee their places on committees from one year to the next, and to help them acquire expertise in the programs that fall within their committee's jurisdiction. State legislatures suffer badly by comparison. Only thirty-three of them have staff units for budget review, and these do not provide the expertise available to the House and Senate Appropriations Committees; twenty-eight provide for a legislative audit of agency spending, but these audits do not match the activities of the GAO. Many state legislatures cannot maintain the guarantees of a seniority system because so few members choose to remain for long. Upward of 40 percent of state legislators are freshmen in any session, and this figure exceeded 80 percent in some legislatures during the reapportionment activities of the mid-1960s. Most of this turnover is voluntary and reflects the members' unwillingness to pursue another term. In contrast, congressional turnover was only 16 percent after the 1972 election. In all, this lack of staff assistance and personal expertise means that the average state legislator has little opportunity to make an impact on public policy.

City Councils

All that is said about the low prestige, few amenities, and meager powers of state legislatures is even more true of city councils. Their chief additional limitations come from the constraints imposed on local governments by the state constitution and statutes (see pages 187–188). The city council of New York, like those of many other cities, must compete with numerous other centers of political power. The only activity it can pursue unhindered is public debate, frequently about minor matters. A well-regarded study of New York's government titles a section on the legislative record of the council "An Abundance of Trifles."[12]

> The meeting place is commonly referred to as "the wind tunnel," and its inhabitants, virtually unknown even to their constituents, are generally thought of by New Yorkers as "gas bags"—when they are thought of at all. . . .
> A councilman's position is the lowest rung on the city's elective ladder. . . . It is a job with few powers and even less prestige. Until fairly recently it was the final resting place for elderly hacks in the Democratic Party.[13]

Chicago's city council is often cited as a legislature dominated by the chief executive. A recent collection of quotations about—and by—Mayor Richard J. Daley reflects the attitude of councilmen toward the Mayor, and the Mayor's attitude toward the council.[14] First, the expressions of two councilmen:

> "God bless Mayor Daley."

> "Thank God for Mayor Daley."

These comments from the Mayor reflect his view of the council, and his relationship with it:

> "Boss" should apply to someone who unreasonably imposes his way. I thought I was the leader of the city. You don't call the leader of a church or synagogue a boss.

> You'll need another haircut. (commenting on an alderman's hairstyle in

response to the alderman's attempt to raise a point of order in a council meeting).

Put the alderman of the 40th ward in his seat if he refuses to obey the rules.

In his book on Chicago politics, and more particularly Mayor Daley, Mike Royko provides the following description of the relationship between the city council and the Mayor:

If there is a council meeting, everybody marches downstairs at a few minutes before ten. Bush [the Mayor's press aid] and the department heads and personal aides form a proud parade. The meeting begins when the seat of the mayor's pants touch the council president's chair, placed beneath the great seal of the city of Chicago and above the heads of the aldermen, who sit in a semi-bowl auditorium.

It is his council, and in all the years it has never once defied him as a body. [Alderman Thomas] Keane manages it for him, and most of its members do what they are told. In other eras, the aldermen ran the city and plundered it. In his boyhood they were so constantly on the prowl that they were known as "the Gray Wolves." His council is known as "the Rubber Stamp."

He looks down at them, bestowing a nod or a benign smile on a few favorites, and they smile back gratefully. He seldom nods or smiles at the small minority of white and black independents. The independents anger him more than the Republicans do, because they accuse him of racism, fascism, and of being a dictator. The Republicans bluster about loafing payrollers, crumbling gutters, inflated budgets—traditional, comfortable accusations that don't stir the blood.

That is what Keane is for. When the minority goes on the attack, Keane himself, or one of the administration aldermen he had groomed for the purpose, will rise and answer the criticism by shouting that the critic is a fool, a hypocrite, ignorant, and misguided. . . .

But sometimes Keane and his trained orators can't shout down the minority, so Daley has to do it himself. If provoked, he'll break into a rambling, ranting speech, waving his arms, shaking his fists, defending his judgment, defending his administration, always with the familiar "It is easy to criticize . . . to find fault . . . but where are your programs . . . where are your ideas . . ."

If that doesn't shut off the critics, he will declare them to be out of order, threaten to have the sergeant at arms force them into their seats, and invoke *Robert's Rules of Orders*, which, in the heat of debate, he once described as "the greatest book ever written."

All else failing, he will look toward a glass booth above the spectator's balcony and make a gesture known only to the man in the booth who operates the sound system that controls the microphones on each alderman's desk. The man in the booth will touch a switch and the offending critic's microphone will go dead and stay dead until he sinks into his chair and closes his mouth.[15]

Legislatures in the United States and Elsewhere

It is one thing to say that the status of American legislatures has declined relative to that of other branches of government. It is quite another thing, however, to examine our legislatures (especially Congress) in comparison to legislatures in other countries. All over the world, legislatures seem to be on the decline and executive and administrative bodies on the ascendancy. Within this broader context, Sir Denis Brogan, a distinguished British political scientist, compared Congress favorably with other national legislatures. In his view, "the Congress of the United States is the last really important legislative body."[16]

> . . . this is an age of legislative decline. Even the House of Commons, "the Mother of Parliaments," is now almost completely under the control of the executive branch. France, "Mother of Revolutions," has chosen to give herself a government very heavily weighted on the executive side. . . . The future of parliamentary government is uncertain in countries as diverse as Italy, India and Japan. But, negatively, at any rate, the Congress of the United States possesses in fact, the powers given to it in form by the Constitution. Congress can and does hold up the program of even the most forceful and popular president, Congress can and does thwart with impunity the wishes of the American electors. An American election cannot be a mandate to the temporary detainers of the national sovereignty as it is in Great Britain. It can only give a broad hint or a polite suggestion to the men who, in fact, keep in their custody the legislative power of the United States.

Thus, the status of American legislatures is mixed. They seem to lack the capacity or the will to take the lead in policy making. As we shall see, Congress, state legislatures, and city councils respond to the policy initiatives that come from executive and administrative branches. This passivity represents a startling change from the eighteenth century, when the framers of the Constitution and the early state constitutions saw the legislature as potentially the most aggressive branch and tried to rein it in with bicameralism, an executive veto, and a host of detailed restrictions. Even though legislatures seldom take the initiative, however, they have not become impotent. They have real and frequently exercised authority to alter the recommendations of the other branches, and to investigate the performance of public officials. More than in any other major country, American legislatures are independent in the policy system. As we continue to examine the policy relevant structures and behaviors of legislators, we must pursue the seemingly contrary goals of asking *What makes them weaker than other branches as policy makers?* and *What makes them continue to be viable participants in the policy system?*

AMERICAN LEGISLATORS

In order to understand the contributions of legislators to the policy delivery system, it may help to know something about the character of American legislators. *Who are* the legislators?

In many respects, the personal backgrounds of American legislators do not appear very different from those of other individuals who reach important positions in government or the private sector. Most of them come from the middle class, have college educations, and possess mainly professional, technical, or managerial backgrounds. The single most prominent occupation of American legislators is law. In recent years, lawyers have accounted for over one-half the members of the U.S. Congress, and about one-quarter of the members of state legislatures. In general, U.S. Congressmen have a more prestigious background than do members of state legislatures. While over 90 percent of the U.S. House and Senate members have come from professional or managerial backgrounds since World War II, studies of nine state legislatures during recent years found this to be true of only 43 to 83 percent of their members. State legislators are more likely than members of the U.S. Congress to list themselves as farmers, craftsmen, or clerks.[17]

These differences between national and state legislators are not surprising. The job of a Senator or Congressman is higher on the political pecking order; individuals who succeed in state legislatures and aspire to more attractive political careers often seek them in Congress. The functions of state legislatures in the policy delivery system, then, include training prospective Congressmen and screening out those who do not make the grade as legislators.

U.S. Congressmen, as compared to executives and bureaucrats in both government and private business, are more likely to come from small-town and rural backgrounds.

> 64 percent (of the Senators in 1959) were raised in rural areas or in small towns, and only 19 percent in metropolitan centers. In contrast, 52 percent of the presidents of the largest industrial corporations grew up in metropolitan centers, as did a large proportion of the political executives appointed during the Roosevelt, Truman, Eisenhower, and Kennedy administrations.[18]

Congressmen are also less mobile than administrators. In 1971, nearly 80 percent of the congressional leaders were still living in the states of their birth, as compared to only 40 percent of administrators. Samuel Huntington sees considerable significance in these differences.

> Congressmen have tended to be oriented toward local needs and smalltown ways of thought. The leaders of the administration and of the great private national institutions are more likely to think in national terms. . . . The Congressman is part of a local consensus of local politicians, local businessmen, local bankers, local trade union leaders, and local newspaper editors who constitute the opinion-making elite of their districts. As Senator Richard Neuberger noted: "If there is one maxim which seems to prevail among many members of our national legislature, it is that local matters must come first and global problems a poor second—that is, if the member of Congress is to survive politically."[19]

A middle-class bias of American legislators also appears at the local level. However, within a range, city councilmen may be more or less middle class depending on the nature of their communities.

> The more uneducated the population, the less well-educated the councilmen; the poorer the community, the less wealthy its leaders; the more working-class the city, the fewer white collar councilors. . . . Although never proportionately drawn from the various social categories, municipal leadership is relatively representative.[20]

The more or less middle-class character of most city councils reveals itself in their policy stances. Rather than proving a stimulus for major change, they generally align themselves with the city-booster elements of the chamber of commerce and lean heavily on the proposals of the mayor or city manager. Where local procedures call for nonpartisan elections, there is a tendency for middle- and upper-class residents and Republicans to swing more weight on the council than their population warrants. Under these conditions, there is little likelihood that the council will strive to meet the social and economic grievances of the cities' minorities and the poor.[21]

THE STRUCTURE AND PROCEDURES OF AMERICAN LEGISLATURES: PERVASIVE FRAGMENTATION

Fragmentation is as prominent in legislatures as it is elsewhere in American governments. Indeed, fragmentation may be the most pervasive feature of our legislative bodies. It appears in bicameralism, which is important not only for the existence of two houses, but also for the differences between them. The presence of two houses simply means that any proposal must find two separate acceptances before it can become law. However, the differences between the houses at the national level means that the second acceptance is not a simple repetition of the first. Different kinds of people act on a proposal in the second house, and thus its advocates and opponents must reckon with different policy orientations there. Supporters of any major item must tailor their proposal for two different sets of hurdles in the U.S. Congress.

House and Senate Differences

The major differences between the House of Representatives and the Senate include their size; the rigidity of leaders' control over the members; the individuality, power, and prestige of the members; and the members' tendencies toward liberalism or conservatism. Size appears to be the most crucial difference. Because the House is more than four times the size of the Senate, there is a compelling need for strong leaders. This means more formality, hierarchical organization, rigid rules, and—despite its large size—more rapid action than in the Senate. These traits, in turn, work to diminish the individuality, prestige, and power of the average Representative as compared to the average Senator, and require the Representative to serve a longer apprenticeship before reaching an important position.

    The greater conservatism of the House seems to reflect the nature of its members' constituencies. Senators represent whole states, Representatives only parts of states. Senators' constituencies are more diverse, and are likely to include liberals and radicals, as well as conservatives. There are relatively few Senators who could make their career by representing the interests of only one congressional district and by taking a conservative position on most items of interest to other groups.[22] Of interest, in this regard, will be the career of Senator James Buckley of New York. Claiming to be a strict conservative, yet representing one of the largest and most diverse constituencies in the country, Buckley may find it difficult to maintain both his ideology and his seat beyond his first term. An example of greater liberalism in the Senate appears in its budget decisions. For fifteen years after World War II the Senate Appropriations Committee recommended an increase of at least 6 percent over the House's appropriation in about 24 percent of the cases, and recommended a decrease of at least 6 percent in the House's appropriation in only 1 percent of the cases. The departments increased by these Senate actions were—in the order of their benefits—Interior, HEW, Commerce, Agriculture, and Labor.[23]

    In earlier chapters, we discussed fragmentation as a means of achieving desirable political values—namely, limited government and democratic government (or political accountability). In the case of Congress, however, fragmentation works to lessen democratic rule. Congress is organized in such a way that almost everything "is sacrificed to see to it that majorities are not easily mustered and registered. The rules of Congress—both the codified, formal rules and the informal, traditional rules—distribute power to small groups and even to individuals so as to restrain activists."[24] The procedures by which schedules are established, the role played by committees and subcommittees, and the informal norms or folkways which are quickly transmitted to freshmen all contribute to this dispersion of political power.

Committees

The fragmentation of Congress is most visible in the committee system. Students of legislative politics have long recognized the significance of congressional committees. Writing in 1885, Woodrow Wilson (who was a political scientist before he was President) observed that "Congressional government is committee government."

> The House sits . . . to sanction the conclusions of its committees. . . . It legislates in its committee-rooms; not by the determinations of majorities, but by the resolutions of specially-commissioned minorities; so that it is not far from the truth to say that Congress in session is Congress on public exhibition, whilst Congress in its committee-rooms is Congress at work.[25]

While Wilson is correct in naming congressional committees as crucial to the legislative process, his description exaggerates their role today. They are not autonomous decision-making units; their decisions can be modified or even rejected by the entire House or Senate. Yet their contribution to the policy delivery system is considerable. Committees make crucial decisions about bills that become law; and without their support, few pieces of legislation have any chance of acceptance.

Committees form the basis of the division of labor which characterizes law-making activity. Legislative proposals are distributed among twenty-one House and sixteen Senate committees, which are organized according to subject matter. They have a formidable set of prerogatives and control whether, and when, a bill will be considered and approved by each house. The committees determine not only if a bill is going to get a serious chance at passage, but which ingredients of the original bill will get that chance. For the Congressman not on a particular committee, there are procedures for extracting a bill from an unwilling committee and for amending the bill once its gets onto the floor. As we shall see, however, these procedures are biased to favor the committee. The best way for a congressman to get approval for his bill is to write one that will appeal to the committee that reviews it. The vast majority of bills are buried in committee and never get to the floor for an actual vote of the entire House or Senate. During the Ninety-first Congress (1969–1970), for example, only 2,591 or the 20,015 bills introduced in the House of Representatives were reported by the committees to which the Speaker had referred them.[26]

Congressional committees also provide the settings for secret deliberations, where members can shape policy in ways that differ from the reputations they wish to maintain in public. In recent years over one-third of the committee sessions have been secret despite a requirement in the 1970 Legislative Reorganization Act that meetings be open to the public unless the committee majority votes otherwise. The same act requires committees to announce their roll-call votes, indicating how members decide on each issue, but chairmen have avoided that requirement by not taking roll-call votes.

The secrecy of committee deliberations can make a difference in matters of policy. According to one member:

> You certainly get some different attitudes in a [secret committee] conference than you would anticipate by listening to speeches on the floor. . . . There is one senator, for example, who is known primarily for a particular position on foreign aid. Yet in conference I never saw anyone fight more ardently for a different position.[27]

Committee Members   Given the importance of committees in the legislative process, two important questions concern their members: *On what basis are committee assignments made?* and *Who has greatest influence over committee activities?* The question of committee membership has several answers. First, the majority party in Congress makes sure that its members constitute a majority on every committee, and that every committee chairman is a member of the majority party. Secondly, the leaders of each party in the House and the Senate make the crucial decisions as to which party members go on each committee. In the House, Democratic committee assignments are made by the Democratic members of the Ways and Means Committee, while Republican assignments come from that party's Committee on Committees (which is composed of one member from each state with a Republican congressman). In the Senate, assignments are made by the Democratic Steering Committee and the Republican Committee on Committees. These different procedures have one thing in common: the party leaders in each chamber directly control committee assignments, and only rarely are their decisions challenged successfully by rank-and-file members. Once made, the "rec-ommendations" of these groups are usually ratified by the members of each house at the beginning of each session.

In the seniority system, a member keeps his committee seat from one session of Congress to the next; the seats to be filled at the beginning of each session are those left vacant by retired members or by those who have sought and received assignments to other committees. Some committee assignments are more desirable than others. In the House, members of the three most prestigious committees—Rules, Appropriations, and Ways and Means—are in a position to influence legislation in a wide range of policy areas. In contrast, members of the House Administration, Merchant Marine and Fisheries, Post Office and Civil Service, and Veterans' Affairs Committees influence fewer and less prominent issues. Thus, committee assignments are matters of considerable controversy. Most congressmen want a say over such topics as appropriations, taxes, military affairs, or agriculture.

In making committee assignments, party leaders consider several factors. Where two members are seeking to fill the same vacancy, the member with greater seniority will generally win. In making assignments to major committees, party leaders look for "responsible legislators," those who have shown a willingness to work hard, to accommodate the views of fellow legislators, and to observe other congressional norms. Committee assignments also reflect a concern for "constituency representation." Where possible, legislators are given assignments that correspond to an interest that prevails in their district and will improve their chances of reelection. Agriculture Committee members generally come from farming areas, Interior Committee members from the West.[28]

Committee seats are too valuable to be passed out without reference to a member's policy inclinations. In the period when Texas Congressman Sam Rayburn was Speaker of the House, and Lyndon Johnson was Senator Majority Leader, it is said that they never let anyone sit in House Ways and Means or Senate Finance without asking what they thought about the oil depletion allowance. Also, when a Maryland congressman was being considered for membership in the House Interstate and Foreign Commerce Committee, he was asked by Kentucky's John Watts, "What's your position on tobacco?" The congressman replied, "I don't smoke"—and was not appointed to the committee.[29]

Because of the importance of committees, the selection of committee members can have a direct effect on policy decisions.

> If there are enough vacancies on a given committee, the impact of committee assignments on committee policy may be immediate—as happened in the

filling of six vacancies on the Education and Labor Committee in 1959. In this case, a new majority was created which pushed a new set of rules through the committee, overrode the chairman, and got the first general aid-to-education bill in history through the House. If the policy balance is close, a single appointment may be decisive. Those Democrats who in 1962 defeated Representative Landrum's bid for a seat on the Ways and Means Committee, in caucus and against the wishes of Speaker McCormick, believed that the fate of President Kennedy's trade program, of his tax program, and of the Medicare bill might be at stake in that single assignment.[30]

Committee Chairmen The committee chairman has extensive powers. He defines the committee's agenda, presides at committee hearings, selects the members and privileges of the subcommittees within his committee, and determines how the committee will choose its professional staff aides. If the chairman uses these powers with skill and assertiveness, he will select the bills that are reviewed by his committee *and* have a significant impact on the language of the bill when it is reported to the full House or Senate.

Representative Wilbur Mills of the House Ways and Means Committee stands out as one of the most effective committee leaders. Mills' influence is not based solely upon his position as the chairman of this key committee. "Contrary to the impression one sometimes receives from newspaper stories about the 'all powerful' Chairman Mills, he is perhaps as responsive to the Committee as the Committee is to him."[31] Instead of trying to impose his will upon the committee, Mills cultivates the support of committee members through bargaining, compromise, and consensus building; his position is strengthened further by his subject matter expertise and his sensitivity to opinions in the committee and in the House itself. In the words of committee members and other close observers:[32]

He is a consensus seeker. He never pushes things to votes, we reach a compromise.

He leads by compromising.

He knows the tax code inside and out, and he knows what Ways and Means has done for the last twenty years.

He counts the heads in Committee, and he counts the heads in the House; he's always counting.

You hear some criticism of Wilbur, but he has a high regard for the Committee. He takes care of it, respects it, and acts to insure its effectiveness on the floor.

The Seniority System

The seniority system determines the question of committee leadership. With rare exceptions, the chairmen and ranking minority members of standing committees are those who have had the longest consecutive service on the committee. The powers of committee chairmen, and the fact that their jobs are locked into the seniority system, have been matters of ritual uproar for years.

Those in Favor The advantages of the seniority system include simplicity and expertise. By passing out the chairmanships according to the automatic criterion of seniority, the legislators save themselves inevitable squabbles over selection. According to friends of the system, the most senior person of the majority party, simply because of his longevity, is likely to know the most about programs within the committee's jurisdiction. Furthermore, by holding out an eventual chairmanship as a reward for seniority, the legislature provides an incentive for its junior and middle-range members to stay with their committee assignments through many sessions of Congress, and so acquire the expertise that will aid Congress in its conflicts with the other branches of government.

Those Opposed Critics of the seniority system say that rewards for length of service give far too much influence to members who are old, often out of touch with social realities, and from "safe" seats (i.e., districts where they face little or no competition at election time). Critics allege that safe seats tend to be rural (i.e., those represented by Southern Democrats and Midwestern Republicans) and conservative. Thus, the seniority system builds a safe rural-conservative bias into Congress by giving committee chairmanships to members with these traits.

Some research by Professor Barbara Hinckley casts doubt on this last argument. For one thing, she finds that "safeness" is a characteristic not of conservative, rural districts per se, but of congressional districts in general. One party is dominant in a majority of districts, and most incumbents are returned to office if they seek reelection. A majority of congressmen receive 60 percent or more of the vote. A relatively small number of districts are marginal. For example, in 1972, 308 "safe" congressmen received 60 percent or more of the vote, while only 67 were elected from "marginal" districts where they received less than 55 percent of the vote.

Safeness is not merely a Southern phenomenon; nor is it found only in states lacking two-party competition. As Hinckley observes, many safe seats are located in what can be considered competitive two-party states.

Take the case of New Jersey. In 1972, this state sent thirteen Democrats and twelve Republicans to the House of Representatives. Of these, twenty were elected by more than 60 percent of the vote, and none received less than 55 percent of the vote. Nor do safe seats favor rural legislators. Metropolitan and small-town legislators enjoy the benefits of safeness just as often as—if not more so than—rural representatives.

According to Hinckley, the seniority system has only limited influence on the character of committee chairmen. The "reason for the preponderance of southern Democrats in committee chairs is not so much a 'bias' of the seniority system as, simply the preponderance of southerners in the Democratic congressional membership in that twenty-year span."[33] Hinckley does, however, show a bias among Democratic committee chairmen.

> In the Democratic party, the requirement of congressional seniority gave the South and the West, regions of greatest Democratic strength to start with, an increased advantage, and these areas tended to be weakest in "liberalism" and support for presidential Democratic programs. But congressional seniority is only one factor contributing to the conservative cast of Democratic chairmen. Most notably conservative Democrats, weakest in support of party programs, were more likely to stay with their committees than their more liberal colleagues—suggesting that patterns of initial assignment or subsequent changes also influenced the results.[34]

Changing the System Critics of the seniority system have scored some success in recent years. Since the rule of seniority is nowhere in the statutes, it is a matter for the Democratic and Republican party caucuses. The new, more open procedures adopted by House Democrats in 1971 call for that party's members of the Ways and Means Committee to report their recommendations for committee chairmen and memberships to the party caucus. Any ten members can demand a vote on any portion of the recommendations. If certain nominees fail to receive the support of a majority of those voting, new nominees must be selected. The new rules also limit the number of committee assignments that a single representative can hold: no legislator can be a member of more than two committees; no representative can head more than one subcommittee; and no chairman can head more than one subcommittee within his own committee. As a result of these rule changes, junior members should receive more desirable committee assignments, and more of them should serve as chairmen of subcommittees. For the Senate, Majority Leader Mike Mansfield confirmed in 1971 that a majority of Democrats could nullify any committee assignment, including that of a chairman. He further stated that they are "empowered to decide all questions of committee membership, including chairmen, ratios, distribution and the basis on which assignments are made."[35] The net result may be committees whose membership in terms of age and ideologies will accurately reflect our diversified society.

Since Republicans have not been the majority party in Congress, and therefore have been without committee chairmanships, since 1955, the seniority controversy has been less troublesome for the GOP. The Republican Committee on Committees' nominees for the positions of committee chairmen or ranking minority members are submitted to the party caucus, where a formal vote is taken. If a nominee is rejected by a majority of those voting, the Committee on Committees is required to submit another name. While it is assumed that the most senior members will be given committee chairmanships, the Committee on Committees does not have to follow the rule of seniority. Republicans in the Senate have limited the number of committee assignments permitted a Senator, thus opening desirable assignments to junior members. To date, these reforms in both houses of Congress have not resulted in a rejection of the seniority rule. As one observer says: "Piecemeal exceptions might now occur; but, as the accepted method for selecting committee chairmen, seniority remains intact."[36]

The Unwritten Rules

Seniority is only one of the informal rules which govern the behavior of legislators. Such traditions prescribe "how things are done" and ensure a certain predictability in behavior from one session to the next. This stability is important for the orderly functioning of government: "the House or the Senate or a state legislature, must transmit its norms to legislative newcomers in order to insure the continued, unaltered operation of the institution, and . . . the member himself must learn these norms if he is to be an effective legislator."[37]

The norm of seniority runs throughout Congress. Freshman senators and representatives are expected to work hard, attend to their committee assignments, and keep quiet. (The last rule is being followed less and less often.) Specialization is another important norm. Legislators are encouraged to concentrate their interests and to establish their credentials in a particular area. The heavy workload facing legislators does not permit them familiarity with all issues; rather, they must attend to one area and depend upon the advice of colleagues in others. Specialization offers rewards as well as work. A legislator with known expertise in one area is listened to with respect; his advice is asked, and he gains muscle as well as friends when his own turn comes to push through a favored piece of legislation.

This last area is known as "reciprocity"—or, less politely but perhaps more honestly, as "trading votes" or "logrolling":

I'll listen to you on housing and you listen to me on feed grains.

You support my legislation and I'll support yours.

It depends on the importance of the bill. On local bills, I think I would. For example, I am interested in a potato referendum bill in 48 states and I'm sure that my good friend _____ of New York couldn't care at all about the bill, but he'll probably support it because we're friends. And I'd do the same for him.

I won't be an S.O.B. if you won't be one.[38]

This norm of reciprocity applies to committees as well as to individual legislators. Members of the House Appropriations Committee are most concerned with the issues before their respective subcommittees (e.g., Subcommittee on Agriculture, Subcommittee on Defense). Consequently, the whole Appropriations Committee tends to defer to the expertise of each of its subcommittees, and in turn the decisions of the full committee are ordinarily adopted by the entire House.

Norms of specialization and reciprocity reinforce the fragmentation of the legislatures. These norms strengthen the committees and distribute power widely in the Senate and House. Yet the strength of these norms has lessened in recent years. Junior members have shown an increased willingness to advance new policies and speak openly in support of favored programs; no longer, as we have said, are freshmen content to sit back and quietly serve their apprenticeship period.

A LEGISLATIVE ARM FOR POLICY SUPERVISION: THE GENERAL ACCOUNTING OFFICE

Elected members of Congress are not alone in their efforts to make policy and supervise its implementation. Individual members have personal staff assistants; committees have extensive staffs; the Congressional Research Service of the Library of Congress is available to all members; and the General Accounting Office (GAO) is an impressive unit that provides administrators with daily reminders that another branch is looking over their shoulders. The GAO is a little known actor with great importance.[39] No state or local government gives its legislature the range of expertise and the formal powers of the GAO.

The GAO's function is to determine whether expenditures are legal and whether programs are being administered efficiently. It decides this after Congress and the White House have passed upon a program, and after the administrators have begun to operate. Despite the lateness of their entry, the GAO auditors can impose themselves heavily into a program's operation. If the GAO determines that an expenditure is illegal, the U.S. Treasury will not pay for goods ordered or services rendered. With no payments forthcoming, the program will probably be halted. The auditor's task is not always simple. Different statutes may apply to the same program, and some inconsistencies may appear in their language. For clues to legislative "intent," an auditor may go beneath formal enactments to debates on the floor of Congress or to statements in committee hearings or committee reports. This kind of a search increases the alternative standards open to the auditor and broadens his power to determine which activities he will allow.

Relations between the GAO and administrative departments are typically cooperative. The reports of illegal or inefficient operations are welcomed by the President, the Office of Management and Budget, and administrators interested in their subordinates' activities. Most adverse rulings of the GAO are accepted with little more than grumbling in the agency and among the clients and contractors who are affected by the decision. Yet there are times when the GAO runs into a bureaucratic barrier. Some information about agency programs is denied to the GAO by administration officials who cite "executive privilege" and the need to keep certain affairs confidential. On occasion, administrative officials strongly disagree with GAO decisions. These confrontations indicate the potential power of the GAO, and its threat to officials in the various departments.

In one confrontation in the late 1960s, the GAO tried to outlaw an important item of President Nixon's domestic program. This was the Philadelphia Plan, whereby government contracts would require contractors to make genuine efforts to hire members of minority groups. The issue gained its political importance from the virtually all-white nature of skilled workers in construction projects, the focus of militant and moderate black organizations against the alleged discriminatory practices of craft unions and contractors, and the widely perceived conservative record of the Nixon administration on racial policies. Because of its "Southern strategy," the administration was said to be ignoring the needs of black Americans. The Philadelphia Plan was an important—some said the *most* important—move of the administration in the direction of equal economic opportunity. The clash rested upon the claim of the GAO's chief (the Comptroller General) that the plan ran afoul of the Civil Rights Act of 1964; in particular, Section 703(j), stating that the act does not require an employer to grant preferential treatment to any individual or group because of race, color, religion, sex, or national origin. The GAO alleged that the Labor Department would "obligate bidders, contractors or subcontractors to consider the race or national origin of their employees or prospective employees."[40] The Labor Department responded that the plan only required contractors to take "affirmative action" that would achieve reasonable goals of "minority manpower utilization." The debate posed legislators against one another, and produced the unusual alliance of labor *and* management in the construction industry against a grouping of President Nixon, Attorney General John Mitchell, and numerous black organizations. The protagonists drew fine distinctions between "quotas" and "goals." A major constitutional clash between the legislative and executive branches was avoided when the Senate failed to sustain the Comptroller General's ruling, and he announced his willingness to permit expenditures under the Plan.

PROFESSIONALISM IN STATE LEGISLATURES

We have already seen in Chapter 7 that state legislatures resemble the structure of the U.S. Congress on certain traits even while they differ from it in powers and procedures. All the states but Nebraska have a bicameral structure. Yet the states no longer follow the senatorial model of apportioning seats equally to jurisdictions within the states—thanks to the decision of the United States Supreme Court in *Reynolds v. Sims* (1964). We have already seen that numerous state legislatures differ widely from Congress on such features as the seniority system, the experience and status of individual legislators, and the policy-making options available to legislators. No state legislature enjoys the proportion of experienced members who are in the Congress, and none has the staff assistance comparable to the aides of Congress, the Congressional Reference Service in the Library of Congress, or the General Accounting Office. However, the state legislatures do vary from one another in several traits of the members, their staffs, and their activities; and these differences seem to affect both policies and services of several kinds.

Professor John G. Grumm has devised a summary measure for the "professionalism" of each state legislature that takes account of several traits mentioned above: legislators' salary, spending for legislative staff and services, the nature of staff services available, the length of legislative sessions, plus a measure of activity—the number of bills introduced in a session. Table 8-1 ranks the states from the most professional (California, Massachusetts, and New York) to the least professional (Wyoming, Montana, and Idaho) on Grumm's index.

Table 8-1 Legislative Professionalism Index: State Rankings

Calif.	1	Ariz.	26
Mass.	2	Okla.	27
N. Y.	3	Nebr.	28
Pa.	4	Me.	29
Mich.	5	Miss.	30
N. J.	6	Ind.	31
Ill.	7	Colo.	32
Haw.	8	Alas.	33
Wisc.	9	Ky.	34
Tex.	10	Kansas	35
Ohio	11	W. V.	36
Ore.	12	Iowa	37
S. C.	13	Va.	38
Dela.	14	Nev.	39
Fla.	15	Ark.	40
La.	16	S. D.	41
Ga.	17	N. M.	42
Conn.	18	Tenn.	43
Md.	19	Vt.	44
Minn.	20	N. H.	45
Mo.	21	N. D.	46
Wash.	22	Utah	47
Ala.	23	Ida.	48
R. I.	24	Mont.	49
N. C.	25	Wyo.	50

Source: John G. Grumm: "The Effects of Legislative Structure on Legislative Performance," in Richard I. Hofferbert and Ira Sharkansky (eds.), *State and Urban Politics: Readings in Comparative Public Policy* (Boston: Little, Brown and Company, 1971), pp. 298–322.

State scores on professionalism are related to current social and economic conditions as well as to regional histories. High scores coincide with the socioeconomic traits of urbanization, personal income, and industrialization. Perhaps the wealth provided by such an economy encourages the state to spend money on its legislature. The complexity of such an economy and the numerous demands for public services and regulations may generate the large number of bills that characterize a professional legislature. Moreover, the models of efficiency and good practice set by industrial and commercial firms may spill over to the state government. Where prestigious citizens urge good staff work and higher salaries, it may be easy for legislatures to acquire the trappings of a professional body.[41]

Regional histories also relate to the condition of legislatures. Each of the New England states has a large number of legislators, with many bills introduced and passed, and long sessions; but except in Massachusetts, legislators' salaries are low.[42] These findings fit the pattern of hyperactive but amateur law making that has characterized New England since its settlement. Legislatures are an extension of town-meeting democracy in which each settlement is entitled to at least one representative in the colonial (and later state) legislature. Today, the largest legislatures in the country are New Hampshire (424 members), Connecticut (213), Vermont (180), and Massachusetts (280). Rhode Island has a relatively small membership of 149, but even that appears large when compared to the state's area of 1,214 square miles and a population of 947,000. With the exception of Massachusetts, New England salaries are designed for part-time, amateur lawmakers. At the bottom is New Hampshire, with a two-year salary of $200.

The professionalism of state legislatures has some bearing on state policies and performance. High scores on Grumm's index of professionalism go along with generous payments for public aid and unemployment compensation, high salaries for state employees and school teachers, and high spending for police protection and education. Professionalism may reflect the lawmakers' increased capacity to perceive and respond to social and economic conditions.[43]

VARIOUS FUNCTIONS OF AMERICAN LEGISLATURES

While legislators are important actors in the policy delivery system, they also have other responsibilities that are related only indirectly to policy. A record of the tasks that compete for a legislator's time includes:

1   Personal advertisement and campaigning—birthday and condolence letters to constituents, congratulations to graduating high school seniors, news letters, press releases, trips back home.
2   Seeing visitors and shaking hands.
3   Personal service—rectifying bureaucratic injustices; facilitating immigration of relatives of constituents; arranging military leaves, transfers, and hardship releases, helping confused constituents to route their inquiries to the right administrative offices; providing information on social security rights, etc.
4   Participation in national political organizations or campaigns . . .
5   Development of local political organization and leadership . . .[44]

Some political scientists are interested in the full range of legislative activities. However, our concern with the policy delivery system leads us back to those aspects of legislatures that contribute to policy making. In the final sections of this chapter we examine three such aspects: (1) representation of constituents and the issue of apportionment, (2) oversight, and (3) law making.

Representation of Constituents in Policy Making and the Issue of Apportionment

As instruments of democratic government, American legislatures are integrally tied to the concept of representation. Since citizens cannot participate directly in policy making, this power is given to a small group of legislators who, in theory, represent them. Yet democratic theory requires some sort of mechanism by which private citizens can hold representatives accountable. Elections serve as this mechanism; the threat of non-reelection may keep legislators responsive to the public's needs and preferences.

The real nature of this constituent-legislator relationship is difficult to define. Some legislators appear more responsive to organized interest groups than to their constituents; other legislators have sacrificed the interests of some constituents in order to cultivate the support of an incensed faction (e.g., some white, Southern legislators who favor the needs of white constituents over those of blacks).

Legislators differ in the way they define their roles. Some view themselves as "delegates" who should carry the views of constituents into the legislative chamber. Those who see themselves as "trustees," in contrast, feel more independent of the voters; once elected, they expect to use their own judgment, even if some of their decisions run counter to constituents' preferences. Other legislators describe themselves in ways that fit a "politico" model; they are "flexible," shifting between the roles of delegate and trustee, depending on the situation. On those issues of greatest concern to his constituents, the politico may follow their wishes (even if only to avoid difficulties on election day); on those matters which are of little importance in the district, a politico will follow his own convictions.[45]

The Problem of Representation and Apportionment   As we saw above in the discussion of committees, the secrecy that surrounds some decisions may allow a politico to represent some groups in private and their opponents in public. How well do American legislatures represent the people? This issue has been percolating for years. At the state level, it has developed for two reasons. First, a number of state constitutions have called for equal representation of districts regardless of population. Thus, Sussex county's 49,255 residents and Essex county's 923,545 inhabitants each sent one member to the New Jersey State Senate. In California, the 14,196 residents of Mono, Inyo, and Alpine counties each had the same representation in the state senate as did the more than 6 million inhabitants of Los Angeles.

A second problem stemmed from the failure of state officials to reapportion seats in accordance with population shifts. Equally represented districts became sharply out of balance as rural areas became depleted and urban districts more populated. By the 1960s many state legislatures exhibited ludicrous disparities between the districts of largest and smallest sizes. In New Hampshire, the largest district for the lower house had a population 1,081 times that of the smallest district; in Vermont, the ratio was 987 to 1. The greatest disparity in an upper house was in California, where the largest district had a population 422 times that of the smallest. Generally, the cities and suburbs were very underrepresented. In fourteen state legislatures less than 20 percent of the population could elect a majority of the members to one or both houses. Over the country as a whole, one-third of the electorate could choose a majority in over half the state senates and in two-fifths of the lower houses.[46] The representativeness of Congress was also askew. There were four states whose most densely populated congressional districts had 80 percent more people than the least-populous district.[47] In practical terms, this meant that a rural and small-town minority could pack the state houses and Congress with "representatives" prepared to minimize the issues of congestion, pollution, education, welfare, transportation, and racial problems which were besetting the urban majority.

The Solution The apportionment controversy came to a head in the 1962 Supreme Court case of *Baker v. Carr.* In laying the groundwork for a legislative revolution, the Court asserted the right of federal courts to judge cases of apportionment. This decision reversed the Court's position as stated in the 1946 case of *Colgrove v. Green.* Writing for the majority in this earlier case, Justice Felix Frankfurter argued that the "courts ought not to enter this political thicket. The remedy for unfairness in districting is to secure State legislators that will apportion properly, or to invoke the ample powers of Congress."[48]

But the courts did enter this political thicket. In 1964, the Supreme Court returned to this question and decided a group of fifteen companion cases. In this packet, headed by *Reynolds v. Sims*, the Court ruled that representation in all legislative bodies must be based upon population. Applying a "one-man, one-vote" principle, Chief Justice Earl Warren argued:

> Legislators represent people, not trees or acres. Legislators are elected by voters, not farms or cities or economic interests. As long as ours is a representative form of government, and our legislatures are those instruments of government elected directly by and directly representative of the people, the right to elect legislators in a free and unimpaired fashion is a bedrock of our political system.[49]

The Effects of Reapportionment With these decisions, legislatures in most states became vulnerable to challenge. Critics of the Court's
position viewed these decisions as an attack on our constitutional system;
they saw the Court's "interference" in the affairs of legislative bodies as
a blow to the separation of powers and checks and balances. Defenders of
the Court hailed the decisions as landmarks in the development of
representative government. They hoped that reapportionment would
make a reality of political equality (one man, one vote), and that it would
make legislatures more responsive to citizen demands. Reapportionment
was to make the legislatures—and thereby the state and national governments—more sensitive to the needs of hitherto underrepresented urban
(and suburban) areas.

These expectations were not shared by all political scientists.
Thomas R. Dye compared the equity of population apportionment in state
legislatures before 1962 with the nature of state policies and found no
substantial differences between the states that were well and poorly
apportioned in policies for education, welfare, health, highways natural
resources, and taxation. Dye therefore predicted that the individual
state's *economy* was the key; reapportionment itself would have little
effect on policy decisions:

> Most of the policy differences which do occur turn out to be a product of
> socio-economic differences among the states rather than a direct product of
> apportionment practices. Relationships . . . between malapportionment and
> public policy are so slight that reapportionment is not likely to bring about
> any significant policy changes.[50]

Since that prediction, one study of Georgia's experiences suggests
that Dye was premature: changes in districting did have an effect on
legislative personnel and practices. Georgia's case is particularly interesting because it was so lopsided. In one pre-1962 study, it ranked last on a
scale that measured the fairness of apportionment in state legislatures.[51]
Before reapportionment, the most heavily urbanized districts had only 6
seats in the state House and 1 seat in the state Senate. After reapportionment, these districts had 57 seats in the House and 21 in the Senate. The
5-county Atlanta area went from 13 representatives and 4 senators to 46
representatives and 13 senators. The average age of legislators declined
from 51 to 35 years and the number of farmers in the state House declined
from 52 to 36. In the House, the number of legislators with college
experience increased from 69 to 85, and the number of Republicans
increased from 2 to 23. Most strikingly, the number of blacks increased
from 1 to 9. By 1966, there were more blacks in the legislature of Georgia
than any other state in the nation.[52]

It is easier to define changes in the makeup of a legislature than in the policies it enacts. It can take years to enact laws on the spectrum of a state's programs, and even longer to change agency precedents and traditions. By 1966, however, there were some indications in Georgia—in the assignment of urban legislators to leadership positions and in the voting records of urban legislators—that policy changes to favor urban areas were on the way. A post-reapportionment survey found that urban legislators were more liberal than their rural counterparts on issues of jury selection, the expansion of government services, federal aid, and state aid to cities. Urban legislators appeared more often as chamber leaders, chairmen and vice chairmen of key committees, and members of key committees. Also, legislators from urban districts began voting together more often and winning more roll calls than before reapportionment on such urban-oriented issues as the structure of state government; taxation; local government powers; state aid to local governments; and the regulation of business, labor, and the professions.

Two nationwide studies of state legislatures after reapportionment have also shown changes in the allocations of state funds. States now tend to give urban areas more money, particularly in the field of education. Policy changes have been most striking in poor states with safe districts and low voter turnout, low levels of urbanization, education, and minimal legislative professionalism and activity.[53]

Oversight

At the same time that Watergate and its related activities have focused attention on the more sordid aspects of American politics, it has also alerted many people to Congress's ability to investigate the other branches of government. Various committees of the House and Senate have investigated the Watergate break-in, the Nixon administration's use of the Internal Revenue Service as a means of punishing its critics and/or enemies, alleged improprieties by officials of the Securities and Exchange Commission, the administration's handling of the Russian wheat deal, the administration's secret policy of bombing Cambodia without congressional authorization, and alleged concessions given to ITT and milk producers in exchange for campaign contributions.

Legislative investigations cover a variety of questions. Are laws being correctly interpreted and enforced? How do government programs affect particular individuals and groups? Are existing laws and programs appropriate for current needs and conditions? Are any groups or individuals exceeding their authority? We have already described the work of the GAO in reviewing the spending of government agencies. In reviewing the administration's activities, congressmen and their aides uncover waste and abuse, push particular projects and innovations, highlight inconsis-

tencies, correct injustices, and compel the exposure and defense of
bureaucratic decisions.[54]

> . . . it is a major means for legislators to secure information on the operation
> of the administration and the impact of public policy. Legislators may
> uncover instances of callous, arbitrary or capricious administrative actions,
> or areas of discontent and dissatisfaction within the public may come to light.
> Because it exists as a "watchdog" over the administration, the legislature
> also exists as a sounding board for those interest groups who feel the
> administration is not sympathetic toward them. Finally, monitoring is a
> weapon which Congress can utilize in its rivalry with the administration to
> force respect and recognition for its position and powers.[55]

Law Making

We began this chapter by noting the erosion of legislative prestige and
power. Some commentators feel that legislators merely respond to
proposals initiated by the executive—whether the governor or the President. Some have gone further, arguing that executives not only dominate legislative agendas but also determine the legislature's response.

At the national level, this view received support from a congressional
committee in 1962. Viewing its role as one of acquiescence, the committee
observed:

> To any student of government, it is eminently clear that the role of the
> Congress in determining national policy, defense or otherwise, has deteri-
> orated over the years. More and more the role of Congress has come to be
> that of a sometimes querulous but essentially kindly uncle who complains
> while furiously puffing on his pipe but who finally, as everyone expects, gives
> in and hands over the allowance, grants the permission, or raises his hand in
> blessing, and then returns to the rocking chair for another year of somno-
> lence broken only by an occasional anxious glance down the avenue and a
> muttered doubt as to whether he had done the right thing.[56]

Yet the events of the past decade suggest at least a partial lessening
of paralysis. The war in Laos, Cambodia, and Vietnam inspired Congress
to challenge the President's leadership in the areas of defense and foreign
affairs. In 1969, the Senate fell one vote short of cutting off funding for the
administration's ABM system. In both 1969 and 1970, Congress limited
the use of government funds to support combat troops in Cambodia,
Laos, and Thailand. In 1971, the President speeded up a cutback in
military strength because of congressional limits on the size of the army.
After numerous efforts to restrict the President's war-making powers,
Congress passed, in 1973, a "war powers bill" that placed a sixty-day limit

on any presidential commitment of U.S. troops abroad without specific congressional authorization. In November 1973, both houses voted to override the President's earlier veto of this measure.

An emerging assertiveness of Congress also appears in other policy areas. Presidents Johnson and Nixon both had nominees for Supreme Court Justices rejected by the Senate. In the period preceding his resignation, Congress twice "persuaded" President Nixon to appoint an independent prosecutor to handle Watergate-related investigations. Efforts to reform our system of campaign financing have generally come more from Congress than from the White House. *Newsweek* reflected the mood of Congress in its review of 1973 activities:

> To hear Richard Nixon tell it, the 93rd was a do-nothing Congress, much more interested in wallowing in Watergate than in carrying out the nation's business—and there was no denying that the White House scandals were Topic A on Capitol Hill for most of the year. But as Congress closed its first session last week and headed home for the holidays, its members had put in nearly 2,000 hours in debate, racked up a new record for roll-call votes—and enacted a staggering total of more than 200 new laws.

> The dominant theme of the session was the continuing clash between the White House and the Democratic majority on the Hill. Some of Congress's most conspicuous activities reflected the President's scandal problems: the Watergate committee hearings, the confirmation of Gerald Ford as Vice President and the first steps toward impeachment. But others grew out of a struggle for power that had been brewing long before Watergate—and Congress managed to exploit the President's problems to reverse a long slide toward ineffectuality. In foreign affairs, the Congress reaffirmed its policymaking role by forcing an end to U.S. bombing in Cambodia and by putting sharp new limits on the President's war-making powers. Domestically, the clash centered on the White House tactic of "impounding" funds authorized by Congress—and after losing a string of court decisions, White House aides showed a new interest in compromise.

> Congress also passed landmark legislation ranging from agricultural subsidies to last week's 11 per cent hike in social-security benefits. The legislators moved to streamline their own budgeting procedures, and the House took a major step toward internal reform by limiting the role seniority plays in the choice of committee chairmen. . . .[57]

One can only speculate about the future policy-making role of Congress. The new search for congressional leadership derives largely from Vietnam and Watergate. As the Executive became embroiled in unpopular military policies and domestic scandals that seemed endless, the Congress was handed numerous opportunities to reassert itself. But as Vietnam and Watergate are resolved and become less pressing problems, Congress will most likely face a revitalized White House. The unity of the Executive and its greater access to information, publicity, and—in the case of foreign affairs—sheer power may make it difficult for Congress to assert itself except in those instances when, as in Vietnam and Watergate, the Executive weakens itself by overreaching its own considerable strength.

SUMMARY

This is the first of four chapters that deal with the major branches of American governments. In the legislature, we see an institution that seemed initially to be the primary source—and threat—of policy. In the 200 years since Independence, however, legislatures have been challenged and eclipsed by executive and administrative branches that possess the specialization and technical expertise demanded by public service today.

The legislature's eclipse is worldwide. In many respects, American legislatures, especially Congress, have withstood this erosion fairly well. When we compare the status, powers, and aides of Congress to those of state legislatures and city councils, we get some clues to the staying power of Congress. Membership in that body still commands political prestige, and thus attracts high-caliber politicians willing to devote their careers to it and become experts in one or more areas. Members of the House and Senate also surround themselves with well-trained and well-paid personal and committee staffs, the Congressional Reference Service, and the General Accounting Office. Some *state* legislatures have gone further than others in attracting able members and providing them with assistance; and these professional legislatures have left their mark on state programs in such fields as welfare, education, and public safety.

Not all the concerns of legislators deal directly with public policy. Indeed, the diversity of their interests and energy is one factor that keeps legislators from being more forceful policy makers. However, although many legislators do not see themselves essentially as lawmakers, they nevertheless contribute significantly to the policy delivery system. They may give their constituents the feeling that someone is looking after their interests; they may prod bureaucrats to reexamine a constituent's case; or they may uncover injustice, inefficiency, and inconsistency in administrative practices.

From a policy-making perspective, three legislative issues have been prominent. *Representation of constituents in policy making and legislative reapportionment* was the central issue in the legislative reapportionment controversy of the 1960s. By making Congress and the state legislatures more representative of their populations, this controversy may strengthen them in relation to other branches. There is some evidence that state legislatures are now more responsive to the demands of urban residents. although reformers may still feel that there is a long way to go. *Administrative oversight* permits legislators to judge the implementation and impact of public policy, and to control the abuses of administrators or executives. Oversight allows legislators to identify areas where existing programs are inadequate and gives them an opportunity to prod the other branches. Finally, there is *law making.* Conventional wisdom has it that legislatures make few waves; they discuss and ratify proposals initiated by the executive. If such a view has always been somewhat unrealistic, it is particularly so today. Legislatures are currently experiencing a period of revitalization, although they have not yet acquired the prestige and power of the executive and the bureaucracy. The legislatures' strengths may depend on temporary declines in the strength of other branches.

REFERENCES

1 Warren Weaver, Jr., *Both Your Houses: The Truth about Congress* (New York: Frederick A. Praeger, Inc., 1972), p. 3.
2 Samuel P. Huntington, "Congressional Responses to the Twentieth Century," in David B. Truman (ed.), *The Congress and America's Future*, 2d ed. (Englewood Cliffs, N.J.: Prentice-Hall, Inc., 1973), pp. 6–38.
3 The "such Persons" referred to in this clause were slaves.
4 Joseph S. Clark, *Congress: The Sapless Branch* (New York: Colophon Books, Harper & Row, Publishers, Incorporated, 1965), p. 22.
5 Ibid., p. 24.
6 Ibid., p. 25.
7 Taylor Branch, "Profiles in Caution," *Harper's Magazine* (July 1973), p. 63.
8 Citizens Conference on State Legislatures, *The Sometime Governments: A Critical Study of the 50 American Legislatures* (New York: Bantam Books, Inc., 1971), pp. 2, 23–24.
9 Committee for Economic Development, *Modernizing State Government* (New York: Committee for Economic Development, 1967), p. 32.
10 Citizens Conference on State Legislatures, op. cit., p. 59.
11 David Ogle, *Strengthening the Connecticut Legislature*, A Report of the Eagleton Institute of Politics (New Brunswick, N.J.: Rutgers University Press, 1970), p. 230. Copyright © 1970 by Rutgers University, the State University of New Jersey. Reprinted by permission of the Rutgers University Press.
12 Wallace Sayre and Herbert Kaufman, *Governing New York City* (New York: W. W. Norton & Company, Inc., 1965), p. 611.
13 Martin Arnold, "City Councilman: Man in a 'Wind Tunnel,'" as published in Duane Lockard, *Governing the States and Localities*; *Selected Readings* (New York: The Macmillan Company, 1969), p. 164.
14 The following quotations are taken from Peter Yessne (ed.), *Quotations from Mayor Daley* (New York: Bantam Books, Inc., 1970), pp. 5, 92, 94.
15 Mike Royko, *Boss: Richard J. Daley of Chicago* (New York: E. P. Dutton &

Co., Inc., 1970), pp. 13–14. Copyright © 1971 by Mike Royko. Reprinted by permission of the publishers, E. P. Dutton & Co., Inc.

16 See his "introduction" in Clark, op. cit., pp. vii–viii.

17 See Malcolm E. Jewell and Samuel C. Patterson, *The Legislative Process in the United States* (New York: Random House, Inc., 1966), pp. 108, 115.

18 Huntington, op. cit., p. 15.

19 Ibid, pp. 17–18.

20 Kenneth Prewitt, *The Recruitment of Political Leaders: A Study of Citizen-Politicians* (Indianapolis: The Bobbs-Merrill Company, Inc., 1970), p. 36.

21 Willis D. Hawley, *Nonpartisan Elections and the Case for Party Politics* (New York: John Wiley & Sons, Inc., 1973).

22 Lewis A. Froman, Jr., *The Congressional Process: Strategies, Rules, and Procedures* (Boston: Little, Brown and Company, 1967), pp. 12–15.

23 Richard Fenno, Jr., *The Power of the Purse: Appropriations Politics in Congress* (Boston: Little, Brown and Company, 1966), p. 578.

24 Duane Lockard, *The Perverted Priorities of American Politics* (New York: The Macmillan Company, 1971), pp. 130–131.

25 Woodrow Wilson, *Congressional Government* (New York: Meridian Books, Inc., 1956), p. 69.

26 Richard Fenno, Jr., "The Internal Distribution of Influence: The House," in David B. Truman (ed.), *The Congress and America's Future*, 2d ed. (Englewood Cliffs, N.J.: Prentice-Hall, Inc., 1973), p. 65.

27 Mark J. Green, James M. Fallows, and David R. Zwich, *Who Runs Congress?*, Ralph Nader Congress Project, (New York: Bantam Books, Inc. / Grossman Publishers, 1972), p. 64.

28 Nicholas Masters, "Committee Assignments in The House of Representatives," *American Political Science Review* (June 1961), pp. 345–357.

29 Green et al., op. cit., p. 55.

30 Fenno, "The Internal Distribution of Influence: The House," p. 77.

31 John Manley, "Wilbur Mills: A Study in Congressional Influence," *American Political Science Review* (June 1969), p. 464.

32 Richard Fenno, Jr., *Congressmen in Committees* (Boston: Little, Brown and Company, 1973), pp. 114–137. Copyright 1973 © by Little, Brown and Company (Inc.). Reprinted by permission.

33 Barbara Hinckley, *Stability and Change in Congress* (New York: Harper & Row, Publishers, Incorporated, 1971), p. 76.

34 Barbara Hinckley, *The Seniority System in Congress* (Bloomington: Indiana University Press, 1971), p. 82.

35 John F. Bibby and Roger H. Davidson, *On Capitol Hill*, 2d ed. (Hindsdale, Ill,: The Dryden Press, Inc., 1967), p. 174.

36 Fenno, "The Internal Distribution of Influence: The House," p. 69.

37 Herbert B. Asher, "The Learning of Legislative Norms," *American Political Science Review* (June 1973), p. 449.

38 See ibid., p. 503; and Hinckley, *Stability and Change in Congress*, p. 63.

39 See Richard E. Brown, *The GAO: Untapped Source of Congressional Powers* (Knoxville: University of Tennessee Press, 1970).

40 U.S., Senate, *The Philadelphia Plan: Congressional Oversight of Administra-*

tive Agencies (The Department of Labor), Hearings before the Subcommittee on Separation of Powers of the Committee on the Judiciary, 91st Cong., 1st sess., Act 27–28, 1969, p. 133.

41   See John G. Grumm, "The Effects of Legislative Structure on Legislative Performance," in Richard I. Hofferbert and Ira Sharkansky (ed.), *State and Urban Politics: Readings in Comparative Public Policy* (Boston: Little, Brown and Company, 1971), pp. 298–322.

42   See Ira Sharkansky, *Regionalism in American Politics* (Indianapolis: The Bobbs-Merrill Company, Inc., 1970), chaps. 3 and 6.

43   See Grumm, op. cit.; and Herbert B. Asher and Donald S. Van Meter, "Determinants of Public Welfare Policies: A Causal Approach," *Sage Professional Papers in American Politics* (Beverly Hills: Sage Publications, 1970), 104–109.

44   Raymond A. Bauer, Ithiel de Sola Pool, and Lewis Anthony Dexter, *American Business and Public Policy: The Politics of Foreign Trade* (New York: Atherton Press, Inc., 1967), pp. 409–410.

45   This discussion of legislative roles relies on Duane Lockard, "The State Legislator," in Alexander Heard (ed.), *State Legislatures in American Politics* (Englewood Cliffs, N.J.: Prentice-Hall, Inc., 1966), pp. 98–125; James David Barber, *The Lawmakers: Recruitment and Adaptation to Legislative Life* (New Haven, Conn.: Yale University Press, 1965); and John C. Wahlke et al., *The Legislative System* (New York: John Wiley & Sons, Inc., 1962).

46   Malcolm E. Jewell, *The State Legislature: Politics and Practice* (New York: Random House, Inc., 1969), p. 17.

47   *Representation and Apportionment* (Washington: Congressional Quarterly Service, 1966), p. 87.

48   *Colegrove v. Green*, 328 U.S. 549 (1946).

49   *Reynolds v. Sims*, 377 U.S. 533 (1964).

50   Thomas R. Dye, *Politics, Economics, and the Public: Policy Outcomes in the American States* (Chicago: Rand McNally, 1966), p. 280.

51   Charles Press and Glendon Schubert, "Measuring Malapportionment," *The American Political Science Review*, vol. 18 (December 1964), pp. 969–970.

52   See Brett W. Hawkins, "Consequences of Reapportionment in Georgia," in Richard I. Hofferbert and Ira Sharkansky (ed.), *State and Urban Politics: Readings in Comparative Public Policy* (Boston: Little, Brown and Company, 1971), pp. 273–297.

53   See Donald S. Van Meter, *The Policy Implications of State Legislative Reapportionment: A Longitudinal Analysis,* unpublished Ph.D. dissertation, University of Wisconsin, 1972; and H. George Frederickson and Yong Hyo Cho, "Legislative Reapportionment and Public Policy in the American States," a paper given at the 1970 meeting of the American Political Science Association, Los Angeles.

54   Huntington, op. cit., pp. 31–32.

55   Dale Vinyard, *Congress* (New York: Charles Scribner's Sons, 1968), p. 29.

56   *House Report 1406*, 87th Cong., 2d sess., 1962, p. 7.

57   *Newsweek*, Dec. 31, 1973, p. 12. Copyright Newsweek, Inc. 1973. Reprinted by permission.

Chapter 9

Executive Politics and Policy Making

With the sudden deaths of Presidents Franklin Roosevelt and John Kennedy, many Americans experienced strong emotional responses and a sense of personal loss. When President Lyndon Johnson announced in 1968 that he would neither seek nor accept nomination for another term of office, the intensity of the public response—whether elation or anger—also indicated that this was no ordinary political event. And few issues have aroused the public as has the Watergate affair, with Richard Nixon's resignation after disclosing his complicity in illegal acts. Each of these incidents cut deeply into the awareness of people throughout the nation because each involved the individual whom most Americans see as the chief architect and protector of government—the President of the United States.

The President's popular image as "the great engine of democracy," the "American people's one authentic trumpet," and "probably the most important governmental institution in the world" is well established. The President is the most powerful figure in American politics. With his legal authority and extensive staff assistance, the President has enough policy-making power to match, and probably surpass, that of Congress. In most instances, his capacity to name the administrators of government programs is greater than that of any other person. The President gets much of the attention that is given to national political affairs by the mass media, the public, and officials of other governments.

As a consequence of his image, the President is the object of the highest expectations. We expect presidents to protect us from foreign hostility, guard against economic deprivation, and preserve social harmony. When wars become unpopular, economic crises severe, and social tensions explosive, it is the President whom we hold most responsible. And given these expectations, it is not surprising that public confidence in President Nixon would fall so much in the wake of Watergate.

One writer has portrayed this image of an all-powerful President in the following manner:

> Franklin D. Roosevelt personally rescued the nation from the depths of the great Depression. Roosevelt, together with Harry Truman, brought World War II to a proud conclusion. Courageous Truman personally committed us to resist Communist aggression around the globe. General Eisenhower pledged that as President he would "go to Korea" and end that war—and he did. These are prevailing images that most American school children read and remember. For convenience, if not for simplicity, textbooks label certain periods as the "Wilson years," the "Hoover depression," the "Roosevelt revolution," the "Eisenhower period," and so forth.[1]

With the agony of Vietnam and Watergate, this idealized image of the President has come under increasing attack in recent years. Popular mythology often exaggerates the President's powers and capabilities; there are many problems, both international and domestic, over which he has little control. The ironic contrast between the authority of the President and his actual capacity to shape policy is one of the great fascinations of American politics. The President is formally the Commander in Chief of the Armed Forces, though this does not mean that he controls the activities of all military personnel. All administrative officials are theoretically answerable to the President, but this does not guarantee that they will respond to his preferences and directives.

Many of the observations about the President can be applied—at a greatly reduced scale—to chief executives of state and local governments. Their legal authority and staff aides are generally equal to or greater than those of their legislative branches. They are the single most important policy makers in their governments, though, like the President, they have no assurance that their legal authority will yield actual power.

In this chapter we examine the role of American chief executives in their policy delivery systems. We inquire into the constitutional basis and historical development of the Presidency. We also discuss the relationship between the President and other political actors, and the ever-expanding White House staff, which serves as a source of information, as a means of achieving the President's objectives, and recently as a considerable embarrassment. We use the President as a standard of comparison for the governors of the fifty states and the mayors and managers of cities. As in the treatment of legislatures, we find that executive offices of states and localities pale in contrast with the national model. Not only does the President's economic, military, and political influence extend around the world, but he has more power within his government departments than do governors, mayors, and managers within theirs. In contrast to the President, most state and local executives are more limited in selecting their important subordinates, allocating funds to existing programs, and designing new activities. They must share more of their legal authority and political power with other officials, whose positions are relatively independent of their own.

CONSTITUTIONAL AND HISTORICAL ROOTS OF THE PRESIDENCY

Any analysis of the President's role in the policy delivery system that focused exclusively upon constitutional provisions would be grossly inadequate. Article II of the original Constitution, and the Twelfth, Twentieth, Twenty-second, Twenty-third, and Twenty-fifth Amendments concern his office, dealing mainly with his selection and tenure.[2] Those concerning his formal authority are generally ambiguous. For example, Article II stipulates that all "executive power shall be vested in the President of the United States," but at no point does the Constitution tell us what "executive power" is. Article II also states that the President shall nominate and, with the "advice and consent" of the Senate, appoint a variety of federal officials; but nowhere is there any mention of the President's authority to remove these officials once in office. Elsewhere in the Constitution we find statements indicating that Congress—but not the President—has authority to declare war and to control the appropriation of federal funds. Yet, these provisions were of cold comfort to a Congress confronted with a raging war in Southeast Asia that it had not declared and a President's refusal to spend funds that it had authorized. It is obvious that to understand the sources of the President's power, we must look beyond the original Constitution and its twenty-six amendments.

The language of the Constitution provides a series of empty vessels which could have evolved into either weak or strong grants of power. At least some framers of the Constitution wanted a Chief Executive with severely limited powers. During their colonial years, the American people had come to fear the tyrannical and repressive power of some colonial governors and other representatives of the British crown. As we have already noted, the founding fathers deliberately created a fragmented political system with protections against the growth of tyranny from any one branch.

Yet, by the time of the Constitutional Conventions in 1787, after ten years of chaos, the men who met in Philadelphia recognized the need to make the President a more powerful figure than had existed under the Articles of Confederation. As its name suggests, that former government was a loose confederation of state governments. Congress was the dominant body in the national government, but it depended on the voluntary cooperation of state officials to take any important action. There was no full-time national executive. When Congress was not in session, a "committee of states" (consisting of one legislator from each state) ran the government. This committee named one of its members as the chief executive, though he had little power and was limited to a single one-year term.

The political confusion that characterized the period of the Articles of Confederation demonstrated the need for a strong executive to provide for the common defense, facilitate economic growth and stability, and maintain social order and tranquility. As Alexander Hamilton asserted:

> Energy in the executive is a leading character in the definition of good government. It is essential to the protection of the community against foreign attacks; it is not less essential to the steady administration of the laws; to the protection of property against those irregular and high-handed combinations which sometimes interrupt the ordinary course of justice; to the security of liberty against the enterprises and assaults of ambition, of faction, and of anarchy. . . . A government ill executed, whatever it may be in theory, must be, in practice, a bad government.[3]

Hamilton also wrote that elements of a strong executive are "unity; duration; an adequate provision for its support; and competent powers."[4] The Constitution provided unity by creating a single President rather than government by committee; it provided duration by a term of four years without any limitation on self-succession (which changed only with the ratification of the Twenty-second Amendment in 1951). "Adequate" support, however, depended on the cooperation of a Senate willing to accept almost all the President's appointees and a Congress willing to provide the personnel and funds he wanted. Hamilton's notion of "competent powers" is not spelled out in the Constitution; it depended on a combination of a strong President and a relatively weak legislature. These two tendencies began in the administration of George Washington and have developed sporadically from then until now.

The ambiguities in the Constitution are partly a result of its authors' cross purposes. Conflicts at the Constitutional Convention often led to compromised, vague, and imprecise provisions. One effect of this ambiguity has been flexibility; various Presidents were able to redefine their role in the policy delivery system. And though the evolution of the Presidency has been uneven, the trend has been toward the expansion of its powers. George Washington's staff of aides bears no resemblance to the huge Executive Office today (see pages 248–253). Early Presidents exercised little direct control over the country's economic affairs. Twentieth-century Presidents reshape our social and economic lives through New Deals, Square Deals, New Frontiers, and Great Societies; impose wage and price controls; establish import quotas and export subsidies; and initiate other policies designed to protect and stimulate the American economy. The President's role as Commander in Chief originally meant only that he could choose the generals who were responsible for developing and carrying out battlefield strategies. Today the President has, apart from the heads of the Armed Forces, his own military brain trust—the National Security Council. He can plan the conduct of military affairs that begin and end without formal declarations by Congress. Recent examples include the Kennedy administration's Bay of Pigs, the dispatch of troops to the Dominican Republic under Lyndon Johnson—and, of course, Vietnam. This enlargement of the Presidency reflects, in part, the enormously increased role of the national government in the twentieth century. The responsibilities of all government officials, including the President, have expanded as government activity has grown. But the role of the President as compared with that of other government officials has also expanded greatly since George Washington's day, and most strikingly since the Great Depression.

THE CONTEMPORARY PRESIDENCY

The proper role of the President in the policy system has been a subject of great controversy. Only a few years ago, political scientists tended to applaud a strong President. As the only official elected by the whole country and as head of his political party, he was supposedly in the best position to provide leadership for policy making across the areas separated from each other by checks and balances. More recently, in the Nixon administration, Americans became accustomed to hearing about grave constitutional crises centering on the war powers shared by the President and Congress; the President's exercise of "executive privilege" during the Watergate investigations; and the President's impounding of funds earmarked by Congress for highway, urban, and pollution-control programs. Even though the Constitution created a system of divided authority, the growing dominance of the President has altered any balance that existed earlier.

The President's dramatic increase in power is directly linked to the growing role of the United States in world affairs. Since World War II, we have faced one major international involvement after another, with each one seeming to increase the President's role in foreign affairs. On the domestic side, however, his powers have not grown so greatly, for reasons which will become clear in the next paragraph. The events of Fall 1973 illustrate this contrast beautifully. While President Nixon's domestic proposals virtually disappeared under the pressure of Watergate and related matters, he was able to take decisive actions independent of Congress after the Yom Kippur War: calling a worldwide military alert; beginning a massive logistical operation to resupply Israel; and initiating negotiations, via Henry Kissinger, between Israel and the Arabs.

While it is too simple to say that the President controls the policy delivery system, it is appropriate to conclude that he dominates it. The President's role has expanded far beyond that described in the Constitution. This document lists five presidential functions: the ceremonial head of the government, the Chief Executive, the Commander in Chief of the Armed Forces, the chief diplomat, and the legislative leader. In reality, the President exercises power by his leadership of several important constituencies: the federal bureaucracy, his political party, a variety of interest groups, and officials of other governments who see him as the embodiment of his own government, and—especially when his party is in control of it—Congress.[5] He is the primary molder of public opinion, the keeper of domestic peace and tranquility, the foremost guardian of the economy, and the leader of an international coalition.[6] In looking to the President for leadership, each of his constituencies permits him to influence their affairs in exchange for his help. Yet in so doing, it also hedges his capacity for action. In this give-and-take process, he cannot take initiatives in many policy areas without taking into account the preferences and demands of other actors. Consider what happened when President Johnson wanted to request a 10 percent surcharge on corporate and personal income taxes:

[He] waited 19 months after his economic advisers recommended increasing taxes before asking Congress to pass the tax surcharge. Early in 1966, the president could find little support in the country or in Congress for a recommended tax increase. Rather than try to persuade the public and Congress to accept one and risk what he feared most—renewed confrontations between the hawks and the doves over Vietnam—the president and his advisers devised a package of piecemeal fiscal measures to control excessive demand. . . . By the summer of 1967, increased government spending for Vietnam had intensified the inflationary condition of the economy, so that the president had no other reasonable choice but to propose a tax increase.[7]

In trying to serve any one of his constituencies, a President must reckon with the implications of his every action for many others. A decision to seek a compromise with congressional critics on an important policy question (e.g., the use of busing to achieve school desegregation) must not clash so much with powerful interest groups that he will lose their support on other occasions. In considering actions designed to protect American economic interests (e.g., controls on imports or exports), the President must anticipate the responses of foreign governments, which see themselves as the targets of such policies.

While the President can be said to dominate the policy delivery system, his powers are not without limitation. As we have just noted, some of the very elements that expand his influence also limit his capacity to use it. Furthermore, with so much power and so many problems, the President must decide which issues to delegate and which to concentrate on himself. During the past thirty years, the President's job has focused increasingly on international activities. The great preoccupations have been World War II, the cold war, Korea, the Middle East, Cuba, Southeast Asia—and all the while keeping up with or trying to solve the problem of the arms race and maintaining our international political relationships. The time and energy left for domestic concerns have been limited to a small number of highly visible issues: medicare, desegregation, federal aid to education, economic growth and stability, and public welfare. In other areas, and to a considerable extent even in these highly visible ones, the President has depended heavily upon other actors—members of the White House staff, federal administrators, and members of Congress.

PRESIDENTIAL PERSUASION

It is not sufficient to list the powers and responsibilities of the President. Knowing something about *what* the President is tells us little about *how* he achieves his goals and objectives and provides no assurance of his success. Fundamental questions remain: How can the President best lead? How can he make his will felt within the policy delivery system?

In answer to these questions, Richard Neustadt has argued that "presidential power is the power to persuade." Since the President's formal authority does not guarantee his exercise of power, he must convince other actors in the system that his goals deserve their support or that his interests are also theirs: "The essence of a President's persuasive task, with congressmen and everybody else, *is to induce them to believe that what he wants of them is what their own appraisal of their own responsibilities requires them to do in their interest, not his*."[8]

The separation of powers and the divided authority of the policy delivery system make it necessary for the President to become an expert at persuasion. He cannot command Congress to approve his legislative proposals; he cannot even be sure that administrative officials—his supposed subordinates—will obey his orders. During his last months in office, President Truman looked ahead to the Eisenhower administration and wondered how a well-disciplined general would accommodate himself to such a situation: "He'll sit here, and he'll say, 'Do this! Do that!' *And nothing will happen*. Poor Ike—it won't be a bit like the Army. He'll find it very frustrating."[9]

A President's persuasiveness depends upon his skill as a bargainer. Three factors are particularly important here: (1) the bargaining position of the office; (2) the President's professional reputation; and (3) his public prestige.[10] The President enjoys an advantage in most bargaining situations. Bargaining involves an exchange of values; thus, one who has many negotiable resources is in a better position to gain concessions than one who has few. The President's resources are extensive: he can make appointments to federal offices, endorse an incumbent seeking reelection, support programs favored by interest groups, and offer economic and military aid to other nations. In the hands of a skillful President, these resources can help persuade others that what he wants is what their own responsibilities and interests require them to do.

A President's bargaining power also depends on his professional reputation—how other actors in the system view his use of the resources at his disposal. President Johnson's reputation as an effective congressional leader provided him with a reservoir of support when he entered the White House in 1963. Later, however, growing opposition to the war in Southeast Asia eroded his leadership position. Similarly, while President Nixon's handling of the war won him the support of many officials, his apparent unwillingness or inability to cope with the Watergate scandal seriously damaged his bargaining position and ultimately brought down his Presidency.

The President's bargaining success also reflects his public prestige and popularity. In responding to the President's efforts at persuasion, constituents are sensitive to his reputation. During the first three years of the Nixon administration, some congressmen were slow to oppose the President's policies in Vietnam since public acceptance of his actions was high; at that point, their criticism could only lead to trouble with their own constituencies. In contrast, as Nixon's popularity dropped in the wake of Watergate their opposition became much more free and outspoken.

While subject to many pressures and constraints at home, the President is relatively free in determining foreign policy. Presidents often find their domestic programs thwarted by a hostile Congress, dissident party leaders, or passive citizens. Yet they seldom fail to gain support in the area of defense and foreign affairs.

Why is the President's position superior here? One reason is the nature of foreign policy concerns. They frequently involve crisis situations that require a quick response (e.g., the Soviet placement of missiles in Cuba or Vietcong attacks on South Vietnamese villages). The President, as Commander in Chief, has the formal authority to act; and once he has acted, it is difficult for Congress to restrict him. Further, public opinion polls show that voters are rarely knowledgeable about foreign affairs. They expect the President to act and depend upon him for information. And while numerous interest groups are busy trying to sway the President on domestic policies, in defense and foreign affairs he has a relatively clear field. There is less interest in and information about foreign affairs, and pressure groups are less likely—and less able—to mobilize public or congressional opposition to the President's policies.[11]

THE INSTITUTIONALIZED PRESIDENCY: THE EXECUTIVE OFFICE

The White House Office (WHO)

One of the more fascinating trends in the policy delivery system has been the institutionalization of the American Presidency. When we talk of the Presidency, we are speaking not of one individual but rather of an assortment of groups and persons organized around the President to give him information and advice, and to help with the many details of presidential life. The White House Office includes the President's most intimate staff in the extensive Executive Office. The President's staff is a most significant resource. Besides providing him with information on a variety of activities and problems, its members represent him in meetings; write speeches and draft bills; screen individuals and groups who would monopolize his time; coordinate the activities of administrators outside the White House; negotiate with legislators, agencies, business firms, and foreign governments; and check to see how his directives are carried out.

Only forty years ago, President Franklin Roosevelt dealt with the Great Depression, and other responsibilities of the Presidency, with six aides and a small number of clerical assistants. Understandably, his Committee on Administrative Management reported in 1937 that "the President has too much to do" and recommended an expanded Executive Office of the President.[12] Roosevelt made additional appointments, transferred the Bureau of the Budget from the Treasury Department to the new unit, and thus began a process of executive growth that now employs thousands and spends millions. By 1974, the White House Office had grown to about 600 persons and accounted for some $12 million of government spending.

One result of this growth is that the White House staff has replaced the Cabinet as the President's primary source of information and advice. The President's closest associates have been men like Harry Hopkins (Roosevelt); Sherman Adams (Eisenhower); Theodore Sorenson (Kennedy); Bill Moyers and Jack Valenti (Johnson); and Henry Kissinger, John Ehrlichman, and H.R. Haldeman (Nixon), who occupied advisory positions and only later (i.e., Hopkins and Kissinger) joined the Cabinet. The power of these officials appears in the comment of a former White House aide who responded, when asked if he was interested in running for the United States Senate: "I had more power over national affairs in a few years in the White House than I could if I spent the rest of my life in the Senate."[13]

The Executive Office is a mixed blessing. On the positive side, staff assistance provides the President with the information and tools to strengthen his position in relation to other policy makers. On the negative side, the President can become a servant to his staff, devoting large amounts of time to directing them. Even more troublesome, the staff can isolate the President from other parts of the system, and from reality itself: "Presidential aides, attuned to his style and thoughts, may become simply 'yes' men, fearing that negative thoughts or challenges to presidential thinking may imperil their standing and career."[14] In this context, one cannot help but think of President Johnson, whose aides were slow to alert him to the rapidly deteriorating conditions in South Vietnam for fear that their reports and recommendations would be rejected or their careers endangered. Even more, one is reminded of the so-called White House horrors described during the 1973–1974 Watergate investigations. The break-ins at the Democratic national headquarters were planned, according to President Nixon, without his approval or knowledge. Watergate may finally prove the truth of a criticism made more and more often: that the White House staff has grown beyond the President's capacity to control its activities or beyond a citizen's ability to know whom to hold responsible for wrongdoing.

Every President is free to organize and use his advisors in a manner that suits his own style. Franklin Roosevelt built a system of "creative chaos," whereby aides were given overlapping and sometimes conflicting assignments. There were no meaningful chains of command, and aides found themselves shifted from one area of activity to another without explanation. Roosevelt delighted in this game of keeping his people a little off balance, on guard; presumably, the creative juices would flow more freely when people were not allowed to become smug and secure in their jobs. Further, Roosevelt was more likely to hear of trouble on a program when he assigned different aides to the same post, keeping them in competition with one another. In contrast, Dwight Eisenhower, the former Army general, established a hierarchy in which aides had well-defined and specialized responsibilities, numerous committee assignments, and little direct access to the President. Presidents Kennedy and Johnson established staffs that resembled Roosevelt's more than Eisenhower's, though they lacked some of the free-wheeling, chaotic traits of Roosevelt's creation. Nixon, like Eisenhower, left much to the discretion of such aides as Haldeman and Ehrlichman. And, as in Eisenhower's sorry experiences with Sherman Adams (who departed under allegations of influence peddling), Nixon encountered serious problems when his key people ran afoul of public confidence.

The Office of Management and Budget (OMB)

This is the executive unit with the most awesome collection of formal powers. First, it prepares the President's budget and defends it before congressional committees. Since the OMB works on a year-round, full-time basis, its well-researched facts and figures constitute a formidable weapon. In discussing finances with the President, Congress has no comparable source of information—and often wishes it had. The OMB screens administrative requests before they are transmitted to Congress; no administrator can make a financial request of Congress that has not been cleared through the OMB. Since Congress is allowed to grant more funds for a unit than had been requested by the OMB, an administrator's budget may sometimes be larger after Congress has finished with it. In this event, the OMB has another weapon: it controls the allocation of funds from the Treasury to the agencies, so it can prevent an agency from spending more money than it had originally recommended. Finally, the OMB is the unit that actually impounds funds when directed to by the President.

Outside the financial area, the OMB has certain controls over the statutory authority of each department. Before any administrator can ask for new legislation, or even reply formally to a congressman's inquiry about new legislation, he must clear his communication through the OMB. It circulates the proposed communication to other agencies whose programs might be affected by the proposal, and then gathers opinions and defines the implications of the proposal for other features of presidential policy. Without a favorable evaluation from the OMB, a government agency cannot formally support a measure being considered in Congress. The OMB cannot stop Congress from granting to departments powers that had not initially been approved. However, the Office *can* act again after Congress has completed its work. While a measure is awaiting presidential action, the Office circulates it to relevant agencies, gathers their opinions, and then prepares a recommendation for the President's veto or approval.

The Council of Economic Advisers (CEA)

This group consists of three professional economists, plus a staff of assistants. The three professionals are appointed by the President with the consent of the Senate. The CEA traces its origin to the Employment Act of 1946 and is one of the instruments established by that act to give the federal government responsibility for supervising, and hopefully controlling, the nation's economy. The most prominent activity of the Council is the compilation of the annual *Economic Report of the President*. In this and other reports, the Council assesses the current state of economic growth and stability, balance of payments, and other international matters; appraises likely impacts on the economy from certain policy proposals; and recommends corrective measures for inflation, recession, or other symptoms of economic distress. The Council has no direct role in the implementation of policy. However, its advice on the economic implications of current or proposed activities affects policy decisions taken by the Office of Management and Budget and the President.

The National Security Council (NSC)

The Council has, as its members, the President, Vice President, Secretaries of State and Defense, and the Director of Emergency Preparedness. The task of the NSC is to advise the President on issues of domestic, foreign, and military policies pertaining to national security. It is the body that meets during times of great urgency, as in the Cuban missile crisis of 1962 and the Yom Kippur War of 1973. An important feature of the NSC is its staff, which prepares the assessments that form the basis of many key decisions. It was Henry Kissinger's job, before he became Nixon's Secretary of State, to head the NSC staff.

The Central Intelligence Agency (CIA)

This is a unit which, although it has considerable power in its own right, is part of the NSC's staff arm. Most readers will recognize the CIA as a supersecret entity, reputedly huge in budget and manpower, and allegedly responsible for spying and government manipulation abroad and perhaps at home. During the domestic anti-Vietnam demonstrations of the 1960s, it was credited with infiltrating campus activist groups, compiling dossiers on antiwar leaders, and cooperating with the FBI in establishing a nationwide security blanket. In the antiseptic language of the *U.S. Government Organization Manual*, the Agency

> correlates and evaluates intelligence relating to the national security ... performs, for the benefit of the existing intelligence agencies, such additional sources of common concern as the National Security Council determines can be more efficiently accomplished centrally. Performs such other functions and duties related to intelligence affecting the national security as the National Security Council may from time to time direct.

Ad Hoc Bodies

Beyond these components of the Presidency are various individuals consulted on an *ad hoc* basis: as members of advisory commissions, or as consultants for research institutions that specialize in policy research, e.g., RAND, whose experts identify and assess policy choices that face the national government. The President can also assemble groups of experts to deal with a pressing issue: crime, the needs of higher education, alleged inadequacies in federal programs; the economic feasibility of new programs; the anticipated threat of automation to employment levels; or racial discrimination by unions. There were sixty-two of these *ad hoc* bodies in the first sixteen months of the Hoover administration; more than 100 during the first eight years of the Roosevelt administration; twenty "major commissions" in the Truman years; and eleven groups which had all the characteristics of an *ad hoc* policy commission during the first $4^{1}/_2$ years of the Eisenhower administration.[15] The Johnson administration set new records with more than 2,500 citizens named to approximately 170 presidential advisory commissions or boards.[16]

Some observers have found it curious that the sprawling national bureaucracy would need still more people for information and advice. However, there frequently seems a need for new ideas, or at least old ideas in new formats, or given the status of support by well-known individuals. A prestigious advisory board can help the President focus public attention on certain recommendations. Its reports attract widespread attention from people who count: members of Congress, officials of state and local governments, corporate executives and labor leaders, and others who may shape public opinion. The President must choose board members carefully. Although he may be tempted to "pack" a board with people who agree with him, the nature of a problem often requires a balanced commission; and even a packed board sometimes gets out of control. The 1967 Kerner Commission lost White House support with its aggressive report about the causes of civil disorder, especially its claims about "white racism." President Nixon clashed even more directly with the Presidential Commission on Obscenity and Pornography, most of whose members were holdovers from the Johnson administration. Even before the Commission's report had been published, the President announced that his mind was made up; he would offer no support to any recommendation that would liberalize restrictions against pornography.

CHIEF EXECUTIVES IN STATES AND LOCALITIES

The chief executives of states and localities are sufficiently different from the President of the United States to require separate consideration. Most of the differences result in their having less formal control over the policies and performance of their jurisdiction. They must often work with the heads of administrative departments whose positions do not depend on them, and they make up the budget with the help of bureaucrats who are independent of them. At the local level we find city commissions and professional city managers who are hired by, and thus dependent upon, their councils.

The severe limitations placed on many state and local executives do not necessarily weaken them. They do, however, place a premium on the executive's skills in using whatever political and statutory resources are available. We saw that the President must employ persuasiveness and bargaining skills to get what he wants. For governors, mayors, and city managers, this is even more true.

The Governor

It is misleading to talk about *the* governor since the office varies considerably from one state to another. In some instances, the governor's formal authority allows him to dominate policy making; elsewhere he has little formal authority to get what he wants. We noted in Chapter 7 some differences between state governments. Here we explore variations in the governors' powers, seeking to identify the economic, social, and political influences on these differences, and the state-to-state differences in policy that reflect them.

The governor's role, like that of the President, is multifaceted; he is the living symbol of his state, the primary spokesman for its people, the chief executive, the commander in chief of the National Guard (state militia), legislative leader, and leader of his political party. But in comparison with the President's, the formal authority of most governors is quite restricted.

Professor Joseph Schlesinger has compared the governors' authority in four areas (see Table 9-1):[17]

A   *Tenure Potential.* One constraint facing most governors is the length of time they are permitted to serve. The governor's power grows with tenure; bureaucrats and politicians will listen to him if he seems capable of dispensing help and patronage for a long time. Schlesinger identifies five

Table 9-1   A Combined Index of the Formal Powers of the Governors

	Tenure potential	Appointive powers	Budget powers	Veto powers	Total index
New York	5	5	5	5	20
Illinois	5	5	5	5	20
Hawaii	5	5	5	5	20
California	5	4	5	5	19
Michigan	5	4	5	5	19
Minnesota	5	4	5	5	19
New Jersey	4	5	5	5	19
Pennsylvania	4	5	5	5	19
Maryland	4	5	5	5	19
Utah	5	3	5	5	18
Washington	5	3	5	5	18
Ohio	4	4	5	5	18
Massachusetts	5	5	5	3	18
Wyoming	5	2	5	5	17
Missouri	4	3	5	5	17
Alaska	4	3	5	5	17
Tennessee	3	5	5	5	17
Idaho	5	4	5	3	17
North Dakota	5	1	5	5	16
Kentucky	3	4	5	4	16
Virginia	3	5	5	3	16
Montana	5	3	5	3	16
Nebraska	4	3	4	5	16
Connecticut	5	4	4	3	16
Delaware	4	1	5	5	15

categories of tenure potential, depending on the length of a governor's term and his ability to succeed himself through reelection.

B *Appointive Power.* It is commonly believed that the ability to appoint and remove officials is one means of influencing their actions. If a governor can name an official, he can choose someone whose values are close to his own and also acquire some loyalty from the appointee as a *quid pro quo* for the job. Schlesinger places the governors into one of six categories according to whether the heads of sixteen major state units are appointed by the governor directly, receive their positions through election, or through appointments by other individuals over whom the governor has little control.

C *Budgetary Power.* Control over the preparation of the budget for the legislature's consideration can be an important tool in the hands of a skillful governor. But not all governors have such control. Schlesinger ranks them according to their independence in preparing the budget.

D *Veto Power.* The governor's ability to veto legislation is another means by which he can strengthen his position vis-a-vis legislators and administrators. The Governor of North Carolina has no veto power. The veto power

Table 9-1 (Continued)

	Tenure potential	Appointive powers	Budget powers	Veto powers	Total index
Oklahoma	4	1	5	5	15
Alabama	3	3	5	4	15
Wisconsin	5	2	5	3	15
Colorado	5	1	4	5	15
Louisiana	4	2	4	5	15
Georgia	3	1	5	5	14
Oregon	4	2	5	3	14
Nevada	5	2	5	2	14
Arizona	2	1	5	5	13
South Dakota	1	4	5	3	13
Maine	4	2	5	2	13
Vermont	2	4	5	2	13
Kansas	2	2	4	5	13
Arkansas	2	4	3	4	13
Iowa	2	3	5	2	12
New Hampshire	2	2	5	2	11
Rhode Island	2	3	4	2	11
New Mexico	1	1	5	3	10
North Carolina	3	2	4	1	10
Mississippi	3	1	1	5	10
Indiana	3	5	1	1	10
Florida	3	2	1	3	9
South Carolina	3	1	1	3	8
West Virginia	3	3	1	1	8
Texas	2	1	1	3	7

of other governors can be assessed according to (1) the size of the legislative majority needed to override his veto and (2) the governor's power to veto individual items in a bill while leaving the others intact.

With these criteria, Schlesinger created an index of the governors' formal power (with 20 the highest rating and 5 the lowest). New York, Illinois, and Hawaii lead the list of powerful governors, with California, Michigan, Minnesota, New Jersey, Pennsylvania, and Maryland close behind. At the bottom are Texas, West Virginia, South Carolina, and Florida. The standing of each governor on the individual traits and the summary scores appear in Table 9-1.

The formal powers given to a governor have much to do with the size and prominence of the state's population, economy, and political clout. Rich, powerful states may put a premium on dealing firmly with complex and conflict-ridden issues. Such states require a powerful chief executive, who, once elected, has the authority to enact needed programs. Also, such states are likely to be on the leading edge of new political as well as cultural styles. It has been the fashion since World War II—at least until the excesses of Watergate—to believe that a strong chief executive is a system's best guarantor of efficient decision making. Furthermore, large urban states are usually the homes of the country's leading industrialists and bankers, who often appear on prestigious boards that are established to make recommendations on government structure. Just as these persons are likely to recommend strong leadership in business, so do they wish strong executives for their state governments.

Two-party competition and the prominence of certain governors in national politics may also have something to do with a strong governorship, either as cause or as effect. The competition between parties may encourage politicians to establish a strong governor's office—that is, a plum worthy of a good fight. And the strong governor is likely to be a prominent person in his own right (e.g., Nelson Rockefeller, Ronald Reagan, George Romney), whose formal authority, along with the importance of his state, may aid his own rise or that of his allies in national politics.

One should be cautious with an index of formal powers. Like the President, a governor with strong legal authority has no assurance that it will yield political power. If he is unable to persuade others of the merits in his position, or is unwilling to bargain, he may find himself no better off than the governor with fewer powers. On the other side of the coin, a weak governor, as defined by Schlesinger's index, need not accept a situation of powerlessness.

Such a governor can still be a successful politician with more public visibility than any other state official. He claims the whole state as his constituency, and his position at the top of the ballot gives him more stature than separately elected *department* heads who also have statewide constituencies. No other state official holds the frequent press conferences that are customary for many governors and none receives his volume of mail. The governors of such diverse states as Michigan, California, and North Carolina receive 40,000 to 65,000 letters a year.[18]

No governor stands entirely on his own in the policy delivery system; they all have staffs of professional and clerical assistants. A study of the governor's office in California found that 85 percent of the people who wanted to see "the Governor" actually saw a member of his staff. Titles and assignments vary from one state to another, as do the number of people assigned to each category. Governors in the large states usually have staffers assigned to handle pardons and clemency, press and public relations, legislative relations, administrative management, invitations and travel, and personal correspondence. During the rush of business in the midst of a legislative session, the function of "legislative liaison" may expand to include most of the staff.

The size of a governor's staff varies with the state's population. An early study found that governors of Vermont, Utah, Nevada, Wyoming, South Dakota, and New Mexico had only three persons on their staff, while the governors of New York and California had over forty.[19] In many states the outer limits of the "governor's staff" are flexible. People are "borrowed" from administrative departments, and student interns work without pay for a summer term. Political activists donate their time for the good of the party or for the prestige of working with the governor. In some states a whole department (e.g., Wisconsin's Department of Administration) may not actually be part of the governor's office but will be considered to be within his orbit for the purposes of budgetary and personnel management. As organizations move further away from the governor's intimate supervision, however, the problems of competing loyalties keep them from his effective control.

Mayors and City Managers

The local executive is not simply a smaller version of the governor; ironically the job of mayor or manager is generally more difficult. The cities are the most explosive areas of American government. Because the mayor or manager is at the top, he gets more than his share of the blame whenever discontent flares into violence. One sign of the mayor's problems is the dead-end nature of his job. Since 1928, one-half of the major party nominations for President have gone to former governors; only one of those nominations has gone to a former big-city mayor (Hubert Humphrey).

Writing in the preface to the second edition of *The Mayor's Game*, Allan Talbot, a former assistant to New Haven's Mayor Richard Lee, offered the following insights into the tenuous nature of the mayor's status:

> In the two years since this book was published, four of the nation's more prominent mayors have announced their retirement: Jerome Cavanaugh of Detroit, Ivan Allen of Atlanta, Arthur Naftalin of Minneapolis, and Richard Lee of New Haven. While there are surely personal reasons in all of this—and, with just a few exceptions, a mayorship has seldom served as a stepping stone to higher office—the decision of these men still reflects the colossal frustrations posed by the American city.
>
> Are our cities beyond repair? In the introduction to the original edition I observed that New Haven's message to other cities is "written in optimism," and I went on to predict that progress in the cities "is possible and success is feasible." I suggested that New Haven demonstrated that the work of restoring our cities "can be challenging, fruitful, and even fun." Five months after the book came out, New Haven had a riot.[20]

In terms of its constitutional and legal status, the city is at the bottom of the heap. As we saw in Chapter 7, cities have no guarantees in the U.S. Constitution like those of the states. Further, they are hemmed in by state restrictions on the kinds and amounts of taxes they can raise, their borrowing limits, and numerous details of program design and administration. However, the cities do have some clout. Their concentrations of voters and problems are earning them increased attention from national and state governments. Yet the cities' demands are subject to reassessment as national or state authorities find themselves beset with problems that compete with urban crises for priority treatment.

Much of the mayor or manager's power comes from his own skills in finding a common course that his numerous constituents can pursue. Like the President and the governors, he is at the center of different arenas. Because the city is smaller in scale, the actions of the chief executive in working with different interests are often more visible than in the state or nation. The local chief executive must play several "games" at the same time. He must deal with the city council; professional city administrators; the press; spokesmen for industrial, commercial, and financial sectors of the local economy; religious, cultural, and labor leaders; and the pressure groups that represent such diverse clients of local services as the PTA and welfare mothers.

THE CHIEF EXECUTIVE AS POLICY LEADER

Despite the vulnerability of the chief executive as the favorite target of unhappy citizens and officials, he is still the most powerful single individual in his jurisdiction. Whether President, governor, or mayor, his position at the head of numerous constituencies gives him strengths as well as heartaches. His primacy is evident in his relations with the legislature. Although his proposals are often bitterly attacked and some-times significantly changed, legislators take them seriously; almost in-variably, they provide the focus of debate. Much of the time, legislative enactments closely resemble his recommendations.

Budgeting provides a convenient subject of inquiry into executive-legislative relations.[21] Budget proposals and decisions appear in readily measured dollar amounts that lend themselves to statistical analysis. Chief executives have several advantages in budgeting. First, they themselves usually prepare the budget, which serves as the focus of the legislature's work. They also have extensive staff assistance—in the case of the President and some governors, more than is available to the entire legislature for budget review. The chief executive also benefits from his intermediary role between the legislature and program administrators. Administrators naturally try to expand their activities and seek increased funding. Legislators generally distrust administrators' requests; they feel that such requests are often padded unjustifiably. Even if legislators also distrust the executive budget, it is usually lower—and thus more attrac-tive—than administrative requests. The executive's budget is therefore the best answer for a legislature that wants to brake the self-generated growth of the administration and yet has too small a staff of its own to make up a separate budget.

The funds voted by Congress are typically in line with those requested by the President. From 1947 to 1963, only seven of thirty-six selected agencies received funds from the House of Representatives that varied by as much as 10 percent from the President's recommendations. During this same period, the Senate departed from the President's recommendations by 10 percent for only one of the thirty-six agencies.[22]

In the states, also, most legislatures enact budgets that closely resemble their governor's recommendations. The lawmakers typically allow those agencies supported by the governor to grow, and either hold the line or reduce funding for agencies the governor wishes to curb. State legislatures seldom make independent assessments of agency budget requests, although they may disagree with the governor on some details.[23] Members of the Georgia legislature accepted budget recom-mendations from the Governor's office even when there was virtually no incumbent. The budget for fiscal 1968 was submitted by outgoing Governor Carl Sanders, whose term was supposed to have expired at the end of 1966. However, neither Republican candidate Howard Callaway nor his Democratic opponent, Lester Maddox, had received a majority of the popular vote, and several weeks passed before Maddox was chosen as the next governor by the legislature. With his late selection, Maddox had little opportunity to review Sanders' "lame duck" budget and make his own recommendations during the time the legislature was permitted to meet. Even so, the legislature gave almost the same support to the "executive's" recommendations that year as during each normal budget cycle in the 1963 to 1969 period.[24]

Mayors also have strong influence on the budget decisions of city councils. Councils in Cleveland, Detroit, and Pittsburgh "traditionally hold a series of public hearings on various portions of the (mayor's) budget, but rarely make alterations of any significance."[25] Most local governments must balance revenue and expenditures. For the council to increase one part of the mayor's budget, it must reduce another part or take upon itself the uncomfortable job of raising taxes. Local legislatures are less well-staffed than any others. They lack the capacity to reexamine the mayor's budget to determine which areas could receive less money without hurting services.

While the executive's budget recommendation is generally the most important consideration in the legislature, it does not always have a controlling effect. Congress has often deviated from customary budget practices during periods of political change. In 1948, Republicans in control of the Eightieth Congress tried to reduce President Truman's recommendations. In 1953 to 1955 the Republicans gained control of both Congress and the Presidency for the first time in twenty years, and the Democrats were in a comparable position during the early 1960s. Perhaps in an effort to depart from the opposition's previous policies, in both periods executive-legislative conflict ran high.[26] On the state level, legislatures are most likely to change the governor's budget when he cannot succeed himself in office and when he does not appoint the heads of key departments.

Although the legislature generally accepts the executive's budget recommendation, individual legislators can still be—and are—the nemesis of the President, governor, or mayor. Recognizing this fact, chief executives try to anticipate the reaction of potentially hostile legislators as they prepare the budget. In this way, some legislators may influence executive decisions before the budget is given to the legislature. Yet, once the budget is presented, it tends to dominate the legislature's actions.

SUMMARY

The chief executive is the single most visible and influential policy maker at all levels of government. With often broad formal powers, constituencies looking to him for leadership, and numerous roles to play within his jurisdiction and as liaison between his jurisdiction and others, the chief executive has many opportunities to achieve his policy goals. Yet in no sense is he free of limitations. The very number and variety of friends as well as adversaries confine his policy options.

The power of the chief executive depends largely on his reputation and his skills at persuasion and bargaining. He must persuade others of the correctness of his position; see that his reputation is that of an able and effective leader; and guard against anything that threatens his prestige. If he is successful, an executive with strong formal powers can have much of what he wants; an executive with few formal powers can dominate policy making in his jurisdiction by force of personality.

One of the most valuable resources of chief executives is a team of staff aides and advisers. The President has an Executive Office, appointees at the top layer of the bureaucracy, and a host of advisory bodies that can help him master complex issues. Yet, while this institutionalized Presidency can collect needed information and attend to time-consuming tasks, it can also hinder the President's effectiveness. Aides can sometimes add to his glut of information rather than boil it down to its essence; they can increase his political problems by advancing proposals that clash with his own; and they can isolate him from others in a way that distorts his view of reality.

While all executives are the targets of dissident political factions, the mayor has the greatest difficulties. He is not only the most convenient target during local crises but also the chief executive with the shortest supply of formal powers and economic resources. His authority is typically limited by independent government bodies within his local area and by state-imposed limits on what local governments can do. As Lyndon Johnson once observed: "Things could be worse. I could be a mayor."[27]

In our concern with the limitations on the power of chief executives, we must not lose sight of their varied opportunities. They remain the single most powerful figures in their jurisdictions. Their budgetary recommendations, for example, are usually passed by the legislature with few major changes. Nonbudgetary decisions of legislatures, too, usually reflect executive proposals. The chief executive is not alone as a power holder and policy maker, but he is definitely the most important actor.

REFERENCES

1 Thomas Cronin, "The Textbook Presidency and Political Science," paper delivered at the Annual Meeting of the American Political Science Association, September 1970, Los Angeles, p. 1.

2 The Twelfth Amendment concerns joint balloting for the President and Vice President; the Twentieth Amendment sets the beginnings of a presidential term at January 20; the Twenty-Second Amendment limits a President to two terms; the Twenty-Third Amendment provides for the allocation of three presidential electors to the District of Columbia; and the Twenty-fifth Amendment defines the line of succession in case of the President's death, disability, or removal from office.

3 *The Federalist Papers, Number 70* (New York: Mentor Books, New American Library, Inc., 1961), p. 423.

4 Ibid., p. 424.

5 Richard Neustadt, *Presidential Power: The Politics of Leadership* (New York: John Wiley & Sons, Inc., 1960), p. 7.

6 Clinton Rossiter, *The American Presidency* (New York: Signet Books, New American Library, Inc., 1966), chap. 1.

7 Lawrence Pierce, *The Politics of Fiscal Policy Formation* (Pacific Palisades, Calif.: Goodyear, 1971), p. 8.

8 Neustadt, op. cit., p. 46.

9 Thomas A. Bailey, *Presidential Greatness: The Image and the Man from George Washington to the Present* (New York: Appleton Century Crofts, 1966), p. 78.

10 Neustadt, op. cit., chap. 3–5.

11 See Aaron Wildavsky, "The Two Presidencies," *Transaction*, vol. 4, no. 2 (December 1966).

12 See Barry Karl, *Executive Reorganization and Reform in the New Deal* (Cambridge, Mass.: Harvard University Press, 1963).

13 Patrick Anderson, *The Presidents' Men* (Garden City, N.Y.: Doubleday & Company, 1968), p. 1.

14 Dale Vinyard, *The Presidency* (New York: Charles Scribner's Sons, 1971), pp. 28–29.

15 Alan L. Dean, "Ad Hoc Commissions for Policy Formulation," in Thomas E. Cronin and Sanford D. Greenberg (eds.) *The Presidential Advisory System* (New York: Harper and Row Publishers, Incorporated, 1969), pp. 101–116.

16 Cronin and Greenberg, op. cit., pp. xvi–xvii.

17 Joseph A. Schlesinger, "The Politics of the Executive," in Herbert Jacob and Kenneth N. Vines, *Politics in the American States: A Comparative Analysis*, 2d ed. (Boston: Little, Brown and Company, 1971), pp. 210–237.

18 See Coleman B. Ransone, Jr., *The Office of Governor in the United States* (University: University of Alabama Press, 1956), pp. 128–129. These figures date to the 1940s and 1950s, and are presumably higher today.

19 Ransone, op. cit., chap. 10. These figures are out of date (1949–1951), and might be treated as medieval history.

20 Allan R. Talbot, *The Mayor's Game* (New York: Frederick A. Praeger, Inc., 1970), p. xiii.

21 See Ira Sharkansky, *The Routines of Politics* (New York: Van Nostrand Reinhold Company, 1970), chap. 5.

22 Richard F. Fenno, Jr., *The Power of the Purse: Appropriations Politics in Congress* (Boston: Little, Brown and Company, 1966), pp. 368, 585.

23 Ira Sharkansky, "Agency Requests, Gubernatorial Support, and Budget Success in State Legislatures," *The American Political Science Review*, vol. 62 (December 1968), pp. 1220–1231.

24 Ira Sharkansky and Augustus B. Turnbull, III, "Budget-Making in Georgia and Wisconsin: A Test of a Model," *Midwest Journal of Political Science*, vol. 12 (November 1969), pp. 631–645.

25 John P. Crecine, *Governmental Problem-Solving: A Computer Simulation of Municipal Budgeting* (Chicago: Rand McNally & Company, 1969), p. 99.

26 Otto A. Davis, M. A. H. Dempster, and A. Wildavsky, "A Theory of the Budgetary Process," *The American Political Science Review*, vol. 4 (September 1966), pp. 529–547.

27 *Newsweek*, Mar. 13, 1967, p. 38.

Chapter 10

Bureaucratic Politics
and Policy Making

In his controversial bestseller *Future Shock*, Alvin Toffler argues that most Americans are anxious about the growth of bureaucracy. According to him, many of us see our future at the mercy of overpowering, complex organizations.

> It is difficult to overestimate the force with which this pessimistic prophecy grips the popular mind, especially among young people. . . . In the United States everyone "knows" that it is just such faceless bureaucrats who invent all-digit telephone numbers, who send out cards marked "do not fold, spindle or mutilate," who ruthlessly dehumanize students, and whom you cannot fight City Hall.[1]

Toffler himself feels that the future may bring the debureaucratization of American society. Instead of Americans being crushed by huge bureaucratic organizations, he sees the emergence of temporary, nonhierarchical, decentralized organizations. Few writers have accepted Toffler's optimistic view of the future, but most agree that complex bureaucracies are now dominant features of our society.

Much of what Americans see as "government" is actually bureaucracy. Bureaucrats (administrators) provide services, collect taxes, and impose regulations. They work in "departments," "bureaus," "agencies," "commissions," "offices," "services," and units with numerous other labels. In the national government, for example, we can find the *Department* of Justice, the *Office* of Education, the *Agency* for International Development, the Public Health *Service,* the *Bureau* of Indian Affairs, the Interstate Commerce *Commission,* and the Selective Service *System.* Over 98 percent of all United States government personnel are employed by administrative units, and these organizations accounted for over 99 percent of the government's expenditures in fiscal 1974. In state government, over 99 percent of the budget is allocated to administrative activities.[2]

The U.S. Constitution does not mention administrators or any limitations on their powers. It defines the legislative, executive, and judicial branches. Administrators are supposedly the subordinates of these "constitutional" branches and appear in organization charts as the underlings of the Chief Executive. The Constitution limits the activities of the three branches individually and the United States government as a whole. Only from these descriptions and limitations can we *infer* the authority that may be passed on to administrators by Congress, the President, and the courts.

THE GROWTH OF THE FEDERAL ADMINISTRATION

The administration is mentioned several times in the *Federalist Papers,* but always as subordinate to the constitutional offices. Alexander Hamilton argued that the President should control the appointments of administrators and should be responsible for supervising them. He defended a long term for the President on the grounds that "there is an intimate connection between the duration of the executive magistrate [the President] in office and the stability of the system of administration."[3]

Hamilton could focus on the roles of the President and Congress because of the small roles then played by administrators. He argued that the bureaucracy would remain small, and although he may have underestimated its size, he was not far from the truth. In 1792, the federal service numbered only 780 employees, plus some deputy postmasters; by 1801, there were only 2,120 civilian employees in addition to 880 deputy postmasters. Few of these employees were engaged in anything more complicated than tax collecting, record keeping, and copying. The professionals consisted of surveyors, lawyers, and some physicians and engineers employed by the military. The civil service was hardly the body of experts that it has now become, and seemed to pose very little threat to the executive, legislative, or judicial branches as a maker of important decisions.[4]

For many years, students of administration assumed that one could distinguish clearly between politics and administration. Politics involved *making* public policies and the decisions that grew out of them; administration was the straightforward *implementation* of those policies and decisions. More recently, this traditional view has been seriously challenged. More and more observers recognize the crucial role of administrators in creating policy. In 1964, it was a group of administrators that developed the core of President Johnson's War on Poverty. Many other policies originate in administrative agencies rather than in Congress or the White House.

The power given to administrators in carrying out policy also adds to their importance. In ordering that public schools be desegregated in 1954, the Supreme Court gave the state and local education agencies wide discretion in determining the appropriate speed and procedures of integration. Even in its more recent busing decisions, the Court has spoken in terms vague enough to give the agencies a wide field of action, and the agencies involved have come to include the U.S. Departments of Justice and Health, Education, and Welfare.

> The Nixon administration's views on school busing have resulted in tortured and twisted moves by the Justice Department, as the Civil Rights Division walks a path between Nixon's "Southern strategy" designed not to antagonize the South and the rulings of the courts requiring busing. . . . Administrative practices and organizational policies have profound and immediate implications for public policy, and are political in every important way.[5]

BUREAUCRATIC POWER

Related to this political perspective on administration is the notion of "bureaucratic power." As with Presidents, governors, and mayors, the *formal* authority given to administrators does not tell the whole story. We must go beyond the statutes, constitutional provisions, and executive orders to examine the administrators' *power*—their capacity to win in the policy delivery system. And to determine their precise role, we must ask, How do administrators achieve their goals?

Professor Francis Rourke writes that administrators derive power from two sources: the mobilization of political support and technical expertise.[6] They create support by reaching out to several con-stituencies—for example, individual legislators and legislative commit-tees. Without such support, bureaucrats may find it difficult to secure approval for new programs or money to carry out existing ones. Adminis-trators also woo the President, who, in making up the budget, places a ceiling on spending for their agencies. President Johnson's refusal to defend the Office of Economic Opportunity against its critics in 1966 proved especially damaging; President Nixon's outspoken opposition to OEO limited its capacity to protect key programs like the Job Corps.

Outside the government, administrators must cultivate the support of private citizens and special interest groups. Depending upon private citizens for support can prove risky, since they are often poorly informed about agency activities. For this reason, administrators generally seek the support of already established groups"which have a salient interest in the agency."[7] One finds well-developed relationships between the Depart-ment of Agriculture and the American Farm Bureau Federation, the Veterans Administration and the American Legion, and the Office of Education and the National Education Association. These connections give administrators the political clout required to achieve their objectives. Yet alliances of this type can also cause administrators to lose control over their activities. The Interstate Commerce Commission, for example, developed numerous ties with the railroads through the early years of the twentieth century, thereby limiting its support of competing transporta-tion interests (e.g., airlines and truckers) that emerged later. Philip Selznick's study of the Tennessee Valley Authority, a government corporation engaged in flood control and the production of electric power, shows some of the disadvantages of linkages between administrative agencies and special interest groups. These local alliances assured the TVA's continued existence when it came under fire from anti-New Dealers, but as a *quid pro quo*, the TVA found it necessary to serve them at the expense of its own goals in the field of conservation.[8]

Bureaucratic expertise derives both from the specialized nature of administrative agencies and from the skills of administrators themselves. Unlike the generalists in the constitutional branches, bureaucrats can give concentrated and extended attention to specific problems. Expertise also gives administrators a near monopoly on available information. This is especially true in those units that depend heavily on the skills of economists, engineers, and natural scientists. When it comes to a dispute with elected politicians—who are generalists—agencies with this special-ized knowledge have a decided advantage. The National Institutes of Health are good examples; few senators or congressmen have the knowledge—much less the nerve—to question recommendations on medical research.

In this chapter, we examine the characteristics of administrative structures and procedures and their implications for policy making in American governments. Five concerns receive attention: (1) administration in national government; (2) administration in state and local governments; (3) the role of administrators in making and implementing public policy; (4) the internal workings of administrative units; and (5) the impact of private citizens on their activities.

ADMINISTRATION IN NATIONAL GOVERNMENT

National administrative activities are nominally the responsibility of the President. The official organization chart of the national government (Figure 10-1) portrays the administration as a hierarchy, with each department and independent office linked to the President through his power to appoint their top officials. This chart also locates the Executive Office of the President between the Chief Executive and the administration, reflecting its role as the President's most intimate source of advice and as one of his primary tools for controlling the bureaucracy.

Cabinet Departments and Independent Offices

The most prominent units in the national administration are the Cabinet departments. There are eleven of them, which fall just below the Executive Office of the President in Figure 10-1. Although these are the most distinctive, they are not the only units in the administrative branch. Figure 10-1 lists some thirty-four independent offices as well. The principal distinction between Cabinet departments and independent offices appears to be one of prestige and the salary paid to the top officials. The President may receive advice on matters of policy from members of his Cabinet, but this group does not consist solely of the Secretaries of executive departments. Presidents often invite officials who are not department Secretaries to attend Cabinet meetings on a regular basis. For several years, the Vice President and the Ambassador to the United Nations have been regular participants. The heads of certain independent offices have also attended. Robert Weaver was a regular participant in John F. Kennedy's Cabinet when he served as Administrator of the Housing and Home Finance Agency, before that body became the Department of Housing and Urban Development.

The policy-making role of Cabinet members varies considerably from one President to another, and from one Cabinet member to another. President Eisenhower met with his Cabinet on a weekly basis, seeking their advice in a highly formal setting. Presidents Franklin Roosevelt, John Kennedy, and Lyndon Johnson spent relatively little time in formal

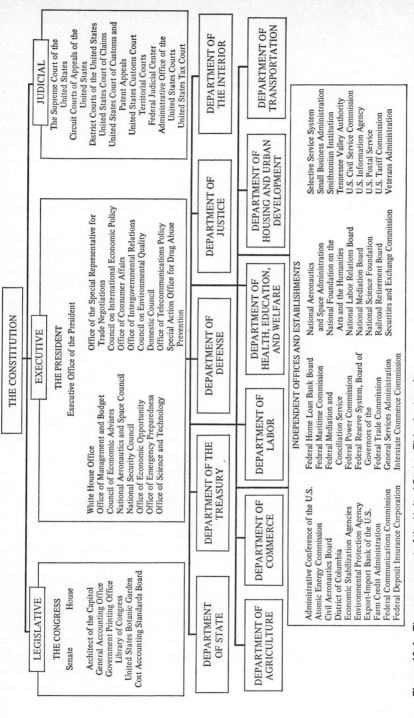

Figure 10-1 The government of the United States. This chart seeks to show only the more important agencies of the government.

Cabinet meetings. Viewing such meetings as an ineffective way of obtaining important information, they relied heavily on advice received privately from individual Cabinet members, from officials holding non-Cabinet posts, and from trusted private citizens. During the first years of the Nixon administration, the President convened his Cabinet more regularly than his two predecessors, but less and less as time passed. Through the later years of the first term, he relied heavily on advisers like Henry Kissinger, John Ehrlichman, and H. R. Haldeman, who did not have seats in the Cabinet. With the departure from government of Ehrlichman and Haldeman in 1973, General Alexander Haig joined Henry Kissinger—by then elevated to Secretary of State—and Press Secretary Ron Zeigler as the President's chief advisers.

Presidents do seek advice from department Secretaries. When this happens frequently, however, it reflects the adviser's personal qualities and not his position as Secretary. Robert Kennedy's advisory role in his brother's administration, and that of John Mitchell during Nixon's first administration, was based on respect and confidence, and not on their positions as Attorney General.

In their number of personnel and the size of their budgets, the Cabinet departments are generally larger than independent offices. However, this difference is not uniform. The Veterans Administration spends more money than eight of the Cabinet departments; only the Departments of Health, Education, and Welfare, Defense, and Treasury have bigger budgets. Also, the budgets of the National Aeronautics and Space Administration, the Atomic Energy Commission, and the Environmental Protection Agency exceed those of four Cabinet departments. In number of employees, the United States Postal Service and the Veterans Administration are topped only by the Department of Defense.

With the exception of those few units that were already established at the time of the Constitutional Convention in 1787 (the Departments of State, War, and Treasury),[9] all the Cabinet departments began as independent offices or as parts of other departments. Their acquisition of Cabinet-level status was a triumph for themselves, their clients, and other supporters who recognized their importance. For a department to become a member of the Cabinet is indeed a victory; it gains increased visibility and support from the White House, Congress, and citizens' groups, which presumably allows it to push through more programs. For this reason, proposals to elevate a unit to Cabinet status usually provoke controversy. The evolution of the Federal Security Agency into the Department of Health, Education, and Welfare, and that of the Housing and Home Finance Agency into the Department of Housing and Urban Development, brought resistance from conservatives who opposed the expansion of domestic programs. The Housing and Home Finance Agency faced an additional hurdle when President Kennedy proposed it for Cabinet rank: its administrator, Robert Weaver, was to be the first black person in the Cabinet.

The Postal Service is the only case of demotion from the Cabinet. Before the establishment of the United States Postal Service in 1971, the Post Office Department was the most politically oriented of all Cabinet departments. Characterizing this department as poorly managed and patronage-dominated, President Nixon transformed it into a government corporation somewhat removed from the interest groups that demand low rates and from their spokesmen in Congress.

Aside from the Cabinet departments and independent offices, other organizations related to the President and Congress include independent regulatory commissions, government corporations, and government contractors.

Independent Regulatory Commissions

Eleven "independent regulatory commissions" make rules and regulate activities in the fields of commerce, transportation, finance, communications, and labor relations.[10] Each of them is headed by a board of directors rather than by one secretary. Furthermore, fixed terms of commissions, bipartisanship, and vague guarantees of job protection ensure some independence from the President. Commissioners are appointed for terms ranging up to fourteen years; their terms overlap, making it unlikely that any one President could staff an entire commission with his own appointees; and each commission must include members from both major parties. Members of several commissions cannot be removed by the President except for certain "causes," which include inefficiency, neglect of duty, or corruption. But in spite of this, commissions can be pressured by the President, investigated by Congress, or cut financially by both the President and Congress.

The regulatory commissions have delicate assignments. They make rules within broad statutory grants of power, apply their own rules to specific cases, and judge cases in which parties appeal the commission's first decision. Because they appear to be more independent of the President than other agencies, regulatory commissions take on the reputation of impartial courts. This image may help them win some groups' acceptance of adverse decisions.

One of the continuing tasks of regulatory commissions is to guard their independence. In spite of statutory limitations, the President's removal power is actually quite broad. In addition to the causes for removal cited above, the President may "also force the commissioners to comply, in the absence of specific legislative requirements to the contrary, with Executive Orders of general application, under pain of dismissal for refusing to do so. The commissions may also be directed to undertake investigations at the direction of the President."[11] Congressmen also try to influence regulatory commissions. They make inquiries and conduct investigations of commission practices, and pass laws restricting a commission's authority:

> In 1965, following the conclusion of the Surgeon General's advisory committee that "cigarette smoking is a health hazard of sufficient importance in the United States to warrant appropriate remedial action," the FTC (Federal Trade Commission) issued regulations warning cigarette users. Congress thereupon drafted a bill which forbade both the FTC and state and local governments from regulating cigarette advertising for the next four years. *The New York Times* referred to the bill as "a surrender to the tobacco interests," and a threat to the "integrity and independence of the Federal Trade Commission."[12]

Regulatory commissions also find their independence challenged by the very groups they have been established to regulate. According to former Senator Paul Douglas, there is a

> tendency of independent regulatory agencies to surrender their regulatory zeal as they age, and to become more and more the protagonists of a clientele industry, and less and less the vigilant defenders of the welfare of the consumers or the general public. All too often, those who are supposedly being regulated, actually regulate their nominal regulators.[13]

Publications of Ralph Nader and his Center for the Study of Responsive Law show ample evidence of collusion between regulators and those being regulated, as noted in Chapter 6 (see pages 156–158).

Government Corporations

Several corporations that are wholly owned by the federal government deal with banking, insurance, scientific research, electric power generation, land development, and the delivery of mail.[14] The President appoints their boards of directors with approval of the Senate, and they come under the budget controls of the President and Congress. However, much of their funding comes from the sale of products or services in the private sector. The justification of these groups is that, as corporations, they can use economic rather than political criteria in deciding about products, services, and prices. Yet government corporations are not protected from all political controversy. Throughout its forty years, the Tennessee Valley Authority has been enmeshed in conflicts with individual landowners in deciding whose land would be taken for a TVA project; with producers of electricity, fertilizer, and other commodities or services, who feel the TVA moves into their markets with an unfair price advantage; with local governments, which feel their tax base is being eroded by taxfree TVA facilities or by the flooding caused by the TVA dams; with environmentalists, who object to TVA-sanctioned stripmining; and with other units of the federal government (e.g., the U.S. Army Corps of Engineers, the National Park Service, and the Fish and Wildlife Service, which collide with the TVA as a result of overlapping responsibilities).

Government Contractors

Government contractors are private companies that serve important functions for government agencies. They build weapons for the military; construct post offices and other buildings for lease to the government; provide janitorial and protection services for government installations; and conduct research in numerous fields of social and natural science. What some agencies do for themselves, others (or the same agencies under other conditions) hire out to a contractor. Some decisions to contract are motivated by the agency's desire not to tie up its funds in capital construction. In a given year, the Postal Service may find it less expensive to lease a building than to build one itself. At times, the temporary nature of a program leads an agency to contract for services rather than to enlarge its own staff. A contractor can also pay higher wages and more easily attract talent than can government agencies, being free of the salary scales of the U.S. Civil Service Commission. On other features, however, contractors are subject to official procedures. Contractors must provide equal opportunity to minorities in hiring and may not segregate their employees according to race; and they are subject to audits by the General Accounting Office, which has the option of making their expenditures and profits public.

Contractors also come in for their share of the public criticism normally directed at government. In other words, the contractor becomes identified as part of the policy delivery system. Citizens who object to activities of the Defense Department, the State Department, or the Central Intelligence Agency are militant in their insistence that universities and industrial firms sever their contracts with these units. Those who assess the impact of government on the opportunities of minority groups must take account of equal opportunity standards which apply to federal contractors. And any assessment of the goods and services produced by the national government must include the numerous business firms, research organizations, and universities that do part of their work under government contract.

ADMINISTRATION IN STATE AND LOCAL GOVERNMENTS

The greatest bureaucratic expansion in recent years has taken place at the state and local levels. From 1952 to 1972, federal civilian employment increased by approximately 8 percent; during the same period, state and local employment increased by about 2½ times. This growth has been especially pronounced in education, health and hospitals, and police protection, areas in which administrators of state and local governments directly provide services to the public (see Table 10-1).

Not all states and localities have expanded equally. Table 10-2 measures these state-to-state variations by the expenditures they make for public services.[15] State administrators seem to compensate for weaknesses that exist elsewhere in their jurisdictions. Their expenditures

Table 10-1   Civilian Employment by Level of Government and Function, 1970 and 1952

(In Thousands)

Function	1970			1952		
	Total	Federal	State-Local	Total	Federal	State-Local
National defense	1,200	1,200	. . .	1,342	1,342	. . .
Post office	731	731	. . .	525	525	. . .
Education	5,316	19	5,297	1,884	11	1,873
Highways	612	5	607	460	4	456
Hospitals and health	1,202	193	. . . 1,009	589	157	432
Police protection	538	30	508	254	16	238
Natural resources	404	221	183	292	171	121
Public welfare	259	. . .	259	. . .	. . .	. . .
Corrections	146	. . .	146	. . .	. . .	. . .
Local utilities	277	. . .	277	. . .	. . .	. . .
Financial administration	334	94	240	. . .	. . .	. . .
General control	412	43	369	. . .	. . .	. . .
Other	1,567	317	1,252	1,959	358	1,042
Total	12,998	2,851	10,147	7,105	2,583	4,522

Source: United States Bureau of the Census, *Historical Statistics on Government Finances and Employment* (1963), pp. 60–61; *Compendium of Public Employment* (1969), p. 20; and *Public Employment in 1970* (1971), p. 7.

are highest where locally administered services are relatively scarce, and where private resources (as measured by population and industrialization) are meager. Where citizens and local governments are poor, state authorities render a disproportionately large number of services. Of all the states, Ohio makes the smallest investment in state-administered services. Other wealthy states scoring near the bottom are Missouri, Indiana, and New Jersey. Administrative agencies in these states have been sluggish in supporting programs that are popular elsewhere, leaving massive responsibilities to local governments. Since we often hear about the rather meager public services provided by poor states such as Mississippi, it is surprising that this state does not score low. When spending for the services administered by both state and local governments is combined, however, Mississippi takes its usual place near the bottom.

The professionalism of government employees is a second feature that shows wide state-to-state variations. "Professional" administrators are those who have advanced training in their fields of specialization, an active concern to keep up with the latest developments, and a desire to provide the most sophisticated services available. A jurisdiction that wants creditable professionals would, presumably, offer high salaries and fringe benefits to recruit the best possible candidates and support their activities with generous budgets.

In evaluating state and local government employees, one writer has observed that only about 6 percent of them can be called professional. He argues, however, that although small, this is an especially significant group.

> To the extent that key social functions of government are rendered by organizations largely built on professional expertise, this small group exercises influence out of proportion to its numbers. A great deal of social power rests in the hands and on the judgment of the heads of these agencies, particularly when they are "professionals" also.[16]

Various services show the influences of professional administrators who set policies for subordinates. Policies concerning welfare payments and the supervision of clients' affairs likewise reflect the attitudes of social work professionals in local welfare offices.[17] In police departments, something as mundane as ticketing policies may reflect the chief's determination of the best ways to deal with the enforcement of speed limits, parking congestion, or rambunctious teenagers.[18]

Table 10-2   State Government Total General Expenditures per Capita by Rank, 1972

	Rank	Expenditures per capita*
Alaska	1	$1,769.84
Hawaii	2	945.79
Delaware	3	727.23
Vermont	4	701.25
Wyoming	5	679.64
New York	6	672.61
New Mexico	7	596.87
Minnesota	8	557.65
Washington	9	554.27
Nevada	10	550.33
West Virginia	11	547.27
Utah	12	546.98
California	13	540.44
Louisiana	14	526.74
Wisconsin	15	523.65
North Dakota	16	521.46
Maryland	17	519.30
Montana	18	515.53
Massachusetts	19	509.61
Connecticut	20	505.92
Rhode Island	21	501.67
Michigan	22	499.01
Oregon	23	495.95
Arizona	24	486.46
Colorado	25	480.93
Pennsylvania	26	479.68

THE ROLE OF ADMINISTRATORS IN THE POLICY DELIVERY SYSTEM

Any discussion of administrators in the policy delivery system must take account of two activities: the efforts of executive and legislative officials to control administrative units, and the efforts of top administrators to control their subordinates. In order to assess the control of administrative units, we can examine the executive-legislative-administrative relationships that occur in the budgetary process. To examine the controls on individual administrators, we must look within departments to assess the procedures that superiors use to supervise and control subordinates.

Executive and Legislative Control of Administrators

The question of administrative control is not simply academic. To some observers, American democracy may not long survive the growth of

Table 10-2 (Continued)

	Rank	Expenditures per capita*
Kentucky	27	477.84
Oklahoma	28	476.03
Maine	29	475.26
Mississippi	30	466.66
Idaho	31	462.54
Illinois	32	453.44
South Dakota	33	445.43
Iowa	34	442.44
Alabama	35	428.05
North Carolina	36	419.91
Georgia	37	413.29
New Jersey	38	407.05
New Hampshire	39	403.53
Virginia	40	403.30
South Carolina	41	402.85
Kansas	42	394.72
Arkansas	43	377.78
Florida	44	375.40
Nebraska	45	366.14
Tennessee	46	358.99
Indiana	47	355.96
Texas	48	355.38
Missouri	49	353.76
Ohio	50	326.53

*General expenditures are for those functions pursued in common by almost all the states. They exclude expenditures of state liquor stores and insurance trust funds.

Source: U.S. Bureau of the Census, *State Government Finances in 1972* (Washington, D.C.: Government Printing Office, 1973).

bureaucracy and the vast responsibilities of nonelected officials. Others, though recognizing that administrators do most of the work we think of as "government," and that they have broad policy-making powers, take a more optimistic view. One question important in this debate is: To what extent can the activities of bureaucrats be influenced and controlled by elected officials in executive and legislative branches? As Professor Charles Hyneman states this concern:

> Government has enormous power over us, and most of the acts of govern-
> ment are put into effect by the men and women who constitute the
> bureaucracy. It is in the power of these men and women to do us great injury,
> as it is in their power to advance our well-being. It is essential that they do
> what we want done, the way we want it done. Our concept of democratic
> government requires that these men and women be subject to direction and

control that compel them to conform to the wishes of the people as a whole whether they wish to do so or not.[19]

We have already questioned the capacity of executive and legislative officials to comprehend and control the activities of administrators. Some of the most important controls used by elected officials (e.g., budget appropriations) depend on the recommendations made by administrators themselves. For the control of administrators, we rely on procedures that are devised and operated by upper-level administrators. The United States is a collection of "administrative states." This does not mean that our individual liberties have succumbed to power-seeking bureaucrats in Washington, state capitols, and city halls. It does mean, however, that we depend heavily on administrators for our guarantees of liberty as well as for our public services. And therefore, we cannot really understand the policy delivery system without seriously considering the policy-making role of administrators.

Budgetary Process

The budget cycle of the national government provides a convenient device for identifying the ways in which executive, legislative, and administrative personnel interact to shape policy. Although this process varies somewhat in state and local governments, the general features remain the same: (1) administrators formally request funds for their departments; (2) these requests are reviewed by top-level administrators and the executive budget staff; (3) their recommendations, in turn, are submitted for a final review by the legislature, which allocates money as it sees fit.

The budget cycle of the national government takes twenty-eight months and includes four well-defined phases: (1) administrative and executive preparation and submission, (2) legislative authorization and appropriation, (3) execution, and (4) audit.[20]

Administrative and Executive Preparation and Submission This is an almost year-long process which culminates each January, when the President sends his proposed budget to Congress. Program planning and preparation for fiscal year 1976 (which runs from July 1, 1975, through June 30, 1976), for example, began in March 1974. Prior to that time, program planning within each administrative agency had provided the basis for financial estimates (in this discussion, the term "agency" refers to an operating subunit of a Cabinet department). The agency first defends its own estimates in the budget office of its department. The departmental budget office plays an intermediate role between the operating agencies and the President's Office of Management and Budget (OMB). The hearings of the department budget office provide the agency with the only opportunity to defend its own requests. While many factors are examined in these hearings, agency and department officials are particularly interested in comparing budget requests with directives issued by the White House (or the OMB) and with the actions taken by Congress in previous years.

At the conclusion of these hearings, the department budget office makes a recommendation to the OMB. Typically, this recommendation is lower than the agency's original request. Subsequently, the agency must defend the budget that the department has recommended for it (rather than seek restoration of departmental cuts) before the examiners of the OMB. At the agency's next opportunity to defend a budget request (before an appropriations subcommittee in the House of Representatives), it must support the recommendation made for it by the OMB, even though this recommendation is likely to be below that of the department budget office.

While the formal rules obligate the agency to accept the recommendations of the department budget office and the OMB, there are certain opportunities to evade these rules. An agency willing to assert itself might mobilize support at the White House while its budget is still within the executive branch. Also, an agency might seek the support of interest groups or members of Congress, thus circumventing the controls of department and OMB officials.

> Through the assiduous cultivation of legislative and public support, it is possible for an administrative agency to establish a position of virtually complete autonomy within the executive branch. Agencies like the FBI and the Corps of Engineers are—as compared with other administrative units—largely immune from the hierarchical controls exercised by either the President or officials in their own executive department. Historically, therefore, the quest for outside support has often been a divisive force within the organizational structure of American bureaucracy, weakening the identification of departments with the President or of bureaus with their department.[21]

The President does not play a continuing role in the making of agency budgets. He establishes the broad guidelines used by the OMB in evaluating agency requests, reviews the decisions of the OMB, and hears appeals from the agencies. With more than one hundred agencies and a total budget of more than $300 billion, it is obvious that the President cannot give equal, or in many cases any, attention to all that wish more money. Most agencies use a variety of devices to attract the President's attention, including influential clients and lobbyists. Some agencies, however, consider it wrong to use interest groups. According to their view, each of the agencies is part of the "President's team" that is governed by the OMB. To try to change the OMB's recommendations would be to work against the team.

Legislative Appropriation The second phase of the budget cycle begins with the President's submission of his budget for *legislative appropriation*. In two distinct processes, the Congress must *authorize* the programs of each agency and *appropriate funds* for each program. Authorization typically occurs once at the start of a program's life, whereas appropriations occur every year. Our concern here is with appropriations.

When the budget proposals of Cabinet departments and independent offices reach Congress, they go first to specialized subcommittees of the Appropriations Committee in the House of Representatives. Agency heads testify before these subcommittees; and while they cannot ask for more funds than have been recommended by the OMB, they are frequently able to suggest that their agency's "real needs" are greater than those reflected in the President's budget. The actions of these subcommittees are extremely important.

> The subcommittee's recommendations and report are . . . sent to the full committee for action. They are rarely discussed or even studied in detail; the full committee almost automatically approves the recommendations of the subcommittee and sends them on as a bill to the House, where they are debated with the House sitting as a committee of the whole. On the floor . . . extended debate is a rare occurrence, and the bill usually passes expeditiously.[22]

In the Senate, appropriations follow a similar movement from subcommittees to the full Senate Appropriations Committee, and ultimately to the floor of the Senate. However, debate is somewhat more extensive at each stage, thus giving administrators additional leverage.

When appropriations subcommittees examine agency budgets, they are thorough in their investigation of those agencies requesting large increases. In dealing with these more assertive agencies, subcommittee members ask more questions during the hearings. They are more likely to demand that the agencies justify certain items, to ask the Department Secretary and his budget officer about the agency's budget, and to reduce the agency's request and add special restrictions to the agency's use of its funds. Thus, assertive agencies get some rough treatment from Congress. But in the long run, these agencies may wind up with bigger budgets than more timid agencies. While the agencies that ask for the largest increases and pursue their goals most aggressively suffer the largest cuts, they also have the largest increases remaining after the fray.

Budget Execution and Audit These final two phases of the budget cycle have not received much attention from political scientists. In part, this is because these activities are considered dull and routine. However, certain events in recent years have pointed to the fallacy of this view. Legislative appropriations do not guarantee that funds will be spent as directed. An agency may find that it has more money than it needs for a given task, and may use the excess in a manner not intended by Congress and the President. In the early 1960s, the Office of Education was found to be spending more on certain conferences than "allowed" by law, having gathered the funds from its own savings on other items. The same pattern, on a much more important level, was repeated during the Vietnam war, when persons in the White House and the Defense Department hinted that they might find money to pursue the war in other accounts if Congress did not appropriate enough money directly for that purpose. Further, the President may impound funds already earmarked for an agency's use (see pages 142–146). Administrators sometimes find themselves in a cross fire between the President and Congress. In some instances, they sympathize with the President; in others, they feel constrained by his unwillingness to support programs they see as vital.

The General Accounting Office, an arm of Congress, is the principal auditing unit of the national government. Most of its activities are routine, even when it finds inequalities or inefficiency in agency allocations (see pages 225–227). Occasionally, however, the GAO finds itself the center of a major controversy verging on a crisis of separation of powers. One of its most prominent recent investigations involved the use of government funds to renovate and provide security for President Nixon's homes in Key Biscayne and San Clemente.[23]

Incrementalism One of the striking features of budget decisions at all levels of government is *incrementalism*, which works as follows: public officials do not ask questions about broadly defined social goals currently being pursued by existing programs; they do not consider all the alternative courses of action open to them; and they do not examine all available information in making policy decisions. Rather, they agree to accept past decisions and concentrate their investigations on the *increments*, or amounts, of change that are requested. Thus, they could be characterized by inertia—working in the same general directions year after year, with differences not of kind but of degree.

The use of incremental budgeting is evident in the preoccupation with the "base" of expenditures established by earlier decisions. Agency personnel concentrate on the percentage of increase they should request for the coming year; reviewers in the departmental budget offices and in the OMB think in terms of percentage cuts to be imposed on the agencies' requests. The House of Representatives examines increments of change in the President's budget from one year to the next and discusses its own percentage changes in his proposals. As one House subcommittee chairman has said: "The past is prologue. Look to the past. That's what I do. I always check this year's testimony against last year's testimony." Senators talk about the percentage changes they will make in the House decisions.[24]

Incrementalism also pervades state and local budget making. The paperwork of budgeting requires administrators to list current and previous expenditures and to compare these figures with their estimates for the coming year. Budget examiners in the executive and legislative branches are most likely to question proposed increases and to cut from those requests in order to minimize budget growth.[25]

If anything can be said about the differences in incremental budgeting in national, state, and local governments, it is that state and local officials seem to be even more fascinated with the dollar increment of change in an agency's proposal. Budget reviewers in Washington often question the substance of programs that are to be financed with the budget increment. However, one study of state decision makers indicates that there is a fixation on the increment itself, with virtually no attention paid to the program involved.[26] There are several explanations for the narrower inquiry of state and local budget-makers. The central budget offices of state governments have smaller staffs than the OMB. State legislators have less staff assistance than congressmen, and state appropriations committees are therefore less prepared to make detailed investigations. At the local level, there are even more serious constraints, since local governments have even fewer of the resources listed above.

It is not difficult to understand why incremental budgeting is so popular at all levels of government. To do otherwise would mean renegotiating every program for every budgetary cycle. This would require continuous and extensive investigation, and would make every program always controversial. At the present time, officals at all levels of government are hard-pressed to complete their budgets in time to pay the salaries of government employees and to fund agency activities. Imagine the chaos if the entire budget were open to serious inspection every year! And so, rather than attempt this impossible task, administrators, executives, and legislators begin by agreeing to keep on funding existing programs. The programs themselves receive little attention; what *does* is the increment of change in spending and, perhaps, changes in program details.

The popularity of incrementalism also reflects the commitments that are implicit in many budget decisions. A legislative body that appropriates several million dollars to establish a new housing or education program is not likely to terminate that program the next year. Administrators and clients can usually anticipate that the program will continue; large numbers of employees know that they will keep their jobs and not be threatened with dismissal or transfer during each year's budget review; and the public is assured that the level and nature of the services provided will remain the same. These inflexibilities, reflecting common agreements as to what is "practical," are good because they ensure stability; they are bad because they impose real limits on the thorough review of an agency's budget.

Our discussion of incrementalism reveals its conservative force in the policy delivery system. To budget-makers, no single criterion is as important as their own decisions of the recent past. They accept established levels of spending and focus their inquiries (and their budget cutting) on new funds that are requested.

In stating that incrementalism is *pervasive* in the policy delivery system, we are not so bold as to argue that all budget decisions are incremental. This is simply not true. In defense and foreign affairs, many policy decisions involve sweeping change. For example, appropriations made to finance American activities in Southeast Asia since the mid-1960s cannot be explained in incremental terms. Similarly, incrementalism has hardly existed in funding policies for strategic forces, such as bombers, antiballistic missiles, and ICBMs, during the past two decades.

Even in domestic policy, one can find important deviations from incremental budget making. President Johnson's War on Poverty, the space program of the early 1960s, and revenue-sharing were not at first incremental; they were major innovations. Arguing that we need to pay attention to both incremental and sweeping, or "fundamental," decisions, Amitai Etzioni writes that while fundamental decisions are relatively few in number, their impact on our lives is so great that they must be weighted more heavily than they are; they are too important to be relegated "to the category of exceptions."[27]

THE INTERNAL WORKING OF ADMINISTRATIVE UNITS

Administrative agencies are not simply mechanisms that receive money and instructions from other government officials and produce public services. The picture is more complex. Executives, legislators, and judges do not always agree on policy. Statutes can be vague on important points, and legislators and executives with vested interests may interpret them differently. The administrators themselves come to their jobs from a variety of backgrounds, and with numerous preferences of their own. Many government programs operate without any long-range goals, or with goals made so vague by the need to accommodate different preferences that they can hardly be defined at all.

One of the earliest concerns of political science students was the management of agencies. This is a fascinating topic that deals with policy direction in the midst of ambiguity, as well as many related issues: the capacity of agency managers to work without threatening the rights and privileges of their employees, the rights of administrators to express professional judgments that may conflict with established policy, and the rights of administrators to campaign actively for candidates seeking public office or for certain legislative proposals. It is not easy to distinguish between mechanisms designed to maintain the department head's control over his subordinates (and, thereby, executive and legislative control over the bureaucracy) and the mechanisms that interfere with the civil rights of employees. Some of the sharpest disputes in public affairs reflect competing pressures to loosen and tighten the policy control of superiors over subordinates. When the lawyers of the Civil Rights Division of the U.S. Department of Justice accused Nixon's former Attorney General, John Mitchell, of failing to aggressively combat racial discrimination, they provided evidence of a breakdown in the internal management of the bureaucracy.

The effective leader of an administrative unit must use formal authority, skills of communication, and a variety of incentives to guide and control his people. Leadership is not a simple process. Authority may be questioned; communications go astray or are misinterpreted; and incentives may be inadequate. There is no assurance that the agency head will be an effective leader. A classic study of leadership put it this way: "All leaders are also led; in innumerable cases, the master is the slave of his slaves. Said one of the greatest German party leaders referring to his followers: 'I am their leader, therefore I must follow them.'"[28]

No single leadership style can be most effective; different situations may call for different techniques. Some situations may call for a highly authoritarian leader; others may require subordinates to participate in making policy decisions. These traits vary from one unit to another and from one time to another. One of a leader's primary tasks is to determine the important limits of his situation, what is worth fighting for, and what tactics will gain him most of what he wants.

The techniques used depend partly on the resources available and partly on the leader's view of what it will take to shape his employees' performance. Many assessments are personal and haphazard; most governments, however, do not allow a free-wheeling operation. Their administrators receive detailed instructions on agency management in executive manuals and training sessions. During the past century, these prescriptions (and the assumptions about employee motivation and behavior on which they are based) have changed. The changes did not occur in government alone, but reflected widespread theories about the control of people in public and private organizations.

Scientific Management

Two approaches to administrative management deserve special attention: *scientific management* and *human relations*.[29] Advocates of the former approach viewed organizations as machines, even though many of its parts consist of people; thus, "just as we build a mechanical device with given sets of specifications for accomplishing a task so we construct an organization according to a blueprint to achieve a given purpose."[30] The primary purposes of any administrative unit, they asserted, should be *economy* and *efficiency*. Administration was viewed as the implementation of policy decisions made by other public officials. Therefore, administrative units were expected to fulfill their responsibilities as efficiently as possible, using no more resources than absolutely necessary.

This being the theory, the scientific management school dealt almost exclusively with how organizations should be structured. It favored a neat hierarchy, with clear chains of command; a well-defined division of labor, with extensive specialization of tasks; and close supervision of subordinates. Behind all this was the assumption that an administrator could learn everything he needed to know. There was, presumably, "one best way" to accomplish each particular task. Academic texts and courses in administration offered POSDCORB as an acronym that represented each major component of management science: Planning, Organizing, Staffing, Directing, Coordinating, Reporting, and Budgeting. Each involved procedures that superiors could use to control subordinates.

The most notable failure of scientific management was the neglect of informal procedures within organizations. In focusing on the tasks and tools of management, it ignored the goals, motivations, and norms of employees; it failed to consider the social life of individuals within the organization, including personal disputes and friendships, which do not appear on organization charts. Little consideration was given to the manager's sensitivity toward the interests and desires of his employees; the problems involved in maintaining effective communications or designing incentives tailored to the traits or preferences of employees, or providing leadership to a diverse and demanding group of employees.

Human Relations

The excessive simplicity and narrow focus of scientific management gave rise to a contrary theory. Advocates of this new "human relations" approach argued that individuals could not be treated as objects to be manipulated by managers. Effective management requires that leaders be sensitive to the goals, preferences, and motives of employees. There can be no "one best way" of management because employees do not fit precise molds. Money alone is not enough to win the cooperation of subordinates: employees may also want status, security, respect, freedom to define their own working situation, and an opportunity for their work group to help set the organization's norms.[31]

What are the tasks of management in the human relations approach? They involve more than organizing human and material resources, directing and controlling of subordinate behavior, or modifying behavior in order to achieve organizational objectives. According to Douglas McGregor,

> **1** Management is responsible for organizing the elements of productive enterprise—money, materials, equipment, people—in the interest of economic ends.
> **2** People are *not* by nature passive or resistant to organizational needs. They have become so as a result of experience in organizations.
> **3** The motivation, the potential for development, the capacity for assuming responsibility, and the readiness to direct behavior toward organizational goals are all present in people. Management does not put them there. However, management is responsible for making it possible for people to recognize and develop these characteristics themselves.
> **4** The essential task of management is to arrange organizational conditions and methods of operation so that people can achieve their own goals *best* by directing *their own* efforts toward organizational objectives.[32]

Today, there is dissatisfaction with the human relations approach. Critics maintain that it has two major shortcomings. First, *employee happiness* is too often substituted for *service performance* as the most important objective of leadership. Many advocates of human relations management state, or at least imply, that the "one best way" to run an organization is to maximize the members' happiness. In their fascination with social and psychological incentives, they may use too little economic incentive to increase productivity. This is doubly unfortunate: not only does it overlook the many employees who are motivated by salary, bonuses, and the like, but it places too much emphasis on a kind of incentive that managers can provide only with great difficulty. Consider, for example, a Department of Corrections making decisions about the work conditions of prison guards. Salaries and fringe benefits can be clearly defined and given as deserved. However, if the department seeks to control its members via social and psychological gratifications—such as permitting guards to set rules for the treatment of prisoners or authorizing guards to carry whatever kinds of weapons they consider appropriate—these rewards may be given only at the expense of equally important goals, such as rehabilitation of prisoners.

Second, as the above example shows, the human relations approach fails to cope with persistent conflicts between the goals of the organization and those of employees. An administrative body is not—as some human relations advocates would have it—an idealized "happy family." The organization has its own needs, and these change at different times and for different reasons than do the needs of its employees. The one-happy-family theme can harm the organization: it may keep an organization from making changes that would be in its own best interest, and it leads to the surprise and frustration of employees when they find the organizational father figure making changes that fracture the family. Consider the case of an environmental agency that, in the face of severe energy shortages, relaxes controls on industrial polluters. This decision may create serious discontent among employees with a strong attachment to clean environment goals. However, such a decision might be thought essential if it kept the agency from the attacks of powerful adversaries.

At this time, no one approach to management is dominant. Today's writers and administrators borrow from several approaches. One view, with which we agree, sees administrative units as systems with environments and internal components, all of which are interdependent. By this reasoning, the leaders of particular units must identify their own traits, those of the employees, and those of the environment that influence one another. Under some conditions a leader might pursue a human relations concern with maximizing working satisfaction, while elsewhere he might profit from a more traditional interest in close supervision and tying wages to performance.

CITIZEN IMPACT ON BUREAUCRACY

Herbert Kaufman, writing in 1968, predicted that the last third of the twentieth century would be a period of tension and conflict, with many Americans demanding that administrative agencies be made more responsive to public needs and preferences. As many people had come to feel that administrative agencies were not sufficiently responsive to popular interests, Kaufman anticipated a "growing demand for extreme administrative decentralization, frequently coupled with insistence on local clientele domination of the decentralized organization."[33] Such a movement is present, although its magnitude is not clear. It goes by several names: "client control," "decentralization," "neighborhood control," "community control," or "control-sharing."

Not all demands are the same. There are important differences between arrangements which would *actually decentralize* the power to make program decisions and arrangements that would merely *add clients to a centralized policy-making body*.[34] The differences hinge on the amount of power that administrators would surrender (probably more under "decentralization") and the kinds of public services that would be produced. Presumably there would be more individualized programming with "decentralization" than with "client representation."

The move toward client control of local administration is largely, though not entirely, seen in the black ghetto. It represents an attempt by black communities to obtain a greater say in the governing of their own lives. The struggle to achieve an integrated society, with a fair distribution of public goods and services, has not brought an end to segregation and discrimination. Therefore, many blacks have tabled, at least temporarily, their demands for integration; they are now concentrating on a redistribution of political and economic power. However, any effort to explain the move toward neighborhood control *within* central cities must consider the precedent set by the (largely white) self-governing suburbs. Central city ghetto leaders argue that they merely want the same benefits of local autonomy that the suburbs have enjoyed for years.

The Economic Opportunity Act of 1964 provided important incentives for urban decentralization by calling for "maximum feasible participation" of community residents in the design and implementation of its programs. By 1970, more than 1,000 communities had antipoverty boards with citizen representatives of the poor.[35] According to one study, neither the President nor Congress realized the implications of "maximum feasible participation" when the Economic Opportunity Act was passed. By 1967, however, elected officials in the cities were sufficiently aware of the realities of client control to push for a revision of the law. And therefore, when the act was extended, it carried a requirement that local agencies funded by the Office of Economic Opportunity must be subject to greater control by the mayor and city council.[36] Disliking the concept of "maximum feasible participation," and, more generally, the Office of Economic Opportunity, the Nixon administration largely dismantled the program. This has had the effect of limiting those community programs not tied directly to city hall.

Organized opposition to client control has also come from the unions and professional associations of civil servants. The New York City teachers' strike of 1968 centered on the job rights of teachers and their demands to use their own "professional standards" in the face of neighborhood policy-making bodies that wanted to control hiring in the schools.

Although client control in urban areas sounds almost revolutionary, it actually goes back to the beginning of our country; de Tocqueville noted the attachment of Americans to their local communities. There are also long-standing instances of client control elsewhere in public administration. Committees of local farmers assign soil conservation funds and acreage allotments for various crops within their areas. Boards of physicians, attorneys, teachers, barbers, beauticians, and plumbers certify members of their own professions and trades. According to Alan Altshuler, this preference for political participation and decentralization "has rested in part on a general belief that government should be kept as close to the people as possible, and in part on the desire of particular subgroups within the national system to exercise as much self-rule as possible."[37] Like de Tocqueville, Altshuler ties the client-control movement to the traditional norms of American democracy.

> This has probably been the most persistent theme in American history. Generation after generation, movements have arisen with the aim of improving the common man's ability to control his governors. Such movements have also arisen elsewhere, but in no other country has the democratic principle been given such priority or met so little opposition—at least, with respect to the organization of governments and the participation of whites.[38]

SUMMARY

No effort to understand the policy delivery system can succeed without an examination of administrators. Theirs are the last hands to touch policy in the implementation stage. They have a more direct influence on the *performance* of government than any other group of officials. Administrators also have a substantial role in the *formulation* of policy. Executive and legislative officials often respond to administrators' program initiatives, or ask administrators to refine their own proposals for new programs.

With all their roles in policy making and policy delivery, administrators are hardly mentioned in the U.S. Constitution. Their growth in numbers and importance has occurred mostly in the twentieth century, along with the development of highly sophisticated public services which must be designed by experts and not by (amateur) elected officials. If ours is the century of the specialist in science and private industry, it is also the century of the specialist in government. And for the most part, this means the ascendance of professional administrators.

There is great diversity in the administrative units of American governments. The bureaucracy of the national government includes Cabinet departments, independent offices, regulatory commissions, government corporations, and government contractors. These units have widely varying perspectives. Administrators may present the demands either of their own employees or of their client groups. Policy conflicts run within administrative units, as well as within and among the legislative, executive, or judicial branches.

Insofar as administrators do much of what we think of as "government," it should not surprise us that many groups and individuals try to influence administrative activities. The control efforts of executives and legislators are prominent, but not always successful. Private citizens also want their say. Thus, "client control" or "decentralization" are important issues in local governments. Clashes between administrators and clients occur in education, public health, welfare, and police protection. The strongest pressure for community control in the last few years has come from urban blacks. However, their demands bear a strong resemblance to those of white suburbanites and the members of organized trades and professions. All the efforts to control administrators testify to their importance.

REFERENCES

1 Alvin Toffler, *Future Shock* (New York: Random House, Inc., 1970), pp. 124–125.
2 For a more extensive consideration of some of the topics discussed in this chapter, see Ira Sharkansky, *Public Administration: Policy-Making in Government Agencies, 2d ed. (Chicago: Markham, 1972).*
3 *The Federalist Papers* (New York: Mentor Books, New American Library, Inc., 1961), Number 72.
4 See Leonard D. White, *The Federalists* (New York: The Macmillan Company, 1948).
5 John Rehfuss, *Public Administration as Political Process* (New York: Charles Scribner's Sons, 1973), pp. 1–2.
6 Francis Rourke, *Bureaucracy, Politics, and Public Policy* (Boston: Little, Brown and Company, 1969). Copyright © 1969. Reprinted by permission.
7 Rourke, op. cit., p. 13.
8 Philip Selznick, *TVA and the Grass Roots* (Berkeley: University of California Press, 1949).

9 The Department of War was reorganized and merged with the Department of the Navy (originally created in 1798) in 1947 to form the Department of Defense.

10 The commissions include: Interstate Commerce Commission, Federal Power Commission, Federal Trade Commission, U.S. Maritime Board, U.S. Tariff Commission, Securities and Exchange Commission, Federal Communications Commission, Civil Aeronautics Board, Federal Reserve Board, National Labor Relations Board, and the Federal Aviation Agency.

11 Robert E. Cushman, *The Independent Regulatory Commissions* (Fair Lawn, N.J.: Oxford University Press, 1941), pp. 464–465.

12 John M. Pfiffner and Robert Presthus, *Public Administration,* 5th ed. (New York: The Ronald Press Company, 1967), p. 446. Copyright © 1967.

13 Paul H. Douglas, "Improvement of Ethical Standards in the Federal Government," *Annals of the American Academy of Political and Social Science*, vol. 280 (March 1952), p. 154.

14 Prominent federal corporations are the Commodity Credit Corporation, Export-Import Bank of Washington, Federal Crop Insurance Corporation, Federal Deposit Insurance Corporation, Federal National Mortgage Association, Federal Prison Industries, Federal Savings and Loan Insurance Corporation, Panama Canal Corporation, Postal Service, Smithsonian Institution, and Tennessee Valley Authority.

15 See Ira Sharkansky, "State Administrators in the Political Process," in Herbert Jacob and Kenneth N. Vines (eds.) *Politics in the American States: A Comparative Analysis*, 2d ed. (Boston: Little, Brown and Company, 1971), pp. 252–255. We can use total "general" state government expenditures per capita to measure the fiscal resources allocated to state administrators. Only a small fraction of the total is used to support the executive, legislative, and judicial branches. Figures compiled by the U.S. Bureau of the Census for 1968 show these branches being allocated an average of only 0.7 percent of state government expenditures. Connecticut spent the highest portion of total funds on the constitutional branches; it allocated them only 2.1 percent of its total. "General" expenditures eliminate funds for liquor stores and insurance trust funds.

16 Rehfuss, op. cit., p. 58.

17 Martha Derthick, *The Influence of Federal Grants* (Cambridge, Mass.: Harvard University Press, 1970).

18 John Gardner, "Police Enforcement of Traffic Laws: A Comparative Analysis," in James Q. Wilson (ed.), *City Politics and Public Policy* (New York: John Wiley & Sons, Inc., 1968), pp. 151–172.

19 Charles Hyneman, *Bureaucracy in a Democracy* (New York: Harper & Brothers, 1950), p. 38.

20 This section relies on Ira Sharkansky, *The Politics of Taxing and Spending* (Indianapolis: The Bobbs-Merrill Company, Inc., 1969), chap. 3.

21 Rourke, op. cit., p. 31.

22 David Ott and Attiat F. Ott, *Federal Budget Policy,* rev. ed. (Washington, D.C.: The Brookings Institution, 1969) p. 37.

23 See Richard E. Brown, *The GAO: Untapped Source of Congressional Power* (Knoxville: University of Tennessee Press, 1970).

24 Aaron Wildavsky, *The Politics of the Budgetary Process* (Boston: Little, Brown and Company, 1964).

25 Sharkansky, *The Politics of Taxing and Spending*, chap. 4.

26 Thomas J. Anton, *The Politics of State Expenditure in Illinois* (Urbana: University of Illinois Press, 1966), pp. 253–255.

27 Amitai Etzioni, "Mixed-Scanning: A 'Third' Approach to Decision-Making," *Public Administration Review*, vol. 27 (December 1967), pp. 385–392.

28 Georg Simmel, "On Superordination and Subordination," quoted in John F. Manley, "Wilbur D. Mills: A Study in Congressional Influence," *The American Political Science Review*, vol. 63 (June 1969), pp. 442–462.

29 For a more detailed discussion of these perspectives, see Frederick W. Taylor, *Scientific Management* (New York: Harper & Brothers, 1911); Daniel Katz and Robert L. Kahn, *The Social Psychology of Organizations* (New York: John Wiley & Sons, Inc., 1966); J. Eugene Haas and Thomas E. Drabek, *Complex Organizations: A Sociological Perspective* (New York: The Macmillan Company, 1973); Chris Argyris, *Personality and Organization* (New York: Harper & Brothers, 1957); James March and Herbert Simon, *Organizations* (New York: John Wiley & Sons, 1958), and P. M. Blau and W. R. Scott, *Formal Organizations* (Scanton: Chandler Publishing Company 1962).

30 Katz and Kahn, op. cit., p. 71.

31 See, for example, Argyris, op. cit.

32 Douglas McGregor, "The Human Side of Enterprise," in Fred A. Kramer (ed.), *Perspectives on Public Bureaucracy* (Cambridge: Winthrop, 1973), p. 106.

33 Herbert Kaufman, "Administrative Decentralization and Political Power," *Public Administration Review*, vol. 29 (January–February 1969), pp. 3–15.

34 Peter K. Eisenger, "Control Sharing of Administrative Functions in the City," a paper delivered at the 1970 Annual Meeting of the American Political Science Association, Los Angeles, Calif.

35 Ibid.

36 Richard Blumenthal, "The Bureaucracy: Antipoverty and the Community Action Program," in Allan P. Sindler (ed.), *American Political Institutions and Public Policy: Five Contemporary Studies* (Boston: Little, Brown and Company, 1969), pp. 127–179.

37 Alan Altshuler, *Community Control* (New York: Pegasus, 1970), p. 96.

38 Ibid., p. 71.

Judicial Politics and Policy Making

The proper limits of judicial power have long been a subject of great controversy in the United States. The founding fathers wanted a judiciary with only modest authority, particularly as a policy-making body. Yet the Constitution they drafted was so vague and ambiguous that John Marshall, Chief Justice of the Supreme Court from 1801 to 1835, seized an opportunity to expand its jurisdiction early in the game. Today the courts play prominent roles in the making of public policy. Many of our most pressing controversies have been fueled, if not ignited, by court rulings. It was a ruling of the U.S. Supreme Court in 1954 that began the struggle over school desegregation. Other Court rulings have defined proper criminal procedures, the nature of obscenity, and the separation between church and state; the extent to which governments can regulate private industry; and the legislative reapportionments of the 1960s. Furthermore, some of the other controversies we have already considered—the impoundment of funds, presidential war powers, and the conflict over the Watergate tapes—may well be finally resolved by the Courts.

WHAT CONSTITUTES THE JUDICIARY?

The judicial branches of national and state governments include the courts and the many kinds of people who work in and around them. Defining the judiciary is a problem, given the overlap among judges, members of other government organizations, and private citizens. Consider the police: are they administrators or part of the judiciary? Since there is no sure basis for determining this, we shall treat the police as part of the judiciary on the basis of their close working relations with the courts and other judicial actors. However, we should recognize that they are mainly concerned with applying and enforcing—not making—the law. From this perspective, they have much in common with administrators and bureaucrats. Also, the issues of supervision and control discussed in Chapter 10 are significant problems in police departments. Attorneys, like the police, present some problems of definition. They consider themselves officers of the court, and so we consider them in this chapter. Some lawyers, however, see themselves as adversaries of the court; and many attorneys who do not practice in courtrooms take a carefully neutral position. Our conception of the judiciary includes the judges and their clerks, U.S. attorneys, juries, and law enforcement agencies. As in other chapters, we restrict our consideration of the judiciary to those matters that bear closely on the policy delivery system. This means that we will focus on the judicial powers, structures, and procedures that affect policy. Our treatment of individual cases will be restricted to those affecting large numbers of people or considerable economic resources. Thus, we will ask if the judges' decisions actually make a difference beyond the narrow confines of the case at hand. The impact of judicial decisions involves many factors which influence the delivery of public policy.

NORM ENFORCEMENT AND POLICY MAKING

Much of what occurs in the judicial process falls outside the scope of this chapter. Courts perform "norm enforcement" as well as policy making.[1] Norm enforcement involves the routine aspects of administering justice by applying laws or regulations in particular cases.

Judicial policy making, in contrast, involves creating new norms through court rulings. During the 1960s, the U.S. Supreme Court established norms for processing criminal cases; ruled that prayers in the public schools are unconstitutional; and decided that each community could establish its own standards for obscenity and pornography. Recognizing that the distinction between norm enforcement and policy making is often unclear, Professor Herbert Jacob has written:

In enforcing laws, the courts intend each decision to apply only to the present case. Such decisions (usually by trial courts) are not designed to create precedent or set policy. . . . Although a series of norm-enforcement decisions may constitute a trend and change the law slowly through judicial usage, judges who make such decisions are often unaware of the direction or pace of the trend. . . .

When they make policy, the courts do not exercise more discretion than when they enforce community norms. The difference lies in the intended impact of the decision. Policy decisions are intended to be guideposts for future actions; norm-enforcement decisions are aimed at the instant case alone. Policy-making decisions are usually accompanied by published opinions to which other lawyers can refer in other courts.[2]

It is judicial policy making that interests us in this chapter. While we explore the diversity of powers, structures, and procedures found in the judiciary, we emphasize those courts that make policy most often. In trial courts, the lowest on both the national and state levels, attorneys, juries, and judges do most of the routine work of trying cases. They make decisions, but rarely make policy. Appellate courts, in contrast, are definitely policy-making courts, functioning squarely in the center of the political arena.

THE CONSTITUTIONAL SOURCES OF JUDICIAL POLICY MAKING

In defining the judiciary's powers, the Constitution is, as usual, vague. Article III concerns the staffing of the judiciary, the definition of cases that fall within its jurisdiction, and certain procedures and standards for trying the crime of treason. Among other things, this Article stipulates that the judicial power of the United States shall be vested in the Supreme Court and inferior courts established by Congress; that judges' terms, assuming good behavior, are for life; that judges will be paid for their services, and such payment shall not be diminished during their tenure in office; that the Supreme Court shall have *original* jurisdiction in cases affecting ambassadors and other "public ministers," and in cases involving states; that all other cases must come to the Supreme Court *on appeal* from inferior courts; and that all trials for crimes, except in cases of impeachment, shall be by jury. It also states: "Treason against the United States, shall consist only in levying War against them, or in adhering to their Enemies, giving them Aid and Comfort. No Person shall be convicted of Treason unless on the Testimony of two Witnesses to the same overt Act, or on Confession in open Court."

Another clause, in Article VI, identifies the Constitution as the "supreme Law of the Land." It also binds *state* judges to the U.S.

Constitution, regardless of conflicting state laws or constitutions, and requires state and national officers to support the constitution by their "oath or affirmation."

The Constitution is vague about many issues. The framers did not anticipate later developments in economics, social relationships, technology, or politics. Yet, trusting the judiciary as little as the executive or the legislature, they wanted to keep it firmly in its place. To accomplish this, they made the judiciary dependent on the other two branches. Alexander Hamilton gave voice to this view when he wrote:

> . . . the judiciary, from the nature of its functions, will always be the least dangerous to the political rights of the Constitution; because it will be least in a capacity to annoy or injure them. The Executive not only dispenses the honors, but holds the sword of the community. The legislature not only commands the purse, but prescribes the rules by which the duties and rights of every citizen are to be regulated. The judiciary, on the contrary, has no influence over either the sword or the purse; no direction either of the strength or of the wealth of the society; and can take no active resolution whatever. It may truly be said to have neither FORCE nor WILL, but merely judgment; and must ultimately depend upon the aid of the executive arm even for the efficacy of its judgments.[3]

There have been many disputes about the interpretations and implications of the Constitution today. One dispute centers on the theory of *judicial review*. The Constitution says nothing about the power of the courts to rule on whether the actions of a legislature, an executive, or any other public official are constitutional. The founding fathers did not indicate which officials should make decisions about the meaning of the Constitution, and thus the permissibility of new policies. In the United Kingdom, Parliament defines basic law; in the United States, the judiciary has taken that role. Establishing the power of judicial review was not a simple matter; it required a contentious decision by the Supreme Court and a shrewd Chief Justice who exploited a ripe opportunity for adding to the powers of the judicial institution.

From one perspective, judicial review was there all the time. Although the words of the Constitution do not clarify the court's powers, Alexander Hamilton—one of the framers—described judicial review in the *Federalist Papers*: "Whenever a particular statute contravenes the Constitution, it will be the duty of the judicial tribunals to adhere to the latter and disregard the former."[4] As we have already noted, Hamilton viewed legislative and executive bodies as the principal threats to our civil rights. He saw the courts as the major guardians of these rights and viewed the independence of the courts as resting on their capacity to judge the acts of the legislature according to the Constitution.

The complete independence of the courts is essential to a limited Constitution. By a *limited* Constitution, Hamilton meant one which spelled out what the legislature could and could not do. Keeping legislatures on the straight and narrow was, according to Hamilton, one vital function of the "courts of justice, whose duty it must be to declare all acts contrary to the manifest tenor of the Constitution void. Without this, all the reservations of particular rights or privileges would amount to nothing."[5]

Despite these sentiments, the Supreme Court had to struggle to assert itself. It was Chief Justice John Marshall who spelled out the power of the Court to render final judgment on the constitutionality of government actions. Marshall, a shrewd politician, did not assert this prerogative without calculating its probable effect on other public officials. He would have risked a great deal if he had announced the power of judicial review when stronger governmental units were disposed to ignore him.

Marshall picked a case in which President Thomas Jefferson and Congress welcomed a decision that canceled out the previous actions of their own branches. The issue concerned William Marbury, appointed as a federal judge by President John Adams (a Federalist) in the final hours of his administration. In the press of business, Marbury's commission of office had not been delivered by the outgoing Secretary of State.[6] James Madison, the new Secretary of State in the administration of Thomas Jefferson (a Republican), was not about to aid the packing of the judiciary by the opposite political party, and he refused to deliver Marbury's commission of appointment. To obtain this crucial document, Marbury sued Madison under a provision of the Judiciary Act of 1789 that empowered the Supreme Court to issue "writs of mandamus," which would command public officials to perform certain duties—in this case, to deliver Marbury's commission.

Here was Marshall's opportunity: by refusing Marbury's petition he could limit the Court's powers in the short run (by refusing to order Secretary of State Madison to act), but at the same time enhance the Court's powers in the long run (by affirming its power to invalidate an act of Congress). The situation almost required this decision. Congress and Jefferson did not want to pack the judiciary with Federalist appointees; they might even have ignored any ruling of the Court to grant Marbury's request—and thereby limit the Court's powers by showing that its decisions could be ignored.

In rejecting Marbury's petition, Marshall ruled that Congress had violated the Constitution by adding the power of mandamus to the original jurisdiction of the Court. The Constitution, argued Marshall, granted original jurisdiction to the Supreme Court in only two types of cases: those involving ambassadors and other public ministers, and those involving a state. This decision may not have been required by the facts of the case or by the wording of the Judiciary Act of 1789. Yet it presented an opportunity for the Court to assert its power to rule on the constitutionality of other officials' actions, while appearing to resist the temptation of expanding its powers greatly. The ploy worked. *Marbury v. Madison* is cited, not only in the United States but in other countries as well, as the case which established judicial review.

Between 1953 and 1969, several actions of the Supreme Court showed the importance of judicial review. Under the leadership of Chief Justice Earl Warren, an active Court made policy by defining what the Constitution required in such matters as racial equality, legislative apportionment, the rights of accused criminals and the police, separation of church and state, and freedom of speech and the press.

THREE JUDICIAL PRINCIPLES: PASSIVITY, PRECEDENT, AND RESTRAINT

To what extent do the Supreme Court and the lower courts define public policy? Most of the courts' business involves routine norm enforcement. An estimated 600,000 criminal cases were heard by major trial courts in 1969, plus additional millions of traffic violations and civil cases.[7] Although these cases contribute little to policy making, they are still important to the individuals involved.

When the courts do get involved in policy making, they find several limits on their activity. Even though the Constitution is brief and often vague, it grants original jurisdiction to the Supreme Court in only two types of cases, and gives Congress the authority to determine the structure and jurisdiction of federal courts.

Passivity

Beyond the Constitution, the courts' policy-making activities are guided by three principles: passivity, precedent, and restraint. The judiciary, unlike the other branches, does not initiate actions; rather, it contributes to policy making by decisions on the cases that others bring to it. Jacob describes the courts as being "available to citizens when they need them but not actively seeking out social conflicts. Whereas a chief executive or a legislature is expected to seize the initiative and suggest solutions for new problems, the courts must wait for litigation on such problems to reach them."[8] This passivity was anticipated by the framers of the Constitution, as reflected in Hamilton's already noted statement " . . . the judiciary . . . may truly be said to have neither FORCE nor WILL but merely judgment." Yet, the judiciary is not totally passive. In *Marbury v. Madison*, for example, Chief Justice Marshall exercised discretion in defining the issues raised by the case at hand.

Precedent

The courts also face the restrictions of the rule of precedent. This principle requires courts to follow rulings of the past in similar cases. The Supreme Court is careful to cite precedents for its decisions and is generally discreet in contradicting earlier decisions. The rule of precedent is also limited, operating only when judges perceive a case to be enough like an earlier one for the earlier ruling to apply. This allows judges to decide when changes in society or technology make older decisions outmoded. It also means that existing decisions set a standard for later cases only if they are recognized as precedents later on. Some precedents have taken a long time to develop. It took more than thirty-five years for the Supreme Court to clarify that racial exclusion or segregation is unconstitutional in all government activities, beginning with a case in 1938 that invalidated the policy of excluding blacks from the University of Missouri School of Law.

Courts sometimes overrule their own prior decisions. The Supreme Court has reversed itself more than one hundred times, with some of its most noteworthy cases violating the rule of precedent. In *Brown v. Board of Education of Topeka* (1954), the Court ruled that school segregation is unconstitutional, regardless of the quality of education offered in black and white schools. This decision overruled *Plessy v. Ferguson* (1896), in which the Court had upheld segregation on the ground that separate-but-equal facilities were consistent with the equal rights provisions of the Constitution. The Court also reversed itself on a state's obligation to provide an attorney for an indigent defendant. In *Betts v. Brady* (1942), the Court argued that states had no such obligation; in *Gideon v. Wainwright* (1963), the Court ruled that states must provide for counsel in all criminal proceedings. The Court reversed itself in 1973 on the definition and prohibition of obscenity. Court rulings between 1957 and 1966 had established a permissive policy that protected all materials except those "utterly without redeeming social importance." These decisions voided many laws against obscenity and censorship. In 1973, however, the Court held that national standards need not be used in determining whether particular materials are pornographic, thus returning obscenity laws to the discretion of state and local officials—and effectively making them more conservative.

Restraint

Another limitation on judicial policy making comes from *judicial restraint*. To the private citizen, judicial power may appear unlimited. To the person found guilty of a crime, a court's word determines his or her fate. To the person burdened with an impossible financial situation or an impossible spouse, the decision of a bankruptcy court or a domestic relations court can mean misery or contentment. However, to the analyst who looks over the whole range of the policy delivery system, the judiciary appears to be more active in some sectors than in others—while in some policy areas there is little or no judicial involvement whatsoever.

The courts have refused to hear some cases on the ground that they involve "political questions." There is a distinction between political questions and legal questions, with the former being outside the proper jurisdiction of the courts. Many court decisions reflect this view. However, the choice of these terms is unfortunate since many of the questions handled by higher courts are indeed political in the sense that they affect—at least indirectly—large numbers of people or basic rights. Yet, the legality of the war in Southeast Asia would not be determined by the courts, which argued that the issue was political and therefore not "justiciable." When Supreme Court Justice William O. Douglas ruled in August 1973 that American military actions in Cambodia were illegal, he was abruptly and unequivocally overruled by his fellow Justices, who argued that the Court did not have proper jurisdiction.[9]

The "political questions" doctrine was of central importance in the Supreme Court's reapportionment rulings of the 1960s. Until 1962, the Court had held that apportionment was a political issue and thus should be handled by the executive and legislative branches (see pages 230–233). However, the Court's reapportionment decision in *Baker v. Carr* (1962) and subsequent cases vividly demonstrated its willingness both to violate the rule of precedent and to alter its own conception of political issues. Not all the Justices approved of this reversal in policy. Dissenting from the Court's reapportionment rulings in 1964, Justice John Harlan wrote: "What is done today saps the political process. The promise of judicial intervention in matters of this sort cannot but encourage popular inertia in efforts for political reform through the political process with the inevitable result that the process is itself weakened." Harlan proceeded to argue against the views that "all deficiencies in our society which have failed of correction by other means should find a cure in the court," and that "where there is a political wrong, there is a judicial remedy."[10]

Some major areas of domestic policy remain, for all practical purposes, outside of the courts' domain. The courts will seldom accept a citizen's plea that certain tax or spending legislation is improper or illegal.[11] Almost all the tax cases that courts decide concern the interpretation of a tax law and/or its application to an individual or a business firm engaged in a controversy with the Internal Revenue Service.

JUDICIAL STRUCTURES AND PROCEDURES

The most important feature of court structure in the United States is its plurality. Despite the supremacy of the Supreme Court, no single court can make policy. The courts of different states, and different courts of the federal system, issue inconsistent rulings on similar cases. For example, *I Am Curious Yellow* was ruled obscene by courts in some parts of the country, while other courts held that it was protected by the First Amendment. Similarly, state courts have handed down conflicting decisions on cases involving such issues as busing to achieve school desegregation, abortion, and drug abuse. Some of this variation reflects differences in state constitutions and the statutes enacted by state legislatures. In other cases, it represents differences in judicial tradition or interpretation. Points of law have evolved differently from one state to another, in spite of the fact that all states—with the exception of Louisiana—share a similar heritage in common law (i.e., a system of law in which courts are obligated to follow prior rulings in similar cases).

The federal court system looks deceptively simple: a neat hierarchy that peaks in the Supreme Court. In practice, however, judges in various district or appellate courts often issue contradictory rulings before a decision is made by the Supreme Court. Even after the Supreme Court has ruled, judges in the lower federal courts may hand down rulings that do not comply with the Supreme Court's decision—because the judge feels there is a difference between his case and the earlier one decided by the Court; because he is sufficiently obstinate to resist the Court's precedent; or because he is unfamiliar with the Court's ruling.

This diversity permits judges to experiment with different kinds of rulings and to assess their impact on the problems involved. It also presents options to litigants; they may choose to try a case in either a federal or a state court, or in the courts of one or another state (e.g., if they are bringing suit against a corporation that does business in numerous states). They can assess the legal precedents in each jurisdiction and choose the one that seems most favorable to their case. Diversity in the court systems also slows down the judicial process. A case can go through numerous routes of appeal within the states that have complex court systems, and then, depending on the circumstances, additional routes of appeal through the federal courts. Convicted rapist Caryl Chessman filed fourteen appeals through the courts of California, plus another twenty-eight appeals in the federal courts between 1948 and 1960, in his unsuccessful effort to avoid execution.

State Courts

The terminology applied to state courts varies widely, with the labels used here being the most common.[12] The lowest state court is the *justice court,* presided over by a justice of the peace. It deals with minor matters— cases involving less than $200 and misdemeanors—and is generally not headed by a lawyer. Justice courts are known for their "speed traps" that invariably find out-of-town motorists guilty of speeding and subject to a fine, and for the tendency to find the defendant guilty as charged. One study of justice courts found a conviction rate of 96 percent in civil cases and 80 percent in criminal cases. One observer of the chief justice of the peace in Philadelphia (there called a magistrate) said, "the only difference between Chief Magistrate Walsh and his 27 cohorts and Ali Baba and the 40 Thieves is that one group is somewhat larger."[13]

While justices of the peace continue to operate in some urban areas, many cities have created their own courts. The *municipal court* is generally specialized. Sometimes called the traffic court, city court, night court, court of common pleas, or police court, it handles civil cases involving $500 to $1,000 and misdemeanors. The judges of these courts, unlike justices of the peace, usually have legal training and devote full time to the job. Most major criminal and civil cases have their first hearing in the *county court*, sometimes called the district or superior court. This is the usual court of first instance for serious criminal actions that are described as felonies—murder, manslaughter, burglary, robbery, and rape.

Above these courts are the appellate bodies. In most states, a *court of appeals* receives cases that were decided earlier in the municipal or county courts. In some instances, cases cannot go beyond this court unless a constitutional question is involved. In most states, however, the court of appeals is an intermediate body whose decisions can be appealed to the final court of appeals, often called the *state supreme court.* While this court receives the major questions of law that are not resolved in the first appeals court, it usually decides the cases that it will hear. It does not accept all the cases that come to it. Typically, the state supreme court considers cases that involve unusual interpretations of law. The decisions of this court are considered binding for similar cases that appear in the state's lower courts. When a state supreme court refuses to accept a case appealed from below, the earlier decision stands—unless there is an issue that will support an appeal to the U.S. Supreme Court. In this case, the Supreme Court determines the outcome of the case.

Federal Courts

The national government maintains two types of courts: constitutional and legislative. The labels reflect the courts' origins: constitutional courts are described in Article III of the Constitution, legislative courts in terms of the powers granted to Congress in Article I. *Legislative* courts have highly specialized functions. The *Court of Claims*, for example, deals with compensation for the taking of property, with construction and supply contracts, and with the salaries and benefits of government employees; the *Customs Court* is concerned with actions arising under tariff laws, reciprocal trade agreements, and other matters dealing with imports. The *Court of Customs and Patent Appeals* reviews certain decisions of the Customs Court and those dealing with patents; and the *Court of Military Appeals* is the final appellate court for military courts martial. The *Tax Court* operates as an independent agency in the administrative branch but functions in much the same way as a judicial unit. It tries controversies arising between taxpayers and the Commissioner of Internal Revenue. The decisions of the Tax Court, like those of other specialized courts and the Federal District Courts, are subject to review by federal Courts of Appeal and/or the U.S. Supreme Court.

Constitutional courts handle the general run of federal cases, and at upper levels they hear appeals from the legislative courts. The basic constitutional courts are the ninety-three Federal District Courts. There is at least one District Court in each state and one in the District of Columbia. Citizens bring cases to the Federal District Court if they feel that a federal administrative action is not consistent with the law; if the law which underlies an administrative action seems inconsistent with the Constitution; or if the actions of a state or local administrator seem inconsistent with the federal law or the Constitution. District courts also hear such civil cases as suits involving the citizens of two states and antitrust actions initiated by the national government. Table 11-1 specifies the kinds of cases handled by the District Courts and the higher constitutional courts.

The U.S. Supreme Court stands at the apex of both the federal and state court systems. It is open to appeals from the decisions of state supreme courts, the U.S. Courts of Appeal, and certain legislative courts of the national government. Table 11-2 outlines the two principal ways in

Table 11-1 The Jurisdiction of the Three Major Federal Constitutional Courts of the United States
Courts Created Under Article III of the Federal Constitution*

I *Supreme Court of the United States*, 9 judges, has:
Original jurisdiction in actions or controversies:
1. Between the United States and a state.†
2. Between two or more states.
3. Involving *foreign* ambassadors, other *foreign* public ministers, and *foreign* consuls or their "domestics or domestic servants, not inconsistent with the law of nations."†
4. *Commenced by a state against* citizens of another state or aliens, or *against* a foreign country. (N.B.: if these actions are *commenced by the citizen or alien against a state*, or by a foreign country *against* a state, the suit must *begin in state court*, according to the provisions of Amendment XI.)†

Appellate jurisdiction from:
1. All lower federal *constitutional* courts, most, but not all, federal *legislative* courts, and the *territorial* courts.
2. The highest state courts having jurisdiction, when a "substantial federal question" is involved.

II *United States (Circuit) Courts of Appeals*, 97 judges, have:
Appellate jurisdiction *only* from:
1. U.S. District Courts.
2. U.S. Territorial Courts, the U.S. Tax Court, and some District of Columbia Courts.
3. The U.S. Independent Regulatory Commissions.
4. Certain federal administrative agencies and departments (for review, but also for *enforcement* of certain of their actions and orders).

III *United States District Courts,* approximately 400 judges, have:
Original jurisdiction *only*†† over:
1. All crimes against the United States.
2. All civil actions arising under the Constitution, laws, or treaties of the United States, wherein the matter in controversy exceeds $10,000 (unless the U.S. Supreme Court has jurisdiction as outlined above).
3. Cases involving citizens of different states or citizens and aliens provided the value of the controversy is in excess of $10,000.*
4. Admiralty, maritime, and prize cases.
5. Review and *enforcement* of orders and actions of certain federal administrative agencies and departments.*
6. All such other cases as Congress may validly prescribe by law.

---

*For the purposes of this chart, the three "special" courts (U.S. Court of Claims, U.S. Court of Customs, and U.S. Court of Customs and Patent Appeals) are omitted.

†*Jurisdiction not exclusive*—i.e. while, according to Article III of the Constitution, cases are to originate here, legal arrangements may be made to have them handled by a different level court. For example, Congress has the power to give the federal District Courts *concurrent original jurisdiction* over cases affecting foreign ambassadors and *some* cases in which a state is a party to the suit.

††A case can be made for the contention that it also has a measure of *appellate* jurisdiction, involving certain actions tried before specially designated U.S. Commissioners.

Source: Adapted from Henry J. Abraham, *The Judicial Process,* 3d ed. (New York: Oxford University Press, 1968), pp. 159–160. Reprinted by permission.

which a case may get to the Supreme Court: by *writ of appeal* or by *writ of certiorari*. Although Table 11-2 suggests that cases falling under the *writ of appeal* get to the Court as a matter of right, this is not true. The statutes limit the Court to those cases in which a "substantial federal question" is raised, and the justices of the Court determine which of the cases seeking a writ of appeal fit this category. Approximately 10 percent of the cases heard by the Court come to it on writ of appeal. Cases sent to the Court under the *writ of certiorari* are more clearly discretionary, and the Justices accept about 10 percent of those submitted.

The Supreme Court enjoys a reputation for hard work and an arduous schedule. In a recent year, it received 3,274 cases, and decided 2,683. Of these, however, the bulk were denied a hearing; thus, the lower court decision was left standing. In an average year, the Court actually hears oral arguments on 100 to 150 cases and hands down formal opinions in 75 to 85 percent of them. The remainder of the cases are decided with brief *per curiam* opinions—that is, they affirm the Court's position using the precedent of earlier cases and do not offer new definitions of law.

THE SELECTION AND BEHAVIOR OF JUDICIAL PERSONNEL

Courts are not simple machines that follow certain rules of behavior. Not only are judicial personnel affected by their own preferences and values, but they also participate in the larger political process. At every level of government, politics has something to do with the staffing of courts.[14] In the national government, and in many states, judgeships and positions as government attorneys, clerks, and marshalls are important rewards for party patronage.

The backgrounds of judicial personnel show something about the career opportunities available to persons of different social and economic origins. Judges are hardly representative of the population as a whole; most of them come from wealthy, white Anglo-Saxon Protestant families, many with a legal tradition. In certain cities—e.g., New York, Chicago, Philadelphia—we find numerous Irish- and Italian-Catholic judges, but nationally, the above pattern prevails. Judges have their own policy preferences, but these—like their decisions—seem largely independent of class origins. Policemen are generally white and from the lower-middle or working class. Do these traits affect work in the judicial branch?

Often the judicial system does appear biased in ways that reflect the social and economic origins of its officials.

1 Cases of business fraud involving the stealing of millions of dollars receive light sentences (six months to a year), while cases

Table 11-2 United States Supreme Court Review

[Cases Normally Reach the U.S. Supreme Court for Purposes of *Review* (As Distinct from Original Jurisdiction) in One of Two Principal Ways:]

(1) on *appeal*, i.e. as a matter of right;

(2) on a *writ of certiorari*, as a matter of Court discretion.

[A third way, by *certification*, will be omitted for present purposes. It is rarely used—presenting the Court with even less cases than those on its original docket. It covers "any question of law in any civil or criminal case as to which instructions are desired" by the lower court, usually a Court of Appeals or the Court of Claims.* The old *writ of error*, a common law process strongly akin to (1) above, was statutorily discontinued in the federal courts in 1928. It brought the entire record of a case proceeding in a lower court before the Supreme Court for its consideration for alleged "errors of law" committed below.]

I *Cases reaching the U.S. Supreme Court on appeal* (i.e. the Court reviews because it *must*).

 A. *From the state court of last resort* having statutory jurisdiction in any particular case (usually, but not always, the *highest state court*, which normally, but not always, is the state supreme court).

 1. When a state court has declared a federal law or a federal treaty, or provisions thereof, unconstitutional.

 2. When a state court has *upheld* a state law or a provision of the state constitution *against* the challenge that it *conflicts* with the federal constitution, a federal law, a federal treaty, or any provision thereof.

 B *From the U.S. (Circuit) Courts of Appeals:*

 1. When a state law or a provision of a state constitution has been *invalidated* because of a conflict with a federal law, a federal treaty, or a provision of the federal constitution.

 2. When a federal law has been held *unconstitutional, provided* the United States, or one of its agencies, officers, or employees is a party to the suit.

 C *From the U.S. District Courts:*

 1. When a federal statute has been held *unconstitutional, provided* the United States, or one of its agencies, officers, or employees is a party to the suit.

 2. When the United States is a party to a *civil* suit under the federal interstate commerce, communication, or antitrust laws.

 3. When a *special three-judge District Court* (which must include at least one

involving far smaller sums through shoplifting or bank robbery draw much heavier penalties. This is the modern equivalent of the principle that he who steals the goose from the land is punished severely, while he who steals the land from under the goose earns public veneration as a great man.

2   Judges from comfortable backgrounds seem unable to understand the backgrounds of minority-group criminals and are unduly harsh and moralistic in sentencing them. Indeed, the heart of the case that abolished capital punishment was the evidence that the death penalty was applied to those who were poor and black far more often than to whites found guilty of capital crimes.

Table 11-2 (Continued)

circuit judge) has granted or denied an interlocutory or permanent injunction in any proceeding required to be heard by such a court. (These three-judge courts usually sit in suits brought to *restrain enforcement, operation, or execution of federal or of state statutes or orders of state administrative agencies* on the grounds of unconstitutionality; *or* because of an order of the Interstate Commerce Commission.)

D. *From "any court of the United States"* (comprising the *constitutional, legislative,* and *territorial* courts)—and specifically including, among others, the *Court of Claims, the Court of Customs and Patent Appeals,* etc.:

 1. When a federal statute has been held *unconstitutional* in any *civil* action, suit, or proceeding, *provided* the United States, or one of its agencies, officers, or employees is a party to it.

II *Cases reaching the U.S. Supreme Court on a* writ of certiorari (i.e. because a minimum of four Supreme Court Justices have agreed to a review.) *Writs of certiorari* are granted or denied at the *discretion* of the Court—subject always to the latent power of Congress to define and limit the *appellate* power of the Court.

A. *From the state court of the last resort having statutory jurisdiction* in any particular case (usually, but not always, the *highest state court*, which normally, but not always, is the state supreme court).

 1. In all cases, *other than* those for which the remedy is *appeal* (see I, A, 1 and 2 above), in which a *"substantial federal question"* has been properly raised. (The Court itself determines just what constitutes such a question.)

B. *From U.S. (Circuit) Courts of Appeals* (and, in all pertinent cases, from the *U.S. Court of Claims*, and the *Court of Customs and Patent Appeals)*:

 1. When a decision involves the *application or interpretation* of a federal law, a federal treaty, the federal Constitution, or provisions thereof.
 2. Where the U.S. Court of Appeals has *upheld* a state law or a provision of a state constitution *against* the challenge that it conflicts with a federal law, a federal treaty, the federal Constitution or provisions thereof.

---

*One of the very infrequent illustrations of its use is that by the Fifth United States Circuit Court of Appeals in 1963, which certified the question of whether its criminal contempt citation of Governor Ross R. Barnett and Lieutenant-Governor Paul B. Johnson, Jr., of Mississippi necessitated a trial by jury. The intermediate appellate tribunal was evenly divided (4:4) when it turned to the Supreme Court in this ticklish case arising out of the admission of Negro James H. Meredith to the University of Mississippi at Oxford. The highest tribunal ruled 5:4 against Barnett and Johnson in 1964. But one year later the Circuit Court cleared the two because of "changed circumstances and conditions."

Source: Adapted from Abraham, op. cit., pp. 182–183. Reprinted by permission.

3 Police officers reflect the influences of their own racial and class prejudices, and seem especially tough on minority groups and on those deviant-appearing white youths who run afoul of police standards in respect to drugs, sex, personal appearance, and political protest.

Judges

The appointment of judges has a political importance that is warranted by the status of the jobs and—for some judgeships—their influence over policy. At the national level, the President and the Senate are most directly involved in making appointments, but several other actors participate, and still others seek access on an informal basis. In the case of federal district judges, the Attorney General and senators of the President's party from the state that has the opening list nominees; the FBI investigates each serious candidate; and evaluations of candidates come from the Standing Committee on Federal Judiciary of the American Bar Association, interested senators, and existing federal judges. When an appointment becomes controversial (perhaps because someone's favored candidate is not getting the job or because the likely nominee meets strong opposition), the Attorney General handles the matter. He makes the crucial decisions as to the merit of the favorite's opposition. The controversies may take in a wide range of political interests, and when the issue is an appointment to the Supreme Court, it will occupy prime space in the mass media. During the last months of the Johnson administration and the first months of the Nixon administration, there were few items of greater interest than the unsuccessful nominations of Abe Fortas for Chief Justice and Clement Haynsworth and Harold Carswell for Associate Justice.

The bar associations receive special consideration in the selection of judges. In Congress and many state legislatures, all members of the judiciary committees are lawyers. In the national government, the American Bar Association's Standing Committee on Federal Judiciary investigates every candidate. Its report and vote on qualifications go to the Attorney General and are given great weight by the Senate Judiciary Committee—especially if a person nominated does not have the support of the ABA Committee.

In most cases, the Senate gives the President's judicial nominees the same support it gives most nominees for administrative posts. However, the 1968 to 1970 period saw three dramatic instances of senatorial rejection. First, Lyndon Johnson's nomination of Abe Fortas as Chief Justice was rejected, largely on the basis of conflict-of-interest charges which led him—under threat of impeachment—to resign his seat as an Associate Justice in May 1969. President Nixon had no easy time finding a replacement for Fortas. His initial nominee, Clement J. Haynsworth, was rejected in November 1969 after being charged with conflict-of-interest while sitting as a lower court federal judge. G. Harrold Carswell was rejected in April 1970 amidst charges of an undesirable record on civil rights and a general lack of professional competence.

Supreme Court Justices   With the Supreme Court at the apex of the American judicial systems, its status is second only to that of the President. As of 1974, only 100 persons had occupied seats on the Court, and most have had upper-class backgrounds. Of the Justices appointed through 1959, only 9 percent came from humble origins.[15] The large majority came from families with social prestige and political influence. Over one-third had relatives who were judges, including justices in the highest state court or the Supreme Court. Almost 90 percent were members of WASP families coming from northwestern Europe. Most were affiliated with high-prestige denominations: Episcopalian, Presbyterian, Congregational, and Unitarian. The order of minority groups' ascendancy to the Court has corresponded roughly to their political gains in other areas. The first Catholic on the Court was Chief Justice Roger Brooke Taney, appointed by President Andrew Jackson; the first Jew was Louis D. Brandeis, appointed by Woodrow Wilson; and the first black was Thurgood Marshall, appointed by Lyndon B. Johnson.

The educational opportunities and early occupations of Supreme Court Justices have corresponded to their social backgrounds. Fully one-third of the Justices attended prestigious Ivy League schools, and about an equal number studied law in those same schools. All but four of the Justices appointed through 1959 had practiced law as their major previous occupation, and the four exceptions were professors or deans at major law schools.

As we noted in our discussion of political parties (in Chapter 4), almost all Supreme Court Justices have shared the party affiliation of the President who appointed them. Partisanship was especially important to Franklin Roosevelt, John Kennedy, Lyndon Johnson, and Richard Nixon. This is even more true in appointments to the lower federal courts.[16] Because Presidents are less involved at this level, they tend to rely more heavily on party patronage as their criterion.

When Chief Executives do make choices, they weigh heavily the candidate's record, plus some estimate of the decisions he is likely to render on major issues coming before the Court. In a classic letter to Senator Henry Cabot Lodge, President Theodore Roosevelt showed that policy inclinations were more important than partisanship for one Supreme Court nomination.

> Nothing has been so strongly born in on me concerning lawyers on the bench as that the nominal politics of the man has nothing to do with his actions on the bench. His *real* politics are all-important. In Lurton's case, Taft and Day, his two former associates, are very desirous of having him on. He is right on the Negro question; he is right on the power of the federal government; he is right on the Insular business; he is right about corporations, he is right about labor. On every question that would come before the bench, he has so far shown himself to be in much closer touch with the policies in which you and I believe than even White because he has been right about corporations where White has been wrong.[17]

The backgrounds of Supreme Court Justices seem more important in determining their appointment than in shaping their decisions once they are on the bench. Family background, especially when judicial connections are prominent, and the right education and professional and political contacts produce the visibility that is needed for a judicial appointment. However, when political scientists have tried to relate specific decisions to the backgrounds of Supreme Court Justices, they have been impressed by the seeming inconsistencies: the incidence of Justices from humble backgrounds who have taken conservative positions, and those from upper-class families with a progressive record. In contrast to what seems to be class or ethnic bias in lower court judges, those who reach the U.S. Supreme Court may be above these influences.

Professor John P. Frank has examined the decisions made on the Court by men who had earlier reputations as liberals or conservatives. Noting that "unpredictability is almost the clearest feature of the appointment process," he found that

> the number of surprises is great, and no President can be sure of what he is getting. Wilson chose McReynolds, who proved to be the total antithesis of everything Wilson stood for and became the most fanatic and hard-bitten conservative extremist ever to grace the Court. Coolidge chose his own Attorney General, Harlan Stone, and Stone is commonly regarded as one of the great liberal Justices. Anti-Federalist Presidents sent Justice after Justice to the Court only to see them captivated by Marshall.[18]

If Frank had written this passage a few years later, he could have added President Eisenhower's selection of Earl Warren to this list. Like Coolidge and Wilson, Eisenhower chose a Justice who, in combination with the appointees of other Presidents, went on to write a distinctive and contrary judicial record that embarrassed many members of his own party. Frank could also have pointed to Byron White, whose record has been far less liberal than one might expect of a Kennedy appointee.

Rating the Justices and the Court   Classifying judicial behavior requires much sophistication. Two types of analysis can aid our understanding of the judiciary's place in the policy delivery system: the study of decision patterns by individual justices, and the study of general trends in the policies set by the Supreme Court. Professor Glendon Schubert is the most prominent scholar of Supreme Court voting patterns. As a result of his work, political scientists can speak in precise terms about the liberal and conservative members of the Court, and document the issues that align one group of Justices against another. Schubert finds that 66 percent of the divided opinions between 1946 and 1963 saw the Justices voting "on the basis of their acceptance of relatively liberal or relatively conservative ideologies."[19] He discovered two kinds of liberalism-conservatism on the Court. One is political and deals with cases involving political and religious freedom, the right to fair procedures in criminal cases, and individual privacy. During the 1962 term of the Court, the Justices were arrayed from most-liberal to most-conservative on this scale as: Douglas, Black, Warren, Brennan, Goldberg, White, Stewart, Harlan, and Clark. Another kind of liberalism-conservatism involves economic issues: labor-management disputes, government regulation of business activities, financial claims of workers against their employers, and suits between small and large businesses. On these cases, the Justices arrayed themselves differently than on the political cases. From liberal to conservative, the order for 1962 was Black, Douglas, Warren, Brennan, Clark, White, Goldberg, Stewart, and Harlan.

Another kind of analysis focuses on the trends in major decisions that mark each era of the Supreme Court. One of the earliest and most significant periods in the Court's history was that of John Marshall as Chief Justice (1801–1835). This was an era of nation building, with an increase in powers for the Supreme Court (especially in *Marbury v. Madison*) and other national institutions. In *McCulloch v. Maryland* (1819) the Court, concerned with the power of Congress to establish a National Bank and the power of the states to tax that Bank, offered a broad ruling that helped to expand the law-making powers of Congress. It also interpreted the supremacy clause of the Constitution in a way that strengthened the national government against the states. More recently, the Warren Court (1953–1969) appears every bit as distinct as the Marshall Court. It is cited for the expansion of equal rights (as in race) and majority rights (as in legislative apportionment) and for the general enlargement of national standards and institutions (as in the role of the Supreme Court itself in the development of law). Warren's landmark cases have reduced racial inequalities in public facilities and some areas that have been considered private (e.g., housing); guaranteed equal political opportunities in voting and legislative apportionment; bolstered the separation of church and state; added to the rights of defendants in criminal cases; and made available books, films, and live entertainment that had been barred earlier as "obscene."[20] The decisions of this Court did not go uncriticized, as is evident to all who remember campaigns to "Impeach Earl Warren" and "Support Your Local Police."

In his 1968 presidential campaign, Richard Nixon charged that the Warren Court was too liberal and activist. As President, he accused the Court of "weakening the peace forces as against the criminal forces in our society" and vowed to correct this by filling the Court with judicial "conservatives" and "strict constructionists." The President's opportunity to deliver on this promise came with the resignations of Justices Warren and Fortas in 1969, and the resignations two years later of Justices Hugo Black and John Harlan. With the appointments of Chief Justice Warren Burger, and Associate Justices Harry Blackmun, Lewis Powell, Jr., and William Rehnquist, Nixon created a new Court. However, it does not appear that the "Nixon Court" has staged a massive retreat from the decisions of the Warren Court. The Nixon Court has been more timid in advancing new positions. Except in the areas of criminal procedures and obscenity, the new Court has accepted the Warren Court's status quo. But this does not mean that there is no "Nixon Court." Paul Bender argues that policy changes have occurred, even though the new Court has not dramatically rejected or overruled previous decisions. Rather, through the techniques of subtle erosion, the Court has consciously and gradually produced a change in judicial policy. Describing one such technique, Bender observes:

> Several years ago, . . . the Court established the right of a criminal suspect to have a lawyer witness a police lineup in which the suspect is forced to participate. The Court majority held that the presence of counsel was essential in preventing an unfair or overly suggestive lineup, which might result in the identification and conviction of the wrong person. By happenstance, the cases at issue involved lineups that were held after the defendants' formal indictment by a grand jury (most lineups are held *prior* to indictment), but the Court did not seem to rely heavily upon the fact in holding counsel necessary. . . .
>
> Yet . . . the four Nixon Justices, joined by one of the dissenters from the earlier cases, seized upon the fact that those cases involved lineups occurring *after* indictments—and thereby held that counsel is not required at the vast majority of lineups that occur *before* indictment. The Court explained that it did not wish to "extend" the earlier ruling. What it seems to have done, in practical effect, is to obliterate that ruling.[21]

Despite these moves that counter the trends of the Warren Court, other decisions since Warren's retirement seem, ironically, to have given the spirit of his court a new lease on life. Two major examples are the decisions providing widespread access to abortions, and the decision holding the death penalty, where it is still used, to be unconstitutional.

United States Attorneys

United States attorneys play important roles in the judicial branch. Representing the national government in the federal court districts, these attorneys prosecute violations of federal law and represent the national government in most civil cases. As federal prosecutors, they are largely responsible for implementing the policies of the Justice Department.

The President makes the formal appointment of United States attorneys but actually plays only an indirect role in their recruitment and selection. The key role is that of the Justice Department, in cooperation with White House aides in charge of patronage. Justice Department spokesmen negotiate with several groups seeking to influence the final selection, including senators of the President's party who represent states with vacancies, state and local party activists, prominent members of the bar, federal judges, and other United States attorneys. Successful appointees are attorneys, residents of the judicial districts where the vacancy occurs, at least nominal members of the President's party, and usually active politically.[22]

Once in office, the United States attorney is subject to numerous pressures. He is formally controlled by the Department of Justice, which spells out standard policies and procedures in a *United States Attorney's Manual*, inspects the activities of attorneys' offices, uses special attorneys to oversee particular cases, and chooses its attorneys carefully. Because the United States attorney is also subject to other pressures, the Justice Department's efforts are not always successful. In addition to his own preferences and desires, the United States attorney feels the weight of local attitudes (e.g., resistance to school desegregation in the South) and is bound by the rulings of federal judges. As in other cases of bureaucratic control (see pages 283–287), the controls of the Justice Department over United States attorneys are imperfect because of lack of information.

> The department can succeed in securing compliance with any given policy or decision. But it lacks the manpower to prevail in very many of them. It must pick and choose. U.S. attorneys can make it costly to the department to enforce its will—costly in terms of manpower, time, money, and psychic energy. . . . It also helps to explain why a U.S. attorney, if he is inclined to fight hard, is able to prevail in disputes that do not fall into the limited group the department assigns top priority. Of course, the U.S. attorney faces similar limitations; there are only so many battles he can wage with the department.[22]

The Police

Our conception of the judiciary includes the police. By discussing the police in the same chapter as the courts, we have the opportunity to observe some sharp differences in social and economic background that separate these two closely related areas of government. In contrast to the upper-class background of the courts, police departments recruit almost entirely from the lower-middle and working classes. The records of the New York City police department seem to reflect conditions elsewhere. They show that approximately 78 percent of new policemen come from blue-collar families. The recruits' performance on an intelligence test showed average IQs of 105, which is barely above the national average.[23] Studies of police attitudes and behavior have found many traits of the authoritarian personality: conservatism in dress and behavior; suspicion of others; aggression; and a tendency to accept the stereotypes of ethnic, religious, and racial groups. These traits are generally more apparent in the working class than in other social groups.[24] The class backgrounds and attitudes of police recruits help prepare them for the rough aspects of the jobs.

> From a practical point of view, the working-class youth may develop into a more dependable policeman than the middle-class college student, simply because he has already been tested in a gang and street-corner society. . . . The police occupational system is geared to manufacture the "take charge guy," and it succeeds in doing so with outstanding efficiency.[25]

One of the most controversial issues is that of the control of the police and the ideological conflict between them and the judges. This controversy stems partly from the differences in background, and from the temperaments that grow out of those backgrounds. From one perspective, there is an inherent conflict between the police and the courts, just as there is between "law" and "order."

> Law is not merely an instrument of order, but may frequently be its adversary. . . . The police in democratic society are required to maintain order and to do so under the rule of law. . . . [Their ideology] emphasizes initiative rather than disciplined adherence to rules and regulations. By contrast, the rule of law emphasizes the rights of individual citizens and constraints upon the initiative of legal officials. This tension between the operational consequences of ideas of order, efficiency, and initiative, on the one hand, and legality, on the other, constitutes the principle problem of police as a democratic legal organization.[26]

There had been a period of sharply increased restrictions on police activities during the latter years of the Warren Court, followed by some retrenchment during the first years of the Burger Court. The Warren years were marked by frequent verbal attacks against the Court by spokesmen of the police, and by the sometimes related campaigns of the John Birch Society. Some of the most important changes in police procedures concerned the guarantees of legal counsel for indigents when serious penalities are involved; the insistence that arrested persons be advised of their rights to obtain counsel and to remain silent at any interrogation; and the exclusion from trials of evidence gathered by improper means, such as wire-tapping, unlawful searches, and interrogation without advising the suspect of his rights. According to spokesmen who claimed to represent the police, these rulings hamstrung law enforcement by limiting police maneuverability in apprehending and convicting criminals. As we shall see in the next section, these assertions do not always square with the evidence.

What of police corruption? Admittedly, the problems of police departments include patrolmen, plainclothesmen, and administrators who overlook or accept bribes to protect various forms of crime—ranging from overtime parking to the organized dealing in sex, drugs, gambling, or extortion. Periodically an exposé will rock a department and threaten police morale or police effectiveness in dealing with the community. The community, which becomes contemptuous of police hypocrisy in maintaining "law and order," is encouraged to believe that crime does pay and to act accordingly. Like other forms of corruption in the policy delivery system, however, that of police departments operates underground, is seldom open to systematic study, and evades any serious consideration of its true extent or impact.

JUDICIAL POLICIES AND THEIR IMPACTS

We saw in Chapter 2 that nearly twenty years passed before an even modest implementation of the Supreme Court's 1954 school desegregation decision. Many factors contributed to the delays, including subsequent actions of executive, legislative, administrative, and judicial officials at all levels of government. One of the lessons to be learned from this is that the judiciary, like other parts of the policy delivery system, does not operate alone.

Justices of the Supreme Court anticipate that their rulings will make a difference not only to the persons involved in the case at hand but also to others who later find themselves in similar circumstances. As we have already noted, the Court considers only important issues and seeks to create the law at the same time that it decides particular cases. Yet, for the Justices' policies to have effect, they must guide both the decisions of lower courts in subsequent cases and the actions of administrators or private citizens. In recent years, the Court's decisions about desegregation, the constitutionality of prayers and other religious exercises in the public schools, and the treatment of accused criminals by the police have been widely criticized and evaded by private citizens and government officials alike. Thus, decisions of the Supreme Court do not always have their intended impact on the delivery of public services.

It is helpful to think about three kinds of judicial impact:

1 *Primary impact*: the decisions of the Supreme Court influence (or fail to influence) the subsequent decisions of judges in the lower courts;
2 *Secondary impact*: the decisions of the Supreme Court influence (or fail to influence) non-judicial officials or citizens whose behavior is the target of the Court's decisions;
3 *Tertiary impacts*: the decisions of the Supreme Court influence (or fail to influence) the benefits that citizens receive from public policy.

Primary Impacts

Our concern with *primary impacts* grows out of the alleged key place of the Supreme Court in the American judiciary. Because of the "supremacy clause" of the Constitution, the pyramid structure of the federal and state court systems, and judges' professional commitments to accept the rulings of prior courts in similar cases, we often assume that decisions of the Supreme Court will guide the lower courts. For example, when the Court says that racial segregation in public schools is unconstitutional, we expect lower court judges to rule against segregated school districts.

However, applying Supreme Court decisions may often raise legitimate questions. If the Court has ruled on the constitutionality of school segregation alone, for example, one can argue that this decision does not automatically apply to other kinds of state-supported services—such as public parks or hospitals, or private schools or hospitals that receive limited state aid. Some federal judges and many state judges have offered bizarre reasons to delay or alter the application of Supreme Court rulings in specific cases. When a U.S. District Judge in South Carolina received a case brought by blacks against a segregated public golf course, the judge disqualified himself with this direct attack on the Supreme Court's interpretation of the constitution: "Since as a Federal judge I have to follow that decision I will disqualify myself because I have taken an oath to sustain the Constitution."[27] And in refusing to set a date for the desegregation of schools, a Federal District Judge in Texas commented: "I believe that it will be seen that the [Supreme] Court based its decision on no law but rather on what the Court regarded as more authoritative, more psychological knowledge."[28]

U.S. District Court Judge John J. Parker once took on himself the task of altering Supreme Court precedent when he refused to follow the Court's ruling in *Minersville School District v. Gobitis* (1940). In this case the Court had held that the children of Jehovah's Witnesses attending public schools (in Pennsylvania) could be compelled to salute the flag, despite the freedom of religion provision of the Constitution. In an almost identical case two years later, Judge Parker invalidated this law. He asserted that he was not defying the Supreme Court, since three of the *Gobitis* majority had later reversed themselves and another two had retired from the Court. Consequently, arguing that the supporters of the *Gobitis* decision now represented a minority of three, Parker ruled

> that the flag salute here required is violative of religious liberty when required of persons holding the religious views of plaintiffs, [and] we feel that we would be recreant to our duty as judges, if through a blind following of a decision which the Supreme Court itself has thus impaired as an authority, we should deny protection to rights which we regard as among the most sacred of those protected by constitutional guarantees.[29]

One reason Supreme Court decisions fail to influence the subsequent rulings of lower courts is the vague language in which they are expressed. Professor Jack Peltason examined the reaction of Southern federal judges to the Supreme Court's school desegregation ruling. Having ordered the desegregation of public schools "with all deliberate speed," the Court depended upon lower courts to determine what a reasonable rate of speed might be. Peltason found that the vagueness of the Court's decision permitted judges to do almost anything they pleased. The obvious happened: lower courts in the South let themselves be guided by the segregationist views of their districts, and integration was achieved as slowly as possible. One writer observed that "the Court was its own undoing; a man will not bring undue hardship upon himself and his family if he does not have to—even if he is a federal district court judge."[30] [For additional evidence of the secondary and tertiary impacts of these decisions, see Chapter 2 (pages 33–35).]

Secondary and Tertiary Impacts: Legislative Apportionment

The Supreme Court's rulings on legislative apportionment reveal interesting cases of secondary and tertiary impacts. The legislatures in most states were vulnerable to challenge following the Supreme Court's ruling in *Reynolds v. Sims*, which required the equal representation of urban and rural voters. The Court had active supporters in states that considered themselves disadvantaged by the old styles of apportionment. There were many lower court cases and appeals to the higher federal courts when compliance was not quick in coming. Secondary impacts come quickly. The Court was in a position to threaten state governments with severe inconvenience by ruling that the business conducted by unlawfully apportioned legislatures was invalid, and thus subject to litigation. Futhermore, the lower courts were willing to design apportionment plans and order them put into effect if the state legislatures themselves did not do so. Within four years of the first apportionment decision, forty-nine of the fifty state legislatures had reapportioned themselves or had been reapportioned by commissions and/or judicial decisions.[31] In Chapter 8, we examined the tertiary effects of these reapportionment decisions on the composition of legislatures and the kinds of policies enacted (see pages 232–233).

School Prayer

The Court entered an area of great controversy in the 1960s with a series of school prayer decisions. These were a direct challenge to practices considered important by large numbers of school boards, principals, teachers, and parents. In *Engel v. Vitale* (1962), the Court outlawed the use of a Regent's prescribed prayer in New York public schools. One year later, in *Abington School District v. Schempp*, the Court held that Bible reading or the recitation of the Lord's Prayer in public schools was unconstitutional. The secondary effects of these decisions were resentment and resistance. Congress was hostile; many legislators condemned the rulings as an attack on America's spiritual values. "Any opposition to religious activities in the public schools was an attack upon religion and upon God Himself."[32] One congressman suggested that the *Engel* decision constituted "a deliberately and carefully planned conspiracy to substitute materialism for spiritual values and thus to communize America"; and another asserted that it would be "most pleasing to a few atheists and world Communism."[33] While the reaction to *Schempp* was somewhat milder, Congress was not pleased. In the nine months following this decision, nearly one hundred and fifty constitutional amendments intending to reverse the *Schempp* decision were introduced. None of these was supported by a majority of either house, although it appeared for a while that they might be.

For many years there were opponents of prayer reading in the public schools, and some states outlawed it before the Court's decisions. However, the opponents of school prayer were not as numerous, as vocal, or as well-placed politically as were those pushing for legislative reapportionment. Furthermore, the Court's targets were not the relatively few legislatures of the fifty states, but thousands of school districts and individual classrooms. For this reason alone, there were many more opportunities for the evasion of the Court in the prayer cases than in the apportionment cases. Exploring the secondary impacts of these decisions, surveys in Kentucky, Indiana, and Texas (all in the "Bible belt") found only 6 to 30 percent of the school districts changing their practices to comply with the Court's rulings.[34]

In Tennessee, some 58 percent of school districts continued the Bible reading required by state law two years after the Court had ruled it unconstitutional. One of the elements explaining why some districts complied while others did not was the local official's view of the Court. Where the official accepted the Court's right to make the ruling, even if he did not agree with it, he would be likely to comply. Consider the statements of policy makers in districts that *did* comply with the Court's order:[35]

> We must conform with Federal law. If we are to teach our children to obey laws we must set an example.

> We did not want to violate any federal law.

> I think the Supreme Court is correct. Very few people understand the religious issue, less seem to understand what is meant by religious freedom, and relatively few seem to understand the Supreme Court's role in our government.

> We are commanded by the Bible to be subject to civil powers as long as their laws do not conflict with laws of God.

In contrast, policy makers who *did not* comply with the Court's ruling offered the following challenges to its authority:

> Impeach Earl Warren.

> The Supreme Court decision didn't mean a damn.

> The general public in this country do not have the respect for the U.S. Supreme Court as they once did. They think it is packed, so to speak, and doubt very much if all are qualified and unbiased and listen to the whims of the President that gave them the appointment. The standards are on a lower level than back several years ago.

> I am at a loss to understand the necessity for this survey. I am of the opinion that 99% of the people in the United States feel as I do about the Supreme Court's decision—that it was an outrage and that Congress should have it amended. The remaining 1% do not belong in this free world.

There are regional differences in the impacts of the prayer decisions. Eastern states had generally required religious exercises in the schools, but they showed the highest rate of compliance with the new decision.

Western states, which had earlier prohibited religious observances, remained largely unaffected. Southern practices were changed the least, reflecting perhaps the more deeply seated religiosity of the region and anti-Court tendencies that had been formed during the earlier desegregation struggle. Some variations in compliance reflect the attitudes of the classroom teachers. Teachers who attended church frequently were more likely to conduct religious observances in their classrooms before the Court's decisions and to continue them afterward. Roman Catholic and Jewish teachers complied most often with the decisions, followed by liberal Protestants. Conservative Protestants were those least likely to follow the Court's rulings.

We know little about the tertiary effects of the prayer decisions. Presumably, they will depend on changes—if any—in the religious feelings of children who are no longer allowed to pray in the classroom, and in the self-esteem of children who are no longer required to pray.

Criminal Procedures

The issue of criminal procedures has surfaced in recent years as the Supreme Court handed down several decisions designed to protect the rights of the accused. Critics of the Court charged that the rulings would damage the law enforcement process; some blamed the Court for a breakdown of "law and order." In *Gideon v. Wainwright* (1963), the Court ruled that the "right to counsel" required that states supply indigents with competent attorneys in all criminal proceedings. A year later, the Court's *Escobedo v. Illinois* decision held that a suspect must be told that he can remain silent; that he has a right to consult with an attorney; and that if he is not informed of these rights, any incriminating information—such as a confession—that is acquired cannot be used in court. In *Miranda v. Arizona* (1966), the Court tried to clarify some of the issues arising from the *Escobedo* decision. Arguing that an interrogation is basically coercive and can lead to a violation of a suspect's rights, the Court laid down strict procedures for law enforcement agencies (see pages 313–315).

Not all police departments complied with these rulings. Studies of secondary effects found that only 25 of 118 suspects in New Haven, Connecticut, received all the information required. Ninety of them were informed of their right to remain silent; 51 were warned that anything they said could be used against them; 81 were told that they could see their lawyer; and 27 were informed of their right to counsel.[36] In Washington, D.C., only 30 percent of post-*Miranda* defendants reported that they had received all the four warnings prescribed by the Court; almost one-third said that they had been told nothing.[37]

The tertiary effects of the *Escobedo* and *Miranda* decisions were also limited. For one thing, confessions and other information gained from the suspect aid in obtaining convictions in only about 15 percent of felony arrests.[38] Defendants do not always understand the meaning of the *Miranda* warnings; and where the warnings are understood, they may not be needed. In Washington, D.C., 34 percent of the suspects knew of their right to counsel but did not request an attorney. Another 41 percent talked, even though they realized that they had the right to remain silent.[39]

SUMMARY

The judiciary, like the executive and the legislature, reflects the fragmentation of political power that characterizes American governments. The judiciary must depend on other actors to implement its rulings. These include government attorneys, the police (whose relations with courts are not always friendly), lower federal and state courts, state legislatures (for reapportionment), local school boards and teachers (for racial integration and school prayers), and the operators of numerous public and private institutions (for racial integration in public accommodations).

There are important differences between the judiciary and other branches of government, most of which seem to work against the judiciary. Judges take a passive role in policy making, waiting for litigants to initiate actions that raise "justiciable" questions. Also, the judiciary has avoided major "political" questions in the areas of taxation and international affairs. By leaving these to the other branches, the courts limit their own policy-making role. Yet the boundaries established by the judiciary's definition of "political" questions are subject to change. It was only in 1962 that the Supreme Court decided that legislative apportionment cases fell within the jurisdiction of the courts; and in less than a decade they managed to remap legislative districts for all fifty states and the United States Congress.

The courts' involvement in politics is evident to all who would examine judicial appointments, the behavior of judicial actors, and the public's attitude toward important court decisions. The courts may interpret the laws in the quiet decorum of richly paneled chambers, but once their decisions are aired, they arouse some of the most bitter public controversies. The decisions of the Warren Court drew criticism from many quarters, including the White House, Capitol Hill, state legislatures, police precincts, and churches. Few public officials in recent years have felt such strong and concerted attack as former Chief Justice Earl Warren. Warren did not establish the most liberal record during his tenure; that honor goes to either Justices Black or Douglas, depending on the nature of the issue. Yet Warren personified the tenor of decisions made while he was Chief Justice, and it is his name (like that of John Marshall more than one hundred years earlier) that marks the most recent distinctive era of the judiciary and reminds us that courts have major roles in policy delivery systems.

REFERENCES

1 Herbert Jacob, *Justice in America: Courts, Lawyers, and the Judicial Process,* 2d ed. (Boston: Little, Brown and Company, 1972), pp. 21–39. Copyright © 1972, 1965. Reprinted by permission.
2 Ibid., p. 31.
3 *The Federalist Papers,* Number 78 (New York: Mentor Books, New American Library, Inc., 1961), p. 465.
4 Ibid., p. 468.
5 Ibid., pp. 465–466.
6 Henry J. Abraham, *The Judicial Process* (New York: Oxford Book Company, Inc., 1968), pp. 307ff.
7 Jacob, op. cit., p. 23.
8 Ibid., p. 212.
9 For a more extensive discussion of this matter see Anthony A. D'Amato and Robert M. O'Neil, *The Judiciary and Vietnam* (New York: St. Martin's, 1972).
10 *Reynolds v. Sims,* 377 U.S. 533 (1964).
11 Jacob, op. cit., p. 36.
12 For a more extensive discussion of the structures and procedures of American courts, see Abraham, op. cit., pp. 139ff.
13 Ibid., p. 141.
14 See Joel B. Grossman, *Lawyers and Judges* (New York: John Wiley and Sons, Inc., 1965).
15 See John R. Schmidhauser, *The Supreme Court: Its Politics, Personalities, and Procedures* (New York: Holt, 1960).
16 Joel B. Grossman, "The Politics of Judicial Selection," in Herbert Jacob (ed.), *Law, Politics, and the Federal Courts* (Boston: Little, Brown and Company, 1967), p. 59.
17 Quoted in ibid., p. 49.
18 Quoted in Glendon Schubert, *Constitutional Politics: The Political Behavior of Supreme Court Justices and the Constitutional Policies That They Make* (New York: Holt, 1960), p. 52.
19 See Glendon Schubert, *The Judicial Mind: Attitudes and Ideologies of Supreme Court Justices 1946–1963* (Evanston: Northwestern University Press, 1965), chap. 5. This quotation comes from p. 97.
20 For a critical assessment of the Warren period see Alexander M. Bickel, *The Supreme Court and the Idea of Progress* (New York: Harper & Row, Publishers, Incorporated, 1970).
21 Paul Bender, "The Techniques of Subtle Erosion," *Harper's Magazine* (December 1972), p. 20.

22 James Eisenstein, *Politics and the Legal Process* (New York: Harper & Row, Publishers, Incorporated, 1973), pp. 163–164.

23 See Arthur Niederhoffer, *Behind the Shield: The Police in Urban Society* (Garden City, N.Y.: Anchor Books, Doubleday & Company, Inc., 1969), pp. 35–40.

24 See Seymour Martin Lipset, *Political Man: Where, How and Way Democracy Works in the Modern World* (Garden City, N.Y.: Doubleday & Company, Inc., 1960), especially chap. 4.

25 Niederhoffer, op. cit., p. 160.

26 Jerome H. Skolnick, *Justice without Trial: Law Enforcement in Democratic Society* (New York: John Wiley & Sons, Inc., 1967), pp. 6, 7.

27 Abraham, op. cit., p. 226.

28 Ibid.

29 *Barnette v. West Virginia*, 47 F. Supp. 251, 253 (1942).

30 Theodore L. Becker and Malcolm M. Feeley (eds.), *The Impact of Supreme Court Decisions*, 2d ed. (New York: Oxford Book Company, Inc. 1973), p. 63.

31 *Representation and Apportionment* (Washington, D.C.: Congressional Quarterly Service, 1966), p. 65.

32 William M. Beaney and Edward N. Beiser, "Prayer and Politics: The Impact of *Engel and Schempp* on the Political Process," *Journal of Public Law*, vol. 13, no. 2 (1964), pp. 475–503.

33 108 *Congressional Record*, 11734, 11718 (1962).

34 These and a number of additional studies are summarized in Stephen L. Wasby, *The Impact of the United States Supreme Court: Some Perspectives* (Homewood, Ill.: The Dorsey Press, 1970), pp. 131ff.

35 Robert H. Birkby, "The Supreme Court and the Bible Belt: Tennessee Reaction to the 'Schempp' Decision," *Midwest Journal of Political Science*, vol. 10 (August 1966), pp. 304–315. Reprinted by permission of Wayne State University Press.

36 Michael Wald et al., "Interrogations in New Haven: The Impact of *Miranda*," *Yale Law Review*, vol. 76 (July 1967), pp. 1521–1648.

37 Richard J. Medalie et al., "Custodial Police Interrogation in Our Nation's Capital: The Attempt to Implement *Miranda*," *Michigan Law Review*, vol. 66 (May 1968), pp. 1347–1422.

38 Eisenstein, op. cit., p. 290.

39 Ibid., p. 293.

Chapter 12

The Performance of American Governments

American governments have faced a number of crises and conflicts during the last decade. During this period, the United States fought a tragic war in Vietnam. Unrest and bitterness spread throughout the nation, even though (and perhaps because) most Americans never understood the reasons for this commitment of men and material in a struggle beyond the nation's massive military capacity. There remain serious problems of poverty, in spite of decades of government involvement and the spending of billions of dollars. Washington's fiscal policies have failed to control inflation and unemployment; indeed, some critics assert that they have aggravated the situation. The picture is no more encouraging in other areas, as the costs of health care skyrocket; environmental pollution continues to engulf the cities; cities are riddled with crime and decay; and racial justice and equality remain unrealized dreams for many Americans. Most recently, the scandals of Nixon and Agnew have threatened the credibility and integrity of government officials and institutions alike, have produced our first presidential resignation and the selections of President Gerald Ford and Vice President Nelson Rockefeller, neither of whom faced the voters in a national election. And though the full effect of all these problems has yet to be felt, they will leave scars on the American political system for years to come.

Taken together, these controversies have resulted in a crisis of confidence. Americans have become increasingly worried and cynical about government paralysis in identifying and solving social and economic problems. Yet, it would be unfair to let this indictment stand by itself without a balanced assessment. As we observed in Chapter 1, the staying power and worth of the American political system are reflected in two centuries of stability and orderly change. Admittedly, these changes have usually been marginal, intended to strengthen the status quo. Only once did the demands for a basic change in economic, social, and political institutions reach a critical level: during the Civil War era. All other crises have been resolved by incremental structural or policy changes, with the backing of most Americans.[1]

It is a measure of our political system's flexibility that few people seriously question its basic structure. Racial tensions, memories of Vietnam, an unstable economy, and the horrors of Watergate have undermined public support. And yet, it is unlikely that the existing coolness, cynicism, and distrust will jeopardize the future of the political system or lead to a basic change in our political institutions and public policies.

HOW CAN WE ASSESS GOVERNMENT PERFORMANCE?

Joyce M. and William C. Mitchell have proposed five criteria to evaluate the performance of political systems. According to them, every political system should:[2]

1 Provide a minimal level of public goods and services, including such generalized goods as order and safety and such symbolic goods as dignity and regard.
2 Distribute these goods and services as fairly, effectively, and efficiently as possible.
3 Be as adaptable to changing conditions and as responsive to citizen preferences as its resources and priorities allow.
4 Provide the opportunities to develop its members' talents, motivations, and resources as effectively as possible.
5 Solve problems as satisfactorily and inexpensively as possible.

According to these standards, the American political system receives both good and bad marks. American governments provide a wide range of goods and services, although not with equal effectiveness and efficiency. It is more difficult to assess the fairness of distribution. Take the equity of tax policies. In principle, an equitable tax is one that distributes the costs of public services fairly among different economic groups. But does this mean an *equal* assignment of taxes among citizens and business firms, a *progressive* system (whereby people with large incomes pay the highest taxes, in both dollar and percentage terms), or a *regressive* system (whereby taxes take larger income percentages from the poor than the rich)?

The tax systems of most urban governments tend to be regressive. This is particularly true of the property tax. State sales taxes are generally regressive because they weigh more heavily on the poor, who must spend most of their incomes on basic necessities that are subject to the tax. At the federal level, income taxes are moderately progressive. At the local level, however, taxes on incomes tend to be fixed, typically at 1 percent. Considered as a whole, then, the American tax system is not so progressive as we sometimes suppose. More important, the tax system shows that assessing how well a government performs depends upon the definition of equity used.

It is no easier to assess how fairly public goods and services are distributed in other areas. In education, some students enjoy far greater opportunities than others. The legal services available to the poor and minorities are far inferior to those of most other Americans. Similar gaps can be found in the areas of health, transportation, agriculture, and housing. The *persistence* of these gulfs—between rich and poor, black and white, central cities and suburbs, and different regions—has contributed to the recurring problems of recent years. According to one study that examines the total programs of all governments, however, low-income families receive proportionately more benefits than middle- and upper-income families.[3]

Efforts to help the poor do not come easily. Our political system responds more readily to the needs of some individuals and groups than others. Take the long-standing controversy over the government's role in providing medical services. Although demands for government involvement date back to the beginning of the twentieth century, it was not until 1948 that public medical care was seriously considered. That year, President Truman proposed a program of compulsory health insurance. Such a program, he asserted, would pave the way for a national health insurance plan. But even though public opinion polls reported that a majority of Americans favored this move, Congress failed to approve it; it was defeated mainly by the American Medical Association's nationwide lobbying. In what amounted to a multimillion-dollar effort, the AMA "enlisted hundreds of voluntary organizations and pressure groups to oppose compulsory health insurance, and their crusade was conducted on a note of hysteria, holding out horrific visions of a socialized America ruled by an autocratic federal government."[4]

The opposition of the AMA continued through the 1950s and early 1960s. In 1961, President Kennedy proposed a new hospital insurance program for the aged. In spite of the President's vigorous support and strongly favorable public opinion polls, however, this and other Medicare proposals remained buried in the House Ways and Means Committee for four years. It was not until 1965, after the massive Democratic landslide of the previous year, that Medicare finally made it through Congress. It took President Johnson's overwhelming electoral victory, and a significant change in the composition of Congress, to overcome the AMA's forty-five year, multimillion-dollar fight against public health legislation.[5]

WHAT DOES IT ALL MEAN?

It is not our purpose to answer the question, How well do American governments work? The answers would be affected by the criteria used and the way they are applied. They would also rely heavily upon the authors' perceptions, experiences, and biases. Thoughtful readers should be able to evaluate the system on their own. Depending on their personal observations, experiences, and political philosophies, widely varying assessments will be made.

It is our purpose here to explain how American governments identify economic and social needs, design policies to meet them, and achieve their goals. To do this, we should step back and reexamine our discussions of voters, political parties, and interest groups as policy makers; national, state, and local governments; and legislative, executive, judicial, and bureaucratic politics and policy making. What does it all mean? What does it tell us about the impact of governments on our lives? What does it say about the capacity of governments to adapt to changing environmental conditions, to solve economic and social problems, or to minimize dissatisfaction or eliminate injustice?

RATIONAL POLICY MAKING

"Rationality" is a widely held value in American society. It is often supposed that policies derived from a rational decision-making process —one in which all important issues are taken into consideration—will have a good chance of realizing their objectives. Yet, the demands of a completely rational decision-making process are severe. Policy makers are seldom rational, in the pure sense of that term. This does not mean that officials make choices in an irrational fashion, ignoring some of the factors that most observers would consider important. Most policy making is neither completely rational nor completely irrational. Major decisions appear to be made after several—but not all—important issues have been assessed.

According to one common formula, a perfectly rational policy maker would:

1   Identify the problem;
2   Clarify the goals, and then rank them according to importance;
3   List all possible means—or policies—for achieving each goal;
4   Assess all the costs and benefits that would seem to follow from each policy;
5   Select the package of goals and associated policies that would bring the greatest relative benefits and the least relative disadvantages.[6]

Following these procedures, policy makers should inform themselves about *all* possible opportunities and *all* possible consequences of each option. Yet, this is an enormous job. Behind it are two assumptions: (1) that public officials have vast resources to gather information about the environment and how each proposal will affect it, and (2) that decision makers are not committed in advance to any one set of goals or policies, and, therefore, can choose on the basis of the information collected. However, this rational model is unrealistic when public officials are under pressure to produce policies quickly, or when they are hampered by prior commitments. Furthermore, political demands often force policy makers to favor certain goals and policies at the expense of others, regardless of the merits of the case. For instance, it was easier for President Nixon, a Republican, to move the United States toward diplomatic relations with the People's Republic of China than it would have been for a Democratic President, whose party was identified in some minds as having "lost" China to the Communists in the 1950s. Similarly, the financial backing and votes that Democratic presidential candidates traditionally receive from organized labor inhibits them from taking economic positions which alienate labor.

Four features of the policy delivery system undermine rational policy making. These are:

1   The many problems, goals, and policy commitments that are imposed on—or kept from—policy makers by other groups in government or in the private sector;
2   Barriers to collecting adequate information about "acceptable" goals and policies;
3   The needs, commitments, and inhibitions of policy makers, which interfere with their assessment of "acceptable" goals and policies;

4 Structural barriers to the identification and assessment of alternative goals and policies, such as seniority rules, which give special influence to the biases of certain legislators.

These four factors are interrelated; each includes elements that also appear in others. And each imposes its own limits on decision makers who might, in an ideal world, want to make rational choices. By exploring these factors, we can reexamine the major features of policy delivery systems that have been covered in this book, and see how they fit into a larger view of politics.

The Many Problems, Goals, and Policy Commitments

This is actually a combination of two factors: (1) the variety of problems and goals that concern government activity, and (2) the commitments that prevent a thorough assessment of each. Frequently, the full range of possibilities is so great that even defining the problem becomes difficult. "Symptoms" of something wrong in the environment may be misunderstood. What are the problems that lie beneath urban riots, rising drug use, or an increasing number of inflationary wage settlements? Should each be handled with separate goals and policies? Or do they point to other underlying difficulties which are themselves the problems to be treated? If so, what are they? If there *is* a common problem, the way in which it is defined will influence the goals and policies chosen to solve it. The problem behind increased drug use may include mass dissatisfaction with our foreign policy, short-range social and/or economic pressures, or a loss in the basic sense of community that once united the country. Unless they can agree on what the problems are, policy makers cannot design goals and programs rationally to eliminate them. Defining the problem is, at best, a difficult and ambiguous process. Problems do not simply exist; they must be defined through a process of observing, assessing, and abstracting from reality. This is done by officials who are influenced by their own prior experiences and commitments. Thus, the process is somewhat less than "rational."

Limits on Information

The high cost of obtaining information makes rational policy making almost impossible. Public officials seldom have time to assess thoroughly their environment and the pros and cons attached to each set of goals and policies. Even after spending much time acquiring information, some ignorance remains. Information gathering is hampered in two ways:

1 It is impossible to acquire all the information needed. Public officials must often make decisions quickly without knowing the full range of constituents' demands.

2 More troublesome, officials must often use the present to make inferences about the future. Some inferences are based on the assumption that past trends will continue into the near future; these are not too risky if the trend is a simple one and has, in the past, been consistent in repeating itself. However, no one can predict with certainty what particular persons or organizations will do in the future. To try to do so is to invite error.[7]

The Needs, Commitments, and Inhibitions of Policy Makers

American governments receive information and evaluations from a vast number of sources—sometimes, it seems, almost too many. When selecting goals, assessing information, and developing policies, government units must work through members who have subjective values and attitudes. These may reflect professional training or personal bias, and shape how the individual perceives the environment and establishes goals and policies.[8]

This diversity can be seen in the bureaucracy, where a wide range of professions (law, medicine, engineering, and various social and natural sciences) is represented. There are different schools of thought, both within each profession and between different professions, that may generate disputes. Some disputes are personality conflicts. Antagonisms developed in one context may carry over to other encounters between administrative departments and/or legislative committees. These ongoing conflicts may generate arguments about the definition of problems or about the choice of goals or policies.

Structural Barriers to Rationality

If making rational decisions requires us to develop a *method*—a series of steps—by which we can move toward certain goals rather than others, the structure of American governments defeats this purpose. Fragmentation at all levels hinders the system's capacity to define problems, establish goals, and survey alternate policies comprehensively. This should not be surprising, since the founding fathers were more concerned with preventing tyranny than with establishing a smooth-running government machine. The implications for rational policy making are obvious. Instead of being attacked in a coordinated manner, problems are dealt with by three levels of government, each of which may be pursuing different policies to achieve the same or different goals. Within each level of government, legal authority is fragmented. This means that decision makers can pursue different goals and policies. However, none can make important decisions "rationally" without fear of a veto from other officials with different perspectives.

COMPROMISES WITH RATIONALITY

All this is not meant to imply that policy makers are completely irrational. The rational model requires a central decision maker who can—with the cooperation of subordinates—define problems, establish goals, and survey all possible policies before choosing those that will prove (relatively) successful and inexpensive. Since the American policy delivery system hardly works this way, public officials have devised a number of ways of coping with the many demands they face. *Incremental* budgeting is one of them. As we observed in Chapter 10, incrementalists do not debate social goals. They generally accept the legitimacy of established programs and continue to pay for them. They concentrate their inquiries only on the increments of change proposed in the new budget (see pages 281–283).

In the absence of rational decision making, officials make policy by the pull and push of politics. Professor Charles E. Lindblom refers to this as a process of *mutual adjustment*, with policy making as a process of "muddling through" rather than one of long-range planning. Many techniques combine to make for mutual adjustment: participation of various interest groups; maintenance of a flexible position; a willingness to bargain; the expectation that people will bargain in good faith and agree to make concessions; and the view that goal formation and policy making are continuing processes, so that desires that are not satisfied today may be tomorrow—or in next year's budget.[9]

Flexibility is the main feature of mutual adjustment. Decision makers have no hard-and-fast evidence that any one set of goals or policies is "the one best way" to resolve their problems. "Rational" search and discovery is not emphasized; rather, mutual adjustment places a priority on assessing the persons who support a demand, their intensity, their alliances with key officials, and the possibility of modifying a position so that it appeals to an even wider group. Decisions are not made once and for all, but in a sequence of continuing interactions; later decisions serve to modify the impact of earlier ones. Annual or biennial budget reviews provide a good opportunity for mutual adjustment. Demands that are not met in one phase of the sequence return again, often in a different form and with different supporters. If, meanwhile, either the environment or the wording of the demand has changed, a once-rejected demand may find acceptance and financial backing.

PPB AND THE PURSUIT OF RATIONALITY

Dissatisfaction with these nonrational approaches to policy making reached a climax in the early 1960s, when a planning, programming, and budgeting system (PPB) was introduced in the Department of Defense. Decision makers were urged to take more factors into consideration when choosing goals and the policies to realize them. Former Director of the Bureau of the Budget Charles L. Schultze has described PPB as an attempt to *integrate* policy formulation with budgetary resource allocation, and to provide a means for regularly bringing systematic analysis to bear on both policy formulation and budget allocation.[10]

PPB seeks greater rationality in decision making by clarifying the steps used to attain certain goals. The policy maker using PPB would:

1 Identify and examine goals and objectives in each major area of government activity;
2 Analyze how well a given program meets these objectives;
3 Measure total program costs for *several* years, not merely one or two;
4 Formulate long-range goals and policies beyond the year in which the budget is submitted;
5 Analyze alternatives to find the most effective and least expensive means of reaching program objectives;
6 Make these procedures part of the program and budget review.[11]

PPB is a major departure from nonrational approaches to policy making; emphasis is placed on analysis of goals and programs, and measurement of costs. In practice, however, PPB has met with only limited success. At the federal level, President Johnson directed all major civilian agencies to initiate a PPB system in August 1965. Less than six years later, PPB "died" when the Office of Management and Budget informed all federal agencies that they would no longer be required to submit with their budget requests the long-range program and financing plans, and other program memoranda, that had become part of this system of policy making.[12] The Nixon administration's abandonment of PPB reflects the failures and shortcomings of this system. As Allen Schick has reported:

PPB died because of the manner in which it was introduced, across-the-board without much preparation. PPB died because new men of power were arrogantly insensitive to budgetary traditions, institutional loyalties, and personal relationships. PPB died because of inadequate support and leadership with meager resources invested in its behalf. . . . PPB died because good analysts and data were in short supply and it takes a great deal of time to make up the deficit.[13]

Beyond the specifics listed here, Schick is arguing—perhaps more importantly—that PPB failed because it ran counter to some basic American political values. The policy delivery system does not encourage centralization. Instead, it invites bargaining, compromise, trade-offs, and logrolling; it favors the push and pull of diverse political interests which could be neglected if policy choices rested with technical analysts.[13]

PPB, which still exists in some state and local governments, has encountered many of these problems. While state agencies may go through the motions of preparing PPB documents and other memoranda, this paperwork is often ignored when policy decisions are actually made. "In the final days of budget decision, months of promotional and analytic work can go down the drain as budgeters forsake the long view in favor of the short run, and the analytic in favor of the justificatory material. (Analyses raise questions, justifications give answers, and these are what decision makers want in the final stages.)"[15]

Finally, if PPB—or any of its successors—is going to survive, policy makers must be shown that it seeks to *modify* the political process, not to *replace* it. So long as "rational" approaches are seen as threats to the democratic processes of advocacy, bargaining, and negotiated settlement, they are doomed to failure. Their survival depends on the recognition that political limits and considerations are not being neglected, but that systematic analysis adds a new dimension. It can aid policy making by identifying problems, clarifying goals and objectives, determining how resources have been used and what has been accomplished, and defining alternative policies for the future.

THE POLITICS OF POLICY IMPLEMENTATION

Even when, after long or brief analysis of alternative goals and programs, policy is actually made, there is no assurance that its goals will be realized. This brings us to *implementation*, the process whereby general policies are converted into concrete, meaningful public services. This is seldom a simple task. When faced with an unsuccessful program, it is all too easy to cite insufficient planning or the inadequacy of the program itself. This rationalization is often unjustified. One of the planners of the War on Poverty has lamented that "implementation was the Achilles' heel of the Johnson administration's social policy."[16] Viewing social policies generally, Robert A. Levine concluded that much of the trouble resulted "not so much from the nature of the programs as from difficulties of administration."[17]

Unfortunately, we know little about how policies are implemented. Pointing to the possible gap between the intentions and statements of public officials (policy) on the one hand and the delivery of public services (performance) on the other, Kenneth M. Dolbeare and Philip E. Hammond argue that very little may really be decided by the words of a decision or a statute: the enunciation of such a national policy may be just the beginning of the decisive process of determining what will happen to whom, and understanding this further stage is essential to a full understanding of politics.[18]

An inquiry about policy implementation "seeks to determine whether an organization can bring together men and material in a cohesive organizational unit and motivate them in such a way as to carry out the organization's stated objectives."[19] The fragmentation of American governments greatly complicates this task, making it difficult to realize program objectives. The system provides no guarantee that one group of public officials will implement a program authorized by another. At the federal level, this fact is illustrated by the impoundment controversy. To promote his own domestic priorities over those of Congress, President Nixon refused to spend funds that had been appropriated by Congress. Futhermore, the Nixon administration has often been criticized for not fully executing numerous federal civil rights laws, even though they had been enacted by Congress and/or upheld by the Supreme Court.

Fragmentation is a serious problem for the implementation of policies that cut across federal, state, and local lines. Programs are sometimes initiated and funded by the federal government, while much administration rests with state and local officials. This pattern is common in the fields of public welfare, housing and community development, and education. Take, for example, the Elementary and Secondary Education Act of 1965. As enacted by Congress, this law was intended to "provide financial assistance . . . to local educational agencies serving areas with concentrations of children from low-income families; and to expand and improve their educational programs by various means . . . which contribute particularly to meeting the special educational needs of educationally deprived children." In administering this program, the U.S. Office of Education was constrained by legislation and appropriations acts. Yet it had wide latitude in defining the options available to state and local educational agencies, and in establishing criteria to be used in evaluating state and local funding requests. Stephen K. Bailey and Edith K. Mosher have written that

> the implementation stage offered Federal officials their most important opportunity to exercise initiative and foresight in exploring policy alternatives, in ventilating controversies, and in testing strategies for obtaining a high degree of voluntary compliance with legislative intent.[20]

There is no guarantee, however, that state and local officials will comply with federal guidelines and standards. Noncompliance may result from several factors. First, state and local officials may not know what federal officials want, because of vague or ambiguous language in legislation or in administrative instructions. Second, state and local policy makers may not be able to do what federal officials want.

> Because of the uncertainty and late availability of funds, a circumstance which has prevented educators from being able to plan for Title I as they develop their program months in advance of the school year, ESEA money has largely gone for a variety of special ancillary programs and has not been utilized to upgrade the central portion of the educational curriculum presented to disadvantaged children.[21]

Finally, state and local officials may reject the goals and objectives of federal officials, and therefore, refuse to do what Washington wants them to do. Title I of ESEA, for example, provided funds to aid educationally deprived children; yet, many school districts tried to use the funds for general school purposes. Similarly, Title I funds were not meant to substitute for state and local revenue, although in some instances they have. Finally, in spite of the law and the Constitution, Title I funds were used by some Southern school systems to frustrate desegregation efforts by improving the services available in all-black schools.[22]

A CONCLUDING NOTE

We are neither bold enough nor foolish enough to end this book with a definite prediction about the future of American governments; the scene is shifting too quickly.[23] It is almost impossible to predict future developments in the great crises which face the nation: racial antagonisms, economic instability, the decay of cities, the paradox of poverty amid vast wealth, and America's international responsibilities. Many of these problems may be ultimately insoluble in a democratic political system. Some of them—crime, congestion, and decay—may simply be inherent in an industrialized, urban society. Others—pollution, for example—seem to be the inevitable by-products of this society. The solutions to still other problems—poverty and racial discrimination—may be politically unworkable. Elected officials are rarely willing to risk their chances for reelection by supporting unpopular policies, especially when they can rationalize that they are simply doing what their constituents want. Perhaps the most effective solution to the problem of poverty is a form of guaranteed income for all; and busing may be the only way to desegregate the schools in the near future. Politically, however, such proposals are likely to prove so unpopular that most politicians will avoid them.

In some instances, solving one problem will aggravate another. The pollution of air and water, for example, cannot be ended without great cost to the economic system, which in turn would make the fight against poverty even more difficult. Similarly, many of the nation's social problems may be helped by increased federal spending, but perhaps at the risk of straining our already overexpanded economy and serious problems of inflation.

We have not tried to evaluate in detail how well American governments perform. Clearly, the policy delivery system has succeeded in sustaining itself; it has coped with—or actually solved—many economic, social, and political problems. The system continues to protect many conflicting interests. This does not mean that change is impossible; it does mean that it is difficult to make any *basic* change that will severely affect particular interest groups. In many cases only marginal changes are made. From another perspective, the system has shown itself to be a creaking gate rather than a well-oiled machine, incapable of responding quickly and coherently to social problems.

Nor have we tried to explore the issue of political values. Obviously, the individual's personality and political philosophy have a lot to do with his or her evaluation of American governments. Take, for example, the division of authority. If you place a high priority on efficiency and effectiveness, fragmentation will seem ponderous and stupid. If, on the other hand, you fear centralized authority and feel that many people should have a voice, divided authority will seem to be an advantage.

Since the authors' own perspectives on many of these issues are very different, they cannot provide detailed assessments of American governments. Perhaps this is wise; ultimately, you alone must choose. And you can choose wisely only after becoming familiar with the many problems that cry for public attention; appreciating the limits and opportunities which face policy makers; knowing that policy systems have complex components; and understanding how each of these contributes to policy making and implementation.

REFERENCES

1 For a more detailed discussion of the notion of political change, see Kenneth M. Dolbeare, *Political Change in the United States: A Framework for Analysis* (New York: McGraw-Hill Book Company, 1974).
2 Joyce M. Mitchell and William C. Mitchell, *Political Analysis and Public Policy: An Introduction to Political Science* (Chicago: Rand McNally & Company, 1969), p. 485.

3 *Allocating Tax Benefits and Burdens by Income Class* (New York: Tax Foundation, Inc., 1967), p.6.

4 Theodore R. Marmor, *The Politics of Medicare* (Chicago: Aldine Publishing Co.-Atherton Press Inc., 1973). pp. 12–13.

5 Richard Harris, *A Sacred Trust* (Baltimore: Penguin Books, Inc., 1969), p. 3.

6 Charles E. Lindblom, *The Policy-Making Process* (Englewood Cliffs, N.J.: Prentice-Hall, Inc., 1968), p. 13.

7 See Herbert Simon, *Administrative Behavior* (New York: The Macmillan Company, 1961); and Anthony Downs, *Inside Bureaucracy* (Boston: Little, Brown and Company, 1967).

8 See Richard M. Cyert and James G. March, *A Behavioral Theory of the Firm* (Englewood Cliffs, N.J.: Prentice-Hall, Inc., 1963), chap. 3.

9 See Lindblom, *The Policy-Making Process*; and Charles E. Lindblom, "The Science of 'Muddling Through,'" *Public Administration Review*, vol. 19 (Spring 1959), pp. 79–88.

10 Charles L. Schultze, *The Politics and Economics of Public Spending* (Washington: The Brookings Institution, 1968), p. 15.

11 Ibid., pp. 19–24.

12 See Allen Schick, "A Death in the Bureaucracy: The Demise of Federal PPB," *Public Administration Review* (March—April 1973), pp. 146–56.

13 Ibid., pp. 148–149.

14 For criticisms of PPB and other "rational" approaches to decision making, see Aaron Wildavsky, "The Political Economy of Efficiency: Cost-Benefit Analysis, Systems Analysis, and Program Budgeting," *Public Administration Review* (December 1966), pp. 292–310; Lindblom, *The Policy-Making Process*; and Lindbolm, "The Science of 'Muddling Through.'"

15 Allen Schick, *Budget Innovation in the States* (Washington: The Brookings Institution, 1971), p. 115.

16 Walter Williams, *Social Policy Research and Analysis* (New York: American Elsevier Publishing Company, Inc., 1971), p. 9.

17 Robert A. Levine, "Rethinking Our Social Strategies," *Public Interest* (Winter 1968), p. 86.

18 Kenneth M. Dolbeare and Philip E. Hammond, *The School Prayer Decisions* (Chicago: The University of Chicago Press, 1971), p. 149.

19 Williams, op. cit., p. 144.

20 Stephen K. Bailey and Edith K. Mosher, *ESEA: The Office of Education Administers of Law* (Syracuse: Sycracuse University Press, 1968), p. 99.

21 Joel S. Berke and Michael W. Kirst, *Federal Aid to Education: Who Benefits? Who Governs?* (Lexington, Mass.: Lexington Books, 1972), p. 44.

22 See *Title I of ESEA: Is It Helping Poor Children?* Report by the Washington Research Project of the Southern Center for Studies in Public Policy and the NAACP Legal Defense and Educational Fund, Inc., December 1969.

23 For some attempts, however, see the computerized futurism of Herman Kahn and Anthony Wiener, *Toward the Year 2000* (New York: The Macmillan Company, 1967); andHarvey S. Perloff (ed.), *The Future of the U.S. Government: Toward the Year 2000* (Englewood Cliffs, N.J.: Prentice-Hall, Inc., 1971).

Selected Bibliography

CHAPTER 1

Churchman, C. West. *The Systems Approach.* New York: Dell Publishing Co., Inc., 1968.

Cobb, Roger W., and Charles D. Elder. *Participation in American Politics: The Dynamics of Agenda-Building.* Boston: Allyn and Bacon, Inc., 1972.

Deutsch, Karl W. *The Nerves of Government.* New York: The Free Press, 1968.

Dolbeare, Kenneth M. *Political Change in the United States: A Framework for Analysis.* New York: McGraw-Hill Book Company, 1974.

Easton, David. *A Systems Analysis of Political Life.* New York: John Wiley & Sons, Inc., 1965.

Jones, Charles O. *An Introduction to the Study of Public Policy.* Belmont, Calif.: Wadsworth Publishing Company, Inc. 1970.

Lasswell, Harold D. *Politics: Who Gets What, When, How.* Cleveland: The World Publishing Company, 1958.

CHAPTER 2

Blaustein, Albert P., and Clarence C. Ferguson, Jr. *Desegregation and the Law.* New Brunswick, N.J.: Rutgers University Press, 1957.

Crain, Robert L. *The Politics of School Desegregation.* Garden City, N.Y.: Doubleday & Company, Inc., 1969.

Jencks, Christopher. *Inequality: A Reassessment of the Effect of Family and Schooling in America.* New York: Harper & Row, Publishers, Incorporated, 1972.

Kirby, David J., et al. *Political Strategies in Northern School Desegregation.* Lexington, Mass.: Lexington, 1973.

Orfield, Gary. *The Reconstruction of Southern Education.* New York: John Wiley & Sons, Inc., 1969.

Peltason, Jack W. *Fifty-eight Lonely Men: Southern Federal Judges and School Desegregation.* New York: Harcourt Brace Jovanovich, 1961.

Revolution in Civil Rights. Washington, D.C.: Congressional Quarterly Service, 1968.

Rodgers, Harrell R., Jr., and Charles S. Bullock, III. *Law and Social Change: Civil Rights Laws and Their Consequences.* New York: McGraw-Hill Book Company, 1972.

Rogers, David. *110 Livingston Street.* New York: Random House, Inc., 1968.

Smith, Al, Anthony Downs, and M. Leanne Lachman. *Achieving Effective Desegregation.* Lexington, Mass.: Lexington, 1973.

U.S. Commission on Civil Rights. *Racial Isolation in the Public Schools.* Washington, D.C.: Government Printing Office, 1967.

Wirt, Frederick M. *Politics of Southern Equality: Law and Social Change in a Mississippi County.* Chicago: Aldine Publishing Company, 1970.

CHAPTER 3

Draper, Theodore. *The Abuse of Power.* New York: The Viking Press, Inc., 1967.

Enthoven, Alain C., and K. Wayne Smith. *How Much Is Enough? Shaping the Defense Program, 1961–1969.* New York: Harper & Row, Publishers, Incorporated, 1971.

Evans, Rowland, Jr., and Robert D. Novak. *Nixon in the White House: The Frustration of Power.* New York: Random House, Inc., 1971.

Gregg, Robert W., and Charles W. Kegley, Jr., eds. *After Vietnam: The Future of American Foreign Policy.* Garden City, N.Y.: Doubleday & Company, Inc., 1971.

Handelman, John R., Howard B. Shapiro, and John A. Vasquez. *Introductory Case Studies for International Relations: Vietnam/The Middle East/The Environmental Crisis.* Chicago: Rand McNally & Company, 1974.

Hoopes, Townsend. *The Limits of Intervention.* New York: David McKay Company, Inc., 1969.

Huntington, Samuel P. *The Common Defense: Strategic Programs in National Politics.* New York: Columbia University Press, 1962.

Kissinger, Henry A. *American Foreign Policy: Three Essays.* New York: W. W. Norton & Company, Inc., 1969.

Mueller, John E. *War, Presidents, and Public Opinion.* New York: John Wiley & Sons, Inc., 1973.

The Pentagon Papers. New York: Bantam Books, Inc., 1971.

Robinson, James A. *Congress and Foreign Policy-Making: A Study in Legislative Influence and Initiative.* Homewood, Ill.: The Dorsey Press, 1967.

Rosenberg, Milton J., Sidney Verba, and Philip E. Converse. *Vietnam and the Silent Majority.* New York: Harper & Row, Publishers, Incorporated, 1970.

Russett, Bruce M. *What Price Vigilance? The Burdens of National Defense.* New Haven, Conn.: Yale University Press, 1970.

Spanier, John. *American Foreign Policy since World War II.* 6th ed. New York: Frederick A. Praeger, Inc. 1973.

—————— and Eric M. Uslaner. *How American Foreign Policy Is Made.* New York: Frederick A. Praeger, Inc., 1974.

CHAPTER 4

Barber, James David. *Citizen Politics: An Introduction to Political Behavior.* 2d ed. Chicago: Markham, 1972.

Bone, Hugh A., and Austin Ranney. *Politics and Voters.* 3d ed. New York: McGraw-Hill Book Company, 1971.

Broder, David S. *The Party's Over: The Failure of Politics in America.* New York: Harper & Row, Publishers, Incorporated, 1971.

Campbell, Angus, et al. *The American Voter.* New York: John Wiley & Sons, Inc., 1960.

——————. *Elections and the Political Order.* New York: John Wiley & Sons, Inc., 1966.

Dawson, Richard E. *Public Opinion and Contemporary Disarray.* New York: Harper & Row, Publishers, Incorporated, 1973.

Dexter, Lewis A. *How Organizations Are Represented in Washington.* Indianapolis: The Bobbs-Merrill Company, Inc., 1969.

Flanigan, William H. *Political Behavior of the American Electorate.* 2d ed. Boston: Allyn and Bacon, Inc., 1972.

Greenstein, Fred I. *The American Party System and the American People.* 2d ed. Englewood Cliffs, N.J.: Prentice-Hall, Inc., 1970.

Greenstone, David. *Labor in American Politics.* New York: Alfred A. Knopf, Inc., 1969.

Harris, Louis. *The Anguish of Change.* New York: W. W. Norton & Company, Inc., 1974.

Harris, Richard. *A Sacred Trust.* Baltimore: Penguin Books, Inc., 1969.

Keefe, William J. *Parties, Politics, and Public Policy in America.* New York: Holt, Rinehart and Winston, Inc., 1972.

Key, V. O., Jr. *Public Opinion and American Democracy.* New York: Alfred A. Knopf, Inc., 1964.

——————. *The Responsible Electorate.* Cambridge: Harvard University Press, 1966.

Ladd, Everett C., Jr. *American Political Parties: Social Change and Political Response.* New York: W. W. Norton & Company, Inc., 1970.

Lakoff, Sanford A., ed. *Private Government.* Glenview, Ill.: Scott, Foresman & Company, 1973.

Lipset, Seymour Martin. *Political Man: The Social Bases of Politics.* Garden City, N.Y.: Doubleday & Company, Inc., 1960.

Lipsky, Michael. *Protest in City Politics.* Chicago: Rand McNally & Company, 1970.

Lubell, Samuel. *The Hidden Crisis in American Politics.* New York: W. W. Norton & Company, Inc., 1970.

McConnell, Grant. *Private Power and American Democracy.* New York: Alfred A. Knopf, Inc., 1966.

Mendelsohn, Harold, and Irving Crespi. *Polls, Television, and the New Politics.* Scranton: Chandler, 1970.

Milbrath, Lester W. *The Washington Lobbyists.* Chicago: Rand McNally & Company, 1963.

Pomper, Gerald M. *Elections in America.* New York: Dodd, Mead & Company, Inc., 1968.

Scammon, Richard M., and Ben J. Wattenberg. *The Real Majority.* New York: Coward-McCann, Inc., 1970.

Schattschneider, E. E. *The Semi-Sovereign People.* New York: Holt, Rinehart and Winston, Inc., 1960.

Sorauf, Frank. *Party Politics in America.* 2d ed. Boston: Little, Brown & Company, 1972.

Sundquist, James L. *Dynamics of the Party System: Alignment and Realignment of Political Parties in the United States.* Washington: The Brookings Institution, 1973.

Thompson, Hunter S. *Fear and Loathing on the Campaign Trail '72.* New York: Popular Library, Inc., 1973.

Truman, David B. *The Governmental Process.* New York: Alfred A. Knopf, Inc., 1951.

Watts, William, and Lloyd A. Free, eds. *State of the Nation.* New York: Universe Books, 1973.

White, Theodore H. *The Making of the President, 1960.* New York: Atheneum Publishers, 1962.

————. *The Making of the President, 1964.* New York: Atheneum Publishers, 1965.

————. *The Making of the President, 1968.* New York: Atheneum Publishers, 1969.

————. *The Making of the President, 1972.* New York: Atheneum Publishers, 1973.

Wilson, James Q. *The Amateur Democrat: Club Politics in Three Cities.* Chicago: University of Chicago Press, 1966.

CHAPTER 5

Anderson, Martin. *The Federal Bulldozer.* New York: McGraw-Hill Book Company, 1964.

Derthick, Martha. *Between State and Nation: Regional Organizations of the United States.* Washington: The Brookings Institution, 1974.

————. *The Influence of Federal Grants.* Cambridge, Mass.: Harvard University Press, 1970.

Elazar, Daniel J. *American Federalism: A View from the States.* 2d ed. New York: Thomas Y. Crowell Company, 1972.

Feld, Richard D., and Carl Grafton, eds. *The Uneasy Partnership: The Dynamics of Federal, State, and Urban Relations.* Palo Alto, Calif.: National Press Books, 1973.

Leach, Richard H. *American Federalism.* New York: W. W. Norton & Company, Inc., 1970.

MacMahon, Arthur W. *Administering Federalism in a Democracy.* New York: Oxford University Press, 1972.

Martin, Roscoe C. *The Cities and the Federal System.* New York: Atherton Press, Inc., 1965.

Patterson, James T. *The New Deal and the States: Federalism in Transition.* Princeton, N.J.: Princeton University Press, 1969.

Reagan, Michael. *The New Federalism.* New York: W. W. Norton & Company, Inc., 1970.

Reuss, Henry S. *Revenue-Sharing: Crutch or Catalyst for State and Local Governments?* New York: Frederick A. Praeger, Inc., 1970.

Riker, William H. *Federalism: Origin, Operation, Significance.* Boston: Little, Brown and Company, 1964.

Sundquist, James L. *Making Federalism Work: A Study of Program Coordination at the Community Level.* Washington: The Brookings Institution, 1969.

Wildavsky, Aaron, ed. *American Federalism in Perspective.* Boston: Little, Brown and Company, 1967.

Wolman, Harold. *Politics of Federal Housing.* New York: Dodd, Mead & Company, Inc., 1971.

CHAPTER 6

Bachrach, Peter, and Morton S. Baratz. *Power and Poverty.* New York: Oxford University Press, 1970.

Blechman, Barry M., Edward M. Gramlich, and Robert W. Hartman. *Setting National Priorities: The 1975 Budget.* Washington: The Brookings Institution, 1974.

Cox, Edward F., Robert C. Fellmeth, and John E. Schulz. *Nader's Raiders.* New York: Grove Press, Inc., 1969.

Davis, James, Jr., and Kenneth M. Dolbeare. *Little Groups of Neighbors: The Selective Service System.* Chicago: Markham, 1968.

Donovan, John C. *The Politics of Poverty.* 2d ed. Indianapolis: The Bobbs-Merrill Company, Inc., 1973.

Esposito, John C. *Vanishing Air.* New York: Grossman, 1970.

Fellmeth, Robert C. *The Interstate Commerce Omission.* New York: Grossman, 1970.

Fried, Edward R., Alice M. Rivlin, Charles L. Schultze, and Nancy H. Teeters.

Setting National Priorities: The 1974 Budget. Washington: The Brookings Institution, 1973.

Fried, Joseph P. *Housing Crisis U.S.A.* New York: Frederick A. Praeger, Inc., 1971.

Halberstam, David. *The Best and the Brightest.* New York: Random House, Inc., 1973.

Haveman, Robert H., and Robert D. Hamrin, eds. *The Political Economy of Federal Policy.* New York: Harper & Row, Publishers, Incorporated, 1973.

James, Dorothy B. *Poverty, Politics, and Change.* Englewood Cliffs, N.J.: Prentice-Hall, Inc., 1972.

Kershaw, Joseph A. *Government against Poverty.* Chicago: Markham, 1970.

Kotz, Nick. *Let Them Eat Promises: The Politics of Hunger in America.* Garden City, N.Y.: Doubleday & Company, Inc., 1969.

Lowi, Theodore. *The End of Liberalism.* New York: W. W. Norton & Company, Inc., 1969.

Marmor, Theodore R. *The Politics of Medicare.* Chicago: Aldine Publishing Co., 1973.

Miller, S. M., and Pamela Roby. *The Future of Inequality.* New York: Basic Books, Inc., 1970.

Moynihan, Daniel P. *Maximum Feasible Misunderstanding: Community Action in the War on Poverty.* New York: The Free Press, 1969.

————. *The Politics of a Guaranteed Income: The Nixon Administration and the Family Assistance Plan.* New York: Random House, Inc., 1973.

Ott, David J., and Attiat F. Ott. *Federal Budget Policy.* Rev. ed. Washington, D.C.: The Brookings Institution, 1969.

Pechman, Joseph A., and Benjamin A. Okner. *Who Bears the Tax Burden?* Washington: The Brookings Institution, 1974.

Peters, Charles, and Taylor Branch, eds. *Blowing the Whistle: Dissent in the Public Interest.* New York: Frederick A. Praeger, Inc., 1972.

———— and John Rothchild, eds. *Inside the System.* 2d ed. New York: Frederick A. Praeger, Inc., 1973.

Schultze, Charles L., Edward R. Fried, Alice M. Rivlin, and Nancy H. Teeters. *Setting National Priorities: The 1973 Budget.* Washington: The Brookings Institution, 1972.

Steiner, Gilbert Y. *The State of Welfare.* Washington: The Brookings Institution, 1971.

Sundquist, James L. *Politics and Policy: The Eisenhower, Kennedy, and Johnson Years.* Washington: The Brookings Institution, 1968.

Turner, James S. *The Chemical Feast.* New York: Grossman, 1970.

CHAPTER 7

Altshuler, Alan A. *Community Control: The Black Demand for Participation in Large American Cities.* Indianapolis: The Bobbs-Merrill Company, Inc., 1971.

Banfield, Edward C. *Big City Politics*. New York: Random House, Inc., 1965.

———. *The Unheavenly City Revisited*. Boston: Little, Brown and Company, 1974.

——— and James Q. Wilson. *City Politics*. Cambridge, Mass.: Harvard University Press, 1963.

Campbell, Alan K., ed. *The States and the Urban Crisis*. Englewood Cliffs, N.J.: Prentice-Hall, Inc., 1970.

Crain, Robert L., Elihu Katz, and Donald B. Rosenthal, *The Politics of Community Conflict: The Fluoridation Decision*. Indianapolis: The Bobbs-Merrill Company, Inc., 1969.

Dahl, Robert A. *Who Governs? Democracy and Power in an American City*. New Haven, Conn.: Yale University Press, 1961.

David, Stephen M., and Paul E. Peterson, eds. *Urban Politics and Public Policy: The City in Crisis*. New York: Frederick A. Praeger, Inc., 1973.

Downs, Anthony. *Urban Problems and Prospects*. Chicago: Markham, 1970.

Fenton, John. *Midwest Politics*. New York: Holt, Rinehart and Winston, Inc., 1966.

Hawkins, Brett W. *Politics and Urban Policies*. Indianapolis: The Bobbs-Merrill Company, Inc., 1971.

Hayes, Edward C. *Power Structure and Urban Policy: Who Rules in Oakland?* New York: McGraw-Hill Book Company, 1972.

Jacob, Herbert, and Kenneth N. Vines, eds. *Politics in the American States*. 2d ed. Boston: Little, Brown and Company, 1971.

Key, V. O., Jr. *Southern Politics*. New York: Alfred A. Knopf, Inc., 1949.

Kotler, Milton. *Neighborhood Government: The Local Foundations of Political Life*. Indianapolis: The Bobbs-Merrill Company, Inc., 1969.

Lineberry, Robert L., and Ira Sharkansky. *Urban Politics and Public Policy*. 2d ed. New York: Harper & Row, Publishers, Incorporated, 1974.

Royko, Mike. *Boss: Richard J. Daley of Chicago*. New York: E.P. Dutton & Co., 1970.

Sanford, Terry. *Storm over the States*. New York: McGraw-Hill Book Company, 1967.

Sharkansky, Ira. *The Maligned States*. New York: McGraw-Hill Book Company, 1972.

———. *Regionalism in American Politics*. Indianapolis: The Bobbs-Merrill Company, Inc., 1970.

Williams, T. Harry. *Huey Long*. Boston: Little, Brown and Company, 1970.

Wilson, James Q., ed. *City Politics and Public Policy*. New York: John Wiley & Sons, Inc., 1968.

Wirt, Frederick M., et al. *On the City's Rim: Politics and Policy in Suburbia*. Lexington, Mass.: Heath, 1972.

Wood, Robert C. *Suburbia*. Boston: Houghton Mifflin Company, 1959.

CHAPTER 8

Bailey, Stephen K. *Congress in the Seventies.* New York: St. Martin's Press, Inc., 1970.

Barber, James David. *The Lawmakers: Recruitment and Adaptation to Legislative Life.* New Haven, Conn.: Yale University Press, 1965.

Bibby, John F., and Roger H. Davidson. *On Capital Hill.* 2d ed. Hinsdale, Ill.: The Dryden Press, Inc., 1967.

Bolling, Richard. *Power in the House.* New York: Capricorn Books, G. P. Putnam's Sons, 1974.

Citizens Conference on State Legislatures. *The Sometimes Governments: A Critical Study of the 50 American Legislatures.* New York: Bantam Books, Inc., 1971.

Clark, Joseph S. *Congress: The Sapless Branch.* New York: Harper & Row, Publishers, Incorporated, 1965.

Cleaveland, Frederick, ed. *Congress and Urban Problems.* Washington: The Brookings Institution, 1969.

Fenno, Richard F., Jr. *Congressmen in Committees.* Boston: Little, Brown and Company, 1973.

————. *The Power of the Purse: Appropriations Politics in Congress.* Boston: Little, Brown and Company, 1966.

Green, Mark J., James M. Fallows, and David R. Zwick. *Who Runs Congress?* New York: Bantam Books, Inc., 1972.

Heard, Alexander, ed. *State Legislatures in American Politics.* Englewood Cliffs, N.J.: Prentice-Hall, Inc., 1966.

Hinckley, Barbara. *The Seniority System in Congress.* Bloomington: Indiana University Press, 1971.

————. *Stability and Change in Congress.* New York: Harper & Row, Publishers, Incorporated, 1971.

Jewell, Malcolm E., and Samuel C. Patterson. *The Legislative Process in the United States.* New York: Random House, Inc., 1966.

————. *The State Legislature: Politics and Practice.* New York: Random House, Inc., 1969.

Manley, John F. *The Politics of Finance.* Boston: Little, Brown and Company, 1970.

Peabody, Robert L., ed. *Education of a Congressman: The Newsletters of Morris K. Udall.* Indianapolis: The Bobbs-Merrill Company, Inc., 1972.

———— and Nelson W. Polsby, eds. *New Perspectives on the House of Representatives.* 2d ed. Chicago: Rand McNally & Company, 1969.

———— et al. *To Enact a Law: Congress and Campaign Financing.* New York: Frederick A. Praeger, Inc., 1972.

Pettit, Lawrence, and Edward Keynes, eds. *The Legislative Process in the U.S. Senate.* Chicago: Rand McNally & Company, 1969.

Saloma, John S., III. *Congress and the New Politics.* Boston: Little, Brown and Company, 1969.

Tacheron, Donald G., and Morris K. Udall. *The Job of the Congressman.* 2d ed. Indianapolis: The Bobbs-Merrill Company, Inc., 1970.

Truman, David B., ed. *The Congress and America's Future.* 2d ed. Englewood Cliffs, N.J.: Prentice-Hall, Inc., 1973.

Vinyard, Dale. *Congress.* New York: Charles Scribner's Sons, 1968.

Wahlke, John C., et al. *The Legislative System.* New York: John Wiley & Sons, Inc., 1962.

Weaver, Warren, Jr. *Both Your Houses: The Truth about Congress.* New York: Frederick A. Praeger, Inc., 1972.

CHAPTER 9

Anderson, Patrick. *The Presidents' Men.* Garden City, N.Y.: Doubleday & Company, Inc., 1968.

Berger, Raoul. *Executive Privilege: A Constitutional Myth.* Cambridge, Mass.: Harvard University Press, 1974.

———. *Impeachment: The Constitutional Problems.* Cambridge, Mass.: Harvard University Press, 1973.

Bollens, John C., and John C. Ries. *The City Manager Profession: Myths and Realities.* Chicago: Public Administration Service, 1969.

Evans, Rowland, Jr., and Robert D. Novak. *Lyndon B. Johnson: The Exercise of Power.* New York: New American Library, Inc., 1966.

———. *Nixon in the White House: The Frustration of Power.* New York: Random House, Inc., 1971.

Fisher, Louis. *President and Congress: Power and Policy.* New York: The Free Press, 1972.

George, Alexander L., and Juliette L. George. *Woodrow Wilson and Colonel House: A Personality Study.* New York: Dover Publications, Inc., 1964.

Goldman, Eric F. *The Tragedy of Lyndon Johnson.* New York: Dell Publishing Co., Inc., 1968.

Holtzman, Abraham. *Legislative Liaison: Executive Leadership in Congress.* Chicago: Rand McNally & Company, 1970.

Hughes, Emmet John. *The Living Presidency.* Baltimore: Penguin Books, Inc., 1974.

James, Dorothy Buckton. *The Contemporary Presidency.* 2d ed. Indianapolis: The Bobbs-Merrill Company, Inc., 1974.

Kennedy, Robert F. *Thirteen Days: A Memoir of the Cuban Missile Crisis.* New York: W. W Norton & Company, Inc., 1969.

Koenig, Louis. *The Chief Executive.* Rev. ed. New York: Harcourt Brace Jovanovich, 1968.

Lowi, Theodore J. *At the Pleasure of the Mayor.* New York: The Free Press, 1964.

McConnell, Grant. *The Modern Presidency.* New York: St. Martin's Press, Inc., 1967.

———. *Steel and the Presidency—1962.* New York: W. W. Norton & Company, Inc., 1963.

Neustadt, Richard E. *Presidential Power.* New York: John Wiley & Sons, Inc., 1960.

Phillips, Cabell. *The Truman Presidency: The History of a Triumphant Succession.* Baltimore: Penguin Books, Inc., 1966.

Ransome, Coleman B., Jr. *The Office of the Governor in the United States.* University: University of Alabama Press, 1956.

Rossiter, Clinton. *The American Presidency.* New York: Harcourt Brace Jovanovich, 1956.

Ruchelman, Leonard I., ed. *Big City Mayors: The Crisis in Urban Politics.* Bloomington: Indiana University Press, 1970.

Sorenson, Theodore C. *Kennedy.* New York: Harper & Row, Publishers, Incorporated, 1965.

Talbot, Allan R. *The Mayor's Game.* New York: Frederick A. Praeger, Inc., 1970.

Tugwell, Rexford G., and Thomas E. Cronin, eds. *The Presidency Reappraised.* New York: Frederick A. Praeger, Inc., 1974.

Vinyard, Dale. *The Presidency.* New York: Charles Scribner's Sons, 1971.

Wills, Garry. *Nixon Agonistes: The Crisis of the Self-Made Man.* Boston: Houghton Mifflin Company, 1969.

CHAPTER 10

Allison, Graham T. *Essence of Decision: Explaining the Cuban Missile Crisis.* Boston: Little, Brown and Company, 1971.

Art, Robert J. *The TFX Decision.* Boston: Little, Brown and Company, 1968.

Davis, James W., Jr. *An Introduction to Public Administration: Politics, Policy, and Bureaucracy.* New York: The Free Press, 1974.

———*The National Executive Branch.* New York: The Free Press, 1970.

Downs, Anthony. *Inside Bureaucracy.* Boston: Little, Brown and Company, 1967.

Etzioni, Amital. *A Comparative Analysis of Complex Organizations.* New York: The Free Press, 1961.

———. *Modern Organizations.* Englewood Cliffs, N.J.: Prentice-Hall, Inc., 1964.

Heller, Walter W. *New Dimensions of Political Economy.* New York: W. W. Norton & Company, Inc., 1967.

Kaufman, Herbert. *The Forest Ranger: A Study in Administrative Behavior.* Baltimore: Johns Hopkins Press, 1960.

———. *The Limits of Organizational Change.* University: University of Alabama Press, 1971.

Kohlmeier, Louis M., Jr. *The Regulators: Watchdog Agencies and the Public Interest.* New York: Harper & Row, Publishers, Incorporated, 1969.

Lindblom, Charles E. *The Policy-making Process.* Englewood Cliffs, N.J.: Prentice-Hall, Inc., 1968.

MacAvoy, Paul W., ed. *The Crisis of the Regulatory Commissions.* New York: W. W. Norton & Company, Inc., 1970.

Mainzer, Lewis C. *Political Bureaucracy.* Glenview, Ill.: Scott, Foresman and Company, 1973.

March, James, and Herbert Simon. *Organizations.* New York: John Wiley & Sons, Inc., 1958.

Marini, Frank, ed. *Toward a New Public Administration.* San Francisco: Chandler Publishing Company, 1971.

Rehfuss, John. *Public Administration as Political Process.* New York: Charles Scribner's Sons, 1973.

Rourke, Francis. *Bureaucracy, Politics, and Public Policy.* Boston: Little, Brown and Company, 1969.

Seidman, Harold. *Politics, Position, and Power: The Dynamics of Federal Organization.* New York: Oxford University Press, 1970.

Selznick, Philip. *TVA and the Grass Roots.* Berkeley: University of California Press, 1949.

Sharkansky, Ira. *The Politics of Taxing and Spending.* Indianapolis: The Bobbs-Merrill Company, Inc., 1969.

————. *Public Administration: Policy-making in Government Agencies.* 2d ed. Chicago: Markham, 1972.

Wildavsky, Aaron. *The Politics of the Budgetary Process.* Boston: Little, Brown and Company, 1964.

CHAPTER 11

Abraham, Henry J. *Freedom and the Court: Civil Rights and Liberties in the United States.* 2d ed. New York: Oxford University Press, 1972.

Becker, Theodore L., and Malcolm M. Feeley, eds. *The Impact of Supreme Court Decisions.* 2d ed. New York: Oxford University Press, 1973.

Berman, Daniel M. *It Is So Ordered: The Supreme Court Rules on School Segregation.* New York: W. W. Norton & Company, Inc., 1966.

Bickel, Alexander M. *The Least Dangerous Branch: The Supreme Court at the Bar of Politics.* Indianapolis: The Bobbs-Merrill Company, Inc., 1962.

Bordua, David, ed. *The Police.* New York: John Wiley & Sons, Inc., 1967.

Casper, Jonathan D. *The Politics of Civil Liberties.* New York: Harper & Row, Publishers, Incorporated, 1972.

D'Amato, Anthony A., and Robert M. O'Neil. *The Judiciary and Vietnam.* New York: St. Martin's Press, Inc., 1972.

Dolbeare, Kenneth M., and Philip E. Hammond. *The School Prayer Decisions: From Court Policy to Local Practice.* Chicago: University of Chicago Press, 1971.

Eisenstein, James. *Politics and the Legal Process.* New York: Harper & Row, Publishers, Incorporated, 1973.

Grossman, Joel B. *Lawyers and Judges.* New York: John Wiley & Sons, Inc., 1965.

Harris, Richard. *Decision.* New York: E. P. Dutton & Co., Inc., 1971.

Jacob, Herbert. *Justice in America: Courts, Lawyers, and the Judicial Process.* 2d ed. Boston: Little, Brown and Company, 1972.

Klonoski, James R., and Robert I. Mendelsohn, eds. *The Politics of Local Justice.* Boston: Little, Brown and Company, 1970.

Krislov, Samuel. *The Supreme Court and Political Freedom.* New York: The Free Press, 1971.

——. *The Supreme Court in the Political Process.* New York: The Macmillan Company, 1965.

Lewis, Anthony. *Gideon's Trumpet.* New York: Random House, Inc., 1964.

McCloskey, Robert G. *The American Supreme Court.* Chicago: University of Chicago Press, 1960.

Murphy, Walter F. *Congress and the Court.* Chicago: University of Chicago Press, 1962.

Niederhoffer, Arthur. *Behind the Shield: The Police in Urban Society.* Garden City, N.Y.: Doubleday & Company, Inc., 1969.

President's Commission on Law Enforcement and the Administration of Justice. *Task Force Report: The Police.* 1967.

Reiss, Albert J., Jr. *The Police and the Public.* New Haven, Conn.: Yale University Press, 1971.

Richardson, Richard J., and Kenneth N. Vines. *The Politics of Federal Courts.* Boston: Little, Brown and Company, 1970.

Schmidhauser, John R., and Larry L. Berg. *The Supreme Court and Congress. Conflict and Interaction, 1945–1968.* New York: The Free Press, 1972.

Schubert, Glendon. *Judicial Policy-Making.* 2d ed. Glenview, Ill.: Scott, Foresman and Company, 1974.

Scigliano, Robert. *The Supreme Court and the Presidency.* New York: The Free Press, 1971.

Shapiro, Martin. *Law and Politics in the Supreme Court.* New York: The Free Press, 1964.

——. *The Pentagon Papers and the Courts: A Study of Foreign Policy-making versus Freedom of the Press.* San Francisco: Chandler Publishing Company, 1972.

Simon, James F. *In His Own Image: The Supreme Court in Richard Nixon's America.* New York: David McKay Company, Inc., 1973.

Skolnick, Jerome. *Justice without Trial: Law Enforcement in Democratic Society.* New York: John Wiley & Sons, Inc., 1967.

Wasby, Stephen L. *The Impact of the United States Supreme Court: Some Perspectives.* Homewood, Ill.: The Dorsey Press, 1970.

Wilson, James Q. *Varieties of Police Behavior.* Cambridge, Mass.: Harvard University Press, 1968.

CHAPTER 12

Bailey, Stephen K., and Edith K. Mosher. *ESEA: The Office of Education Administers a Law.* Syracuse, N.Y.: Syracuse University Press, 1968.

Berke, Joel S., and Michael W. Kirst. *Federal Aid to Education: Who Benefits? Who Governs?* Lexington, Mass.: Lexington, 1972.

Derthick, Martha. *New Towns In-Town.* Washington: The Urban Institute, 1972.

Gore, William. *Administrative Decision-Making: A Heuristic Model.* New York: John Wiley & Sons, Inc., 1964.

Lyden, Fremont J., and Ernest G. Miller, eds. *Planning-Programming-Budgeting: A Systems Approach to Management.* 2d ed. Chicago: Markham, 1972.

Perloff, Harvey S., ed. *The Future of the U.S. Government: Toward the Year 2000.* Englewood Cliffs, N.J.: Prentice-Hall, Inc., 1971.

Pressman, Jeffrey L., and Aaron B. Wildavsky. *Implementation.* Berkeley: University of California Press, 1972.

Rivlin, Alice M. *Systematic Thinking for Social Action.* Washington: The Brookings Institution, 1971.

Schick, Allen. *Budget Innovation in the States.* Washington: The Brookings Institution, 1971.

Schultze, Charles L. *The Politics and Economics of Public Spending.* Washington: The Brookings Institution, 1968.

Sharkansky, Ira. *The Routines of Politics.* New York: Van Nostrand Reinhold Company, 1970.

Williams, Walter. *Social Policy Research and Analysis: The Experience in the Federal Social Agencies.* New York: American Elsevier Publishing Company, Inc., 1971.

Index